T0254143

# Linux and Solaris Recipes for Oracle DBAs

## Second Edition

Darl Kuhn

Charles Kim

Bernard Lopuz

〈IOUG〉
Independent oracle users group

Apress®

ISBN-13 (pbk): 978-1-4842-1255-4

ISBN-13 (electronic): 978-1-4842-1254-7

Managing Director: Welmoed Spahr
Lead Editor: Jonathan Gennick
Development Editor: Douglas Pundick
Technical Reviewer: Jay Nielsen
Editorial Board: Steve Anglin, Mark Beckner, Gary Cornell, Louise Corrigan, Jim DeWolf, Jonathan Gennick, Robert Hutchinson, Michelle Lowman, James Markham, Susan McDermott, Matthew Moodie, Jeffrey Pepper, Douglas Pundick, Ben Renow-Clarke, Gwenan Spearing, Matt Wade
Coordinating Editor: Jill Balzano
Copy Editor: Nancy Sixsmith
Compositor: SPi Global
Indexer: SPi Global
Artist: SPi Global
Cover Designer: Anna Ishchenko

Distributed to the book trade worldwide by Springer Science+Business Media New York, 233 Spring Street, 6th Floor, New York, NY 10013. Phone 1-800-SPRINGER, fax (201) 348-4505, e-mail orders-ny@springer-sbm.com, or visit www.springeronline.com. Apress Media, LLC is a California LLC and the sole member (owner) is Springer Science + Business Media Finance Inc (SSBM Finance Inc). SSBM Finance Inc is a Delaware corporation.

For information on translations, please e-mail rights@apress.com, or visit www.apress.com.

Apress and friends of ED books may be purchased in bulk for academic, corporate, or promotional use. eBook versions and licenses are also available for most titles. For more information, reference our Special Bulk Sales–eBook Licensing web page at www.apress.com/bulk-sales.

Any source code or other supplementary material referenced by the author in this text is available to readers at www.apress.com. For detailed information about how to locate your book's source code, go to www.apress.com/source-code/.

*To the teachers of Dixie High School and Dixie State University,*
*who challenged and changed the trajectory.*

*—Darl Kuhn*

*I dedicate this book to my father,*
*who passed away this year to be with our Lord and Savior Jesus Christ.*

*—Charles Kim*

# About IOUG Press

*IOUG Press is a joint effort by the **Independent Oracle Users Group (the IOUG)** and **Apress** to deliver some of the highest-quality content possible on Oracle Database and related topics. The IOUG is the world's leading, independent organization for professional users of Oracle products. Apress is a leading, independent technical publisher known for developing high-quality, no-fluff content for serious technology professionals. The IOUG and Apress have joined forces in IOUG Press to provide the best content and publishing opportunities to working professionals who use Oracle products.*

**Our shared goals include:**

- Developing content with excellence
- Helping working professionals to succeed
- Providing authoring and reviewing opportunities
- Networking and raising the profiles of authors and readers

To learn more about Apress, visit our website at **www.apress.com**. Follow the link for IOUG Press to see the great content that is now available on a wide range of topics that matter to those in Oracle's technology sphere.

Visit **www.ioug.org** to learn more about the Independent Oracle Users Group and its mission. Consider joining if you haven't already. Review the many benefits at www.ioug.org/join. Become a member. Get involved with peers. Boost your career.

www.ioug.org/join

## Apress®

# Contents at a Glance

# Contents

# About the Authors

**Darl Kuhn** is a DBA/developer working for Oracle. He also teaches Oracle classes at Regis University in Denver, Colorado, and is an active member of the Rocky Mountain Oracle Users Group. Darl enjoys sharing knowledge, which has led to several book projects over the years.

**Charles Kim** is the president of Viscosity North America, a niche consulting organization specializing in Oracle Exadata/RAC, GoldenGate, big data, Oracle performance tuning, and virtualization. He is an architect in Linux infrastructure, cloud, virtualization, engineered systems, Hadoop/big data, and Oracle clustering technologies. Charles has authored books with Oracle Press, Pearson, and Apress in Oracle, Hadoop, and Linux technology stacks. He holds certifications in Oracle, VMware, Red Hat Linux, and Microsoft; and he has more than 24 years of IT experience on mission- and business-critical systems.

Come see Charles present at Oracle OpenWorld, IOUG, VMWorld, and various local/regional user group conferences. He is an Oracle ACE Director, VMware vExpert, Oracle Certified DBA, Certified Exadata Specialist, and a Certified RAC Expert. Books that Charles has coauthored include these:

- *Expert Exadata Handbook*
- *Virtualizing Hadoop*
- *Virtualizing Business Critical Oracle Databases: Database as a Service*
- *Oracle Database 11g New Features for DBA and Developers*
- *Linux Recipes for Oracle DBAs*
- *Oracle Data Guard 11g Handbook*
- *Oracle ASM 12c Pocket Reference Guide*

Charles serves the Oracle Community as the president of the Cloud Computing (and Virtualization) SIG for the Independent Oracle User Group. He blogs regularly at the DBAExpert.com/blog site. Charles's My LinkedIn profile is http://www.linkedin.com/in/chkim and his Twitter tag is @racdba.

**Bernard Lopuz** is a senior technical support analyst at Oracle Corporation. In the early years of his IT career (before becoming an Oracle DBA), he was a programmer and developed Unisys LINC and Oracle applications, as well as interactive voice response applications such as telephone banking voice-processing applications. He has wide experience using RedHat AS and Oracle Enterprise Linux (OEL). Bernard was the technical reviewer of *emRMAN Recipes for Oracle Database 11g: A Problem-Solution Approach*/ (Apress, 2007), and is an Oracle Certified Professional. He pursued a master's degree in computer information technology at Regis University in Denver, Colorado, and completed a bachelor's degree in computer engineering at the Mapua Institute of Technology in Manila, Philippines. Bernard lives in Toronto, Canada with his wife, Leizle, and daughters, Juliet and Carol.

# About the Technical Reviewer

**Jay Nielsen** is an OCP developer (6i) and OCP DBA (10g), and is right in the middle of upgrading to OCP PL/SQL developer. He has worked in an Oracle environment since January 1989, starting with Oracle version 5.1 while in the U.S. Air Force. He retired from the USAF in 1995 and has continued as a Department of Defense contractor in the DC metro area. Jay has been married since 1975 and has 14 children. He currently works in the Cyber Division of NCIS HQ. Jay has a master's degree in database technology from Regis University. Darl Kuhn was his favorite instructor from Regis University Online.

# Acknowledgments

Thanks to Jonathan Gennick, Jill Balzano, and the Apress staff; it takes a quality team to produce a quality book. Also thanks to the many people I've learned from over the years, the readers providing feedback, as well as Dave Jennings, Bob Suehrstedt, Scott Schulze, Venkatesh Ranganathan, Valerie Eipper, Mike Tanaka, Simon Ip, Nitin Mittal, Mohan Shanmugavelu, Ric Ambridge, Kamal Chamakura, Dallas Powell, Krishna (KP) Tallapaneni, Laurie Bourgeois, Todd Sherman, Radha Ponnapalli, Mohan Koneru, Kevin O'Grady, Peter Schow, Sujit Pattnaik, Roger Murphy, Barb Sannwald, Pete Mullineaux, Janet Bacon, Shawn Heisdorffer. Mehran Sowdaey, Patrick David, Carson Vowles, Aaron Isom, Tim Gorman, Tom Kyte, Max Rose, Doug Drake, Jim Johnson, Marilyn Wenzel, Mert Lovell, Richard Condie, Ralph Christian, Walter Cox, Harley Iverson, William Olsen, Dr. Braunberger, and Jim Stark.

—Darl Kuhn

I thank my wonderful wife, Melissa, who always supported my career aspirations, even when starting a new consulting company and authoring books at the same time. I also want to thank my three precious sons, Isaiah, Jeremiah, and Noah, for always making me smile. Many thanks to the Apress staff for coordinating the book to completion.

—Charles Kim

# Introduction

Successful organizations use data to gain insights about their businesses to make better decisions and discover new growth opportunities. Gathering and storing data and extracting business intelligence is critical for success in today's competitive environment. Database software and server technologies are used in combination to use vital information assets.

The databases that house this important business data require a stable and effective operating system environment. The Linux and Solaris operating systems excel as cost-effective platforms for database servers. As a DBA, you will inevitably shoulder the responsibility of implementing and maintaining databases running on these systems. Your job depends on your ability to work seamlessly with the server hosting your databases. The more you understand the operating system and tools, the better you'll be able to perform. The best DBAs are the ones who know how to use which operating system features and in what situations.

This book provides you with task-oriented, ready-made solutions for DBAs in a Linux or Solaris environment. We cover topics from a DBA's perspective of the operating system. You don't have to read the book cover to cover; instead, each recipe is a how-to guide for a particular problem. This book allows you to focus on a topic and its corresponding solution.

## Audience

This book is for DBAs who work in Linux or Solaris environments. It focuses on command-line tools and techniques for working with the operating system from a DBA's point of view. If you're a DBA who wants to operate expertly with Linux technology, this book is for you. Whether you are new or experienced, we provide solutions to tasks that DBAs perform on Linux servers.

## How this Book Is Structured

The first few chapters are introductory topics for DBAs working in Linux and Solaris environments. These first chapters provide the foundation for the more complex topics covered in the rest of the chapters in the book.

Subsequent chapters cover advanced technical topics, building on the foundation material and allowing you to expertly leverage the Linux operating system. Each recipe title acts as a pointer to the problem at hand. Within each recipe is a to-the-point solution and a detailed explanation of how it works.

# Conventions

The following typographical conventions are used in this book:

- $ is used to denote commands that can be run by the owner of the Oracle binaries (usually named `oracle`).

- # is used to denote commands that should be run as the `root` user.

- Italics are used to highlight a new concept or word.

- Monospaced font is used for inline code examples, utility names, file names, and directory paths.

- Constant width bold is used to highlight the statements being discussed.

- UPPERCASE indicates view names, column names, and column values.

- < > are used where you need to provide input, such as a file name or password.

## Source Code

The code for the examples shown in this book is available on the Apress web site, `www.apress.com`. A link can be found on the book's information page under the Source Code/Downloads tab, which is located underneath the "Related Titles" section of the page.

## Errata

Apress makes every effort to make sure that there are no errors in the text or the code. However, to err is human, and as such we recognize the need to keep you informed of any mistakes as they're discovered and corrected. Errata sheets are available for all our books at `www.apress.com`. If you find an error that hasn't already been reported, please let us know. The Apress web site acts as a focus for other information and support, including the code from all Apress books, sample chapters, previews of forthcoming titles, and articles on related topics.

# Contacting the Authors

You can contact the authors directly at the following email addresses:

- Darl Kuhn: `darl.kuhn@gmail.com`

- Charles Kim: `charles@dbaexpert.com`

- Bernard Lopuz: `bernard.lopuz@hotmail.com`

# CHAPTER 1

■ ■ ■

# Getting Started

Database administrators (DBAs) are crucial members of every information technology team. They are responsible for mission-critical tasks such as the following:

- Installing software and creating databases

- Providing a highly scalable and well-behaving database environment

- Monitoring and maintaining company databases

- Ensuring that corporate data is backed up, secured, and protected

- Troubleshooting system performance and availability issues

- Being the holistic source of database engineering information

These responsibilities require that a DBA possess a combination of database and operating system (OS) expertise. It's a fact that you (the DBA) cannot architect, implement, or maintain a large, high-transaction database environment without being an expert on the underlying OS. In many situations, the OS is your only conduit to the database. Therefore, it's imperative that you be particularly knowledgeable about the OS to competently perform your database administration duties.

When first building a database, DBAs should be able to specify solid, reliable, and scalable system configurations. Furthermore, DBAs are often the cog between system administrators, users, network administrators, managers, and corporate executives. If you're working (after the fact) on a poorly designed system, you have to possess the tools to diagnose and resolve bottlenecks in the entire technology stack. Regardless of the source of the issues, team members often look to the seasoned DBA to resolve systemic performance, security, and availability concerns. We know this to be true because we live it every day (including nights and weekends).

Oracle software runs on a variety of OSs, including many Linux/UNIX variants and Windows. A large number of Oracle installations are on Oracle Linux or Oracle Solaris. Oracle Linux is Oracle's version of Linux based on Red Hat Enterprise Linux (RHEL). Oracle Solaris is a UNIX OS originally created by Sun Microsystems and now owned by Oracle Corporation since Oracle's acquisition of Sun in 2010.

The Linux and Solaris OSs are widely recognized as reliable 24/7, mission-critical, enterprise server platforms. Employers specifically seek out DBAs with Linux/Solaris expertise. In fact, as a DBA, it's inevitable that you'll someday use Linux or Solaris servers to store your data. You will be responsible for ensuring that your database is working seamlessly with the underlying OS. Managers will look to you to guarantee that corporate databases are competently implemented and maintained.

This book focuses on helping you understand how to efficiently manage Oracle software on Linux and Solaris servers. On the surface, you'll find Linux and Solaris are mostly identical in commands and syntax (the same can be said for Linux and any UNIX variant). Having said that, there are occasional differences between the OSs that you have to be aware of. We'll strive to point out these subtle differences where they exist. When there are no differences, we'll simply refer to the OS as "Linux/Solaris," meaning that the concept applies equally to both.

The information in this book will enable you to function as an expert DBA when performing key responsibilities. We provide direct answers to specific problems regarding Oracle database technology running on Linux/Solaris OSs. The recipes in this first chapter assume that you know nothing about Linux/Solaris and cover situations that you'll be presented with when you first connect to a server and use OS commands. If you are already fairly experienced with the Linux/Solaris OS, feel free to skip this chapter.

In this chapter, we start by walking you through some of the most common methods for logging on to a Linux/Solaris server. We then cover the basics of running Linux/Solaris commands and detail how to use the built-in help and online documentation. We finish the chapter by showing techniques for correcting command-line mistakes and resetting a terminal screen.

# 1-1. Connecting Securely to a Remote Server
## Problem

You're using a Windows-based laptop or workstation and want to securely connect to a remote Linux/Solaris database server over the network.

## Solution

This solution shows how to download and use the PuTTY application to initiate secure remote connections over the network:

1. To get started, download PuTTY from an Internet site such as www.putty.org or www.chiark.greenend.org.uk/~sgtatham/putty/download.html.

2. Once on the PuTTY download site, you'll find links that enable you to download the PuTTY application. You can download just the putty.exe file or all utilities available via the putty.zip file.

3. After you download the desired files, navigate on your personal computer to the directory in which you downloaded the PuTTY utility. You should see a screen similar to Figure 1-1. Double-click the PuTTY icon to start the connection utility.

*Figure 1-1.* *PuTTY application icon*

4. Figure 1-2 shows a partial screenshot of what you see next. From this screen, you can enter the hostname or IP address and connection port of the remote server to which you want to connect. Enter the connection details of your Linux/Solaris database server and click the Open button to initiate a remote connection. If you aren't sure about the connection information, contact your system administrator for details.

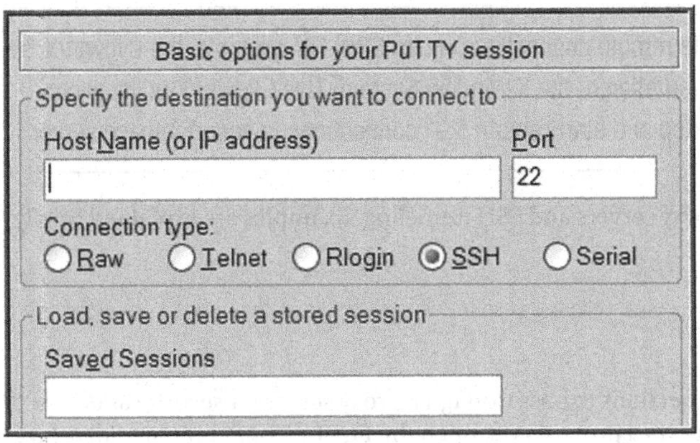

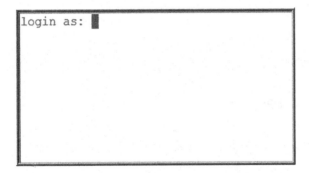

**Figure 1-2.** *PuTTY connection details*

    5.    After you connect to your database server, you should see the screen shown in Figure 1-3. Enter your username and password (contact your system administrator if you don't know them). Once logged on, you can run shell commands to perform tasks on your database server. (Chapter 2 provides more detail about shells.)

```
login as: █
```

**Figure 1-3.** *Linux/Solaris server logon screen*

# How It Works

PuTTY is a free open source utility that allows you to create a secure shell (SSH) connection to a remote database server. This utility is popular because it is a free, easy-to-use application that enables you to connect securely from a Windows client over the network to remote Linux/Solaris database servers. With this tool, you can store your server preferences and connection information, which eliminates the need to retype lengthy hostnames or IP addresses.

---

■ **Note**    Other utilities also allow you to initiate remote connections via an SSH. For example, the Cygwin/X application is a popular Windows-based implementation of the X Window System. This Cygwin/X utility allows you to run X applications on your Windows desktop and start remote SSH connections to your database server.

---

You can also use PuTTY to connect via proxy servers and SSH tunneling. Examples are explained briefly in the next sections.

## Connecting via a Proxy Server

Many companies require all their Internet connections to pass through a proxy server for security and performance reasons. To use PuTTY to connect via a proxy server, open the PuTTY Configuration dialog box and click the Proxy node under the Connection category, as shown in Figure 1-4.

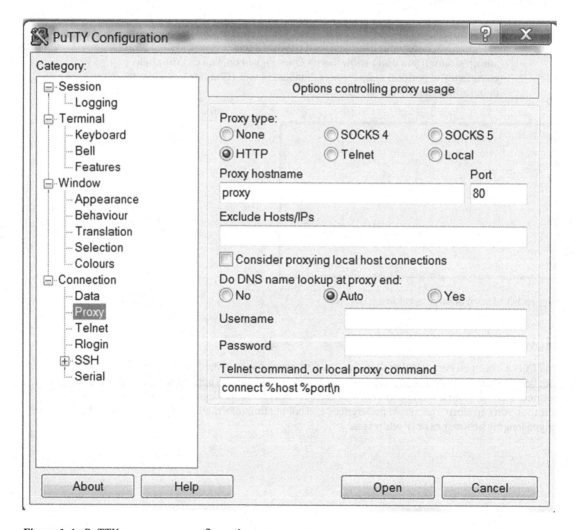

*Figure 1-4.  PuTTY—proxy server configuration*

Select HTTP for the proxy type, provide the hostname or IP address of the proxy server, and provide the corresponding port number. Save the changes to your PuTTY configuration for future use.

## Connecting via SSH Tunneling

You can also use PuTTY for tunneling (also called *port forwarding*) to a remote server. To use tunneling, open the PuTTY Configuration dialog box and then choose the SSH as the connection type. Next, provide the hostname or IP address of the designated SSH server as well as the SSH port number (the default is 22). Afterward, click the Connection node, then the SSH node, and finally the Tunnels node, as shown in Figure 1-5.

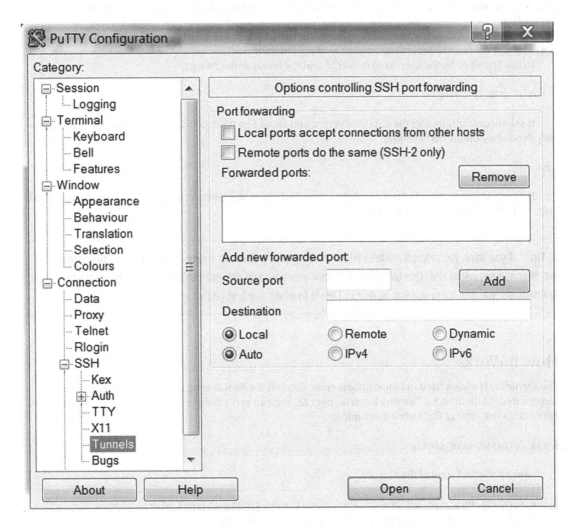

***Figure 1-5.*** *PuTTY—SSH tunneling configuration*

In the "Source port" field under the "Add new forwarded port" section, provide the port number you will connect to at your Windows client. In the Destination field, provide the hostname or IP address of the Linux/Solaris database server, as well as the port number. Save the changes to your PuTTY configuration for future use.

# 1-2. Logging on Remotely via the Command Line

## Problem

Your system administrator has provided you with a username and password for your database server. You now want to log on to the server via a command-line utility such as telnet or ssh.

## Solution

This example assumes that you can access a terminal from which you can initiate an ssh command. Depending on your environment, your "terminal" could be a PuTTY session (see recipe 1-1) on your home PC or workstation. Ask your system administrator for help if you're not sure how to start a terminal session (this can vary quite a bit, depending on your working environment).

In this line of code, the username is oracle and the hostname is rmoug1:

```
$ ssh -l oracle rmoug1
```

If ssh successfully locates the database server, you should be prompted for a password (the prompt can vary depending on the OS version):

```
Password:
```

For security purposes, your password does not display as you type it. After typing your password, press Enter or Return to complete the logon process.

---

■ **Tip**    If you think you made a mistake while entering your password, press Ctrl+U to erase all invisible text from the password line. This technique will save you time and prevent many accidental failed logins. Alternatively, you can try to use Backspace or Delete to erase any text you've entered.

---

## How It Works

The ssh utility is widely used in Linux/Solaris environments for establishing secure connections to remote servers. By default, most SSH servers listen on port 22. You can verify the port by viewing the contents of the /etc/ssh/sshd_config file. Here's an example:

```
$ cat /etc/ssh/sshd_config
```

Here's a partial listing of the output:

```
# The strategy used for options in the default sshd_config shipped with
# OpenSSH is to specify options with their default value where
# possible, but leave them commented. Uncommented options change a
# default value.
#Port 22
```

If your system administrator has set up the server to listen on a port other than 22, you have to explicitly specify it with the -p (port) option. This example connects the oracle user to the rmoug1 server on port 71:

```
$ ssh -p 71 -l oracle rmoug1
```

After a valid username and password are entered, your system might display information such as the last time you logged on, from what machine you initiated the connection, whether your account has unread mail, and so on. Additionally, if your system administrator has entered any text within the /etc/motd (message of the day) file, that information also displays. The following text is a typical login message:

```
Last login: Wed Mar 28 14:12:50 2015 from from hlrn.rmoug.net
```

After your username and password have been successfully authenticated by the Linux/Solaris server, you should see a $ (dollar sign) prompt:

```
$
```

The $ character signifies that you are at the shell command-line prompt. The $ character is the default command-line prompt for most Linux/Solaris systems.

---

■ **Note**    All command-line examples in this book show the $ prompt. You don't have to type the $ prompt as part of any of the example commands in this book.

---

Your system administrator might have configured your account to display a different prompt from the $ character. DBAs sometimes configure the prompt to include information such as the server name and database name. See recipe 2-6 for changing your command-line prompt from something other than the default.

---

■ **Note**    If you are logged in with the root account (sometimes called superuser), the default command-line prompt is the # character.

---

Some servers accept remote connections from telnet clients. For security reasons, we recommend that you do not use telnet to initiate a logon to a server over the network. The telnet utility does not use encryption and is vulnerable to hackers snooping on the network. Whenever possible, you should use the secure ssh tool for remote connections. However, you might occasionally have to use telnet because ssh isn't available. The following example uses telnet to log on to a remote server over the network:

```
$ telnet -l oracle dbsrver
```

# 1-3. Logging off the Server

## Problem

You want to log off the server.

## Solution

Three methods for logging out of the database server are covered in this solution:

- Pressing Ctrl+D
- Typing exit
- Typing logout

The quickest way to log off is to press Ctrl+D, which immediately logs you off your server. In this example, the Ctrl and D keys are pressed at the same time:

```
$ Ctrl+D
```

You should now see a message like this:

```
Connection to <your server> closed.
```

You can also type the exit command to log off your database server:

```
$ exit
```

You should now see a message like this:

```
Connection to <your server> closed.
```

You can also type the logout command to log off the system:

```
$ logout
```

You should now see a message like this:

```
Connection to <your server> closed.
```

## How It Works

If you start a subshell within an existing shell session, the logout techniques described in the "Solution" section exit you from only the innermost shell. For example, suppose that you have logged on to your server and then issued the following command:

```
$ bash
```

You now have started a subshell. If you want to exit the subshell, use one of the techniques described in the "Solution" section:

```
$ exit
```

8

Similarly, if you issue the su command to switch to another user, when you exit that session, you are returned to the shell from which you initiated the su command.

It's a good security practice to log out of your OS session if you plan to be away from your terminal. As a DBA, you'll typically find yourself logged on to the server as the user who owns the database binaries (usually the oracle OS account). The oracle account is like a database superuser account.

The database OS account can do potentially damaging operations such as drop databases, remove database files, and so on. Logging out ensures that your database OS account isn't compromised.

---

■ **Tip**  Set the TMOUT variable to limit the amount of idle time a session can have before it is automatically logged off. This parameter can be set globally in the /etc/bashrc file. See recipe 2-5 for how to automatically set variables when logging on to a server.

---

# 1-4. Running a Command

## Problem

You're new to Linux/Solaris, and you want to run a shell command from the OS prompt.

## Solution

Linux/Solaris commands are run from the command line by typing them and pressing the Enter or Return key. This example uses the df (disk-free) command to display the amount of unused disk space on the database server:

```
$ df
```

There might be some differences in the output of df, depending on your OS version. On a Linux system, you should see output similar to this:

```
Filesystem         1K-blocks       Used Available Use% Mounted on
/dev/xvda2       200095024 123528852  66237984  66% /
/dev/xvda1         1019208    138748    827852  15% /boot
```

On a Solaris system, the output of the df command might look different:

```
$ df

/                  (rpool/ROOT/solaris-1):104676373 blocks  104676373 files
/devices           (/devices           ):        0 blocks          0 files
/dev               (/dev               ):        0 blocks          0 files
/system/contract   (ctfs               ):        0 blocks 2147483592 files
```

Sometimes the output of various OS commands is formatted differently from Linux to Solaris. Usually this is important only if you're trying to write a program (e.g., a shell script) that expects information to consistently be located in certain columns (see Chapter 7 for details on shell scripting). You have to adjust your scripts based on the format of the output for each OS.

# How It Works

When you log on to a Linux or Solaris box, by default you are placed at the command line. (The *command line* is where you type shell commands to accomplish a given DBA task.) The default command-line prompt for most systems is the $ character.

You can modify the default behavior of a command by running it with one or more *options* (sometimes called *flags* or *switches*). This example shows uses the df command with the -h option to display the output in a more human-readable format:

```
$ df -h

Filesystem          Size  Used Avail Use% Mounted on
/dev/xvda2          191G  118G   64G  66% /
/dev/xvda1          996M  136M  809M  15% /boot
```

Commands can also take *arguments*, which typically designate a file or text that the command should use. When running a command, arguments are usually placed after the options. This example uses the df command with the -h option and uses the argument of /dev/sda2 (which is a particular filesystem):

```
$ df -h /dev/xvda2

Filesystem          Size  Used Avail Use% Mounted on
/dev/xvda2          191G  118G   64G  66% /
```

This book does not detail the use of various graphical user interfaces (GUIs), which are helpful when you don't know the actual command. As useful as these graphical tools are, we strongly recommend that you explore using commands from the command-line prompt. As a DBA, you will encounter situations in which the GUI tool doesn't do everything you need to accomplish a task. For some problems, you need access to the command line to debug and troubleshoot issues. Many complicated or custom DBA tasks require that you be proficient with command-line programming techniques. Although some sites have useful GUIs, some do not. All sites have the command line. If you get dependent on a specific GUI to do your work, you might be lost when you get to a site with no GUIs.

If you don't know the appropriate shell commands and their features, you might waste time and effort solving a problem when it could have easily been resolved if you knew which tools and options were available.

## GOLDEN HAMMER RULE

The Golden Hammer Rule can be stated this way: "When the only tool you have is a hammer, everything looks like a nail." What does that mean? When people find a tool that solves a problem, they have a natural tendency to use that tool again and again to solve other problems. This dependence can occur because after you're familiar with a given tool or technique, you'll continue to use it because it's available; you've had training with the tool; and you've developed a skill set.

Nothing is wrong with that approach *per se*. However, if you want to be a more marketable DBA, you should expand your horizons from time to time by learning new skills and investigating up-to-date methods for solving problems. In today's ever-changing technology environment, the DBA with the most current skills is often the one who survives the longest.

It's getting harder and harder to find database environments that don't use Linux/Solaris. As a DBA, you should take the initiative to learn about Linux/Solaris and how this technology is used by companies around the world to provide cost-effective information technology solutions.

# 1-5. Getting Help

## Problem

You want to find more information about how to use a shell command.

## Solution

One extremely nice feature of Linux/Solaris is that there are several options for quickly obtaining more information regarding shell commands. Table 1-1 contains descriptions of command-line help features readily available on most systems:

***Table 1-1.*** *Common Help Features*

| Help Feature | Description |
| --- | --- |
| man | Read the online manual for a command. |
| whatis | View a brief description of a command. |
| which | Find a tool. |
| --help | Show help. |
| apropos | Display man page documentation. |
| info | List extensive documentation. |
| Tab key | Show available commands. |

Each of the help methods in Table 1-1 is described in the following sections.

## Reading Manual Pages

The man (manual) page for a command displays online documentation for almost every shell command. The following command displays information about man:

```
$ man man
```

Here's a partial listing of the output:

```
man(1)

NAME
        man - format and display the on-line manual pages

SYNOPSIS
        man [-acdfFhkKtwW] [--path] [-m system] [-p string] [-C config_file]
[-M pathlist] [-P pager] [-B browser] [-H htmlpager]...
```

The man command uses a screen pager—usually the less command—to display the help page. The less utility displays a : (colon) prompt at the bottom-left corner of the screen. You can use the spacebar to go to the next page and use the up and down arrows to scroll through the documentation line by line.

Table 1-2 lists the less command options available to you while viewing man pages. Press the Q key to exit the man utility.

*Table 1-2.* *The* less *Command Options Available While Viewing* man *Pages*

| Keystroke | Action |
|---|---|
| J, E, or Down arrow | Move down one line. |
| K, Y, or up arrow | Move up one line. |
| Up arrow | Move up one line. |
| Down arrow | Move down one line. |
| /<string> | Search for <string>. |
| n | Repeat the previous search forward. |
| Shift+N | Repeat the previous search backward. |
| H | Display the help page. |
| F, spacebar, or Page Down | Move down one page. |
| B or Page Up | Move up one page. |
| Q | Exit the man page. |

The man pages are usually divided into ten sections. The man command displays the first man page match it finds for a specified command. Sometimes a Linux/Solaris utility is documented in more than one man section. To view all man documentation available for a tool, use the -f option (this is equivalent to running the whatis command). This example views all man pages available with the cd command:

```
$ man -f cd
```

From the output, you can see that cd is documented in several different man sections:

```
cd                  (1p)  - change the working directory
cd                  (n)   - Change working directory
cd [builtins]       (1)   - bash built-in commands, see bash(1)
```

To view the man documentation specific to the cd utility, specify the 1p page:

```
$ man 1p cd
```

To scroll through all man sections associated with a command, use the -a option. Here is an example:

```
$ man -a cd
```

When in this mode, press the Q key to advance to the next man section of information.

## CAPTURING MAN PAGES IN A TEXT FILE

It can sometimes be helpful to capture the output of a man command in a file that can be used later to search and scroll through with a text editor. The following command writes the output of the man page for the find command to a file named find.txt:

```
$ man find >find.txt
```

However, if you inspect the output file, you might notice that it contains unreadable characters that are produced from the man page output. Run the following command to clean up the output of the man page:

```
$ man find | col -b >find.txt
```

The previous command takes the output from the man command and sends it to the col -b (postprocessing filter) command. This filtering command removes the unreadable backspace characters from the man page output and makes them human-readable.

## Viewing a Brief Description of a Command

If you're new to Linux/Solaris (or if you have forgotten the material), use the aptly named whatis command to answer this question: "What is a command's basic information?" The whatis command lists the first line of text from the man page. This example shows how to use the whatis command to find more information about the pwd command:

```
$ whatis pwd
pwd                    (1)  - print name of current/working directory
pwd                    (1p) - return working directory name
pwd                    (n)  - return the absolute path of the current working directory
pwd [builtins]         (1)  - bash built-in commands, see bash(1)
pwd.h [pwd]            (0p) - password structure
```

The number/letter (enclosed in parentheses) specifies the section of the man page in which you can find the command. When you see multiple lines listed by whatis, the command is documented in more than one location in the man pages. The output also indicates that there is a built-in Bash version of the command (see Chapter 2 for more details about built-in commands).

Another interesting use of the whatis command is to view a one-line description of commands in the /bin directory. This example uses whatis with ls, xargs, and less to view the descriptions of all commands in the /bin directory one page at a time:

```
$ cd /bin
$ ls | xargs whatis | less

arch                   (1)  - print machine architecture
awk                    (1p) - pattern scanning and processing language
basename               (1)  - strip directory and suffix from filenames
...
```

The previous code first lists the files in the /bin directory; its output is then piped to the xargs command. The xargs command takes the output of ls and sends it to the whatis utility. The less command displays the output one page at a time. To exit from the documentation (displayed by less), press the Q key (to quit).

---

■ **Note**   The whatis command is identical to the man -f command.

---

## Locating a Command

Use the which command to locate the executable binary file of a command. This line of code locates the binary man executable file:

```
$ which man
/usr/bin/man
```

The which command is extremely useful for determining whether binary files or utilities are available on a server and where they are located. You might find that many commands and utilities are not consistently available, depending on which Linux/Solaris packages have been installed. Talk to your system administrator if you need a utility that is not available.

## Showing Help

On Linux systems, use the --help option to quickly display basic information about a tool's use and syntax. This example demonstrates how to get help for the df command:

```
$ df --help
```

Here's a partial listing of the output:

```
Usage: df [OPTION]... [FILE]...
Show information about the filesystem on which each FILE resides,
or all filesystems by default. Mandatory arguments to long options are mandatory
for short options too.
  -a, --all              include filesystems having 0 blocks
  -B, --block-size=SIZE use SIZE-byte blocks
  -h, --human-readable  print sizes in human readable format (e.g., 1K 234M 2G)
```

Depending on the version of the OS, there might not be a --help option for shell commands. To that point, there is no --help option for Solaris shell commands. If this is the case, you have to use one of the other documentation sources (e.g., man) listed in this recipe.

## Finding Manual Page Documentation

If you can remember only part of the name of the utility you seek, use the apropos command to find more documentation. The apropos command is similar to whatis, except that it searches for any string that matches your input. The following example searches the whatis command for the string find:

```
$ apropos find
```

Here's a partial snippet of the output:

```
find              (1)    - search for files in a directory hierarchy
find              (1p)   - find files
find2perl         (1)    - translate find command lines to Perl code
findchip          (8)    - checks the FIR chipset
findfs            (8)    - find a filesystem by label or UUID
```

The previous output shows that many different types of find commands are available. Use the man command (previously discussed in this recipe) to view more information about a particular find command. The number in the second column (in parentheses) lists the section of the man page in which the documentation is contained.

---

■ **Note**  The apropos command is equivalent to the man -k command.

---

## Listing Extensive Documentation

The info utility often contains extensive documentation for many Linux/Solaris commands. To view all documents available, type info with no parameters, as shown here:

```
$ info
```

Here's a small snippet of the output:

```
File: dir       Node: Top       This is the top of the INFO tree

   This (the Directory node) gives a menu of major topics.
   Typing "q" exits, "?" lists all Info commands, "d" returns here,
   "h" gives a primer for first-timers,
   "mEmacs<Return>" visits the Emacs topic, etc.

   In Emacs, you can click mouse button 2 on a menu item or cross reference
   to select it.

* Menu:

Texinfo documentation system
* Pinfo: (pinfo).            curses based lynx-style info browser.
* Texi2HTML: (texi2html).  Texinfo to HTML Converter.
...
```

Once within the utility, use the N key to go to the next section. The P key takes you to a previous section. Any line that starts with an asterisk (*) is a link to other sections (nodes) in the document. To go to a linked document, navigate to the line containing the asterisk and press Enter or Return. Press the Q key to exit the info page.

Table 1-3 lists some of the commonly used navigational info commands.

***Table 1-3.*** *Commonly Used Navigation Keystrokes Within the info Utility*

| Keystroke | Action |
|---|---|
| N | Move to the next section. |
| P | Move to the previous section. |
| Enter/Return | Move to a linked document. |
| Q | Exit. |
| ? | List all commands. |
| D | Return to the introduction page. |
| H | Go to the tutorial. |

You can also view information regarding specific commands. This example starts the info utility to display help for the cpio command:

```
$ info cpio
```

To view a tutorial on info, type $ info.

## Showing Available Commands

If you're using the Bash shell (see Chapter 2 for details on using a shell), you can use the Tab key to show all executable files that start with a certain string. For example, if you want to view all commands that start with the string ls, type ls and press the Tab key twice (with no space between the ls command and pressing the Tab key):

```
$ ls<Tab><Tab>
ls          lsb_release  lsnrctl        lspgpot
lsattr      lshal        lsnrctlo       lss16toppm
```

After Tab is pressed twice, the Bash shell attempts to find all commands that start with ls that are located in any directories contained in the PATH variable. This feature of automatically looking for files is known as *command completion*. (See recipe 2-2 for more details on command completion.)

## How It Works

The "Solution" section of this recipe contains some of the most useful information you'll need to elevate your Linux/Solaris skills. You should take some time to become familiar with all the helpful techniques described in this recipe.

Linux/Solaris has extensive utilities for easily viewing command documentation. Using these built-in help features allows you to quickly find basic syntax and use of a given shell command. In particular, we suggest that you become familiar with man and info; you'll use these informational tools on a regular basis.

# 1-6. Correcting Command-Line Mistakes

## Problem

You're a typical DBA, so you often mistype things on the command line. You wonder whether there are command-line tools to correct your typing mistakes.

## Solution

If you're using the Bash shell (see Chapter 2 for details on using a shell), press Ctrl+_ (underscore) at the same time to undo what you just typed at the command line. Notice that you have to use the Shift key to get the underscore (_) character. If you type a long command string, pressing Ctrl+_ erases everything to the left of the prompt. If you have backspaced over a command, pressing Ctrl+_ undoes what you have backspaced over.

## How It Works

Other keystrokes are available to help you undo what you just typed. For example, you can use Ctrl+T to transpose two characters just to the left of the prompt (ensure that there is no space between the command characters and Ctrl+T). This next bit of code uses Ctrl+T to transpose the last two characters of the letters pdw:

```
$ pdw Ctrl+T
```

You should now see the following:

```
$ pwd
```

Table 1-4 summarizes the commands available for correcting typing mistakes at the command line.

*Table 1-4.* *Command-Line Keystrokes to Correct Typing Errors*

| Keystroke | Action |
| --- | --- |
| Ctrl+_ | Undo what was just typed in. |
| Ctrl+U | Clear out everything to the left of the prompt. |
| Ctrl+T | Transpose two characters that are immediately to the left of the prompt. |
| Alt+T | Transpose two words that are on the left of the prompt. |

# 1-7. Clearing the Screen

## Problem

Your screen has become cluttered with command output. You want to clear the screen of any previously displayed text or command output.

## Solution

Either use the `clear` command or press Ctrl+L to clear your terminal screen. The `clear` command does what you would expect: it clears the screen. Simply type the command as shown with no options or arguments:

```
$ clear
```

If you're using the Bash shell (see Chapter 2 for details on shells), another method for clearing the screen is to press Ctrl+L:

```
$ Ctrl+L
```

One nice feature about Ctrl+L is that you can enter this command while typing other commands on the command line. Pressing Ctrl+L clears the screen and retains any current commands you have entered on the command line. For example, suppose that you are in the middle of typing a find command; you can enter Ctrl+L as shown here:

```
$ find . -name *.sql Ctrl+L
```

When you press Ctrl+L, it clears the screen and places the command you are currently typing at the top of the screen. In this example, the find command appears at the top of the screen:

```
$ find . -name *.sql
```

## How It Works

The clear command removes all output visible on your screen and retrieves environment information from the terminfo database to determine how to clear the screen (use man terminfo for details regarding your environment).

The Ctrl+L keystroke works with the Bash shell and it can work with other shells, depending on your version of the OS. Unlike the clear command, Ctrl+L retains whatever command you are currently typing and displays it at the top of the cleared-out screen.

# 1-8. Resetting the Screen

## Problem

Your screen has become cluttered with strange, unreadable characters. Using the clear command and Ctrl+L doesn't have any effect.

## Solution

Try to use the reset command to restore the screen to a sane state:

```
$ reset
```

If the reset command doesn't work, try the stty sane command:

```
$ stty sane
```

If that doesn't work, try exiting your terminal session and restarting it. Although it is not the ideal solution, sometimes it is the only thing that does work.

## How It Works

Sometimes your screen can become cluttered with unreadable characters. For example, it can happen if you accidentally use the cat command to display the contents of a binary file. Use either the reset or stty sane command to restore your screen to a normal state.

The reset command is actually a symbolic link (see recipe 5-33 for more details on links) to the tset (terminal initialization) command. (View the man pages for tset for more details on this utility.) The reset command is particularly useful for clearing your screen when a program abnormally aborts and leaves the terminal in an unusual state.

The stty (set terminal type) command displays or changes terminal characteristics. If you type stty without any options, it displays the settings that are different from those set by issuing the stty sane command.

# CHAPTER 2

■ ■ ■

# Working in the Shell

Every Linux/Solaris system includes at least one command-line interpreter that enables you to interact with the OS. This interpreter is known as a *shell*. It is an appropriate moniker because the shell's purpose is to act as a layer that shields you from having to know the internal workings of the OS. The shell allows you to perform complex tasks using simple commands.

If you're a DBA, you should know how to run shell commands from the command line (OS prompt). Yes, you can perform many DBA tasks through various GUIs, but regardless of the robustness of the GUI, you still have to use the command line to perform tasks that the GUI can't handle. For example, you might be in a stressful database restore-and-recovery situation in which you have access only to a terminal to run the appropriate commands. In this scenario, your job depends on being able to work from the command line to diagnose possible media failures and then perform the appropriate database restore-and-recovery operations.

There are many command-line interpreters available (the Bourne Again (Bash) shell, Korn shell, C shell, and so on). Because the Bash shell is usually the default command-line interpreter on many systems, the focus of this chapter (and this book, for that matter) centers on how to perform DBA tasks using the Bash shell. We strongly encourage you to use the Bash shell as your default command-line interpreter because it incorporates most of the useful features of other available shells and provides additional functionality. Where appropriate, we'll also juxtapose key features of the Bash shell with both the Korn shell and C shell.

When you log on to your database server, you are "in" a shell, which means that you can enter commands that the shell will interpret and run for you. The most common default shell prompt is the $ (dollar sign) character, so most examples in this book denote the shell command line with the $ character. Here's an example:

```
$ <commands run here>
```

---

■ **Note**    The # (hash) is used for the prompt to denote operations that need to be performed as the root user.

---

This chapter covers topics such as obtaining information about the shell environment and customizing it. The solutions will enable you to work efficiently at the command line on database servers. The command line is where you will perform most of your database administrator activities.

Because a typical DBA spends several hours per day using commands at the shell prompt, the shell is a tool that all DBAs must thoroughly understand. The solutions in this chapter will form the building blocks for the more complex DBA tasks covered in the rest of this book.

# 2-1. Displaying the Current Shell

## Problem

You want to verify which shell you are currently using.

## Solution

When you first log on to a server, you can verify the default shell viewing the value of the SHELL variable. You must specify a $ in front of the variable to display its contents:

```
$ echo $SHELL
```

In this example, the output indicates that the Bash shell is in use:

```
/bin/bash
```

Many of the recipes in this chapter require the use of the Bash shell. What if the prior output showed that you were using a shell other than the Bash shell? For example, suppose that you view the value contained in $SHELL, and it indicates that your default shell is the C shell after first logging in:

```
$ echo $SHELL
/bin/csh
```

In this situation, to enter a Bash shell session type in the bash command, use the following:

```
$ bash
```

The prior command does not change your default logon shell, so the value of SHELL remains unchanged. However, you can use the $0 variable to show your current working shell. The $0 variable holds the name of the shell or script that is currently running. The following command verifies that the current working shell has been changed to the Bash shell:

```
$ echo $0
bash
```

In this situation, to exit out of the Bash shell session, type the exit command, which returns you to the parent session:

```
exit
```

---

▦ **Tip**    See recipe 2-13 for details on changing your default logon shell.

---

# How It Works

You might occasionally be logged on to a box and wonder why certain Bash shell commands aren't working. This is most likely because your default logon shell is not the Bash shell. In shops that have a large number of Linux/Solaris servers, there might not be a consistent shell used as a common standard. In these types of environments, first verify the default logon shell in use by displaying the contents of the SHELL variable. As shown in the solution section of this recipe, you can modify the current working shell by entering in the name of the shell you want to enter.

---

■ **Note**    On Linux boxes, you can verify which shells are available by viewing the contents of the /etc/shells file. This file isn't a standard file on Solaris systems, but it can be created by the system administrator.

---

Another method for viewing the current shell is to run the ps command without any options:

```
$ ps
```

The first line of the output shows which shell you are currently using. You should see output similar to this:

```
PID  TTY       TIME    CMD
9088 pts/1    00:00:00 bash
9137 pts/1    00:00:00 ps
```

If you enter a shell from a shell (e.g., from the C shell to the Bash shell), you should see all shells in use in the output. The following example demonstrates this. First verify your default shell:

```
$ echo $SHELL
/bin/csh
```

Next, enter the Bash shell:

```
$ bash
$ echo $0
bash
```

Now view the process status:

```
$ ps
  PID TTY        TIME CMD
 1521 pts/13   00:00:00 csh
 5944 pts/13   00:00:00 bash
 5951 pts/13   00:00:00 ps
```

When the ps command is used without any parameters, it displays all processes associated with the current user and terminal. So you might see more processes, depending on which commands you executed in the current session.

---

■ **Tip**　On Linux boxes, use the `pstree` command to view the hierarchical relationship of processes. On Solaris systems, use the `ptree` command to view process ancestry.

---

# 2-2. Running Previously Entered Commands

## Problem

You are spending a lot of time retyping commands that were previously entered. You want to view, edit, and rerun shell commands that were recently executed.

## Solution

One timesaving feature of the Bash shell is that it has several methods for editing and rerunning previously executed commands. This bulleted list highlights several options available for manipulating previously typed commands:

- Scrolling with the up and down arrow keys

- Using Ctrl+P and Ctrl+N

- Listing command history

- Searching in reverse

- Setting the command editor

Each of these techniques is described briefly in the following sections. Keep in mind that some of these techniques might not be available, depending on the OS version.

### Scrolling with the Up and Down Arrow Keys

Use the up arrow to scroll up through your recent command history. As you scroll through previously run commands, you can rerun a desired command by pressing Enter or Return.

If you want to edit a command, use the Backspace key to erase characters or use the left arrow to navigate to the desired location in the command text. After you have scrolled up through the command stack, use the down arrow to scroll back down through previously viewed commands.

---

■ **Note**　If you're familiar with Windows, scrolling through the command stack is similar to the DOSKEY utility.

---

### Pressing Ctrl+P and Ctrl+N

The Ctrl+P keystroke (pressing the Ctrl and P keys at the same time) displays your previously entered command. If you have pressed Ctrl+P several times, you can scroll back down the command stack by pressing Ctrl+N (pressing the Ctrl and N keys at the same time).

## Listing Command History

Use the `history` command to display commands that have been previously entered by the user:

```
$ history
```

Depending on how many commands have previously been executed, you might see a lengthy stack. You can limit the output to the last *n* number of commands by providing a number with the command. For example, the following lists the last five commands that have been run:

```
$ history 5
```

Here is some sample output:

```
273  cd -
274  grep -i ora alert.log
275  ssh -Y -l oracle 65.217.177.98
276  pwd
277  history 5
```

To run a previously listed command in the output, use an exclamation point (!, sometimes called the *bang*) followed by the history number. In this example, to run the `pwd` command on line 276, use ! as follows:

```
$ ! 276
```

To run the last command you ran, use ! !, as shown here:

```
$ !!
```

## Searching in Reverse

Press Ctrl+R (press the Ctrl and R keys at the same time), and you'll see the Bash shell reverse search utility:

```
$ (reverse-i-search)`':
```

As you type each letter from the `reverse-i-search` prompt, the tool automatically searches through previously run commands that have text similar to the string you entered. As soon as you see the desired command match, you can rerun the command by pressing Enter or Return. To view all commands that match a string, press Ctrl+R repeatedly. To exit from the reverse search, press Ctrl+C.

## Setting the Command Editor

You can use the `set -o` command to make your command-line editor to be either `vi` or `emacs`. This example sets the command-line editor to be `vi`:

```
$ set -o vi
```

Now when you press Esc+K, you are placed in a mode in which you can use `vi` commands to search through the stack of previously entered commands.

For example, if you want to scroll up the command stack, you can use the K key and you can scroll down using the J key. When in this mode, you can use the slash (/) key and then type a string to be searched for in the entire command stack.

---

■ **Tip**    Before you attempt to use the command editor feature, ensure that you are thoroughly familiar with either the `vi` or `emacs` editor (see Chapter 4 for details on using `vi`).

---

A short example illustrates the power of this feature. Suppose that you know you ran the `ls -altr` command about an hour ago. You want to run it again, but this time without the r (reverse sort) option. To enter the command stack, press Esc+K:

```
$ Esc+K
```

You should now see the last command you executed. To search the command stack for the `ls` command, type `/ls` and then press Enter or Return:

```
$ /ls
```

The most recently executed `ls` command should appear at the prompt:

```
$ ls -altr
```

To remove the r option, use the right arrow key to place the prompt over the r on the screen and press X to remove the r from the end of the command. After you edit the command, press Enter or Return to have it executed.

## How It Works

Your *command history* is a stored sequential list of all the commands you have previously entered. You can use any of the techniques described in the "Solution" section of this recipe to view and manipulate previously entered commands.

The Bash shell command history is stored in your home directory in a file named `.bash_history`. If your current working directory is your home directory, you can view the contents of this file with a utility such as `cat`. The following example uses the `cd` command to navigate to the home directory and then displays the contents of the `.bash_history` file with the `cat` command:

```
$ cd
$ cat .bash_history
```

The number of entries stored in the `.bash_history` file is determined by the `HISTSIZE` OS variable. You can verify the history size using the `echo` utility. On this system, the command history size is 1000:

```
$ echo $HISTSIZE
1000
```

System administrators usually set the `HISTSIZE` variable in the `/etc/profile` file, which is automatically executed whenever a user logs on to a server. You can override the system's default value for command history by setting the `HISTSIZE` variable in a special startup file (see recipe 2-5 for details).

The easiest way to view the Bash shell command history is to use the up and down arrows to find the command of interest, and use the left and right arrows and/or the Backspace key to modify the command. Other shells typically do not allow the use of the up and down arrows.

Table 2-1 lists some common shells and what types of command history manipulation each tool supports.

***Table 2-1.*** *Command History Options Available in Each Shell*

| Shell | Up/Down Arrows | Reverse Search | Ctrl+P and Ctrl+N | set -o | Command History |
|-------|----------------|----------------|-------------------|--------|-----------------|
| Bash | Yes | Yes | Yes | Yes | Yes |
| Korn | No | No | No | Yes | Yes |
| C | No | No | No | No | Yes |

# 2-3. Automatically Completing Long Commands

## Problem

You are tired of typing long commands and wonder whether there is some way the Bash shell can automatically fill in the text for long command strings.

## Solution

The Tab key can be used for command completion. For example, suppose that there are two files in the current directory: `initRMOUGDB.ora` and `initBRDSTN.ora`:

```
$ ls
initBRDSTN.ora initRMOUGDB.ora
```

In this example, you want to edit the `initRMOUGDB.ora` file with the `vi` utility. All you have to do is type enough characters to make the file name unique within a directory and then press Tab (ensure that there is no space between the text and the Tab key):

```
$ vi initR<Tab>
```

Because there are no other files in the current directory that begin with the string `initR`, the Bash shell automatically fills in the text `initRMOUGDB.ora`:

```
$ vi initRMOUGDB.ora
```

Now you can press Enter or Return to edit this file. Note that you can use this technique on any program, directory, command, or file. For example, if you need to change directories to a subdirectory named `products`, and there are no other directories beneath your current working directory that start with the letter *p*, you can type `cd p` and then press Tab. Your prompt then shows the following:

```
$ cd products/
```

You can now press Enter or Return to execute the `cd products` command.

## How It Works

A timesaving feature of the Bash shell is *command completion*, which allows you to only partially type a program, command, file, or directory. You then press Tab, and the shell attempts to complete the rest of the text.

If the Bash shell can't uniquely identify a program, command, file, or directory, it beeps (or does nothing) after you press Tab. In this situation, if you press Tab again, the shell displays all the possible programs, commands, files, or directories that match the partially typed string.

For example, command completion can be used to show all executable files that start with a certain string. If you want to view all commands that start with the string di, type di and press Tab twice:

```
$ di<Tab><Tab>
diff        diff-jars  dir        dirname   disable    disown
diff3       dig        dircolors  dirs      disol
```

You might hear a bell or beeping sound after you enter the first Tab. The Bash shell will search for commands that start with the string di that are located in any directories contained within the PATH variable.

# 2-4. Viewing Environment Variables

## Problem

You want to view the current settings of your environment variables.

## Solution

You can use any of the following Linux/Solaris commands to display OS variables:

- printenv
- env
- set
- export
- echo

To display all variables set in your environment, use any of these commands (without any options): printenv, env, set, or export. The next bit of code uses the printenv command to show all environment variables:

```
$ printenv
```

Here's a partial listing of the output:

```
HOSTNAME=rmg.rmg.org
TERM=cygwin
SHELL=/bin/bash
HISTSIZE=1000
SSH_TTY=/dev/pts/0
USER=oracle
```

If you know the name of the variable you want to display, you can display it directly with the echo command. To display the contents of an OS variable, you must preface it with a $ (dollar sign) character. This example uses the echo command to display the contents of the USER variable:

```
$ echo $USER
oracle
```

You can also use the printenv command to display environment variables. The following example uses printenv to show the current setting of the USER variable:

```
$ printenv USER
oracle
```

## How It Works

Most DBAs work with multiple database servers. Every time you log on to a server, certain OS variables are automatically set for you. Table 2-2 lists several environment variables you should know. Use any of the commands described in the "Solution" section of this recipe to view variables in your environment.

*Table 2-2.* *Commonly Used Environment Variables*

| Variable | Description |
| --- | --- |
| PATH | Contains a list of directories in which the shell looks to find the executable commands. This variable is usually set by a shell startup script. |
| USER or LOGNAME | Contains the user account you used to log on to the server. It is automatically set for you when you log on. |
| HOME | Holds the home directory for a user. It is set for you when you log on. |
| ~ | Holds the home directory for a user. The tilde character is a shorthand way to reference your home directory. It is set for you when you log on. |
| PWD | Contains the location of the current working directory. It is set whenever you use cd to navigate to a new directory. |
| SHELL | Contains the name of your login shell. |
| EDITOR | Holds the name of the default editor used with some utilities (such as cron). |
| PS1 | Contains the values used for displaying the command prompt. |
| SHLVL | Keeps track of how many subshell levels deep your current shell is. |
| DISPLAY | Is used by X applications to determine the display server used for input and output. |

Sometimes you might not know the exact name of the variable. You can use the grep command to filter the output. This example uses the set command and sends the output to the grep command for filtering any variables:

```
$ set | grep ORA
```

Here's typical output from the previous command:

```
ORACLE_BASE=/oracle
ORACLE_HOME=/oracle/product/10.2
ORACLE_SID=RMDB1
PS1='[\h:\u:${ORACLE_SID}]$ '
```

■ **Tip** For details on all variables set by the Bash shell in your environment, inspect the output of the man bash command. Search the man page for the *Shell Variables* section.

# 2-5. Automatically Setting Shell Variables

## Problem

You want to automatically set various database variables whenever you log on to the database server.

## Solution

Place shell variables that you want automatically set (when you log on) in the .bash_profile file in your home directory. In the next example, the ORACLE_SID variable is set to BRDSTN. The following text is placed in the .bash_profile file:

```
export ORACLE_SID=BRDSTN
```

If you log off and log back on, you can verify that this variable has been set by echoing it:

```
$ echo $ORACLE_SID
BRDSTN
```

If you don't want to log off and back on, run the file manually using the . (dot) command, which executes the lines contained within a file. The following example runs the .bash_profile file:

```
$ . $HOME/.bash_profile
```

The . (dot) instructs the shell to *source* the script. Sourcing tells the shell process that you are currently logged on to inherit any variables set with an export command in an executed script. If you don't use the . (dot) notation, the variables set within the script are visible only within the context of the subshell that is spawned when the script is executed.

■ **Note** In the Bash shell, the source command is equivalent to the . (dot) command.

# How It Works

When you use the Bash shell, several special startup files can be executed for you when you first log on to your database server:

- /etc/profile
- ~/.bash_profile
- ~/.bash_login
- ~/.profile

---

■ **Note**   Depending on the version of the Linux/Solaris OS, there might be different startup files in use. Run the ls -altr command in your home directory to view all the available files. Files beginning with a dot are sometimes referred to as *hidden files* and don't appear in the output of the ls command when it is used with no arguments.

---

The /etc/profile file is maintained by your system administrator, and you need root privileges to modify it. This file sets systemwide variables common to all users logging on to the system. Here is a snippet of some typical entries in the /etc/profile file:

```
# No core files by default
ulimit -S -c 0 > /dev/null 2>&1
# Set OS variables
USER="`id -un`"
LOGNAME=$USER
MAIL="/var/spool/mail/$USER"
HOSTNAME=`/bin/hostname`
HISTSIZE=1000
```

After running the /etc/profile file, the Bash shell next searches for the following files and runs only the first file it locates (in the following order): ~/.bash_profile, ~/.bash_login, ~/.profile.

Here are some typical entries in the oracle user's ~/.bash_profile file:

```
# User specific environment and startup programs
export ORACLE_SID=O1212
export ORACLE_HOME=/u01/app/oracle/product/12.1.0.2/db_1
export PATH=$PATH:$ORACLE_HOME/bin
PS1='[\h:\u:${ORACLE_SID}]$ '
```

You should be aware of two additional important startup type files:

- ~/.bashrc
- ~/.bash_logout

If you start a nonlogin Bash shell by typing bash at the command line, the ~/.bashrc file is automatically executed for you. DBAs place commands in ~/.bashrc to ensure that database-related OS commands are consistently set, regardless of whether they are using a login shell or a nonlogin shell. A common technique to address this is to place the following code in the ~/.bash_profile file:

```
# Run .bashrc if it exists
if [ -f ~/.bashrc ]; then
        . ~/.bashrc
fi
```

When first logging on to a server, the previous bit of code checks to see whether the ~/.bashrc file exists; if so, it runs it. This method ensures that aliases and functions are defined in a consistent manner, regardless of whether it is a login or nonlogin shell.

The ~/.bash_logout file is appropriately named and is executed when you issue the exit command. Typically, you might see the clear command executed in the ~/.bash_logout file to clear text off the terminal when logging out.

# 2-6. Customizing the Command Prompt

## Problem

You work with several database servers and usually have several terminal screens open simultaneously on your screen. To avoid confusion, you want the hostname and username to display in the command prompt.

## Solution

In the Bash shell, the special OS variable PS1 holds the text string of what appears in the command prompt. This example changes the PS1 variable to hold the hostname and username:

```
PS1='[\h:\u]$ '
```

The \h and \u variables are special Bash variables that hold the hostname and username, respectively. After setting PS1 in this example, the prompt now shows the following:

```
[rmougprd1:oracle] $
```

In the prior string, rmougprd1 is the hostname, and oracle is the current OS user. You can also combine special variables and user-defined variables to be displayed in the prompt. For example, the following combination contains current hostname, username, and database SID:

```
PS1='[\h:\u:${ORACLE_SID}] $ '
```

Here's what the command prompt looks like now:

```
[rmougprd1:oracle:ORA12CR1] $
```

If you place the previous line of code in your .bashrc startup file (see recipe 2-5 for details), your prompt will automatically be set to contain hostname, OS user, and the current value of ORACLE_SID every time you log on to the server or start a new Bash shell. Additionally, if you change the value of ORACLE_SID, your prompt will automatically reflect the new setting.

# How It Works

Setting your command prompt to something informational can be invaluable for DBAs who work with multiple servers, OS accounts, and databases. If you work in complex environments, this simple technique will keep you aware of your current surroundings.

---

■ **Tip** You can view all variables available in your environment by issuing a man bash command. Search for *PROMPTING* in the man page.

---

Table 2-3 lists many of the Bash shell backslash–escaped special variables that you can use to customize your command prompt.

*Table 2-3.* *Bash Shell Backslash–Escaped Variables Used to Customize the Command Prompt*

| Variable | Description |
|----------|-------------|
| \a | ASCII bell character. |
| \d | Date in "weekday month date" format (for example, Thu Aug 21). |
| \e | ASCII escape character. |
| \h | Hostname. |
| \j | Number of jobs managed by shell. |
| \l | Base name of shell's terminal device. |
| \n | Newline. |
| \r | Carriage return. |
| \s | Name of shell. |
| \t | Time in 24-hour HH:MM:SS format. |
| \T | Time in 12-hour HH:MM:SS format. |
| \@ | Time in 12-hour a.m./p.m. format. |
| \A | Time in 24-hour HH:MM format. |
| \u | Current username. |
| \v | Version of Bash shell. |
| \V | Release of Bash shell. |
| \w | Current working directory. |
| \W | Base name of current working directory. |
| \! | History number of command. |
| \$ | If effective UID is 0, display #. Otherwise, display $. |

# 2-7. Creating a Command Shortcut

## Problem

You frequently retype long sets of commands and want to create a shortcut to the lengthy commands.

## Solution

There are two very common methods for creating shortcuts to other commands: aliases and functions. These two techniques are described in the following sections.

### Using an Alias

Suppose that you often navigate to a database background process logging destination to view log files. You have to type something similar to this:

```
$ cd /u01/app/oracle/diag/rdbms/o1212/O1212/trace
```

You can use the alias command to create a shortcut to accomplish the same task. This example creates an alias named ad (alert directory) that will change directories to a background location that is dependent on the value of the ORACLE_SID variable:

```
$ alias ad='cd /u01/app/oracle/diag/rdbms/o1212/O1212/trace'
```

Now you can type ad, which is the same as changing your current working directory to the Oracle background dump directory.

### Using a Function

You can also use a function to create command shortcuts. We provide only a brief example of how to use a function in this recipe; for full details on using functions, see Chapter 7. The following line of code creates a simple function named ad:

```
$ function ad { cd /u01/app/oracle/diag/rdbms/o1212/O1212/trace; pwd;}
```

You can now type ad at the command line to change your working directory to the Oracle background dump directory. Notice that the current working directory is displayed by the pwd command after you change directories.

## How It Works

An *alias* is a simple mechanism for creating a short piece of text that executes other shell commands. To show all aliases that have been defined, use the alias command with no arguments:

```
$ alias
```

Listed here are some common examples of alias definitions that DBAs use:

```
alias l.='ls -d .*'
alias ll='ls -l'
alias lsd='ls -altr | grep ^d'
alias ad='cd /u01/app/oracle/diag/rdbms/o1212/O1212/trace'
alias sqlp='sqlplus "/ as sysdba"'
alias shutdb='echo "shutdown immediate;" | sqlp'
alias startdb='echo "startup;" | sqlp'
alias valert='view /u01/app/oracle/diag/rdbms/o1212/O1212/trace/alert_O1212.log'
```

Depending on your implementation of Oracle's Optimal Flexible Architecture (OFA) standard and the version of Oracle, you have to modify some of the previous alias definitions. This is especially true in regard to the location of the alert.log file.

If you want to view a definition for a particular alias, use the following:

```
$ alias ad
alias ad='cd /u01/app/oracle/diag/rdbms/o1212/O1212/trace'
```

You can also use the type command to verify an alias:

```
$ type ad
ad is an alias for 'cd /u01/app/oracle/diag/rdbms/o1212/O1212/trace'
```

If you want to remove an alias definition from your current environment, use the unalias command. The following example removes the alias for ad:

```
$ unalias ad
```

The unalias command affects only your current connection. Although using aliases is a common way to create command shortcuts, we recommend using functions over aliases. Functions are more powerful because of features such as the ability to operate on parameters passed in on the command line and can contain multiple commands.

Functions are described in much more detail in Chapter 7, but we'll take a few minutes to discuss them here. DBAs commonly establish aliases and functions by setting them in the $HOME/.bashrc file. For example, here we created a file named dba_fncs and placed the following lines of code in it:

```
#------------------------------------------
# cd to alert log directory
function ad {
 if [ $ORACLE_SID = "O1212" ]; then
    cd  /u01/app/oracle/diag/rdbms/o1212/O1212/trace
 elif [ $ORACLE_SID = "DWREP" ]; then
    cd /orahome/app/oracle/diag/rdbms/dwrep/DWREP/trace
 fi
 pwd
} # ad
#------------------------------------------
```

A common practice is to create a bin directory beneath the oracle account's home directory and place the dba_fncs file in HOME/bin. The dba_fncs file can be manually sourced as follows:

```
. $HOME/bin/dba_fcns
```

If you put the prior line of code in the $HOME/.bashrc file, the functions in the dba_fncs file are sourced and available for you to use as command shortcuts every time you log on.

If you ever wonder whether a shortcut is an alias or a function, use the type command to verify a command's origin:

```
$ type ad
ad is a function
ad ()
{
  if [ $ORACLE_SID = "O1212" ]; then
    cd /u01/app/oracle/diag/rdbms/o1212/O1212/trace;
    else
      if [ $ORACLE_SID = "DWREP" ]; then
            cd /orahome/app/oracle/diag/rdbms/dwrep/DWREP/trace;
      fi;
  fi;
  pwd
}
```

# 2-8. Providing Input to Commands

## Problem

You want a shell command to receive its input from a file or another process instead of commands typed from the keyboard.

## Solution

In Linux/Solaris, you can instruct a command to receive its input from a file with the < character. This technique is known as *redirection*. In this example, the mailx command is used to send a trace file named to an e-mail address:

```
$ mailx -s "trace file" dba@gmail.com <O1212_ora_21018.trc
```

You can also use the output of one command as the input to another command. This technique is known as *pipelining*. The pipe (|) character instructs a process to receive its input from the output of another process. This example uses the output of the cat command as the input to the mail command:

```
$ cat O1212_ora_21018.trc | mailx -s "trace file" dba@gmail.com
```

This technique of piping the output from one command to another is an extremely powerful tool. It is called a *pipe* because the output of the first command flows through the pipe and becomes the input of the next command. You can also think of the pipe as a temporary memory buffer that holds the output from the command to the left of the pipe. The command to the right of the pipe uses the output stored in the memory buffer as its input. DBAs and developers use this method to chain commands together to perform complex tasks. Many examples of this approach are provided throughout the book.

## How It Works

In Linux/Solaris, there are three data streams associated with a process:

- Standard input (also called *standard in* or *stdin*)
- Standard output (also called *standard out* or *stdout*)
- Standard error (also called *stderr*)

Figure 2-1 displays the three data streams associated with each process. Starting on the left side of the figure, standard input is the data provided to the process, which is usually data entered by you from the keyboard. As demonstrated in the "Solution" section of this recipe, standard input can also come from a file or as the output of another process.

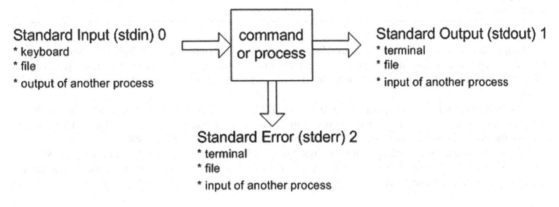

***Figure 2-1.*** *Process input and output data streams*

Shell programs often generate output data. By default, standard output data is directed to the terminal. Standard output can also be redirected to a file or another process.

Sometimes shell programs generate error messages. By default, standard error messages are displayed to your terminal. Like standard output, standard error messages can be redirected to a file or another process.

The process doesn't care where its input comes from or where the output is delivered. This means you can string together combinations of commands that feed output from one command to be used as the input to another command. This piping of command output to another command's input is a very powerful and flexible feature of the shell.

Table 2-4 summarizes the ways in which standard input, output, and errors can be redirected using the Bash shell.

*Table 2-4.* *Command Input and Output Redirection Operators*

| Operation | Bash Shell Redirection Syntax |
|---|---|
| Reads standard input from a file | `command <file` |
| Reads standard input until end of marker | `command <<end of marker` |
| Writes standard output to a file | `command >file` |
| Appends standard output to end of file | `command >>file` |
| Writes standard output and standard error to separate files | `command >file 2>file2` |
| Writes standard output and standard error to the same file | `command >file 2>&1` |
| Writes standard output and standard error to the same file | `command &> file` |
| Appends standard output and standard error to the end of a file | `command >>file 2>&1` |
| Sends (pipe) standard output of first command to input of second command | `command | command2` |
| Sends (pipe) standard output and standard error to input of second command | `command 2>&1 | command2` |

Some additional explanation is required for interpreting the second column of Table 2-4. Notice that the < and << redirection operators are used to redirect standard input. The > and >> redirection operators are used to redirect standard output. Also notice that the redirection operators > and >> are shorthand for 1> and 1>>.

The 2> and 2>> redirection operators are used to redirect standard error. The syntax 2>&1 instructs the shell to redirect the standard error stream to the same location as standard output. In the Bash shell, you can also use the syntax &> to send both standard error and standard output to the same file.

The &0, &1, and &2 file descriptors are synonymous with the /dev/stdin, /dev/stdout, and /dev/stderr files, respectively. To illustrate this point, this example uses the file /dev/stdout to redirect standard error to the same location as standard output:

```
$ cat initBRDSTN.ora 1>myfile.txt 2>/dev/stdout
```

The previous command is equivalent to the following:

```
$ cat initBRDSTN.ora 1>myfile.txt 2>&1
```

The previous command directs the standard output 1> to be sent to myfile.txt. If any errors are encountered when issuing the command (for example, if file initBRDSTN.ora doesn't exist), the standard error stream 2> is sent to the same location as standard out (which is myfile.txt).

# 2-9. Redirecting Command Output

## Problem

You want to save the output of a command to a file.

## Solution

By default, the output from a command displays on your terminal. The > character redirects the output of a command to a specified file. The > character is synonymous with 1>. For example, the following command takes the output of the cat command and places it in a file named output.txt:

```
$ cat init.ora >output.txt
```

If the init.ora file doesn't exist, you'll receive an error message such as this:

```
cat: init.ora: No such file or directory
```

## How It Works

You should know about some other interesting features of redirecting command output. For example, you can also instruct the shell command to redirect any errors that are encountered when running a script to a separate file. The 2> characters specify where errors should be written. Just as > means redirect output to a file, 2> means redirect error messages to a file. This example redirects standard output to the file output.txt and sends any error messages encountered to errors.txt:

```
$ cat init.ora >output.txt 2>errors.txt
```

You can also use a shorthand notation to send both standard output and error messages to the same file:

```
$ cat init.ora >output.txt 2>&1
```

The 2>&1 notation instructs the shell to send output stream number 2 (error output) to the same place as output stream number 1 (standard output). You'll find it useful to use this notation when running scripts such as database-monitoring jobs.

If for any reason you don't want to overwrite the output file, use the >> syntax, which instructs the shell to append any messages to the end of an existing file:

```
$ cat init.ora >>output.txt 2>&1
```

# 2-10. Sending Output to Nowhere

## Problem

You want to run a command, but you don't want the output to be shown or saved anywhere.

## Solution

If you don't want text to appear on your screen or saved in a physical file, you can send it to the proverbial "bit bucket" (referred to as the /dev/null device).

The /dev/null device is useful when you don't want to see all the error messages generated by a command. For example, the following find command generates error messages for directories that it can't read:

```
$ cd /
$ find . -name "alert*.log"
```

Here is a partial snippet of the output:

```
find: cannot read dir ./var/fm/fmd/xprt: Permission denied
find: cannot read dir ./var/fm/fmd/rsrc: Permission denied
find: cannot read dir ./var/fm/fmd/ckpt: Permission denied
```

To eliminate those error messages, send the error output to the /dev/null device:

```
$ find . -name "alert*.log" 2>/dev/null
```

If you know you will run a program or command that generates output you don't need, you can redirect the output to the /dev/null device.

---

■ **Tip**  The /dev/null device can also be used to quickly reduce a large file to 0 bytes without deleting the original file (see recipe 5-31 for details).

---

## How It Works

The /dev/null file is a special file known as the *null device*. It also called *slash dev slash null* or the *bit bucket*. It contains nothing, and any output you send to this special file will never be seen again.

The following is a slightly different example of how to use the /dev/null device. Suppose that you want to test how long it takes to read a file, but you don't want the output of the dd command to actually create a file. In this example, the output is sent to the /dev/null device using the of parameter:

```
$ time dd if=/u01/dbfile/01212/users01.dbf of=/dev/null
```

Here is some sample output:

```
20496+0 records in
20496+0 records out
10493952 bytes (10 MB) copied, 0.0820684 seconds, 128 MB/s
real    0m0.09s
user    0m0.00s
sys     0m0.01s
```

The previous command is useful for troubleshooting disk I/O issues without the overhead of physically creating a file. If you divide the data file size by the total time the command took to run, you get the disk I/O rate. You can compare that value with V$BACKUP_ASYNC_ IO.EFFECTIVE_BYTES_PER_SECOND to help you determine whether the Recovery Manager (RMAN) has a potential I/O problem.

```
CHECKING FOR DATA FILE CORRUPTION
```

In the old days, before there were tools such as `dbverify` and Oracle Recovery Manager (RMAN), DBAs needed a method to detect corrupt blocks in data files. To accomplish this, DBAs used the `export` utility. As the `export` utility runs, it writes information on detected corrupt blocks to the database `alert.log` file.

If the DBA wanted to check only for block corruption without saving the output of the export to a file, the output could be sent to the `/dev/null` file, as shown here:

```
$ exp user/pass full=y file=/dev/null
```

Thus, the DBA could detect database corruption without actually having to create a potentially large export file. Having said that, you should not rely on this approach for detecting database corruption because it has several known limitations (for example, it can't detect corruption in blocks above a table's high water mark—see MOS note 214369.1 for details). You should instead use `dbverify` or RMAN to detect bad blocks in Oracle database data files.

# 2-11. Displaying and Capturing Command Output
## Problem

You want to see the output of a command onscreen and store that output in a file.

## Solution

If you want to capture only the output associated with the execution of a specific OS command, you can use the tee command, which enables any output generated by a command to be written to both the screen and a designated file.

The following example runs the ls command to list all files in a directory. It also saves that output to a file that can later be viewed to determine the names and sizes of files on a particular date:

```
$ ls -altr /ora01/BRDSTN | tee /home/oracle/log/oct15_df.log
```

Here is some sample output of what is displayed to the screen and recorded in the log file:

```
-rw-r----- 1 oracle oinstall 52429312 Oct 15 08:00 redo03a.log
-rw-r----- 1 oracle oinstall 838868992 Oct 15 08:25 undotbs01.dbf
-rw-r----- 1 oracle oinstall 524296192 Oct 15 08:30 system01.dbf
-rw-r----- 1 oracle oinstall 15056896 Oct 15 08:37 control01.ctl
```

## How It Works

The tee command is useful when you want to interactively see the output of a command displayed onscreen and also require that the display be logged to a file that can be inspected later for debugging or troubleshooting activities. For example, when you back up a database and you want to log all output to a file, you can do so with the RMAN utility as follows:

```
$ rman target / | tee rman.log
```

Any output from commands you run while connected to RMAN are displayed onscreen and captured in the log file.

---

■ **Tip** The tee command is similar to a plumbing t-splitter pipe in that it allows one input stream to be split into separate output pipes.

---

# 2-12. Recording All Shell Command Output

## Problem

You're performing a database upgrade and you need to run several SQL scripts. You want to record the output of everything printed to your screen to a log file.

## Solution

The script command enables the recording of all output printed to your screen to also be written to an OS file. This example writes all output to a file named upgrade.log:

```
$ script upgrade.log
Script started, file is upgrade.log
```

From this point on, all output printed to your terminal is also recorded in the script upgrade.log. To end the script logging session, press Ctrl+D or type exit. You should see a message similar to this:

```
Script done, file is upgrade.log
```

## How It Works

The script command is invaluable when you need to capture all output being printed to the terminal. This command stores all output in an OS file that can later be used to verify the tasks performed and whether the operations succeeded or failed.

If you don't specify a file name when using script, a default file with the name of typescript is created. If you need to append to an already existing file, use script with the -a option, as shown here:

```
$ script -a upgrade.log
```

This code enables the capture of all output from all scripts that are being run. It can be extremely useful when you have a mix of OS commands and database commands and want to capture the output of every operation.

DBAs use the script command when the person who developed upgrade scripts (DBA #1) is passing the scripts to a different team member (DBA #2) to have those scripts executed in another database environment. In this scenario, DBA #2 will start a script job, run the upgrade scripts, end the script logging, and send the generated log file to DBA #1 for verification purposes.

# 2-13. Changing the Login Shell

## Problem

Your system administrator has set your OS account to use the Korn shell, and you want to change it to the Bash shell.

## Solution

Use the chsh (change shell) command to change the default login shell. You can specify the desired login shell directly with the -s option. In this example, the default shell for the oracle user is changed to the Bash shell:

```
$ chsh -s /bin/bash
Changing shell for oracle.
Password:
```

After successfully entering the password, a message "shell changed" is displayed. Now when you subsequently log on to the oracle account, the default shell will be the Bash shell.

## How It Works

You might want to change your shell if the default is something other than your preferred shell. We recommend that you use the Bash shell on Linux/Solaris systems. The Bash shell is very robust and incorporates most of the useful features from the Bourne shell, Korn shell, and C shell.

The valid shells available on your server are stored in the /etc/shells file. You can use the chsh -l command or the cat command to view the contents of the /etc/shells file. This example uses the cat command to display the available shells:

```
$ cat /etc/shells
/bin/sh
/bin/bash
/bin/tcsh
/bin/csh
/bin/ksh
```

Table 2-5 describes the various shells available in Linux/Solaris environments.

***Table 2-5.*** *Descriptions of Popular Shells Available*

| Shell | Description |
| --- | --- |
| bsh or sh | The original Bourne shell written by Steve Bourne. |
| bash | The Bourne Again shell is considered to be one of the most robust shells. |
| ash | The Almquist shell has a smaller footprint than the Bash shell and is useful on systems in which disk space is limited. |
| ksh | The Korn shell is popular among DBAs on many varieties of UNIX. |
| pdksh | This shell is a public domain implementation of the Korn shell. |
| tcsh | The TENEX C shell is an enhanced version of the C shell. |
| csh | The C shell is like the C programming language and is popular on many older variants of UNIX. |

You can verify what your default login shell has been set to by viewing the contents of the /etc/passwd file. For example, to view the default shell for the oracle user, use the cat and grep commands:

```
$ cat /etc/passwd | grep -i oracle
oracle:x:2000:500:sb-db1 Oracle Account:/orahome/oracle:/bin/bash
```

■ **Note**    You do not need any special privileges or the assistance of your system administrator to use the chsh command.

# 2-14. Modifying Command Path Search

## Problem

You need your shell to automatically find executable programs that aren't currently in a directory included in your PATH variable. You want to add directories to your PATH variable.

## Solution

You can manually add a directory to your PATH variable by using the export command. The following example prepends the /orahome/app/oracle directory to the current contents of the PATH variable:

```
$ export PATH=/orahome/app/oracle:$PATH
```

In the previous line of code, the PATH variable is defined to be the directory containing the Oracle binaries plus the contents of PATH directory. You separate directories in the PATH variable with a colon (:).

If you want to have a directory added to your PATH variable every time you log on to your database server, place the export command in a special startup file (see recipe 2-5 for details).

## How It Works

The export command allows you to define variables that will be available to subsequently executed commands. You can add directories to the PATH variable by exporting it. To verify the contents of your PATH variable, you can use the echo command:

```
$ echo $PATH
```

Occasionally, you might encounter an Oracle RMAN issue when the directory /usr/X11R6/bin appears in the PATH variable before the ORACLE_HOME/bin directory. You see an error message when you try to start rman:

```
$ rman target /
rman: can't open target
```

You received this error because there is an rman executable in the /usr/X11R6/bin directory that has nothing to do with the Oracle rman backup and recovery utility. In this scenario, you have to modify your PATH variable to ensure that ORACLE_HOME/bin comes before /usr/X11R6/bin:

```
$ export PATH=$ORACLE_HOME/bin:$PATH
```

The other alternative is to rename the rman executable in /usr/X11R6/bin to something like rman.X11.

---

■ **Tip** See MOS note 101050.1 for issues regarding the PATH variable and the rman executable.

---

## CURRENT WORKING DIRECTORY AND PATH

To set your path to include the current working directory, simply use this:

```
$ export PATH=$PATH:.
```

Security experts recommend against having the current working directory referenced near the beginning of a PATH variable because a malicious person could place a program in a directory that does bad things to your system. For example, somebody could place a script named ls in a user's home directory and have commands within the ls script delete files recursively. If the bad ls script is referenced before the ls command in /bin or /usr/bin, the results could be ugly.

# 2-15. Viewing Built-in Commands

## Problem

You wonder whether you're running a built-in version of a shell command or using the binary program located in the /bin directory.

## Solution

Use the help command to view all built-in commands. For example, if you type help with no arguments, all built-in commands display:

```
$ help
```

Here is a partial listing of the output:

```
alias [-p] [name[=value] ... ]      bg [job_spec ...]
 bind [-lpvsPVS] [-m keymap] [-f fi break [n]
 builtin [shell-builtin [arg ...]]  caller [EXPR]
 case WORD in [PATTERN [| PATTERN]. cd [-L|-P] [dir]
 command [-pVv] command [arg ...]    compgen [-abcdefgjksuv] [-o option
 complete [-abcdefgjksuv] [-pr] [-o continue [n]
```

You can also use the type command to determine whether a program is built in. Use the -a option of type to print all locations in the PATH variable that include a command (including all aliases and functions). The following example shows that there is a built-in pwd command and also a pwd program in the /bin directory:

```
$ type -a pwd
pwd is a shell builtin
pwd is /bin/pwd
```

---

■ **Note**   You might wonder why Linux/Solaris provides both a built-in command and a program for pwd. Because some shells might not have a built-in command for pwd, a program is explicitly provided in the /bin or /usr/bin directory.

---

## How It Works

Some commands are built in to the Bash shell. *Built in* simply means that the shell contains its own version of the command. Therefore, if you run a built-in command such as pwd, the Bash shell runs its version of the pwd command instead of the executable program located in the /bin or /usr/bin directory. If you want to explicitly run the pwd command in the /bin directory, specify the complete path and file name. This example shows how to run the pwd program located in the /bin directory:

```
$ /bin/pwd
```

In some situations, it's important to know whether a command is built in to the shell. Built-in commands execute faster than their counterparts in the /bin or /usr/bin directory because there is no overhead of looking in directories for the command and then loading the command into memory for execution.

Additionally, there are code portability issues to consider. Built-in commands typically have the same behavior from one OS to another, whereas the commands in the /bin and /usr/bin directories might behave differently between different ports of Linux/Solaris (especially older versions).

Built-in commands don't start a separate process (sometimes called *forked*, *child*, or *spawned*) when they are executed. This is a requirement of some commands such as cd because a child process can't modify its parent process. If cd were executed as a child process, it couldn't modify the current working directory of the parent process and therefore wouldn't be of much use. For this reason, the Bash shell contains its own executable code for the cd command. Table 2-6 describes some of the more commonly used Bash built-in commands.

*Table 2-6. Commonly Used Bash Built-in Commands*

| Bash Built-in Command | Description |
| --- | --- |
| cd | Changes directories |
| echo | Displays strings and the contents of variables |
| help | Displays help on Bash built-in commands |
| history | Shows recently run commands |
| pwd | Prints the current working directory |
| ulimit | Sets and displays various system resource limits imposed on the shell |

You can instruct the Bash shell to explicitly run a built-in command with the builtin command, which can be useful when porting scripts between different versions of Linux/Solaris.

The builtin command runs the built-in version of the command, even if there is an alias declared for it. This example runs the pwd built-in command:

```
$ builtin pwd
```

Likewise, you can explicitly instruct Bash to run the Linux/Solaris program version of a command, even if there is a built-in command or alias defined with the same name. This example runs the program version of the pwd command located in the /bin directory:

```
$ command pwd
```

You can also use the enable command to enable or disable the use of a built-in command. This example uses enable -n to disable the pwd built-in command:

```
$ enable -n pwd
$ type pwd
pwd is /bin/pwd
```

This example re-enables the pwd command:

```
$ enable pwd
$ type pwd
pwd is a shell builtin
```

---

■ **Tip** You can also use the man bash command to view all built-in commands. When viewing the man page, search for *"shell builtin"* string.

---

# 2-16. Setting the Backspace Key

## Problem

You entered a command incorrectly and you want to backspace over previously entered characters so that you can correct them. When you attempt to use the Backspace key, it shows the ^? characters instead of deleting the previously entered characters.

## Solution

Use the stty command to set your Backspace key to delete characters properly. The following bit of code sets the Backspace key to delete characters:

```
$ stty erase Ctrl+Backspace
```

In the previous command, ensure that you press the Ctrl and Backspace keys at the same time. This might vary depending on your system; for example, the following is an alternative way of setting the Backspace key:

```
$ stty erase <Backspace>
```

In the previous line of code, don't type the word *Backspace*; instead, press the Backspace key.

## How It Works

The stty command is used to view and change terminal settings. To view current stty settings, issue the following command:

```
$ stty -a
speed 38400 baud; rows 36; columns 97; line = 0;
intr = ^C; quit = ^\; erase = ^?; kill = ^U; eof = ^D; eol = <undef>; eol2 = <undef>;
...
```

When you work with older versions of Linux or Solaris, you might be logged on to a server when the Backspace key doesn't work. In such situations, you have to manually set the Backspace key to function correctly. If you want the Backspace key to be automatically set every time you log on to the server, place the stty command in a special startup file (see recipe 2-5 for details).

---

■ **Note** On some older Linux or Solaris systems, you might need to use the stty erase ^H command or the stty erase ^? command to set the Backspace key.

---

# 2-17. Typing a Long Command in Multiple Lines

## Problem

You want to type a long command, but it doesn't fit nicely on one line.

# Solution

To extend a line of code to the next line, use the backslash (\) character, followed by pressing Enter or Return. The following example shows how to break a long rman connection command over several lines:

```
$ /usr/oracle/product/10.2.0/db_1/bin/rman \
> target / \
> catalog rman/rman@db11g_bllnx1 \
> cmdfile=/home/oracle/scripts/rmancheck.rmn \
> msglog=/home/oracle/rmanlog/rmancheck01.log append
```

Although you could have typed the previous command on one line, consider breaking a command up into multiple lines when you have a limited terminal width.

# How It Works

Sometimes it is desirable to extend a command across multiple lines for readability reasons. When you type \ followed by pressing Enter or Return, the next line will be preceded by the > character. This character indicates that the command has been extended to the next line. Both the backslash and the new line marker are ignored when this technique is used.

It doesn't matter which location within the command the backslash is placed; you can break a command over as many lines as necessary.

# CHAPTER 3

■ ■ ■

# Managing Processes and Users

Diagnosing and resolving availability and performance issues is a key part of every DBA's job. When troubleshooting problems, DBAs often start by identifying the processes that are currently running and identifying details about users logged on to the server. It is critical to know how to extract process and user activity from the OS.

When you work with OS users and processes, some of your tasks require root privileges. For example, when you install database software on the server, one of the first steps is to create an OS user and group. Depending on your environment, you might not have a system administrator (SA) to perform these operations. In this scenario, you have to log on to the server with root privileges and perform these tasks yourself. Even if you do have an SA, you have to adequately document and communicate with your SA about the database setup tasks that require root privileges. Therefore, it's important to know which database tasks require root privileges and the commands to execute them.

This chapter starts by showing commands that get information about processes and users. It then progresses to examples of how to access the root account. The chapter wraps up with common database installation tasks that require root privileges, such as adding OS users and groups.

## 3-1. Listing Processes

### Problem

You want to view processes currently running on the database server.

### Solution

To view process information, use the ps (process status) utility. If you type the ps command without any parameters, you see all processes that have been started by the user you're currently logged on as:

```
$ ps
PID    TTY      TIME CMD
12620 pts/1    00:00:00 bash
14103 pts/1    00:00:00 ps
```

If you want to view all processes running on a box, use the -e and -f options to show every process in a full output format:

```
$ ps -ef
```

51

If many processes are running on a box, it is useful to pipe the output of ps to grep and display only a particular user or process name. For example, to determine which Oracle instances are running on the server, you can filter the output to display only Oracle system monitor (SMON) background processes executing. In this example, ps and grep are used to show any processes that contain the string smon (the grep -v grep removes grep from the output):

```
$ ps -ef | grep -i smon | grep -v grep
oracle    7994    1  0 Jan25 ?        00:01:43 ora_smon_TRG
oracle   28035    1  0 Feb23 ?        00:00:50 ora_smon_ORA12CR1
```

The first column indicates that oracle is the OS owner of the processes. The second column contains the process identifier. The fifth column shows that one Oracle instance was started on January 25th, and the other was started on February 23rd. The seventh column indicates that the TRG database SMON process has consumed 1 hour and 43 minutes of CPU time, and the ORA12CR1 database SMON process has consumed 50 minutes. The last column is the name of the process (and the target of the grep command). There are two databases running on this server, as evidenced by two Oracle SMON background processes.

## How It Works

Every time you run a Linux/Solaris command, a process is automatically created for you. Each process is assigned a unique number called a *process identifier* (PID). DBAs use the ps utility for a couple of important reasons:

- Checking on background processes

- Identifying hung or runaway processes that need to be killed

- Troubleshooting performance issues

When there are database connectivity issues, the ps command is useful to quickly identify whether a required database background processes is running. To list all processes for a specific user, use the -u (user) option and specify a username. This example lists all processes running under the oracle user with a full listing of the output:

```
$ ps -fu oracle
```

Here's a snippet of the output:

```
UID        PID  PPID  C STIME TTY      TIME     CMD
oracle    7964    1   0 Jan25 ?        00:03:54 ora_pmon_TRG
oracle    7966    1   0 Jan25 ?        00:11:35 ora_psp0_TRG
oracle    7968    1   0 Jan25 ?        08:55:51 ora_vktm_TRG
oracle    7972    1   0 Jan25 ?        00:02:23 ora_gen0_TRG
oracle    7974    1   0 Jan25 ?        00:01:41 ora_mman_TRG
...
```

When you diagnose database performance issues, it can sometimes be useful to get an overall count of the number of Oracle processes running on a server. Obtaining the overall count of Oracle processes is especially useful when trying to determine whether you have some sort of runaway process that is unnecessarily spawning SQL connections or parallel processes. This example pipes the output of ps to the wc (word count) command. The -l switch instructs wc to count the number of lines in the output:

```
$ ps -fu oracle | wc -l
84
```

This output indicates there are 84 Oracle processes running, which is within the normal range for a server running a database. Although there is no black-and-white rule of thumb to tell you how many processes should be running, if the process count is into the hundreds per database, you should investigate what program is starting the processes and determine whether it is normal for that database and application.

# 3-2. Terminating Processes

## Problem

You're running a database backup job, and you think the process is hung. You want to kill the process.

## Solution

The OS PID can be used to terminate a process with the kill utility. In this example, ps is used to show the PID of an RMAN backup job that seems to be hung and needs to be terminated:

```
$ ps -ef | egrep 'rman|UID' | egrep -v egrep
```

Here is some sample output:

```
UID        PID  PPID  C STIME TTY         TIME CMD
oracle    6822  6234  0 11:40 pts/0    00:00:00 rman target /
```

The PID is 6822 in this example. To terminate that process, issue a kill command, as shown here:

```
$ kill -9 6822
```

The -9 option sends a kill signal to the process, which causes it to terminate. You don't see any output from the kill command because it unceremoniously removes the specified process. Ensure that you don't kill the wrong Oracle process. If you accidentally kill a required Oracle background process, your instance will abort.

---

■ **Note**   To see a list of all available types of kill signals, use the kill -l command.

---

## How It Works

To run the kill command, you either have to own the process or have root privileges. Sometimes it is necessary to use the kill command to terminate unresponsive database processes. For example, you might sometimes need to kill a long-running or hung Oracle process (e.g., RMAN, SQL*Plus, and so on). If you know the process name, you can use the ps command to identify the PID (as shown in the solution section of this recipe).

In some situations, you might not know the OS process name. In these scenarios, you can identify the PID by querying data dictionary views, as shown here:

```
ACCEPT active DEFAULT 'y' PROMPT 'Active only processes y/n? [y is default]: '
SET LINES 200 PAGES 0 HEAD OFF LONG 100000
COL dummy_value NOPRINT
--
```

```
SELECT 'dummy_value' dummy_value,
  'USERNAME      : ' || s.username       || CHR(10) ||
  'SCHEMA        : ' || s.schemaname     || CHR(10) ||
  'OSUSER        : ' || s.osuser         || CHR(10) ||
  'MODULE        : ' || s.program        || CHR(10) ||
  'ACTION        : ' || s.schemaname     || CHR(10) ||
  'CLIENT INFO : ' || s.osuser           || CHR(10) ||
  'PROGRAM       : ' || s.program        || CHR(10) ||
  'SPID          : ' || p.spid           || CHR(10) ||
  'SID           : ' || s.sid            || CHR(10) ||
  'SERIAL#       : ' || s.serial#        || CHR(10) ||
  'KILL STRING : ' || '''' || s.sid || ',' || s.serial# || '''' || CHR(10) ||
  'MACHINE       : ' || s.machine        || CHR(10) ||
  'TYPE          : ' || s.type           || CHR(10) ||
  'TERMINAL      : ' || s.terminal       || CHR(10) ||
  'CPU           : ' || q.cpu_time/1000000     || CHR(10) ||
  'ELAPSED_TIME: ' || q.elapsed_time/1000000 || CHR(10) ||
  'BUFFER_GETS : ' || q.buffer_gets      || CHR(10) ||
  'SQL_ID        : ' || q.sql_id         || CHR(10) ||
  'CHILD_NUM     : ' || q.child_number   || CHR(10) ||
  'START_TIME    : ' || TO_CHAR(s.sql_exec_start,'dd-mon-yy hh24:mi') || CHR(10) ||
  'STATUS        : ' || s.status         || CHR(10) ||
  'SQL_TEXT      : ' || q.sql_fulltext
FROM              v$session s
JOIN              v$process p ON (s.paddr  = p.addr)
LEFT OUTER JOIN v$sql      q ON (s.sql_id = q.sql_id)
WHERE s.username IS NOT NULL -- eliminates background procs
AND NVL(q.sql_text,'x') NOT LIKE '%dummy_value%' -- eliminates this query from output
AND s.status != DECODE('&&active','n','xyz','N','xyz','INACTIVE')
ORDER BY q.cpu_time;
```

You'll be prompted about whether you want to see only active sessions displayed in the output:

```
Active only processes y/n? [y is default]:
```

Press Enter; here's some sample output from the previous query:

```
USERNAME      : SYS
SCHEMA        : SYS
OSUSER        : oracle
MODULE        : rman@cs-xvm (TNS V1-V3)
ACTION        : SYS
CLIENT INFO : oracle
PROGRAM       : rman@cs-xvm (TNS V1-V3)
SPID          : 9458
SID           : 102
SERIAL#       : 49521
KILL STRING : '102,49521'
MACHINE       : cs-xvm
TYPE          : USER
TERMINAL      : pts/0
```

```
CPU           :
ELAPSED_TIME  :
BUFFER_GETS   :
SQL_ID        :
CHILD_NUM     :
START_TIME    :
STATUS        : ACTIVE
SQL_TEXT      :
```

From the name of the program in the prior output, you can tell this is an RMAN process executing. The SPID column in the output is the OS PID. Once the SPID is identified, the `kill` command can be used to terminate the process:

```
$ kill -9 9458
```

---

■ **Caution**    In some rare situations, killing an Oracle process associated with a SQL transaction can have an adverse impact on the stability of the instance. For example, killing a process participating in a distributed transaction might cause the instance to crash. To determine whether this is an issue for the version of the database you're using, see MOS bug IDs 8686128 and 12961905. In older versions of Oracle, various other bugs associated with killing a process have been identified and fixed and are documented in MOS bug IDs 5929055 and 6865378.

---

You can also kill a database connection with the SQL*Plus `alter system kill session` command by using the session ID (SID) and serial number. Here is the general syntax:

```
alter system kill session 'integer1, integer2 [,integer3]' [immediate];
```

In this syntax statement, `integer1` is the value of the SID column, and `integer2` is the value from the SERIAL# column (of V$SESSION). In an RAC environment, you can optionally specify the value of the instance ID for `integer3`. The instance ID can be retrieved from the GV$SESSION view.

As a DBA privileged user, the following command kills the database connection that has an SID of 102 and a serial number of 49521:

```
SQL> alter system kill session '102,49521'
```

If successful, you should see this output:

```
System altered.
```

When you kill a session, the session is marked as terminated, active transactions (within the session) are rolled back, and any locks (held by the session) are released. The session will stay in a terminated state until any dependent transactions are rolled back. If it takes a minute or more to roll back the transaction, Oracle reports the session as "marked to be terminated" and returns control to the SQL prompt. Suppose that you specify IMMEDIATE:

```
SQL> alter system kill session '102,49521' immediate;
```

Oracle will roll back any active transactions and immediately return control back to you.

---

■ **Caution**   Killing a session that is executing a select statement is fairly harmless. However, if you terminate a session that is performing a large insert/update/delete, you might see a great deal of database activity (including I/O in the online redo logs) associated with Oracle rolling back the terminated transaction.

---

# 3-3. Listing the Users Logged On

## Problem

You are experiencing performance problems with your database server. To help diagnose the issues, you first want to view all users currently logged on to the box.

## Solution

Use the who command to display the users logged on to a box:

```
$ who
```

The output consists of four columns: users logged on, terminal name, time they logged on, and location where they logged on. Here's a typical listing of the who command:

```
ptownshend    pts/1        Jun 15 14:17 (vpn-229-150-36-51.com)
rdaltrey      pts/2        Aug 10 22:11 (122.120.44.181)
jentwistle    pts/3        Aug 16 03:14 (111.155.23.114)
kmoon         pts/4        Sep 4  01:23  (10.6.77.121)
kjones        pts/6        Dec 4  06:66  (101.120.23.171)
```

You can also use the who command with the am i option to display your current user information:

```
$ who am i
oracle   pts/2        Aug 4 15:30 (vpn-109-150-32-93.brdstn.com)
```

---

■ **Tip**   You can also use whoami or the id -un to display information about your current user. Contrast this with the who am i command, which always shows which user you initially used to log on to a server. For example, if you su to a different user, whoami displays your current user status, whereas who am i shows which user you originally logged on to the server as.

---

# How It Works

The who command is important for listing a snapshot of users logged on to the server. An alternative to the who command is the w utility. This simply titled but powerful tool is an extension to the who command. The output of the w command is like a combination of the listings from the who, uptime, and ps -a commands. This example uses the w command to eavesdrop on who is logged on to the system and what they are doing:

```
$ w
17:59:54 up 9 days,  5:37,  4 users,  load average: 0.00, 0.00, 0.00
USER     TTY     FROM               LOGIN@  IDLE   JCPU   PCPU   WHAT
enehcd   pts/1   vpn-128-156-33-6   12:32    5:46  0.12s  0.12s  -bash
evork    pts/2   vpn-129-156-33-6   15:22   34:14  0.01s  0.01s  -chmod
aznoga   pts/3   vpn-129-156-32-6   17:22   55:24  0.03s  0.01s  -sleep
wroot    pts/4   vpn-129-150-150-   17:48   0.00s  0.02s  0.00s     w
```

The first line of the w output is similar to that produced by the uptime command; it shows current time, how long the system has been up, number of users, and system load averages. After the header line, it displays users logged on, from where and what time, how long they've been idle, current job CPU (JCPU), foreground process CPU (PCPU), and what command the user is running.

To specifically look at one user, specify the process name as an option. The following command looks at all oracle accounts logged on to the server:

```
$ w oracle
```

The following output indicates that there are two active oracle users on the box:

```
14:14:58 up 130 days, 21:52,  2 users,  load average: 0.00, 0.00, 0.00
USER     TTY     FROM               LOGIN@  IDLE   JCPU   PCPU   WHAT
oracle   pts/1   63-231-82-100.hl   13:10   0.00s  0.03s  0.00s  w oracle
oracle   pts/2   63-231-82-100.hl   14:14   6.00s  0.01s  0.01s  -bash
```

If a user has logged on twice to a server (as in the previous output), you can use the tty command to identify a session. Log on to one of the oracle sessions; here is the tty command and its output:

```
$ tty
/dev/pts/1
```

You can also use the finger command to display information about users logged on to a server. If you don't provide the finger command with a username, it will display all users on a system:

```
$ finger
Login       Name       Tty       Idle  Login Time   Office     Office Phone
oracle                 pts/0           Jun 20 13:29  (br-ea-fw-nat.surg.com)
oracle                 pts/1       2   Jun 20 13:29  (br-ea-fw-nat.surg.com)
```

The pinky command is a lightweight version of the finger command. If no users are specified as a parameter, all users logged on will display:

```
$ pinky
Login       Name       TTY       Idle  When          Where
oracle                 pts/0           Jun 20 13:29   br-ea-fw-nat.surg.com
oracle                 pts/1     00:03 Jun 20 13:29   br-ea-fw-nat.surg.com
```

# 3-4. Listing the Last Logon Time of a User

## Problem

You think that somebody might have hacked into the database OS account, so you want to see when the last time the `oracle` account was logged on to the database server.

## Solution

Use the `last` command to determine a user's last logon time. This bit of code determines the last time the `oracle` account logged on to the database server:

```
$ last oracle
oracle    pts/1    63-227-41-191.hl Fri Dec 21 17:18    still  logged in
oracle    pts/1    63-227-41-191.hl Mon Dec 17 15:55 - 17:53  (01:58)
oracle    pts/1    63-227-41-191.hl Mon Dec 17 11:55 - 13:33  (01:38)
oracle    pts/1    63-227-41-191.hl Mon Dec 17 08:28 - 10:45  (02:17)
oracle    pts/0    63-227-41-191.hl Sat Dec 15 20:59 - 22:00  (01:00)
oracle    pts/0    63-227-41-191.hl Sat Dec 15 20:43 - 20:59  (00:15)
```

The output indicates that the `oracle` user is currently logged on and has logged on several times in the month of December.

## How It Works

If you use the `last` command without any arguments, it displays the last logon time of all users. You can pipe the output of `last` to the `less` command to display one page at a time:

```
$ last | less
```

You can also limit the output of `last` by piping its output to the head command. The following will display the last ten users logged on:

```
$ last | head
```

---

■ **Tip**  On Linux servers, the `last` command retrieves its information from the `/var/log/wtmp` file, which records all logons and logouts on the server. On Solaris servers, the `/var/adm/wtmpx` file is used to record logons and logouts.

---

Another useful command in regard to last logons is the `lastb` utility. This useful command displays a list of recent bad logon attempts. When first using `lastb`, you might see the following output:

```
lastb: /var/log/btmp: No such file or directory
Perhaps this file was removed by the operator to prevent logging lastb info.
```

The previous message means that the `/var/log/btmp` file needs to be created. You can enable `lastb` by running the following commands as `root` (# indicates that the command is run as `root`):

```
# touch /var/log/btmp
# chown --reference=/var/log/wtmp /var/log/btmp
# chmod --reference=/var/log/wtmp /var/log/btmp
```

# 3-5. Limiting the Number of User Processes

## Problem

For security purposes, your database installation instructions indicate that you need to limit the number of processes that can be started by the database OS account. By limiting the number of processes a user can start, you ensure that no single user can consume inordinate amounts of resources on the server.

## Solution

On a Linux system, as the `root` user, add an entry in the `/etc/security/limits.conf` file that restricts the number of concurrently running processes for an OS account. The following lines of code (in the `limits.conf` file) establish a soft limit of 2,047 and impose a hard limit of 16,384 processes for the `oracle` OS user:

```
oracle      soft    nproc        2047
oracle      hard    nproc        16384
```

A soft limit enforces a maximum of 2,047 processes that can be running simultaneously by the `oracle` OS user. The `oracle` user can manually override the soft limit (with the `ulimit` command) and increase the limit on the number of processes up to 16,384 processes. Only the `root` user can modify the hard limit to be higher.

---

■ **Tip**    See Chapter 9 for full details on configuring `oracle` shell limits.

---

To limit the number of processes on a Solaris system, set the `maxusers` parameter in the `/etc/system` file. This parameter doesn't set a hard limit for the number of processes; instead, it is used by Solaris to derive the overall number of processes allowed. The formula Solaris uses to calculate the maximum number of processes varies by release.

## How It Works

For performance and security reasons, you might want to impose a limit on the number of processes allowed on a server. If you're feeling brave, you can test the maximum number of processes allowed by running this function:

```
: () { :|:& };:
```

The previous bit of code creates a `:` function that recursively calls itself and puts its processes in the background. Be warned that you can lock up your system if you don't properly have process limits in place. This type of program is known as a *fork bomb*. It is appropriately named because it continuously creates (forks) new processes on the system. Because the program starts itself in the background, it cannot be stopped by pressing Ctrl+C.

# 3-6. Viewing How Long the Server Has Been Running

## Problem

You want to know how long the server has been running.

## Solution

Use the uptime command to determine how long your database server has been running:

```
$ uptime
08:37:00 up 33 days, 16:14, 1 user, load average: 0.00, 0.00, 0.00
```

This output shows that this server has been up for a little more than 33 days.

## How It Works

When resolving database availability issues, it is sometimes helpful to know when the server was last rebooted because (not surprisingly) there is a direct correlation between the server being down and the database being unavailable. Viewing the server uptime can help determine whether the database was unavailable because of a system reboot.

Interestingly, the output of uptime is identical to the first line of the w command. The next example shows running the w command and the corresponding output:

```
$ w
 08:37:01 up 33 days, 16:14,  1 user,  load average: 0.00, 0.00, 0.00
USER     TTY      FROM             LOGIN@   IDLE   JCPU   PCPU  WHAT
oracle   pts/0    63-227-41-191.hl 07:11    0.00s  0.06s  0.00s w
```

In the first line of the output, 08:37:01 is the current time on the server. Also displayed in the first line are load averages for the past 1, 5, and 15 minutes.

# 3-7. Viewing How Long a Process Has Been Running

## Problem

You wonder how long the Oracle database background processes have been running.

## Solution

Use the ps -ef command to determine how long a process has been running. This line code uses ps with the egrep command to find out when the Oracle system monitor process was started:

```
$ ps -ef | egrep 'smon|UID' | egrep -v egrep
UID        PID PPID C STIME TTY          TIME  CMD
Oracle    8843    1 0 Oct31 ?        00:02:33  ora_smon_RMDB1
```

In this command, the process status output is filtered by egrep to list any lines that contain either smon or UID. When you filter also for the UID string, the header of the ps command displays. In the output, the SMON process was started on October 31 and has consumed 2 hours and 33 minutes of CPU on the database server.

## How It Works

When troubleshooting database problems, you might want to know when your database was last started. For example, you might have had an unexpected server reboot, which caused the databases to stop and restart. You can verify the time your database process was started by using the ps command.

The following is another slight variation of how DBAs use the process status command:

```
$ ps -ef | grep smon | grep -v grep
oracle    8843    1  0 Oct31 ?       00:02:33 ora_smon_RMDB1
```

This command limits the output to just the specific process that you're interested in observing. The grep -v grep code strips out any lines containing the string grep from the output.

# 3-8. Displaying Your Username

## Problem

You want to display your OS username.

## Solution

Use the id command to display the OS account you're current logged on as:

```
$ id
```

Listed next is a sample of output. By default, both the user and group information are displayed:

```
uid=56689(oracle) gid=500(oinstall) groups=500(oinstall),501(dba)
```

---

■ **Tip**    Use the groups command if you just want to display the groups of your current OS account.

---

## How It Works

An effective DBA has to be good at multitasking. You'll find yourself logged on to multiple boxes in a myriad of development, test, and production environments. It is easy to lose your bearings; when you do, you'll want to identify the OS account you're currently using. You can instinctively fulfill this need with the id command.

You can also use the who command with the am i option to display the user you used to log on to the box:

```
$ who am i
oracle    pts/2         Aug 4 15:30 (vpn-109-150-32-93.brdstn.com)
```

You can also use whoami or id -un to display information about your current user; the who am i command shows information about the user you used to originally log on to the box. For example, if you initially log on to a box as oracle and then switch to the root user, the whoami command will display root, whereas the who am i command will display oracle:

```
# who am i
oracle    pts/2        Jun 20 14:20 (br-ea-fw-nat.surg.com)
# whoami
root
# id -un
root
```

# 3-9. Changing Your Password

## Problem

You have just been handed a new database server and want to change your password to something more secure than changeme.

## Solution

Use the passwd command to change your password. Log on to the user account you want to change the password for and type passwd with no options:

```
$ passwd
```

After you type the passwd command, you are prompted to type the current password and then to enter the new password twice:

```
Changing password for user oracle.
Changing password for oracle
(current) UNIX password:
New UNIX password:
Retype new UNIX password:
passwd: all authentication tokens updated successfully.
```

## How It Works

As a DBA, you manage passwords for various OS accounts on the database servers that you log on to. Use the passwd command to ensure that your database OS user is secure and available for your use.

If you have access to the root user, you can change passwords for other users. This example changes the password for the oracle OS user:

```
# passwd oracle
```

You are then prompted to type a new password for the oracle OS user:

```
Changing password for user oracle.
New UNIX password:
Retype new UNIX password:
passwd: all authentication tokens updated successfully.
```

To set up additional password security, use the chage program. This utility can be used to set the maximum amount of time that a password is valid. This example is run as the root user specifies that the oracle user will have to change its password after 60 days:

```
# chage -M 60 oracle
```

To verify the changes to the oracle user, use the -l option:

```
# chage -l oracle
Last password change                                    : Mar 08, 2015
Password expires                                        : May 07, 2015
Password inactive                                       : never
Account expires                                         : never
Minimum number of days between password change          : -1
Maximum number of days between password change          : 60
Number of days of warning before password expires       : -1
```

The chage utility is part of the Shadow Password Suite. This suite includes programs such as chfn, chpasswd, chsh, dpasswd, expiry, faillog, and so on. You can add this group of programs to your system to provide extra security. These utilities allow you to encrypt user passwords in the /etc/shadow file, which is readable only with root privileges.

# 3-10. Becoming the System Privileged (root) User

## Problem

You're installing Oracle on a database server, and an SA is not available. You need to become root (sometimes referred to as the *superuser*) so that you can add new OS groups and user accounts.

## Solution

You need the root user password for this recipe to work. Use the su - command to switch to the root account. The - (hyphen) option specifies that the target user's login shell will be invoked (it runs all login scripts of the target user):

```
$ su - root
```

Or you can simply do this:

```
$ su -
```

You should now see a prompt similar to this:

```
Password:
```

After a successful logon, your shell prompt will change to the # character, indicating that you are now logged on as root:

```
#
```

You can now perform such tasks as adding the groups and users required for the database installation. To exit from the root user, type the following:

```
# exit
```

---

■ **Note**   You can also press Ctrl+D to exit a shell login.

---

## How It Works

Some database installation tasks require root privileges. Sometimes an SA isn't available to perform these tasks, or your SA might be comfortable with temporarily providing you access with the root account. However, competent SAs rarely give out the root password to DBAs (or any non-SA users, for that matter). There are several problems with providing *carte blanche* superuser access:

- It is hard to trace who did what on the system.

- Security is better administered by granting privileges on an "as-needed" basis, not through wide-open system access.

If several people have direct access to the root password, and one of them logs on to the system and accidentally removes critical files, it is hard to tell who did the damaging deed. For this reason, SAs do not usually provide direct root access. Instead, they provide auditable and/or limited access to root privileges through the sudo command (see recipe 3-11 for details).

# 3-11. Running Commands as the root User

## Problem

You want access to commands that can be run only by root, but your security-conscious SA won't give you the root password.

## Solution

Have your SA insert the appropriate entries in the /etc/sudoers file to grant access to restricted commands. You can be granted complete root access or access to only specified commands.

As the root user, use the visudo command to add an entry to the /etc/sudoers file. The visudo command ensures that the /etc/sudoers file is edited in a secure fashion. When using visudo, the sudoers file is locked to disallow multiple users from simultaneously editing the file. The visudo command also performs a syntax check on any edits to the /etc/sudoers file and saves only correct entries.

For example, the SA can provide root access to the oracle account by adding the following line to the /etc/sudoers file:

```
oracle ALL=(ALL) ALL
```

The oracle account can use sudo to execute commands (that would otherwise be required to run as the root user). For example, the groupadd command can now be run by oracle as follows:

```
$ sudo /usr/sbin/groupadd dba
```

The first time you run sudo, you are prompted for your password (not the root password). For a short period of time (5 minutes by default), you can run sudo without being prompted for your password again.

You can also specify that only certain commands can be run with root privileges. For example, if your SA wanted to limit the oracle account to the commands that add groups and users, the /etc/sudoers entry would be as follows:

```
oracle ALL=/usr/sbin/groupadd,/usr/sbin/useradd
```

This method allows your SA to limit access to specific commands that require root privileges. You can view the commands you are allowed to run as sudo with the following command:

```
$ sudo -l
```

The following output shows that this server has been configured to allow the oracle account to run the following commands:

```
User oracle may run the following commands on this host:
(root) /usr/sbin/groupadd, (root) /usr/sbin/useradd
```

## How It Works

The sudo command allows a command to be executed as the root user. The sudo permissions are maintained in the /etc/sudoers file by the SA.

One compelling reason for using sudo is that it allows SAs to grant superuser access without having to give out the root password. This allows SAs to temporarily grant root access to consultants who might have short-term assignments and require root access. SAs can also quickly revoke root access by deleting the appropriate entry from the /etc/sudoers file without affecting other users.

Another advantage of using sudo is that it provides an audit trail. An entry is written to a system log file in the /var/log directory whenever a sudo command is issued. Additionally, you can specify a log file for sudo activity by placing the following line in the /etc/sudoers file:

```
Defaults logfile=/var/log/sudolog
```

After successfully adding the previous line to the /etc/sudoers file, all commands run as sudo are logged on to /var/log/sudolog.

# 3-12. Adding a Group

## Problem

You're performing a database installation and need to add an OS group.

## Solution

Use the groupadd command to add OS groups. Typical Oracle installations require that you add two groups: oinstall and dba. If you have root access, you can run the groupadd command as shown here:

```
# groupadd oinstall
# groupadd dba
```

If you don't have access to a root account, your SA has to run the commands in this recipe. Sometimes SAs are amenable to granting root access via the sudo command (see recipe 3-11 for details).

If you have a company requirement that a group be set up with the same group ID on different servers, use the -g option. This example explicitly sets the group ID to 505:

```
# groupadd -g 505 dba
```

Sometimes it's desirable to consistently create groups with the same group ID across multiple servers. For example, in Network File System (NFS) environments, you might encounter permission problems unless the group is set up with the same group ID across multiple servers.

## How It Works

Sometimes DBAs are required to perform system administration tasks such as adding (or deleting) users and adding (or deleting) groups because an SA might not be available in some environments. Or you might be installing database software on your workstation and you are the SA. Regardless of the situation, you should be familiar with these types of tasks so that you can build and maintain your database server.

You can verify that the group was added successfully by inspecting the contents of the /etc/group file. Here are the entries created in the /etc/group file after running the commands in the "Solution" section of this recipe:

```
oinstall:x:500:
dba:x:501:
```

If you need to remove a group, use the groupdel command (see recipe 3-13 for details). If you need to modify a group, use the groupmod command.

---

■ **Tip**  On Linux systems, if you have access to an X Window terminal, you might want to investigate using the system-config-users utility. This graphical tool allows you to add and delete users and groups.

---

# 3-13. Removing a Group

## Problem

You want to clean up a database server and remove an old dba OS group.

## Solution

Use the groupdel command to remove OS groups. This command requires root access. The following command deletes the dba group:

```
# groupdel dba
```

If you don't have access to a root account, your SA has to run the commands in this recipe. Sometimes SAs are willing to grant root access via the sudo command (see recipe 3-11 for details).

## How It Works

You will not be prompted to confirm whether you really want to delete a group, so make certain you really want to delete a group before using the groupdel command. You can view the /etc/group file to verify that the group has been deleted.

---

■ **Note** You cannot remove a group that is a user's primary group. You must first modify or delete the users who have the group to be deleted (so that the group isn't the primary group of any user on the system).

---

# 3-14. Adding a User

## Problem

You're doing a database installation and need to create an OS user.

## Solution

Use the useradd command to add OS users. This command requires root access. The following command creates an OS account named oracle, with the primary group being oinstall, and the dba group specified as a supplementary group:

```
# useradd -g oinstall -G dba oracle
```

If you don't have access to a root account, your SA has to run the commands in this recipe. Sometimes SAs are agreeable to granting root access via the sudo command (see recipe 3-11 for details).

If you have a company requirement that a user be set up with the same user ID across multiple servers, use the -u option. This example explicitly sets the user ID to 500:

```
# useradd -u 500 -g oinstall -G dba
```

Sometimes it's desirable to consistently create a user with the same user ID on different servers. For example, in NFS environments, you might encounter permission problems unless the user is set up with the same user ID on all servers.

## How It Works

Occasionally as a DBA you will perform system administration–type tasks such as adding (or deleting) users and adding (or deleting) groups. In some environments, an SA might not be available. Or you might be installing database software on your workstation and you are the SA. Regardless of the situation, you should be familiar with these types of tasks so that you are better able to build and maintain your database server.

You can verify user account information by viewing the /etc/passwd file. Here is what you can expect to see after running the useradd command in the "Solution" section of this recipe:

```
oracle:x:500:500::/home/oracle:/bin/bash
```

During the process of creating a new user, the /etc/skel directory contains the files and directories that are automatically created for new users added to the server with the useradd command. Typical files included are .bashrc, .bash_profile, and .bash_logout. The location of the /etc/skel directory can be changed by modifying the value of SKEL in the /etc/default/useradd file.

The userdel command can be used to delete a user (see recipe 3-15 for details). Use the usermod command to modify existing accounts.

---

■ **Tip** If you have access to an X Window terminal, you might want to investigate using the system-config-users utility. This is a graphical tool that allows you to add and delete users and groups.

---

# 3-15. Removing a User

## Problem

You want to clean up a server and remove an old oracle OS account.

## Solution

Use the userdel command to remove an OS account. You need root privileges to run the userdel command. This example removes the oracle user from the server:

```
# userdel oracle
```

If you don't have access to a root account, your SA has to run the commands in this recipe. Sometimes SAs are open to granting root access via the sudo command (see recipe 3-11 for details).

## How It Works

You will not be prompted to confirm whether you really want to delete a user, so make certain you absolutely want to remove a user before using the userdel command. You can view the /etc/ passwd file to verify that the user has been deleted (by the absence of the user).

You can also instruct the userdel -r command to remove the user's home directory and any files in that location. This example removes the oracle account and its home directory:

```
$ userdel oracle -r
```

Before you use this command, make sure the user doesn't need any of the files in his or her home directory tree ever again. You can use a command such as tar to do a quick backup of the files in a user's home directory (see Chapter 6 for details).

# CHAPTER 4

■ ■ ■

# Creating and Editing Files

If you want to survive in a Linux or Solaris environment, you have to be adept with at least one command-line text editor. DBAs use text editors on a daily basis to manipulate database initialization files, create scripts to automate tasks, modify OS scheduler jobs, and so on. In these environments, you won't be an efficient database administrator unless you're proficient with a text editor.

Dozens of text editors are available. To that end, there have been entire books written on the available text editors. The three most common command-line text editors in use are vi, vim, and emacs. This chapter focuses on the vi text editor (pronounced "vee-eye" or sometimes "vie"). We chose to concentrate on this editor for the following reasons:

- The vi editor is universally available on all Linux/Solaris systems.

- Linux/Solaris technologists tend to use vi more than any other editor.

- You can't consider yourself a true geek unless you know vi.

The goal of this chapter is to give you enough information to efficiently use the vi editor. We don't cover every facet of vi; instead, we focus on the features that you'll use most often to perform daily editing tasks. When you first use vi, you might wonder why anybody would use such a confusing text-editing tool. To neophytes, many aspects of vi initially seem counterintuitive.

Not to worry; with some explanation, examples, and hands-on practice, you'll learn how to use this editing tool to efficiently create and manipulate text files. This chapter contains more than enough material to get you started with vi. The problems described are the most commonly encountered editing tasks.

If you are new to vi, we strongly encourage you to not just read the solutions in this chapter but to actually start up a vi session and practice entering the commands shown in the examples. It's like riding a bicycle; you can't learn how to ride until you physically get on the bike and attempt to go forward. It's the same with vi. You can't just read about how to use this tool; you have to type commands before the learning takes place.

---

■ **Note** All the solutions and examples in this chapter also work nearly identically with the vim editor. The vi-improved (vim) editor provides many enhancements to vi. On many systems, you may be using vim and not realize it. The vi editor can be automatically defined as an alias or a soft link to the vim executable.

---

# 4-1. Creating a File

## Problem

You need to create a text file.

## Solution

To create a file named foo.txt, run the vi utility from the command line, as shown here:

```
$ vi foo.txt
```

You should now see a blank screen with several tilde (~) graphemes displayed in the far-left column of the screen. Within a file being edited by vi, the ~ character indicates a line that has no text in it. Depending on your version of vi, you might see the name of your file in the bottom-left corner:

```
"foo.txt" [New file]
```

To enter text, first type i. The lowercase *i* puts the editor in insert mode. You can now enter text into the file. To save your changes and exit from vi, first press Escape to get out of insert mode and into command mode, and then type :wq for write and quit:

```
:wq
```

You should now be back at the OS command prompt. You can verify that the new file has been created with the ls command:

```
$ ls foo.txt
foo.txt
```

---

■ **Note**    See recipe 4-2 to learn how to move your cursor around within a file.

---

## How It Works

The most common way to start vi is to provide it with a file name to operate on:

```
$ vi <filename>
```

Several options are available when first invoking vi. Table 4-1 lists some of the more commonly used command-line choices.

*Table 4-1. Some Helpful vi Command-Line Startup Options*

| Option | Action |
|---|---|
| vi | Starts editing session in memory. |
| vi <file> | Starts session and opens the specified file. |
| vi <file>* | Opens first file that matches the wildcard pattern. Use :n to navigate to the next matched file. |
| view <file> | Opens file in read-only mode. |
| vi -R <file> | Opens file in read-only mode. |
| vi -r <file> | Recovers file and recent edits after abnormal abort from editing session (such as a system crash). |
| vi +n <file> | Opens file at specified line number n. |
| vi + <file> | Opens file at the last line. |
| vi +/<pattern> <file> | Opens file at first occurrence of specified string pattern. |

Once you start a vi session, it's critical to understand that there are two distinct operating modes:

- Command mode
- Insert mode

The vi editor behaves very differently depending on its mode. When you first enter vi, you are in *command* mode by default. In this mode, you can enter commands that control the behavior of vi. For example, you can issue commands to do the following:

- Save a file
- Enter insert mode
- Exit vi

When in command mode, everything you enter is interpreted as a command by vi. You can't enter text into your file while in command mode; you must place vi in *insert* mode before you can start entering text. Table 4-2 lists several methods of placing vi in insert mode. Keep in mind that these commands are case sensitive. For example, the A command comprises pressing the Shift and A keys simultaneously.

*Table 4-2. Common Techniques to Enter vi Insert Mode*

| Enter Insert Command | Action |
|---|---|
| i | Inserts text to the right of the cursor. |
| a | Inserts text at the end of the word to the right of the cursor (appends). |
| I | Inserts text at the beginning of the line. |
| A | Inserts text at the end of the line. |
| o | Inserts text below the current line. |
| O | Inserts text above the current line. |

The easiest way to change from command mode to insert mode is to press i on the keyboard. You can then begin entering text at the place onscreen where your cursor is currently located. When in vi insert mode, you can perform two activities:

- Enter text

- Exit from insert mode

While in insert mode, you should see text at the bottom of your screen indicating that you are in the correct mode (this may vary depending on whether you're using vi or vim):

```
-- INSERT --
```

You can now begin typing text.

To exit from insert mode (and back to command mode), press Escape. There's nothing wrong with pressing Escape multiple times (other than wasting energy). If you are already in command mode and press Escape, you may hear a bell or a beep.

You can exit from vi (back to the OS prompt) after you are in command mode. To save the file and exit, type :wq (write quit):

```
:wq
```

If you made changes to a file and want to exit without saving, type :q!, as shown here:

```
:q!
```

Table 4-3 details some of the more common exit methods. Keep in mind that you have to be in command mode before you can type a vi exit command. If you don't know what mode you're in, press Escape to ensure that you're in command mode. Notice that these commands are case sensitive. For example, the ZZ command is executed by simultaneously pressing Shift and the Z key twice.

***Table 4-3.*** *Useful* vi *Exit Commands*

| Exit Command | Action |
| --- | --- |
| :wq | Saves and exits. |
| ZZ | Saves and exits. |
| :x | Saves and exits. |
| :w | Saves the current edits without exiting. |
| :w! | Overrides file protections and saves. |
| :q | Exits the file. |
| :q! | Exits without saving. |
| :n | Edits next file. |
| :e! | Returns to previously saved version. |

# 4-2. Maneuvering Within a File

## Problem

You want to navigate efficiently within a text file while editing with vi.

## Solution

The most intuitive way to move around is by using the up/down/right/left arrows. These keys will work whether you are in command mode or insert mode. However, you might encounter some keyboards on which the up/down/left/right arrows don't work. In those cases, you have to use the J, K, H, and L keys to move you down, up, left, and right, respectively. You must be in command mode to navigate with these keys. If you're in insert mode and try to use these keys, you'll see a bunch of jjj kkkkk hhh llll letters onscreen.

Using these keys may seem cumbersome at first. However, you'll notice after some time that you can navigate quickly using these keys because you don't have to move your fingers from their natural typing positions.

## How It Works

You can use a myriad of commands for moving around in a text file. Although some of these commands may seem confusing, the navigational commands will soon become second nature to you with a little practice. Keep in mind that the vi editor was designed to allow you to perform most tasks without having to move your hands from the standard keyboard position.

Table 4-4 contains commonly used commands to navigate within vi. Remember that you must be in command mode for these keystrokes to work. Notice that these commands are case sensitive. For example, to navigate to the top of the page, use the 1G command, which is composed of first pressing the 1 key and then simultaneously pressing the Shift and G keys.

***Table 4-4.*** *Common Navigation Commands*

| Command | Action |
| --- | --- |
| j (or down arrow) | Moves down a line. |
| k (or up arrow) | Moves up a line. |
| h (or left arrow) | Moves one character left. |
| l (or right arrow) | Moves one character right. |
| Ctrl+f (or Page Down) | Scrolls down one screen. |
| Ctrl+b (or Page Up) | Scrolls up one screen. |
| 1G | Goes to first line in file. |
| :1 | Goes to first line in file. |
| G | Goes to last line in file. |
| nG | Goes to n line number. |
| H | Goes to top of screen. |
| L | Goes to bottom of screen. |
| w | Moves one word forward. |
| b | Moves one word backward. |
| 0 | Goes to start of line. |
| $ | Goes to end of line. |

# 4-3. Copying and Pasting

## Problem

You want to copy and paste text from one section of a file to another.

## Solution

Use the yy command to yank (copy) lines of text. Use the p command to put (paste) lines of text elsewhere in the file. As with all vi commands, ensure that you are in command mode (press Escape) before using a command. The following example copies five lines of text from the current line that the cursor is on and four lines below the current line (for a total of five lines):

```
5yy
```

You should see an informational line at the bottom of the screen indicating success (or not) of placing the copied lines in the copy buffer:

```
5 lines yanked
```

To paste the lines that have been copied, use the p command. To put the lines beneath the current line your cursor is on, ensure that you are in command mode and issue the p command:

```
p
```

You should see an information line at the bottom that indicates the lines were pasted below the line your cursor is on:

```
5 more lines
```

## How It Works

Copying and pasting are two of the most common tasks of editing a file. Sometimes you may want to cut and paste. This task is similar to the copying and pasting example in the "Solution" section of this recipe. Instead of using the yy command, use the dd (delete) command. For example, to cut five lines of text (inclusive with the line your cursor is currently on), issue the dd command:

```
5dd
```

You should see a message at the bottom of the screen indicating that the lines have been cut (deleted):

```
5 fewer lines
```

Those lines are now in the buffer and can be pasted anywhere in the file. Navigate to the line you want to place the previously cut lines after, and press the p command:

```
p
```

You should see an informational line at the bottom that indicates the lines were pasted after the line your cursor is on:

```
5 more lines
```

There are many commands for cutting and pasting text. Table 4-5 describes the copying, cutting, and pasting commands. Notice that these commands are case sensitive. For example, use the X command to delete one character to the left of the cursor, which means pressing the Shift and X keys simultaneously.

*Table 4-5.* *Common Options for Copying, Deleting, and Pasting Text*

| Option | Action |
|--------|--------|
| yy | Yanks (copies) the current line |
| nyy | Yanks (copies) n number of lines |
| p | Puts yanked line(s) below the cursor |
| P | Puts yanked line(s) above the cursor |
| x | Deletes the character that the cursor is on |
| X | Deletes the character to the left of the cursor |
| dw | Deletes the word the cursor is on |
| dd | Deletes current line of text |
| ndd | Deletes n lines of text |
| D | Deletes to the end of the current line |

# 4-4. Manipulating Text

## Problem

You wonder whether there are some commands to modify the text you're working on, such as changing a character from lowercase to uppercase.

## Solution

Use the ~ (tilde) command to change the case of a character. For example, say you have a string in a file with the text of oracle and you want to change it to Oracle. Place your cursor over the o character. Press Escape to ensure that you're in command mode. Type the ~ character (which requires you to press the Shift key and the ~ key at the same time). You should see the case of the character change from o to O.

## How It Works

Several commands are available for manipulating text. Table 4-6 lists common options used to change text. Notice that these commands are case sensitive. For example, the C command is executed by pressing the Shift and C keys simultaneously.

*Table 4-6.* *Common Options for Changing Text*

| Option | Action |
|--------|--------|
| r | Replaces the character that the curser is on with the next character you type |
| ~ | Changes the case of a character |
| cc | Deletes the current line and inserts text |
| C | Deletes to the end of the line and insert text |
| c$ | Deletes to the end of the line and inserts text |
| cw | Deletes to the end of the word and inserts text |
| R | Types over the characters in the current line |
| s | Deletes the current character and inserts text |
| S | Deletes the current line and inserts text |

# 4-5. Searching for and Replacing Text

## Problem

You want to search for all occurrences of a string and replace it with another string.

## Solution

If you want to search only for a string, use the / command. The following example searches for the string ora01 in the file:

/ora01

To search for the next occurrence of the string, use the n (next) command:

n

To search backward for a previous occurrence of the string, use the N command:

N

If you want to search for text and replace it, use the s option to search for text and replace it with an alternate string. The following example searches for the string ora01 and replaces it with ora02 everywhere in the file:

:%s/ora001/ora02/g

All occurrences of ora01 should now be displayed as ora02.

## How It Works

Searching for strings is one of the most common tasks you'll perform while editing database initialization files. Table 4-7 lists some of the more common options for searching for text.

***Table 4-7.*** *Common Options for Text Searching*

| Option | Action |
| --- | --- |
| /<pattern> | Searches forward for a string |
| ?<pattern> | Searches backward for a string |
| n | Repeats the search forward |
| N | Repeats the search backward |
| f<character> | Searches forward for a character in the current line |
| F<character> | Searches backward for a character in the current line |

# 4-6. Inserting One File into Another

## Problem

While within vi, you want to copy in another file that exists in the current working directory.

## Solution

Use the :r command to read in a file. This has the effect of copying in a file and pasting it starting at the current cursor location. This example reads a file named tnsnames.ora into the current file:

```
:r tnsnames.ora
```

The previous example assumes that the tnsnames.ora file is in your current working directory. If the file you want to bring in is not in your current working directory, you have need to specify a path name. This example reads in a file from a directory that is not the current working directory:

```
:r /oracle/product/11.1/network/admin/tnsnames.ora
```

If you have an OS variable that contains a path, you can use it directly. This example copies in a file contained in a path specified by a variable:

```
:r $TNS_ADMIN/tnsnames.ora
```

## How It Works

You'll often need to insert the content of a file into the current file you're editing. Doing so is a quick and easy way to add text to your current file that you know is stored correctly in a separate file.

You have a few other interesting ways to read in files. This example copies in a file and places it at the beginning of the current file:

```
:0r tnsnames.ora
```

The following bit of code reads in the file at the end of the current file:

```
:$r tnsnames.ora
```

# 4-7. Joining Lines

## Problem

You have one line of text just after the current line you are editing. You want to join the text after the current line to the end of the current line.

## Solution

First, ensure that you are in command mode by pressing Escape. Place your cursor on the first line that you want to join with the line after it. Type the J (capital *J*) command to join the end of the current line to the start of the line after it.

An example helps to illustrate this concept. Say you have these two sentences in a file:

```
select table_name
from dba_tables;
```

If you want to join the first line to the second line, place your cursor anywhere on the first line and type the following:

```
J
```

You should now see both lines joined together:

```
select table_name from dba_tables;
```

## How It Works

You'll often use the J command to join two lines of code together in a text file. You can also join any number of consecutive lines. For example, suppose that you have the following three lines in a file:

```
Select
username
from dba_users;
```

You want the three lines to be joined together on one line. First, place your cursor anywhere on the first line and then type the following while in command mode:

```
3J
```

You should now see the three lines joined together, as shown here:

```
select username from dba_users;
```

# 4-8. Running Operating System Commands

## Problem

While editing text within vi, you want to run an OS command.

## Solution

First make sure you that are in command mode by entering Escape. Use the : ! command to run OS commands. For example, the following bit of code runs the OS date command without exiting vi:

```
:!date
```

Here is the output for this example:

```
Sat Feb 10 14:22:45 MST 2008
~
Hit ENTER or type command to continue
```

Press Enter or Return to get back into vi command mode. To read the output of date directly into the file you're editing, use this syntax:

```
:r !date
```

## How It Works

Running OS commands from within vi saves you the hassle of having to exit the utility, run the OS command, and then re-enter the utility. DBAs commonly use this technique to perform tasks such as listing files in a directory, printing the date, or copying files.

The following example runs the ls (list) command from within vi to view files in the current working directory:

```
:!ls
```

Once the file of interest is identified, you can read it in with the :r syntax. This example reads the script1.sql file into the file currently being edited:

```
:r script1.sql
```

If you want to temporarily place yourself at the shell prompt and run several OS commands, type your favorite shell with the : ! syntax. The following example enters the Bash shell:

```
:!bash
```

To return to vi, use the exit command to log out of the shell. At this point, you need to press Enter or Return to return to vi command mode:

```
Hit ENTER or type command to continue
```

# 4-9. Repeating a Command

## Problem

You are typing commands over and over again. You wonder whether there is a way to repeat the previously entered command.

## Solution

Use the . (period) command to repeat the previously entered command. For example, suppose you delete a large section of code, but want to delete only 10 lines at a time. To achieve this, first ensure you're in command mode (by pressing Escape) and then enter the following:

10dd

To repeat the previous command, type a period:

.

You should see another 10 lines deleted. This technique allows you to quickly repeat the previously run command.

### How It Works

You can use the . command to repeat any previously typed command and you will save a great deal of time and typing when using it. If you often retype lengthy commands, consider creating a shortcut to the keystrokes (see recipe 4-13 for details).

# 4-10. Undoing a Command

## Problem

You want to undo the last command you typed.

## Solution

To undo the last command or text typed, use the u command. Make sure that you are in command mode and then type u, as shown here:

u

You should see the effects of the command that was typed in previously to the u command being undone.

## How It Works

The u command is handy for undoing the previous command. If you want to undo all commands entered on one line, use the U command. Your cursor must be on the last line you changed for this command to work.

If you want to undo changes since the last time you saved the file, type the following:

```
:e!
```

Sometimes the previous command is handy if you want to undo all edits to a file and start over. This is quicker than exiting the file with the :q! (quit without saving) command and reopening the file.

---

■ **Note**   The behavior of u and U can slightly vary depending on your version of vi. For example, with vim, you can use the u command to undo several previous edits.

---

# 4-11. Displaying Line Numbers

## Problem

You want to display line numbers in your text file.

## Solution

Use the set number command. The following command changes the screen to display the line number on the left side of each row:

```
:set number
```

You should now see line numbers on the left side of the screen. The following is a snippet from the init.ora file with the set number option enabled:

```
1 db_name=RMDB1
2 db_block_size=8192
3 compatible=10.2.0.1.0
4 pga_aggregate_target=200M
5 workarea_size_policy=AUTO
6 sga_max_size=400M
7 sga_target=400M
8 processes=200
```

## How It Works

When you deal with files, it is nice to see a line number to assist with debugging. Use the set number and set nonumber commands to toggle the number display.

---

■ **Tip**   Press Ctrl+G (press the Ctrl and G keys simultaneously) to display the current line number.

---

# 4-12. Automatically Configuring Settings

## Problem

You want to configure vi to start up with certain settings. For example, you want vi to always start up in the mode of displaying line numbers.

## Solution

If you want to customize vi to automatically show line numbers, create a file named .exrc in your home directory and place the desired settings within it. The following example creates a file named .exrc in the home directory:

```
$ vi $HOME/.exrc
```

Enter the following text in the .exrc file:

```
set number
```

From now on, every time you start vi, the .exrc file is read, and the settings within it are reflected in the files being edited.

## How It Works

Setting the line numbers to automatically appear is just one aspect that you can configure in the .exrc file. To view all settable attributes in your environment, issue the following command within vi:

```
:set all
```

Here is a very small snippet of the output:

```
--- Options ---
ambiwidth=single   joinspaces          softtabstop=0
noautoindent       keywordprg=man -s   startofline
noautoread         nolazyredraw        swapfile
noautowrite        lines=30            swapsync=fsync
noautowriteall     nolist              switchbuf=
background=light   listchars=eol:$     tabstop=8
```

Options that expect a value contain an equals (=) sign in the output. To view the current setting of a feature, use set and the option name. This example displays the term setting:

```
:set term
term=cygwin
```

To view which options are different from the defaults, use the set command with no options:

```
:set
```

If you use vim, you can place commands in the vim .vimrc startup file. The vim editor also executes the contents of the .exrc file if one is present.

---

■ **Tip**   You can also put shortcuts for commands in your .exrc file. Recipe 4-13 describes how to create command shortcuts (also referred to as *command maps*).

---

# 4-13. Creating Shortcuts for Commands

## Problem

You are using a certain command over and over again and you wonder whether there is a way to create a shortcut for the command.

## Solution

Use the map command to create a shortcut for a sequence of keystrokes. One set of keystrokes that is typed often is xp, which transposes two characters (it performs a delete and then a put). This example creates a macro for the xp command:

```
:map t xp
```

You can now use the t command to perform the same function as the xp command.

## How It Works

Mapping commands is a useful way of creating shortcuts for frequently used sequences of keystrokes. If you want mappings defined for each vi session, place the mappings in your .exrc file (see recipe 4-12 for details).

To view all defined mappings, type :map without any arguments:

```
:map
```

Here is some sample output:

```
up      ^[OA    k
down    ^[OB    j
left    ^[OD    h
right   ^[OC    l
t       t       xp
```

To disable a mapping, use the :unmap command. The following example disables the t mapping:

```
:unmap t
```

# 4-14. Setting the Shell Default Text Editor

## Problem

You're editing the `cron` table on a new database server. The default editor used for `cron` is `emacs`, but you want to set your default editor to be `vi`.

## Solution

Use the `export` command to set the default editor. The following example assumes that you're using the Bash shell and sets the default editor to the `vi` utility:

```
$ export EDITOR=vi
```

You can verify that the variable has been set as follows:

```
$ echo $EDITOR
vi
```

If you're using the C shell, you can set the `EDITOR` variable as follows:

```
$ setenv EDITOR vi
```

## How It Works

Some utilities such as `cron` inspect the OS `EDITOR` variable to determine which editor to use (some older systems use the `VISUAL` variable as well). The following lines can be placed in the `HOME/.bashrc` startup file to ensure that the editor is automatically set when logging in:

```
export EDITOR=vi
export VISUAL=$EDITOR
```

We recommend that you set both the `EDITOR` and `VISUAL` variables because some utilities (such as SQL*Plus) reference one or the other.

# 4-15. Setting the SQL*Plus Text Editor

## Problem

You start a SQL*Plus session and want to edit a file using the `vi` editor. However, you notice that you're placed within an unfamiliar editor when you issue the `EDIT` command:

```
$ sqlplus / as sysdba
SQL> edit test
test.sql: No such file or directory
?
q
```

In this situation, you should set the default SQL*Plus text editor to be `vi`.

# Solution

You can specify the default text editor used by SQL*Plus in one of two ways:

- Set the OS EDITOR variable (see recipe 4-14 for details). By default, SQL*Plus will use the editor specified within the EDITOR variable.

- Define the SQL*Plus _EDITOR variable. Setting this variable overrides any setting in the OS EDITOR variable.

This example sets the default editor to be used by a SQL*Plus session:

```
SQL> define _EDITOR=vi
```

Now when you subsequently edit a file, the vi editor is invoked by default:

```
SQL> edit test
~
"test.sql" [New File]
```

You can verify that the editor has been set by using the DEFINE command and specifying only the name of the variable you're interested in viewing:

```
SQL> DEFINE _EDITOR
DEFINE _EDITOR        = "vi" (CHAR)
```

If you just type in DEFINE by itself, all defined variables will display:

```
SQL> DEFINE
DEFINE _DATE          = "18-APR-15" (CHAR)
DEFINE _USER          = "SYS" (CHAR)
...
DEFINE _EDITOR        = "vi" (CHAR)
```

# How It Works

The solution section demonstrated how to set the default editor for a SQL*Plus session. You'll most likely want to have the default editor defined automatically for you so that you don't have to manually set the editor within each session. To automatically have the _EDITOR variable set, define the _EDITOR variable within the glogin.sql server profile file or the login.sql user profile file. For example, the following line can be placed in either the glogin.sql or login.sql file:

```
define _EDITOR=vi
```

The glogin.sql file is located in the ORACLE_HOME/sqlplus/admin directory. In Linux or Solaris, the login.sql file is executed if it exists in a directory contained within the SQLPATH OS variable. If the SQLPATH variable hasn't been defined, SQL*Plus will look for login.sql in the current working directory from which SQL*Plus was invoked.

If the _EDITOR SQL*Plus variable is not set, the OS EDITOR variable will be used to set the SQL*Plus editor. If the EDITOR variable is not set, the VISUAL variable setting will be used. If neither the EDITOR nor VISUAL variable is set, the ed editor will be used as the default editor within SQL*Plus.

# 4-16. Toggling Syntax Text Color

## Problem

You're using vim or vi to edit a file, and the text appears as multicolored. You're having a hard time reading the text and want to turn the coloring feature off.

## Solution

Within the editor while in command mode, press the Shift key and : simultaneously. This action should place your prompt at the bottom-left side of the screen. You should see the prompt to the right of a : sign. To turn off the syntax coloring, type syntax off and press Return:

```
:syntax off
```

You should see the text font colors displayed in white now. If you want to turn the syntax coloring back on, do so as follows:

```
:syntax on
```

If you want the syntax coloring to be automatically disabled, you can place the syntax off command in the vim .vimrc startup file or the vi .exrc startup file (see recipe 4-12 for details).

## How It Works

Depending on your environment, when you edit a file, some of its text may be shown in various colors. For example, a line that starts with a # sign will be interpreted as a comment line and will therefore appear as dark blue text. This is known as *syntax coloring*. Sometimes this syntax-colored text can be hard to read, depending on the terminal (e.g., it's hard to see dark blue against a black terminal background). In these situations, the easiest way to resolve this issue is to turn off the syntax coloring.

If you prefer the syntax coloring to be enabled but are having a difficult time viewing text of a particular color, you can adjust specific syntax coloring schemes. This line of code sets the font color of a comment line to be dark gray:

```
highlight Comment ctermbg=DarkGray
```

There are various other colors you can control; for example:

```
highlight Constant ctermbg=Blue
highlight Cursor ctermbg=Green
highlight Normal ctermbg=Black
highlight Special ctermbg=DarkMagenta
highlight NonText ctermbg=Black
```

You may want to adjust these colors depending on your terminal type or your ability to see certain colors. For most files that a DBA would edit, the syntax coloring can be more distracting than helpful. However, if you're editing a programming language source code file (e.g., Java) you'll most likely find the syntax coloring quite helpful for identifying segments of code such as comments, constants, variables, and so on.

# CHAPTER 5

■ ■ ■

# Managing Files and Directories

A complex part of the job of every Oracle DBA job involves dealing with files and directories. Therefore, DBAs must be experts in file manipulation. Your job requires skills such as implementing database security, performing backups and recovery, monitoring, and troubleshooting performance issues. These critical tasks are all dependent on a command-line knowledge of managing files. Expert DBAs know how to administer files and navigate within the filesystem.

A file, which is the basic building block of a Linux/Solaris system, is a container for information stored on disk. You access a file by its *file name*. We use the terms *file* and *file name* synonymously in this book. File names can be up to 256 characters long and can contain regular letters; numbers; and the . (period), _ (underscore), and - (hyphen) characters.

A *directory* is like a folder; its purpose is to provide a logical container that facilitates working with groups of files. Every server has a root directory indicated by a forward slash (/); think of the forward slash as a tree falling forward from left to right. The / directory, which is the topmost directory on every server, is like an upside-down tree in which the trunk is the root directory, and the branches of the tree are subdirectories.

Figure 5-1 shows a partial hierarchy directory structure on an Oracle database server. Be aware that Figure 5-1 shows only a fraction of the directories typically created. The main point of the diagram is to give you an idea of the treelike directory structure that is used for a typical Oracle system. Because of the complexity of the directory structures, DBAs must be fluent with command-line directory navigation and file manipulation.

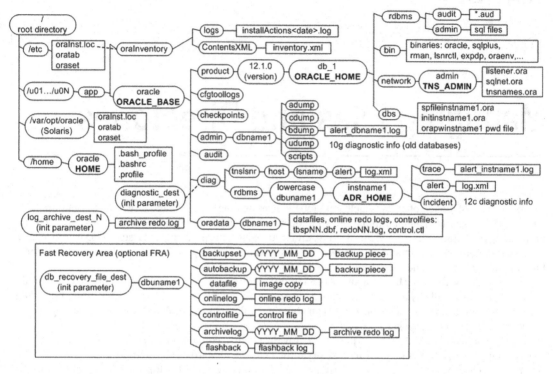

***Figure 5-1.*** *Common directories used on an Oracle database server*

This chapter discusses common problems and solutions that you'll encounter when working with files and directories. It starts with the basics, such as viewing directory structures, and then progresses to more complicated topics such as finding certain types of files.

# 5-1. Showing the Current Working Directory
## Problem

You're logged on to a database server and you want to view the current directory path.

## Solution

Use the pwd (print working directory) command to display the full pathname of your current working directory:

```
$ pwd
/home/oracle
```

From the previous output shows that /home/oracle is the current working directory.

---

■ **Note**    If you're a Windows user, the Linux/Solaris `pwd` command is similar to the DOS `cd` command when issued with no options. The DOS `cd` command without any options simply prints the current working directory.

---

## How It Works

In Linux/Solaris, the directory you are working in is defined to be your *current working directory*. The `pwd` command isn't very complicated; it simply prints the current working directory. As simple as it is, you'll be using it all the time. DBAs constantly use this command to verify that they are in the correct directory. Before you manipulate directories or files, it's wise to verify that you are where you think you should be.

The `pwd` command has two interesting options: `-L` and `-P`. The `-L` option prints the logical path and is the default. It always prints the value of the OS PWD variable. For example, the following two commands always display the same directory:

```
$ echo $PWD
/home/oracle
$ pwd
/home/oracle
```

The `-P` option prints the actual physical path. These options are useful if you're working on systems that have directories that have been navigated to via a symbolic link (see recipe 5-33 for a discussion on soft links). The `-L` option prints the directory name as defined by the symbolic link. The `-P` option displays the directory as defined by the actual physical path.

An example can help illustrate the value of knowing when to use the `-P` option. On a database server, there is a symbolic link defined to be `oradev` that exists under the `root` directory. Here is an example of the long listing of the symbolic link:

```
$ ls -altr /oradev
lrwxrwxrwx 1 root root 9 Apr 15 19:49 oradev -> /oradisk2
```

First, navigate to the directory via the symbolic link and issue a `pwd` command with the `-L` option:

```
$ cd /oradev
$ pwd -L
/oradev
```

Now without changing directories, use the `pwd` command with the `-P` option:

```
$ pwd -P
/oradisk2
```

If you work in environments that use symbolic links, it is important to understand the difference between the `-L` and `-P` options of the `pwd` command.

# 5-2. Changing Directories
## Problem

You want to change your current working directory to a different location.

## Solution

Use the cd (change directory) command to navigate within the filesystem. The basic syntax for this command is as follows:

```
cd <directory>
```

This example changes the current working directory to /orahome/app:

```
$ cd /orahome/app
```

It is usually a good idea to use the pwd command to verify that the cd command worked as expected:

```
$ pwd
/orahome/app
```

You can also navigate to a directory path that is stored in an OS variable. The next set of commands displays the contents of the TNS_ADMIN variable and then navigates to that directory:

```
$ echo $TNS_ADMIN
/orahome/app/oracle/product/12.1.0.2/db_1/network/admin
$ cd $TNS_ADMIN
$ pwd
/orahome/app/oracle/product/12.1.0.2/db_1/network/admin
```

If you attempt to navigate to a directory that doesn't exist, you'll receive an error similar to this one:

```
No such file or directory
```

The owner of a directory must have the execute permission set at the owner level of the directory before the owner can navigate to the directory. An example illustrates this concept; listed here are the permissions for a scripts directory that oracle owns:

```
$ ls -ld scripts
d---rwxrwx 2 oracle oinstall 4096 Jul 30 19:26 scripts
```

As the oracle user, you receive an error when attempting to navigate to the scripts directory:

```
$ cd scripts
-bash: cd: scripts: Permission denied
```

If you modify the directory to include the owner execute permission, you can now navigate to it successfully:

```
$ chmod 100 scripts
$ cd scripts
```

## How It Works

The cd command is a powerful utility that you'll use often in your DBA life. The following sections contain techniques to make you more effective when using this command.

## Navigating HOME

If you don't supply a directory to the cd command, the directory will be changed to the value in the variable of HOME by default. This example demonstrates the concept by viewing the current directory, displaying the value of HOME, and using cd to navigate to that directory:

```
$ pwd
/orahome/app/oracle/product/12.1.0.2/db_1
```

Next, display the contents of the HOME variable:

```
$ echo $HOME
/orahome/oracle
```

Change directories to the value contained in HOME by not supplying a directory name to the cd command:

```
$ cd
$ pwd
/orahome/oracle
```

In the Bash and Korn shells, the ~ (tilde) character is a synonym for the value contained in the HOME OS variable. The following two lines of code also change your directory to the HOME directory:

```
$ cd ~
$ cd $HOME
```

## Navigating to the Parent Directory

The .. (two dots) directory entry contains the value of the parent directory of the current working directory. If you want to change your directory to the parent directory, use the following syntax:

```
$ cd ..
```

You can navigate up as many parent directories as there are in a given path by separating the .. strings with a forward slash character. For example, to navigate up three directories, use this command syntax:

```
$ cd ../../..
```

You can also use the .. directory entry to navigate up a directory tree and then down to a different subdirectory. In the following example, the current working directory is /orahome/oracle/scripts, and the cd command is used to navigate to /orahome/oracle/bin:

```
$ pwd
/orahome/oracle/scripts
$ cd ../bin
$ pwd
/orahome/oracle/bin
```

## Navigating to a Subdirectory

To navigate to a subdirectory, specify the directory name without a forward slash in front of it. This example first prints the current working directory, navigates to the admin subdirectory, and finally verifies success with the pwd command:

```
$ pwd
/home/oracle
$ cd admin
$ pwd
/home/oracle/admin
```

## Using Wildcards

You can also use the wildcard asterisk (*) character with the cd command to navigate to other directories. In this next example, the current working directory is /oracle, and the product subdirectory is the target directory:

```
$ cd p*
$ pwd
/oracle/product
```

When navigating to a subdirectory, you must specify enough of the directory to make its name unique to any other subdirectories beneath the current working directory. If multiple directories match a wildcard string, you might not get the desired directory navigation, depending on your OS version. Always verify your current working directory with the pwd command.

When using the Bash shell, you can also use the Tab key to complete keystroke sequences. For example, if you have only one subdirectory that starts with the letter p, you can cd to it as follows:

```
$ cd p<Tab>
```

In this example, there is only one subdirectory beneath the current working directory that starts with a p, so you now see the following on the terminal:

```
$ cd product/
```

Now you can press Enter or Return to complete the command. This feature of the Bash shell is known as *tab completion* (see recipe 2-2 for more details).

## Navigating to the Previous Directory

The hyphen (-) character is commonly used to navigate to the previous working directory. In the next example, the current working directory is /oracle01, and the previous working directory is /oracle02. To navigate to /oracle02, provide - to the cd command, as shown here:

```
$ cd -
```

Another way to navigate to the previous working directory is via the OLDPWD variable, which contains the location of the previous directory. To navigate to the most recently visited directory, you can change directories, as shown here:

```
$ cd $OLDPWD
```

# 5-3. Creating a Directory

## Problem

You want to store your SQL scripts in a special directory. To do this, you first need to create a directory.

## Solution

Use the mkdir (make directory) command to create a new directory. This example creates the directory named scripts underneath the /home/oracle directory:

```
$ cd /home/oracle
$ mkdir scripts
```

Now use the cd and pwd commands to verify that the directory exists:

```
$ cd scripts
$ pwd
/home/oracle/scripts
```

When navigating to another directory, if the directory doesn't exist, you'll receive an error message similar to this:

```
No such file or directory
```

## How It Works

Before you create a directory, you must have write permission on the parent directory to create a subdirectory. If you attempt to create a directory and don't have write permission on either the user or group level, you'll receive an error. This example attempts to create a directory named oradump under the / directory:

```
$ mkdir /oradump
mkdir: cannot create directory `/oradump': Permission denied
```

The permissions on the / directory show that only the root user has write permissions (and is therefore the only user who can create a directory under /):

```
$ ls -altrd /
drwxr-xr-x 29 root root 4096 Apr 15 19:49 /
```

If you don't have root access, you'll need to work with your SA to create any desired directories under the / directory. See recipe 3-11 for examples of obtaining access to root privileges.

Sometimes you'll find it convenient to create several directories in a path with one command. This example uses the -p (parent) option to create the directory backups and any parent directories that don't already exist in the path:

```
$ mkdir -p /oradump/db/dev/backups
```

The previous directory creation technique is extremely handy when you need to create long complex directory structures and you don't want to create them one directory at a time.

# 5-4. Viewing a List of Directories

## Problem

You want to just list the directories, not the other regular files in your current working location.

## Solution

Use the `ls -l` command in combination with `grep` to list only directories. Here is some sample `ls -l` output without using `grep` to filter anything:

```
$ ls -l
drwxr-x---  3 oracle dba    4096 Apr 25 19:44 orahome
drwxr-xr-x  9 oracle dba    4096 Dec 29 07:43 orainst
-rw-r-----  1 oracle dba  124506 Apr 25 20:10 ora.zip
-rw-r-----  1 oracle dba  112640 Apr 25 18:14 o.tar
-rw-r--r--  1 oracle dba      82 Apr  4 14:30 output.txt
```

Next add in the `grep` filter:

```
$ ls -l | grep '^d'
drwxr-x---  3 oracle dba    4096 Apr 25 19:44 orahome
drwxr-xr-x  9 oracle dba    4096 Dec 29 07:43 orainst
```

In the preceding line of code, the `ls -l` output is piped to `grep`, which looks for files that begin with the d character. The caret ^ (caret) character is a regular expression that tells the `grep` command to match the d character at the beginning of the string. In this manner, you can list out just the directories.

## How It Works

DBAs typically create an alias or function to facilitate typing the command shown in the "Solution" section of this recipe. This command creates an alias named `lsd` that can be used to list directories:

```
$ alias lsd="ls -l | grep '^d'"
```

After the alias is created, type `lsd`. It will run the `ls` and `grep` commands. See recipe 2-7 for details on creating aliases and functions.

Another way to view directories is to use `ls -p` and `grep` for the forward slash character. The next example uses `ls -p`, which instructs the `ls` command to append a / on the end of every directory. The output of `ls -p` is piped to `grep`, which searches for the / character:

```
$ ls -p | grep /
orahome/
orainst/
```

When trying to list out a directory, it can sometimes be convenient to use a wildcard character. For example, say you want to determine all directories and files that are in the ORACLE_HOME directory that begin with the b character. To determine this, you attempt to issue this command:

```
$ ls $ORACLE_HOME/b*
```

The output of this command may not be what you expect. If a wildcard matches a directory name, the files contained in the directory (not the directory name) will be listed. In this example, the output contains all the files listed in the ORACLE_HOME/bin directory; here's a short snippet of the output:

```
acfsroot        exp          lsnrctl0        plshprof0
adapters        expdp        lxchknlb        proc
adrci           expdp0       lxegen          procob
```

To avoid this behavior, use ls -d to list directories, not their contents. The following command lists all directories that begin with the letter b that are beneath ORACLE_HOME:

```
$ ls -d $ORACLE_HOME/b*
/orahome/app/oracle/product/12.1.0.2/db_1/bin
```

# 5-5. Removing a Directory

## Problem

You want to remove a directory and all files that exist beneath that directory.

## Solution

Use the rmdir command to remove a directory. This command can be used only to remove directories that don't contain other files. In this example, the rmdir command is used to remove a directory named scripts that exists beneath the current working directory:

```
$ rmdir scripts
```

If the directory isn't empty, you'll see an error similar to this:

```
rmdir: scripts: Directory not empty
```

If you want to remove directories that contain files, use the rm -r (remove recursively) command. This example removes the directory scripts plus any files and subdirectories that exist beneath the scripts directory:

```
$ rm -r scripts
```

## How It Works

If the rm -r command encounters any files that don't have write permission enabled, a message like this will be displayed:

```
rm: remove write-protected regular file '<file name>'?
```

If you want to remove the file, type y (for yes). If many files are write-protected (such as in oracle-owned directories), typing y over and over again can get tedious.

You can instruct rm to remove write-protected files without being prompted with the -f (force) option. This example removes all files beneath the subdirectory scripts without prompting for protected files:

```
$ rm -rf scripts
```

Sometimes when you're removing old database installations, it is convenient to use the rm -rf command. This command will wipe out entire directory trees without asking for confirmation when deleting write-protected files. Make sure you know exactly what you're removing before running this command.

---

■ **Caution**    Use the rm -rf command judiciously. This command will recursively remove every file and directory beneath the specified directory without prompting you for confirmation.

---

# 5-6. Listing Files

## Problem

You want to see what files exist in a directory.

## Solution

Use the ls (list) command to list the files (and directories) in a specified directory. This line of code uses the ls command without any options to list the files in the current working directory:

```
$ ls
```

Here is a partial listing of the output:

```
dlock.sql  dropem.sql  login.sql  proc.sql  rmfile.bsh
```

## How It Works

The ls command without any options is not very useful; it displays only a limited amount of file information. One of the more useful ways to use ls is to list all the files, protections, ownership, sizes, and modification times—all sorted from most recently created to last. This is achieved with the -altr options:

```
$ ls -altr
```

Here is a partial listing of the output:

```
-rwxr-x--- 1 oracle dba 1543 Mar 29 16:09 proc.sql
-rw-r----- 1 oracle dba 1082 May  7 19:53 dlock.sql
-rw-r----- 1 oracle dba  442 May  7 19:53 login.sql
drwxr-x--- 4 oracle dba 4096 May  7 19:53 ..
-rw-r----- 1 oracle dba    0 May  7 19:54 dropem.sql
-rw-r----- 1 oracle dba    0 May  7 19:54 rmfile.bsh
```

The -a (all) option specifies that all files should be listed, including hidden files. The -l (long listing) option displays permissions, ownership, size, and modification time. The -t (time) option causes the output to be sorted by time (newest first). To have the latest file modified listed at the bottom, use the -r (reverse) option. Table 5-1 shows how to interpret the long listing of the first line of the previous output.

*Table 5-1.* *Interpreting Long Listing Output*

| Type and Permissions | Number of Links | Owner | Group | Size in Bytes | Modification Date | File Name |
|---|---|---|---|---|---|---|
| -rwxr-x--- | 1 | oracle | dba | 1543 | Mar 29 16:09 | proc.sql |

The first column of Table 5-1 has 10 characters. The first character displays the file type. Characters 2 through 10 display the file permissions. The characters r, w, and x indicate read, write, and execute privileges, respectively. A hyphen (-) indicates the absence of a privilege. The following output summarizes the first-column character positions and meanings of the long listing of a file:

```
File Type         User Perms   Group Perms   Other Perms
Column 1          2  3  4      5  6  7       8  9  10
-, d, l, s, c, b  r  w  x      r  w  x       r  w  x
```

In the first character of the first column of output, the hyphen indicates that it is a regular file. Similarly, if the first character is a d, it's a directory. If the first character is an l, it's a symbolic link. Table 5-2 lists the different file types.

*Table 5-2.* *Long Listing First Character File Type Meanings*

| File Type Character | Meaning |
|---|---|
| - | Regular file |
| d | Directory |
| l | Symbolic link |
| s | Socket |
| c | Character device file |
| b | Block device file |

The ls command may vary slightly between versions of Linux/Solaris. This command typically has more than 50 different options. Use the man ls command to view all features available on your system.

One last note: when listing a file with ls -l, you may notice an extra + at the end of the permissions; for example:

```
$ ls -l
drwxr-xr-x+  2 oracle     dba            3 May  2 15:02 scripts
-rw-r--r--+  1 oracle     dba         1627 May  2 15:12 act.sql
```

This means that your file has extended security permissions. Run the getfacl (get file access control lists) command to see the full permissions for the file; for example:

```
$ getfacl scripts
# file: scripts
# owner: oracle
# group: dba
user::rwx
group::r-x
mask::rwx
other::r-x
```

## USING ECHO TO DISPLAY FILES

Interestingly, you can also use the echo command to list files. For example, you can use this command to list files in the current working directory:

```
$ echo *
```

The echo command is a built-in command (see recipe 2-15 for details on built-in commands). This means that if the filesystem that contains the ls executable is unavailable for some reason (perhaps because of corruption), you can still use the echo command to list files.

# 5-7. Creating a File Quickly

## Problem

You're setting up Oracle RMAN backups. You want to quickly create a file so that you can test whether the oracle user has the correct permissions to write to a newly created directory.

## Solution

In the directory in which you want to determine whether you can create a file, use the touch command to quickly determine whether a file can be created. This example uses touch to create a file named test.txt in the current working directory:

```
$ touch test.txt
```

Now use the ls command to verify that the file exists:

```
$ ls -al
-rw-r----- 1 oracle dba 0 May  7 20:00 test.txt
```

From the output, the file is created and has nothing in it (indicated by a 0-byte size).

---

■ **Note**    See Chapter 4 for details on how to edit a text file.

---

## How It Works

Sometimes you'll just need to create a file to test being able to write to a backup location or check the functionality of some aspect of a shell program. You can use the touch command for these purposes. If the file you are touching already exists, the touch command will update the file's last-modified date.

If you touch a file that already exists, its access time and modification time will be set to the current system time (this includes a date component). If you want to modify only the access time, use the -a option of touch. Similarly, the -m option will update only the modification time. Use the --help option to display all options available with touch on your system.

Note that you can also quickly create a file using the following cat command:

```
$ cat /dev/null> test.txt
```

Be careful when running the previous command; if the file already exists, concatenating /dev/null to a file will erase anything contained within the file.

# 5-8. Changing File Permissions
## Problem

You want to change the permission on a file so that there is no public-level access.

## Solution

Use the chmod command to alter a file's permissions. This example changes the permission of the scrub.bsh file to 750:

```
$ chmod 750 scrub.bsh
```

A quick check with the ls command shows that the permissions are set correctly:

```
$ ls -altr scrub.bsh
-rwxr-x--- 1 oracle dba 0 May  7 20:07 scrub.bsh
```

The previous output indicates that the owner has read, write, and execute permissions; the group has read and execute; and the rest of the world has no permissions (see recipe 5-6 for a discussion on file permissions listed by the ls command).

■ **Note**   You must have `root` access or be the owner of the file or directory before you can change its permissions.

## How It Works

DBAs often use the `chmod` command to change the permissions of files and directories. It is important that you know how to use this command. Correct file access is critical for database security. In many circumstances, you will not want to grant any public access to files that contain sensitive information.

You can change a file's permissions by either using the numerical format (such as 750) or by using letters. When using the numerical format, the first number maps to the owner, the second number to the group, and the third number to all other users on the system. The permissions of 750 are translated to indicate read, write, and execute for the owner; read and execute for the group; and no permissions for other users. Inspect Table 5-3 for the translations of the numeric permissions.

*Table 5-3.*  *Meanings of Numeric Permissions*

| Numerical Digit | Permissions | Binary Number | Letter Format |
|---|---|---|---|
| 0 | No permissions | 000 | --- |
| 1 | Execute only | 001 | --x |
| 2 | Write only | 010 | -w- |
| 3 | Write and execute | 011 | -wx |
| 4 | Read-only | 100 | r-- |
| 5 | Read and execute | 101 | r-x |
| 6 | Read and write | 110 | rw- |
| 7 | Read, write, and execute | 111 | rwx |

You can also change a file's permissions by using letters, which is sometimes more intuitive to new Linux/Solaris users. When using letters, keep in mind that the o permission doesn't designate "owner"; it specifies "other." Table 5-4 lists the meanings of to whom the permissions are applied.

*Table 5-4.*  *To Whom the Permissions Are Applied*

| Who Letter | Meaning |
|---|---|
| u | User (owner) |
| g | Group |
| o | Other (all others on the system) |
| a | All (user, group, and other) |

This next example makes the file executable by the user (owner), group, and other:

```
$ chmod ugo+x mvcheck.bsh
```

This line of code takes away write and execute permissions from the group (g) and all others (o) for all files that end with the extension of .bsh:

```
$ chmod go-wx *.bsh
```

You can use three operands to apply permissions: +, -, and =. The plus (+) character adds permissions, and the minus (-) character takes away privileges. The equals (=) sign operand assigns the specified permissions and removes any not listed. For example, the following two lines are equivalent:

```
$ chmod 760 mvcheck.bsh
$ chmod u=rwx,g=rw,o= mvcheck.bsh
```

A quick listing of the file verifies that the permissions are set as expected:

```
$ ls -altr mvcheck.bsh
-rwxrw---- 1 oracle dba 0 May  7 20:10 mvcheck.bsh
```

You can also recursively change file permissions in a directory and its subdirectories. Sometimes this is useful when installing software. The following bit of code recursively changes the permissions for all files in the current directory and any files in subdirectories to 711 (owner read, write, execute; group execute; other execute):

```
$ chmod -R 711 *.*
```

You can also use the chmod utility to change the permissions of files to match the settings on an existing file. This example changes all files ending with the extension of .bsh in the current directory to have the same permissions as the master.bsh file:

```
$ chmod --reference=master.bsh *.bsh
```

## Default File Permissions

Default permissions are assigned to a file upon creation based on the umask setting. The file creation mask determines which permissions are excluded from a file. To view the current setting of your file creation mask, issue umask with no options:

```
$ umask
0022
```

You can also view the character version of the umask settings by using the -S option:

```
$ umask -S
u=rwx,g=rx,o=rx
```

When you create a regular text file, the permissions are set to the value of 0666 minus the umask setting. If the umask setting is 0022, the permissions of the file are set to 0644, or -rw-r--r--.

## Set User ID on Execution

Another concept related to the chmod command is the setuid permission (sometimes referred to as suid). Inspect the permissions of the oracle binary file:

```
$ cd $ORACLE_HOME/bin
$ ls -l oracle
-rwsr-s--x  1 oracle    dba      126812248 Jun 12 15:24 oracle
```

Notice that the owner and group executable setting is an s (not an x), which indicates that the setuid permission bit has been set. This means that when somebody runs the program, it is run with the permissions of the owner of the file, not the permissions of the process running the file. This allows a user to run the oracle binary file as if it had the permissions of the oracle user. Therefore, server processes can execute the oracle binary file as if they were the owner (usually the oracle OS user) to read and write to database files.

To set the setuid permission, you must specify a preceding fourth digit to the numeric permissions when changing file permissions with chmod. If you want to enable the setuid permission on both the user and group level, use a preceding 6, as shown here:

```
$ chmod 6751 $ORACLE_HOME/bin/oracle
$ ls -l oracle
-rwsr-sr-x   1 oracle    dba        118965728 Jun 16  2014 oracle
```

If you want to enable the setuid permission only at the owner level, use a preceding 4, as shown here:

```
$ chmod 4751 $ORACLE_HOME/bin/oracle
$ ls -l oracle
-rwsr-x--x   1 oracle    dba        118965728 Jun 16  2014 oracle
```

As a DBA, it is important to be aware of the setuid permission because you may have to troubleshoot file permission issues, depending on the release of Oracle. For example, see MOS note 271598.1 for issues related to Enterprise Manager Grid Control and setuid dependencies. Additionally, you can run into Oracle accessibility issues when there are non-oracle users on the same server as the database software. In these situations, it's important to understand how the setuid permission affects file access.

## THE STICKY BIT

Do a long listing of the /tmp directory and inspect the permissions:

```
$ ls -altrd /tmp
drwxrwxrwt 4 root root 4096 May 10 17:24 /tmp
```

At first glance, it looks like all users have all permissions on files in the /tmp directory. However, notice that the "other" permissions are set to rwt. The last permission character is a t, which indicates that the sticky bit has been enabled on that directory. When the sticky bit is enabled, only the file owner can delete a file within that directory. The sticky bit is set with the following syntax:

```
chmod +t <shared directory>
```

or

```
chmod 3775 <shared directory>
```

Setting the sticky bit enables file sharing in a directory among many different users, but prevents users from deleting a file that they don't own (within the directory that has the sticky bit enabled).

# 5-9. Changing File Ownership and Group Membership

## Problem

You need to change a file's file ownership and group membership so that it is owned by the oracle OS user and its group is dba.

## Solution

You need root privileges to change the owner of a file. Use the chown (change owner) command to change a file's owner and its group. This example changes the owner on the /var/opt/oracle directory to oracle and its group to dba:

```
# chown oracle:dba /var/opt/oracle
```

The file listing now shows that the directory owner is the oracle user, and the group it belongs to is dba:

```
$ ls -altrd /var/opt/oracle
drwxr-xr-x  2 oracle dba 4096 Dec 28 10:31 /var/opt/oracle
```

If you want to change only the group permissions of a file, use the chgrp command. You must be the file owner or have root privileges to change the group of a file. This example recursively changes the group to dba for all files with the extension of .sql in the current directory and all subdirectories:

```
$ chgrp -R dba *.sql
```

## How It Works

When setting up or maintaining database servers, it is sometimes required to change the ownership on a file or directory. The following lines show the chown syntax for changing various combinations of the owner and/or group:

```
chown user file
chown user:group file
chown :group file
```

If you have root access, you can directly change file ownership. If you don't have root privileges, sometimes SAs will grant you access to commands that require the root privilege through the sudo utility (see recipe 3-11 for details).

# 5-10. Viewing the Contents of a Text File

## Problem

You want to view the contents of a text file, but you don't want to open the file with an editor (such as vi) because you are afraid you might accidentally modify the file.

# Solution

Use either the view, less, or more command to view only (not modify) a file's contents. The view command will open a file using either the vi or vim editor in read-only mode. When you open a file in read-only mode, you are prevented from saving the file with the vi editor :wq (write and then quit) command. The following example views the initBRDSTN.ora file:

```
$ view initBRDSTN.ora
```

Using the view command is the same as running the vi -R command or the vim -R command (see Chapter 4 for more details about vi). To exit the view utility, enter the command :q.

---

■ **Note**    When viewing a file, you can force a write when exiting with the :wq! command.

---

If you want to display the contents of a file one page at a time, use a paging utility such as more or less. This example uses less to view the initBRDSTN.ora file:

```
$ less initBRDSTN.ora
```

The less utility will display a : (colon) prompt at the bottom-left corner of the screen. You can use the spacebar to go to the next page and use the up and down arrows to scroll through the documentation line by line. Enter q to exit less.

This next example uses the more command to page through the file:

```
$ more initBRDSTN.ora
```

Like the less utility, use the spacebar to display the next page and q to exit more.

# How It Works

The more and less utilities are referred to as *pagers* because they display information onscreen one page at a time. These utilities have similar features, and one could argue that they are more or less the same. For the way that DBAs use these utilities, that's mostly true. For hardcore geeks, the less utility is a bit more robust than more. Use the man less and man more commands to view all options available with these utilities.

When using either more or less, you can use vi commands to navigate within the displayed output. For example, if you want to search for a string, you can enter a forward slash and a string to search for text within the more or less output. This example searches for the string "sga_max_size" within the output of less: $ less initBRDSTN.ora

```
/sga_max_size
```

You can also use the cat command to quickly display the contents of a file to your standard output (usually your screen). This example dumps the output of the initBRDSTN.ora file to the screen:

```
$ cat initBRDSTN.ora
```

Using cat to display the contents of files works fine when you have small files. However, if the file is large, you'll see a large amount of text streaming by too fast to make any sense. It's almost always better to use view, less, or more (rather than cat) to view a file's contents. These commands allow you to quickly inspect a file's contents without risking accidental modifications.

# 5-11. Viewing Nonprinting Characters in a File

## Problem

You're trying to load text strings from a file into the database with a utility such as SQL*Loader, but the data appears to be corrupted after it is inserted into the target table. You want to view any control characters that may be embedded into the file.

## Solution

Use the `cat -v` command to view nonprinting and control characters. This example displays nonprinting and control characters in the `data.ctl` file:

```
$ cat -v data.ctl
```

---

■ **Note**  The `cat -v` command does not display linefeed or Tab characters.

---

## How It Works

When dealing with data being loaded into the database from text files, you sometimes might find that your SQL queries don't behave as expected. For example, you might search for a string, yet the SQL query doesn't return the expected data. This might occur because nonprinting characters are being inserted into the database. Use the `cat -v` command as described in this recipe to troubleshoot these kinds of data issues.

To illustrate viewing nonprinting characters, you can spool the following output from a SQL*Plus session:

```
SQL> spool out.txt
SQL> select chr(7) || 'ring the bell' from dual;
SQL> exit;
```

Here you use cat to display the contents of the file out.txt:

```
$ cat out.txt

SQL> select chr(7) || 'ring the bell' from dual;
CHR(7)||'RINGT
--------------
ring the bell

SQL> exit;
```

Notice the ^G ASCII ring bell or beep control character in the last line of the output when you use the -v option:

```
$ cat -v out.txt

SQL> select chr(7) || 'ring the bell' from dual;
CHR(7)||'RINGT
--------------
^Gring the bell

SQL> exit;
```

# 5-12. Viewing Hidden Files

## Problem

You're trying to clean up your home directory and want to view the names of hidden configuration files and/or hidden directories.

## Solution

Use the ls command with the -a (all) option. This bit of code lists all files using a long listing format and sorted in the reverse order in which they were modified:

```
$ ls -altr $HOME
```

Here is a sample of part of the output:

```
drwxr-xr-x 3 root    root      4096 Sep 29 13:30 ..
-rw-r--r-- 1 oracle oinstall  124 Sep 29 13:30 .bashrc
-rw-r--r-- 1 oracle oinstall   24 Sep 29 13:30 .bash_logout
-rw-r--r-- 1 oracle oinstall  223 Sep 29 13:53 .bash_profile
drwxr-xr-x 2 oracle oinstall 4096 Oct  2 17:55 db
drwxr-xr-x 2 oracle oinstall 4096 Oct 15 08:33 scripts
drwx------ 2 oracle oinstall 4096 Oct 15 08:34 .ssh
-rw------- 1 oracle oinstall 6076 Oct 15 13:19 .bash_history
-rw------- 1 oracle oinstall 5662 Oct 15 13:41 .viminfo
drwx------ 5 oracle oinstall 4096 Oct 15 13:55 .
```

Any of the files in the previous listing that begin with a . (dot or period) are classified as hidden files. When using the Bash shell, common hidden files in your home directory are .bash_profile, .bashrc, .bash_logout, and .bash_history (see recipe 2-5 for uses of these files).

If you want to list only hidden files, you can do so as follows:

```
$ ls -d .*
```

Here is the corresponding output:

```
.a              .bash_profile  .lesshst  .sh_history  .viminfo  .Xauthority
..  .bash_history  .history      .ocm      .ssh         .vnc
```

You may want to create an alias for the preceding command, such as this:

```
$ alias ls.='ls -d .*'
```

## How It Works

The only difference between a hidden file and a nonhidden file is that the hidden file begins with a . (dot or period) character. There isn't anything secretive or secure about hidden files. Hidden files are usually well-known files with distinct purposes (such as storing environment configuration commands).

You may not want to muddle the output of an ls command with every file in a directory. The default behavior of the ls command is not to list hidden files. The -a option specifically tells the ls command to list all files, including hidden files. If you want to list all files except the . and .. files, use the -A option:

```
$ ls -A
```

---

■ **Note**    The . file is a special file that refers to the current working directory. The .. file refers to the parent directory of the current working directory.

---

# 5-13. Determining File Type

## Problem

You want to display whether a file is a directory or a regular file.

## Solution

Use the ls command with the -F option to display the file name and file type. This example lists file names and file types within the current working directory:

```
$ ls -F
```

Here is a partial listing of some sample output:

```
alert.log        gcc-3.4.6-3.1.x86_64.rpm  ora01/    ss.bsh*
anaconda-ks.cfg  install.log               ora02/    test/
```

The ls -F command appends a special character to the file name to indicate the file type. In the previous output, the file names appended with / are directories, and the file name appended with * is an executable file.

---

■ **Tip**    Another method of determining file type is to use the ls --color command, which colorizes the file depending on its type.

---

You can also use the `file` command to display characteristics of a file. This command will display whether the file is an ASCII file, a tar file, or a details executable file. For example, one way that DBAs use the `type` command is to tell whether the `oracle` binary file is 32-bit or 64-bit. The following shows the `oracle` binary file on a 64-bit server:

```
$ file $ORACLE_HOME/bin/oracle
```

Here is the corresponding output:

```
/orahome/app/oracle/product/12.1.0.2/db_1/bin/oracle: setuid setgid ELF 64-bit LSB
executable,
AMD x86-64, version 1 (SYSV), for GNU/Linux 2.6.9, dynamically linked (uses shared libs),
not stripped
```

When using the Bash shell, if the file of interest is located in a directory in your PATH variable, you can use command substitution to provide input to the `file` command. Command substitution takes the output of the command enclosed in $( ) and provides that as input to a given command; for example:

```
$ file $(which oracle)
```

In the preceding line of code, the output of the `which` command is used as input to the `file` command.

## How It Works

You can display an indicator for a file by using the `-F` option of the `ls` command. Table 5-5 describes the different file name type indicators. File type indicators allow you to filter the output and look for a certain file type. For example, to list all directories, search the output of the `ls -F` command for the / character:

```
$ ls -F | grep /
```

DBAs often encapsulate strings of commands like this within aliases or functions, which allows them to create shortcuts to long commands (see recipe 2-7 for details).

*Table 5-5.* *File Type Indicator Characters and Meanings*

| Indicator Character | Description |
| --- | --- |
| / | The file is a directory. |
| * | The file is an executable. |
| = | The file is a socket (a special file used in process to process communication). |
| @ | The file is a symbolic link (see recipe 5-33 for more details). |
| \| | The file is a named pipe (a special file used in process-to-process communication). |

---

■ **Tip**   Use the `type` command to determine the characteristics of a command file. It will show whether the command is a utility, a built-in command, an alias, or a function.

---

The `stat` command is another useful command for displaying file characteristics. This command prints in human-readable format the contents of an inode. An *inode* (pronounced "eye-node") is a Linux/Solaris data structure that stores information about the file. The next example displays the inode information for the `oracle` binary file:

```
$ stat $ORACLE_HOME/bin/oracle
```

Here is the corresponding output:

```
  File: `/orahome/app/oracle/product/12.1.0.2/db_1/bin/oracle'
  Size: 323762476      Blocks: 632992    IO Block: 4096   regular file
Device: fd00h/64768d   Inode: 34838017   Links: 1
Access: (6751/-rwsr-s--x) Uid: ( 2000/  oracle) Gid: ( 500/     dba)
Access: 2015-04-21 11:32:14.000000000 -0600
Modify: 2014-12-29 09:17:28.000000000 -0700
Change: 2014-12-29 09:17:28.000000000 -0700
```

You can obtain some of the preceding output from the `ls` command. However, notice that the `stat` output also contains information such as the number of blocks allocated; the inode device type; and the last time a file was accessed, the last time a file was modified, or when its status was changed.

# 5-14. Finding Differences Between Files
## Problem

You have two databases that were supposed to be set up identically. You want to see any differences in the initialization files.

## Solution

Use the `diff` (difference) command to identify differences in files. The general syntax for this command is as follows:

```
$ diff <file1> <file2>
```

This example uses `diff` to view the differences between two files named `initDEV1.ora` and `initDEV2.ora`:

```
$ diff initDEV1.ora initDEV2.ora
```

Here is some sample output showing the differences in the files:

```
6,7c6,7
< sga_max_size=400M
< sga_target=400M
---
> sga_max_size=600M
> sga_target=600M
20a21
> # star_transformation_enabled=true
```

## How It Works

The key to understanding the output from diff is that it provides you with instructions on how to make file1 look like file2. The output tells you how to append, change, and delete lines. These instructions are signified by a, c, or d in the output.

Lines prepended by < are from file1. Lines prepended by > are from file2. The line numbers to the left of a, c, or d apply to file1. The line numbers to the right of a, c, or d apply to file2.

From the previous output in this recipe's solution, the first line, 6,7c6,7, is translated to mean "change lines 6 and 7 in file1 to lines 6 and 7 in file2." The second-to-last line of the output is 20a21, which means "after line 20 in file1, append line 21 from file2."

The output of diff is known as a *difference report*, which can be used in conjunction with the patch command to make file1 look like file2. Before you can use the patch command, you first have to save the difference report output in a file. The following example stores the difference output in a file named init.diff:

```
$ diff initDEV1.ora initDEV2.ora > init.diff
```

To convert initDEV1.ora to initDEV2.ora, use the patch command with the difference report output:

```
$ patch initDEV1.ora init.diff
```

You can also use the sdiff (side-by-side) utility to display file differences. The sdiff output is usually easier to interpret than the diff command because differences are juxtaposed visually in the output. The following example uses sdiff to display the differences between two files:

```
$ sdiff initDEV1.ora initDEV2.ora
```

Here is a snippet of the side-by-side differences:

```
sga_max_size=400M               |  sga_max_size=600M
sga_target=400M                 |  sga_target=600M
...
                                >#star_transformation_enabled=true
```

---

■ **Tip**    Use the diff3 utility to compare the differences between three files.

---

# 5-15. Comparing Contents of Directories

## Problem

You want to ensure that two different directories have identical contents in terms of the number of files, file names, and file contents.

## Solution

You can use the `diff` command to display any differences in two directories in terms of file names and file contents. This example compares the files in the `/ora01/upgrade` directory with the files in the `/cvsroot/prod_scripts` directory:

```
$ diff /cvsroot/prod_scripts /ora01/upgrade
```

If there are no differences, you won't see any output. If there's a file that exists in one directory but not in the other directory, you'll see a message similar to this:

```
Only in /ora01/upgrade: tab.sql
```

If there are differences in any files in each directory, you'll see a message similar to the following:

```
22c22
< # cd to udump
---
> # cd to udump directory.
```

See recipe 5-14 for details on interpreting the output of the `diff` utility. If you want to see only the names of the files that are different (and not how the files differ), use the `--brief` option:

```
$ diff --brief /cvsroot/prod_scripts /ora01/upgrade
```

## How It Works

Occasionally you may need to compare the contents of directories when maintaining database environments. In these situations, use the `diff` command to compare the contents of one directory with another.

If you want to recursively look in subdirectories and compare files with the same name, you can use the `-r` option. This example recursively searches through subdirectories and reports any differences in files that have the same name:

```
diff -r /cvsroot/prod_scripts /ora01/upgrade
```

You can also use the long listing of the recursive option to achieve the same result:

```
diff --recursive /cvsroot/prod_scripts /ora01/upgrade
```

# 5-16. Copying Files

## Problem

You want to make a copy of a file before you modify it.

## Solution

This first example shows how to use the cp (copy) command to create a copy of a file. For example, cp is used here to make a backup of the listener.ora file:

```
$ cp listener.ora listener.old.ora
```

You can verify that the copy worked with the ls command:

```
$ ls listener*.ora
listener.old.ora listener.ora
```

If you need to copy a file over the network, you can use a command-line utility such as scp, ftp, rsync, wget, or curl. We'll show an example of using scp in this recipe. There are examples of using scp and rsync to copy directories and files in recipe 5-17. We generally don't use ftp because it's not considered to be a secure way to copy files over the network. There are examples of using wget and curl to download files in recipe 5-36.

Having said that, let's look at scp; the basic syntax for scp is as follows:

```
scp [options] sourcefile destinationfile
```

The source/destination can be directories and/or files. The source/destination directory/file in the preceding syntax line can take one of the following general forms:

- directory/file
- host:directory/file
- user@host:directory/file

In the next line of code, a file is being copied from the remote host to the local host. The remote user is oracle, the remote host is srv2, the remote file is initTRG.ora in the /u01 directory, and the file is being copied to the local current working directory (signified by a dot):

```
$ scp oracle@srv2:/u01/initTRG.ora  .
```

The scp command prompts you for the password of the remote user. If you've never copied from the remote server, you'll also be prompted to ensure that you want to copy from the specified remote server.

This example copies a file from the local server to the remote host:

```
$ scp startup.sql oracle@srv2:.
```

Inspect the preceding syntax carefully. The local file being copied is `startup.sql` and exists in the current working directory. The file is copied using the remote user `oracle`, to the remote server `srv2`, and to the oracle user's `HOME` directory (specified by a dot immediately following the colon). Assuming that the remote `HOME` directory is `/home/oracle`, the following example copies the file to the same directory as the preceding example:

```
$ scp startup.sql oracle@srv2:/home/oracle
```

## How It Works

DBAs often need to create copies of files. For example, the `cp` utility provides a method to create backups of files or quickly replicate directories. The `cp` command has this basic syntax:

```
cp [options] source_file target_file
```

Be careful when copying files. If the target file exists prior to issuing the `copy` command, it will be overwritten with the contents of the source file. If you want to be warned before overwriting an existing file, use the `-i` (interactive) option. In this example, there already exists a file named `init.old.ora`:

```
$ cp -i init.ora init.old.ora
cp: overwrite `init.old.ora'?
```

Now you can answer y or n (for yes or no, respectively) depending on whether you want the target file overwritten with the source. Many DBAs create a shortcut command for `cp` that maps to `cp -i` (see recipe 2-7 for details on how to create shortcuts). For example, this code helps prevent you from accidentally overwriting previously existing files:

```
$ alias cp='cp -i'
```

You can also copy files directly into an existing directory structure using this syntax:

```
cp [options] source_file(s) directory
```

If the destination is a directory, the `cp` command will copy the file (or files) into the directory. The directory will not be overwritten. This example copies all files in the current working directory with the extension `.sql` to the `scripts` directory:

```
$ cp *.sql scripts
```

When you copy a file, the original timestamp and file permissions may differ between the original file and the file newly created by the `copy` command. Sometimes it's desirable to preserve the original attributes of the source file. For example, you may want to make a copy of a file, but for troubleshooting purposes want to still be able to view the original timestamp and ownership. If you want to preserve the original timestamp, ownership, and file permissions, use the `-p` (preserve) option:

```
$ cp -p listener.ora listener.old.ora
```

You can also use the cp utility to create the directory structure associated with the source file by using the --parents option. For this command to work, the destination must be a directory. This example creates a network/admin/log directory and copies any files ending with the extension of .ora to a directory beneath the destination ~/backup directory:

```
$ cp --parents network/admin/*.ora ~/backup
```

Any files with the extension of .ora in the source directory should now exist in the ~/backup/network/admin destination directory.

# 5-17. Copying Directories
## Problem
You want to copy all files and subdirectories beneath a directory to a new location.

## Solution
Use the cp command with the -r option to recursively copy all files in a directory and subdirectories. This example copies all files in the /orahome/scripts directory tree to the /orahome/backups directory:

```
$ cp -r /orahome/scripts /orahome/backups
```

The /orahome/backups directory now should have an identical copy of the files and subdirectories in the /orahome/scripts source directory. Be aware that existing files in the destination directory will be overwritten if they have the same name as files being copied from the source directory. If you want to be prompted before a file is overwritten, also use the -i (interactive) option:

```
$ cp -ri /orahome/scripts /orahome/backups
```

If you need to copy directories (and files) securely over the network, use the scp (secure copy) command. The basic syntax for scp is as follows:

```
scp [options] sourcefile destinationfile
```

The source/destination can be directories and/or files. The source/destination directory/file in the preceding syntax line can take one of the following general forms:

- directory/file
- host:directory/file
- user@host:directory/file

To recursively copy and preserve directories and files use the -r and -p options of the scp command. This example recursively copies the scripts directory (and any subdirectories and files) from the local box to a remote box named rmougdev2 as the oracle user:

```
$ scp -rp scripts oracle@rmougdev2:/home/oracle/scripts
```

In the preceding line of code, if the destination directory does not exist, it will be created. If the directory already exists, a subdirectory named scripts will be created underneath the existing scripts directory.

The scp command will prompt you for the password of the remote user. If you've never copied from the remote server, you'll also be prompted to ensure that you want to copy from the specified remote server.

## How It Works

As part of the daily routine, DBAs and developers often copy directories and files from one location to another. The location could be local or remote. You might require this if you are installing software or if you just want to ensure that you have a backup of files copied to a different location.

Another powerful utility used to synchronize directories is the rsync command. The basic syntax for rsync is as follows:

```
rsync [options] sourcefiles destinationfile
```

By default, the rsync tool will transfer only the differences that it finds between the source and destination. This makes it an extremely flexible and efficient method to synchronize one directory tree with another.

If the source and destination are on the same server, ordinary file and directory names can be used. Use the -r and -a options to recursively copy a directory tree and preserve permissions and ownership; the --delete option also specifies removing any files that exist in the destination that do not exist in the source. This example ensures that two local directories have the exact same directory structure and files; in other words, it ensures that test2 is identical to test1:

```
$ rsync -ra --delete /home/oracle/test1/ /home/oracle/test2/
```

You can copy locally to a remote server or from a remote server to your local server. If the directory or file is remote, it takes the following general form:

```
user@host:port/filename
```

For example, you can use rsync to synchronize a remote directory structure with a local directory structure. This line of code recursively copies the contents of the local scripts directory to the remote rmougdev2 server as the oracle user:

```
$ rsync -ra --delete --progress scripts/ oracle@rmougdev2:/home/oracle/scripts
```

You'll be prompted for the oracle user's password. The / at the end of the source folder ensures that if the destination folder exists, rsync will synchronize the two directories. If the destination folder doesn't exist, it will be created. Without the / at the end of the source directory, if the destination directory already exists, a subdirectory will be created underneath it.

The rsync command is very flexible and powerful. If you've never used it, you should become familiar with it and incorporate it into your bag of file transfer tricks.

# 5-18. Moving Files and Directories
## Problem

You want to rename or relocate a file.

# Solution

Use the mv (move) command to relocate a file or rename it. This example renames a file from initdw.ora to a new name of initDWDB.ora:

```
$ mv initdw.ora initDWDB.ora
```

You can also use the mv command to relocate a file to a different directory. This bit of code moves a file from the current working directory to its parent directory:

```
$ mv scrub.sql ..
```

Quite often, you'll need to move a file from the current working directory to a subdirectory. This example moves a file from the current working directory to a subdirectory named scripts:

```
$ mv scrub.sql scripts
```

In the previous line of code, if the scripts subdirectory didn't exist, you would end up renaming the scrub.sql file to a file named scripts. In other words, the destination subdirectory must exist before you issue the mv command (otherwise you'll end up renaming the file).

It is also possible to relocate directories. The following example moves the scripts directory to the sqlscripts directory:

```
$ mv scripts sqlscripts
```

In the preceding line of code, if the sqlscripts directory already exists, the scripts directory is created as a subdirectory beneath the sqlscripts directory. This might seem a little confusing if you're not expecting this behavior. One way to think of this is that the mv command does not overwrite directories if they already exist.

# How It Works

The mv command is used to relocate or rename a file or a directory. The mv utility uses the following syntax:

```
mv [options] source(s) target
```

Be aware that the mv command will unceremoniously overwrite a file if it already exists. For example, say you have the following two files in a directory:

```
$ ls
initdw.ora init.ora
```

If you move initdw.ora to the name of init.ora, it will overwrite the contents of the init.ora file without prompting you. To protect yourself against accidentally overwriting files, use the -i (interactive) option:

```
$ mv -i initdw.ora init.ora mv: overwrite `init.ora'?
```

You can now enter a y or an n to indicate a yes or no answer, respectively. You can easily implement the mv command as mv -i via a function or an alias to protect yourself against erroneously overwriting files (see recipe 2-7 for details on command shortcuts).

Table 5-6 describes the various results of the mv operation, depending on the status of the source and target.

*Table 5-6. Results of Moving File(s) and Directories*

| Source | Target | Outcome |
|---|---|---|
| File | File doesn't exist. | Source file is renamed to target. |
| File | File exists. | Source file overwrites target. |
| File(s) | Directory exists. | Source file(s) are moved to target directory. |
| Directory | Directory doesn't exist. | Source directory is renamed to target. |
| Directory | Directory exists. | Source directory created as a subdirectory beneath target directory. |

# 5-19. Renaming a File or Directory

## Problem

You want to change the name of a file or directory.

## Solution

Use the mv (move) command to rename a file. For example, the following line of code renames a file from credb1.sql to credatabase.sql:

```
$ mv credb1.sql credatabase.sql
```

You can also rename a directory. The following renames a directory from dev to test:

```
$ mv dev test
```

Be aware that when renaming directories, if you attempt to rename a directory to the name of an existing directory, a new directory will be created as a subdirectory beneath the already existing directory. See Table 5-6 for details on the behavior of the mv command.

## How It Works

You can also use the rename command to change file names. The rename utility has the following syntax:

```
rename oldname newname files
```

This command has a big advantage over the mv command because it allows you to rename several files at once. For example, here is a way to rename all files in a directory that ends with the extension of .trc to the new extension of .trace:

```
$ rename .trc .trace *.trc
```

You can also use rename to change the name of just one file. Here the file initDEV.ora is renamed to initTEST.ora:

```
$ rename initDEV.ora initTEST.ora initDEV.ora
```

# 5-20. Removing a File
## Problem
You want to remove a file from disk.

## Solution
First, use the ls command to identify the files you want to remove. In this example, any files with the extension of .trc are displayed:

```
$ ls -altr *.trc
```

After visually verifying the files you want to remove, use the rm command to permanently delete files:

```
$ rm *.trc
```

## How It Works
Be very careful when using the rm command. Once the files have been removed, the only way to get them back is from a backup (if there is one). DBAs can get in a lot of trouble by accidentally removing files.

DBAs typically are logged on to a server as the oracle OS user. This special user is usually the owner of all the critical database files, so this user can remove database files, even if they are currently in use.

Because the rm command doesn't prompt you for confirmation, we recommend that you always use the ls command to verify which files will be removed.

If you want confirmation before removing a file, use the -i option:

```
$ rm -i *.trc
```

You will now be prompted for confirmation before each file is deleted:

```
rm: remove regular file `rmdb1_j001_11186.trc'?
```

Type y to have the file removed or n if you want to keep the file. This method takes longer, but gives you some reassurance that you're deleting the correct files.

Another technique for preventing the accidental deletion of the wrong files is to use the !$ variable. The !$ character contains the last string entered on the command line. For example, to use !$ to remove files, first use the ls command to list the files targeted for deletion:

```
$ ls *.trc
```

Here is some sample output:

```
ora.trc
```

Now the value *.trc is stored in the !$ parameter. You can use rm to remove the files listed by the previous ls command:

```
$ rm !$
```

If you're ever unsure of the contents of the !$ variable, use the echo command to display its contents:

```
$ echo !$
echo *.trc
ora.trc
```

# 5-21. Removing Protected Files Without Being Prompted
## Problem
You want to remove all the files associated with an old installation of the database. However, when you issue the rm (remove) command, you are presented with this prompt:

```
rm: remove write-protected regular empty file
```

You wonder whether you can run the rm command without being prompted.

## Solution
There are two techniques for removing write-protected files: rm -f and yes. This example uses rm -rf (remove, recursive, force) to recursively remove all files beneath a directory without being prompted:

```
$ rm -rf /oracle/product/11.0
```

This example uses the yes command to recursively remove all files beneath a directory without being prompted:

```
$ yes | rm -r /oracle/product/11.0
```

If you type the yes command without any options, the subsequent output will be a repeating y on your screen until you press Ctrl+C. You can pipe the output of the yes command to another command that is expecting a y or n as input for it to proceed.

## How It Works
Be very careful when using the removal methods described in the "Solution" section of this recipe. These techniques allow you to easily remove entire directories and subdirectories with one command. Use these techniques only when you're absolutely sure you don't need a directory's contents. Consider using tar or cpio to recursively back up a directory tree before you delete it (see Chapter 6 for details)

# 5-22. Removing Oddly Named Files

## Problem

Somehow a file was created with the odd name of -f, and apparently it cannot be removed with the rm (remove) command. You wonder how you can remove it using the rm command.

## Solution

First use the ls command to view the oddly named file:

```
$ ls
-f
```

You can attempt to remove the file with the rm command:

```
$ rm -f
```

However, the rm command thinks -f is the force argument to the command and does nothing with the -f file. To remove the file, specify the current path with the file name, as shown here:

```
$ rm ./-f
```

## How It Works

Files with odd names are occasionally created by accident. Sometimes you can type a command with the wrong syntax and end up with a file with an undesirable name. For example, the following will create a file name of -f:

```
$ ls > "-f"
```

Now when you list the contents of the directory, you'll see a file named -f:

```
$ ls
-f
```

Worse yet, you might have a malicious user on your system who creates a file like this:

```
$ ls > "-r home"
```

Be *extremely* careful in this situation. If you attempt to remove the file without specifying a path, the command will look like this:

```
$ rm -r home
```

If you happen to have a directory named home in the current directory, this command will remove the home directory. To remove the file, use the current path ./, as shown here:

```
$ rm "./-r home"
```

In the previous command, you need to enclose the pathname and file name in quotes because there is a space in the file name. Without quotes, the rm command will attempt to remove a file named ./-r and another file named home.

# 5-23. Finding Files

## Problem

You want to locate a certain file on the database server.

## Solution

Use the find command to search for a file. The most basic way to search for a file is to instruct find to look for a file recursively in the current working directory and any of its subdirectories. The following command looks in the current directory and any subdirectories for any file that begins with the string "alert" and ends with the extension of .log:

```
$ find . -name "alert*.log"
```

Here's some sample output that indicates the location of the found file relative to the current working directory:

```
./RMDB1/admin/bdump/alert_RMDB1.log
```

## How It Works

It's well worth the effort to spend some time getting to know the find command. This command will allow you to easily search for files from the command line. Because this utility is used in so many different ways, we decided to include individual recipes to document these tasks. The next several recipes of this chapter show examples of how DBAs use the find command.

If your OS account doesn't have correct access permissions on a directory or file, find will display an error message. This example changes directories to the / directory and issues a find command:

```
$ cd /
$ find . -name "alert*.log"
```

Here is a partial listing of output, indicating that there is no access to certain directories:

```
find: ./proc/11686/task/11686/fd: Permission denied
find: ./proc/11688/task/11688/fd: Permission denied
find: ./proc/15638/task/15638/fd: Permission denied
```

To eliminate those error messages, send the error output to the null device:

```
$ find . -name "alert*.log" 2>/dev/null
```

# 5-24. Finding Strings in Files

## Problem

You want to search for a string in a text file that could be located somewhere beneath a given directory path.

## Solution

Use a combination of the find and grep commands to search for a string that exists in a file in a directory tree. The first example uses find to locate all SQL files beneath a directory and pipes the output to xargs, which executes the grep command to search for a create database string:

```
$ find . -name "*.sql" | xargs grep -i "create database"
```

If your system supports it, consider displaying the string being searched for in color:

```
$ find . -name "*.sql" | xargs grep -i --color "create database"
```

You can also use the find command with exec, grep, and print to search for strings within files. The following command is equivalent to the prior command that uses xargs:

```
$ find . -name "*.sql" -exec grep -i "create database" '{}' \; -print
```

In the previous line of code, the find command finds all files in a directory tree with the extension of *.sql. The output is passed to the -exec '{}' command, which feeds each file found to the grep -i command. The \; marks the end of the -exec command, and -print displays any files found.

You can also use command substitution to achieve the same functionality; for example:

```
$ grep -i "create database" $(find . -name "*.sql")
```

Depending on your version of the OS, the grep command may support the -r (recursive search) option. The following command recursively searches all subdirectories and files beneath the current working directory for the create database string:

```
$ grep -ir "create database" .
```

The preceding command can take a long time, depending on the number of files it searches through. Prior examples in this solution section are more efficient because they search for a particular type of file and then search within the file for a string.

## How It Works

Searching through files for a particular string is a very common task. Although the "Solution" section demonstrated several techniques for accomplishing this task, there are a few other examples that you may find relevant. For example, suppose that you want to display only the file name, not instances of the search string. To achieve this, use the -q option of grep. This example searches trace files for the word error and displays only the file name containing the search string:

```
$ find . -name "*.trc" -exec grep -qi "error" '{}' \; -print
```

When you troubleshoot issues, it is also helpful to see the file names and at what time the file was last modified:

```
$ find . -name "*.trc" -exec grep -qi "error" '{}' \; \
-printf "%p %TY-%Tm-%Td %TH:%TM:%TS %Tz\n"
```

---

■ **Note**  On some systems, the -q option may not be available. For example, similar functionality on Solaris would be implemented with the -l option. Use man grep to display all options available on your server.

---

Sometimes you want to search for the incidence of two or more strings in a file. Use grep with the -e option to accomplish this. This command searches for the "error" or "ora-" strings:

```
$ find . -name "*.trc" -exec grep -ie "error" -e "ora-" '{}' \; -print
```

You can also use egrep to search for multiple strings in a file:

```
$ find . -name "*.trc" -exec egrep "error|ora-" '{}' \; -print
```

Occasionally, you might have the need to inspect a binary file. For example, suppose that when using a spfile (server parameter file), you set a parameter erroneously as follows:

```
SQL> alter system set processes=10000000 scope=spfile;
System altered.
```

You then subsequently discover the bad setting when you attempt to stop and start the database:

```
ORA-00821: Specified value of sga_target 512M is too small
```

In this situation, you can't even start your database in nomount mode, so you can't use the ALTER SYSTEM command to modify the spfile. However, you can use the strings command to extract text strings from the binary spfile to quickly create a text-based init.ora file:

```
$ cd $ORACLE_HOME/dbs
$ strings spfileORA12CR1.ora >initORA12CR1.ora
```

Now modify the newly created init.ora file so that the value causing the problem is eliminated and then rename the spfile so that Oracle automatically uses the init.ora file when starting the instance.

This situation is just one example of how a DBA might have to use the strings command; the important thing to keep in mind is that this utility provides you with a way to look for text strings in binary files.

## DOES DATABASE WRITER WRITE TO DATAFILES IN BACKUP MODE?

Back in the days before RMAN, a misconception existed with some DBAs that the database writer stops writing to datafiles while a datafile's tablespace is in hot backup mode. The following example uses the `strings` command to verify that the database writer does indeed continue to write to datafiles, even while in backup mode.

First verify that a string does not exist in a datafile:

```
$ strings users01.dbf | grep -i denver
```

Verify that nothing is returned by the previous command. Next create a table and place it in the USERS tablespace:

```
SQL> create table city(name varchar2(50)) tablespace users;
```

Next alter a tablespace into backup mode:

```
SQL> alter tablespace users begin backup;
```

Now insert a string into the CITY table:

```
SQL> insert into city values('Denver');
```

Connect as SYS and run the following command to flush modified blocks from memory to disk:

```
SQL> alter system checkpoint;
```

From the OS command line, search for the "denver" string in the USERS database file:

```
$ strings users01.dbf | grep -i denver
```

You should see the following output:

```
Denver
```

This verifies that the database writer continues to write to datafiles, even while the corresponding tablespace is in backup mode. Don't forget to take the USERS tablespace out of backup mode.

# 5-25. Finding a Recently Modified File

## Problem

You recently created a file, but can't remember where it is located on the server. You want to find any files with a recent creation date.

## Solution

Use the `find` command with the `-mmin` (modified minutes) option to find very recently modified files. This example finds any files that have changed in the last 30 minutes beneath the current working directory:

```
$ find . -mmin -30
```

To find all files that were modified more than 30 minutes ago, use the + sign instead of the - sign:

```
$ find . -mmin +30
```

Sometimes when you troubleshoot issues, it is helpful to additionally pinpoint the exact time the file was modified; you can use the stat command to accomplish this:

```
$ find . -mmin -30 -exec stat -c "%n %y" {} \;
```

Additionally, the -printf option will show the time of file modification:

```
$ find . -mmin -30 -printf "%p %TY-%Tm-%Td %TH:%TM:%TS %Tz\n"
```

Here's some sample output:

```
./dbcreate.sql 2015-05-09 10:21:46 -0700
./.mozilla/firefox/q5xf2w9k.default 2015-05-09 12:07:05 -0700
```

# How It Works

The find command with a time-related option is useful for locating files that have recently been updated or changed. This command can be useful when you can't remember where you placed recently modified or downloaded files.

If you're using a version of find that does not support the -mmin option, try the -ctime option instead. The following command locates any files that have changed on the server in the last day beneath the ORACLE_HOME directory:

```
$ find $ORACLE_HOME -ctime -1
```

Many options are available when you are trying to find a file. For example, use the -amin (access minutes) option to find a file based on when it was last accessed. This line of code finds all files that were accessed beneath the current working directory exactly 60 minutes ago:

```
$ find . -amin -60
```

Table 5-7 describes a subset of time-related options commonly used with the find command.

**Table 5-7.** *Commonly Used Time-Related Options to Find Files*

| Option | Description |
|---|---|
| -amin | Finds files accessed more than +n, less than -n, or exactly n minutes ago |
| -atime | Finds files accessed more than +n, less than -n, or exactly n days ago |
| -cmin | Finds files changed more than +n, less than -n, or exactly n minutes ago |
| -ctime | Finds files changed more than +n, less than -n, or exactly n days ago |
| -mmin | Finds files modified more than +n, less than -n, or exactly n minutes ago |
| -mtime | Finds files modified more than +n, less than -n, or exactly n days ago |
| -newer <file> | Finds files modified more recently than <file> |

A wide variety of options are available with the find command. Use the man find command to display the options available on your system.

# 5-26. Finding and Removing Old Files

## Problem

You noticed that there are thousands of trace files being created in a diagnostic directory that consume disk space. You want to find old trace files and remove them.

## Solution

Use the find command to locate files older than a certain age. Once the old files are identified, use the rm command to remove them. The following example identifies files greater than 14 days old and removes them all with one line of code:

```
$ find $ORACLE_BASE/diag/rdbms/dwrep/DWREP/trace/*.trc -type f -mtime +14 -exec rm -f {} \;
```

The preceding command finds all files (the option -type f indicates a regular file) in the specified directory and its subdirectories that are older than 14 days. The rm command is executed (-exec) once for each file name located by the find command. The function of {} is to insert each file returned (by find) into the rm -f command line. When using the -f (force) option, you will not be prompted if you really want to remove write-protected files (files without write permission enabled); \; denotes the end of the exec command line.

You can also use the find command in conjunction with xargs to find and remove old files:

```
$ find $ORACLE_BASE/diag/rdbms/dwrep/DWREP/trace/*.trc -mtime +14 | xargs rm
```

In the preceding line of code, the xargs command provides as input to the rm command any file names returned by the find command.

Another variation of this is to use command substitution $(<command>); for example:

```
$ rm $(find $ORACLE_BASE/diag/rdbms/dwrep/DWREP/trace/*.trm -mtime +14)
```

In the preceding line of code, any file names returned by the find command enclosed by $() will be removed by the rm command.

You might be wondering why you cannot directly pipe the standard output of the find command to be used as standard input to the rm command. For example, this *does not* work:

```
$ find $ORACLE_BASE/diag/rdbms/trg1/TRG/trace/*.trm -mtime +14 | rm
rm: missing operand
```

Some commands (e.g., rm and kill) don't directly accept another command's standard output as standard input. To use standard output of the find command as standard input to the rm command, you have to use one of the techniques described in this "Solution section" (e.g., exec, xargs, or command substitution).

## How It Works

An active database will regularly produce trace files as part of its normal operations. These files often contain detailed information about potential problems or issues with your database. You usually don't need to keep trace and audit files lying around on disk forever. As these files grow older, the information in them becomes less valuable.

DBAs will typically write a small shell script to clean up old files. This shell script can be run automatically on a periodic basis from a utility such as cron. See Chapter 7 for details on shell scripting and Chapter 11 for techniques for details on automating tasks through cron.

# 5-27. Finding the Largest Files

## Problem

Your database is experiencing availability issues because a disk is 100 percent full. You want to locate the largest files in a directory tree.

## Solution

Use the find command to locate files recursively in a directory tree. The following command sends the output of the find operation to the sort and head commands to restrict the output to just the five largest files located in any directory beneath the current working directory:

```
$ find . -ls | sort -nrk7 | head -5
```

Here is a sample of the output:

```
6602760 820012 -rw-r-----    1 oracle    oinstall 838868992 Jan 21 14:55
./RMDB1/undotbs01.dbf
6602759 512512 -rw-r-----    1 oracle    oinstall 524296192 Jan 21 14:55
./RMDB1/system01.dbf
6602758 51260 -rw-r-----    1 oracle    oinstall 52429312 Jan 20 22:00
./RMDB1/redo03a.log
6602757 51260 -rw-r-----    1 oracle    oinstall 52429312 Jan 19 06:00
./RMDB1/redo02a.log
6602756 51260 -rw-r-----    1 oracle    oinstall 52429312 Jan 21 14:55
./RMDcB1/redo01a.log
```

The -nrk7 option of the preceding sort command orders the output numerically, in reverse order, based on the seventh column position. As shown in the output, the output is sorted largest to smallest. The top listing shows that the largest file is about 800MB in size.

## How It Works

You can also use the find command to look for certain types of files. To look for a file of a particular extension, use the -name option. For example, the following command looks for the largest files beneath the current working directory and subdirectories that have an extension of .log:

```
$ find . -name "*.log" -ls | sort -nrk7 | head
```

DBAs often create shortcuts (via shell functions or aliases) that encapsulate long strings of commands. This line of code shows how to create an alias command shortcut:

```
$ alias flog='find . -name "*.log" -ls | sort -nrk7 | head'
```

Command shortcuts can save time and prevent typing errors. See recipe 2-7 for details on creating functions and aliases.

# 5-28. Finding a File of a Certain Size
## Problem

You're running out of disk space, and you want to recursively locate all files beneath a directory that exceed a certain size.

## Solution

Use a combination of the find command with the -size option to accomplish this task. This example uses the -size option to find any files more than 1GB in the current working directory and any subdirectories:

```
$ find . -size +1000000k
```

Here's a small snippet of the output:

```
./ORA1212/sysaux01.dbf
./ORA12CR1/users01.dbf
./ORA12CR1/undotbs01.dbf
```

If you want to see the size of the file, use the stat command to do so:

```
$ find . -size +1000000k -exec stat -c "%n %s" {} \;
```

Here's the corresponding output:

```
./ORA1212/sysaux01.dbf 1073750016
./ORA12CR1/users01.dbf 5368717312
./ORA12CR1/undotbs01.dbf 4294975488
```

## How It Works

You can use the -size option of the find command in a number of useful ways. For example, if you want to find a file smaller than a certain size, use the – (minus) sign. This line of code finds any files smaller than 20MB beneath the directory named /home/oracle:

```
$ find . -size -20000k
```

If you want to find a file of an exact size, leave off the plus or minus sign before the size of the file designator. This example finds all files with the size of 16,384 bytes:

```
$ find . -size 16384c
```

# 5-29. Sorting Files by Size

## Problem

You want to list files from largest to smallest.

## Solution

The ls -alS command displays the long listing of all files sorted from largest to smallest; for example:

```
$ ls -alS
```

Here is a sample of the output:

```
total 4001584
-rwxr----- 1 oracle oinstall 2039488512 Jan 21 16:39 o1_mf_undotbs1_3gpysv9n_.dbf
-rwxr----- 1 oracle oinstall 983834624 Jan 21 16:37 o1_mf_sysaux_3gpystwj_.dbf
-rwxr----- 1 oracle oinstall 775954432 Jan 21 16:39 o1_mf_system_3gpysttv_.dbf
-rwxrwxr-x 1 oracle oinstall 176168960 Jan 21 02:31 o1_mf_temp_3gpz8s70_.tmp
```

To eliminate directories from the output, use the following technique:

```
$ ls -lS | grep '^-'
```

If you want to reverse the order of the sort (smallest to largest), include the -r (reverse) switch:

```
$ ls -arlS
```

## How It Works

If there are many files in a directory, you can combine ls and head to just list the "top n" files in a directory. The following example restricts the output of ls to the first five lines:

```
$ ls -alS | head -5
```

If you're using Solaris, it might not have the -S option for the ls command. On Solaris systems, use a command such as the following to display files sorted by size:

```
$ ls -l | sort -nrk5 | head
```

Also be aware that the sort column (5 in the preceding line of code) may differ, depending on the long listing of the output.

# 5-30. Finding the Largest Space-Consuming Directories

## Problem

You have a mount point that is out of space and you need to identify which directories are consuming the most space.

## Solution

Use the du command to report on disk usage. The following example reports the top five directories consuming the most disk space beneath the current working directory:

```
$ du -S . | sort -nr | head -5
```

The -S (do not include size of subdirectories) option instructs du to report the amount of space used in each individual directory. By default, the output of space used is reported in kilobytes. Here's a sample of the output:

```
1068448 ./lib
680104  ./assistants/dbca/templates
550140  ./bin
260136  ./rdbms/audit
227868  ./inventory/Scripts/ext/lib
```

If you want to report the cumulative space consumed by a directory, including its subdirectories, leave off the -S option:

```
$ du . | sort -nr | head -5
```

Here is the corresponding output:

```
6197828 .
1074732 ./lib
695236  ./assistants
684212  ./assistants/dbca
680104  ./assistants/dbca/templates
```

When not using the -S option, the top directory will always report the most consumed space because it is an aggregate of its disk space plus any spaced used by its subdirectories.

On some systems, there may not be an -S option. For example, on Solaris the -o option performs the same feature as the Linux -S option:

```
$ du -o . | sort -nr | head -10
```

Use man du to list all options available on your database server.

## How It Works

The du command recursively lists the amount of disk space used by a directory and every subdirectory beneath it. If you don't supply a directory name as an argument, du starts with the current working directory by default. The du command reports the amount of space consumed and the name of the directory on one line.

The du command has a variety of useful options. For example, the -s (summary) option is used to report a grand total of all space used beneath a directory and its subdirectories. This command reports on the total disk space used beneath the /orahome directory:

```
$ du -s /orahome
3324160 /orahome
```

You can also use the -h option to make the output more readable:

```
$ du -sh /orahome
3.2G /orahome
```

# 5-31. Truncating an Operating System File
## Problem

You have a large trace file that is being written to by a database process. You know that the trace file doesn't contain anything that needs to be retained. The trace file has filled up a disk, and you want to make the size of the file 0 bytes without removing the file because you know that a database process is actively writing to the file.

## Solution

Copy the contents of /dev/null to the file. You can use either the cat command or the echo command to accomplish this. This example uses the cat command to make an existing log file 0 bytes in size:

```
$ cat /dev/null > listener.log
```

The other way to zero out the file is with the cp command. This example copies the contents of /dev/null to the trace file:

```
$ cp /dev/null listener.log
```

## How It Works

One of us recently had a database that hung because one of the mount points was full, which prevented Oracle from writing to disk and subsequently hung the database. Upon further inspection, it was discovered that an Oracle Net trace file had grown to 4GB in size. The file had grown large because a fellow DBA had enabled verbose tracing in this environment and had forgotten to monitor the file or inform the other DBAs about this new level of tracing.

In this case, there was an Oracle Net process actively writing to the file, so we didn't want to simply move or remove the file because we weren't sure how the background process would react. In this case, it is safer to make the file 0 bytes. The /dev/null device is colloquially called the *bit bucket*. It is often used for a location to send output when you don't need to save the output. It can also be used to make a file 0 bytes without removing the file.

---

■ **Caution**    Zeroing out a file permanently deletes its contents. Use the techniques in this recipe only if you're certain you don't need the information contained within the file.

---

# 5-32. Counting Lines and Words in a File
## Problem

You want to count the number of lines and words in a shell script.

## Solution

Use the wc (word count) command to count the number of lines and words in a file. This example counts the number of words in the rmanback.bsh shell script:

```
$ wc rmanback.bsh
35  204 1361 rmanback.bsh
```

The preceding output indicates that there are 35 lines, 204 words, and 1,361 characters in the file.

## How It Works

If you want to see only the number of lines in a file, use wc with the -l option:

```
$ wc -l rmanback.bsh
35 rmanback.bsh
```

Similarly, if you want to display only the number of words, use the -w option:

```
$ wc -w rmanback.bsh
204 rmanback.bsh
```

If you want to see the line count of all files in a directory from smallest to largest, use the following:

```
$ wc -l *.* | sort -nk1
```

The preceding command pipes the output of wc to the sort command (sorting on the first column of the output).

# 5-33. Creating a Second Name for a File

## Problem

When performing a new install of the Oracle binaries, your initialization parameter file is located in an Oracle Flexible Architecture (OFA) directory such as /ora01/admin/DBS/pfile. When starting a database, Oracle looks for the initialization file in the ORACLE_HOME/dbs directory by default.

You don't want to maintain the initialization file in two separate directories. Instead, you want to create a link from the OFA directory to the default directory.

## Solution

Use the ln -s command to create a soft link to another file name. The following creates a soft link for the physical file in /ora01/admin/DEV/pfile/initDEV.ora to the link of /ora01/product/12.1.0/dbs/initDEV.ora:

```
$ ln -s /ora01/admin/DEV/pfile/initDEV.ora /ora01/product/12.1.0/dbs/initDEV.ora
```

A long listing of the soft link shows it pointing to the physical file:

```
$ ls -altr /ora01/product/12.1.0/dbs/initDEV.ora
lrwxrwxrwx    1 oracle dba    39    Apr 15 15:58 initDEV.ora ->
/ora01/admin/DEV/pfile/initDEV.ora
```

If you need to remove a soft link, you can use the rm or unlink commands. As a precaution, you may want to create a copy of the file before you remove the soft link. Be careful that you remove the soft link, not the physical file. For this example, the soft link is removed (and not the physical file):

```
$ unlink /ora01/product/12.1.0/dbs/initDEV.ora
```

The physical file located in the /ora01/admin/DEV directory should still exist.

## How It Works

A *soft link* (also referred to as a *symbolic link*) creates a file that acts as a pointer to another physical file. Soft links are used by DBAs when they need a file to appear as if it were in two separate directories, but physically resides in only one location.

The technique described in the solution of this recipe is commonly used by Oracle DBAs to manage the initialization file. This technique allows DBAs to view and edit the file from either the soft link name or the actual physical file name.

# 5-34. Creating a Second Name for a Directory

## Problem

You want to physically move a datafile to a different disk location without having to change any of the Oracle metadata.

## Solution

Use soft links to make a directory look like it exists, when it is really just a pointer to a physical location. This example shows how to move a tablespace datafile from one mount point to another, without having to change the datafile's name as it appears in the data dictionary. In this example, the datafile will be moved from /oradisk1/DBS to /oradisk2/DBS.

On this server, the following physical mount points exist:

```
/oradisk1/DBS
/oradisk2/DBS
```

A long listing shows the ownership of the mount points as follows:

```
$ ls -altrd /oradisk*
drwxr-xr-x  3 oracle oinstall 4096 Apr 15 19:17 /oradisk2
drwxr-xr-x  3 oracle oinstall 4096 Apr 15 19:19 /oradisk1
```

Create the following soft link as the root user:

```
# ln -s /oradisk1 /oradev
```

Here's a simple test to help you understand what is happening under the hood. Change directories to the soft link directory name:

```
$ cd /oradev/DBS
```

Notice that if you use the built-in Bash pwd command, the soft link directory is reported:

```
$ pwd
/oradev/DBS
```

Compare that with the use of the pwd utility located in the /bin directory, which reports the actual physical location:

```
$ /bin/pwd
/oradisk1/DBS
```

---

■ **Note**    You can also make the Bash built-in pwd command display the physical location by using the -P (physical) option (see recipe 5-1 for more details).

---

Next, create a tablespace that references the soft link directory. Here's an example:

```
SQL> CREATE TABLESPACE td01
    DATAFILE '/oradev/DBS/td01.dbf' SIZE 50M;
```

A query from V$DATAFILE shows the soft link location of the datafile:

```
SQL> select name from v$datafile;
```

Here's the output pertinent to this example:

```
/oradev/DBS/td01.dbf
```

Next, shut down your database:

```
SQL> shutdown immediate;
```

Now move the datafile to the new location:

```
$ mv /oradisk1/DBS/td01.dbf /oradisk2/DBS/td01.dbf
```

Next (as root) remove the previously defined soft link:

```
# rm /oradev
```

Now (as root) redefine the soft link to point to the new location:

```
# ln -s /oradisk2 /oradev
```

Now (as oracle) restart the database:

```
SQL> startup
```

If everything goes correctly, your database should start. You have physically moved a datafile without having to change any data dictionary metadata information.

## How It Works

Using soft links on directories gives you some powerful options when you relocate datafiles. This technique allows you to make Oracle think that a required directory exists when it is really a soft link to a different physical location.

The techniques in the "Solution" section of this recipe are useful when duplicating databases to a remote server using RMAN. In this situation, you can use symbolic links to make the auxiliary database server look similar to the source database server filesystem. It provides a method for relocating databases to servers with different mount points from the original server in which you can make a mount point or directory look like it exists to Oracle when it is really a soft link.

# 5-35. Viewing a Large File
## Problem

The database has dumped a large trace file, and you're troubleshooting the issue and are attempting to view the file with a text editor (e.g., vi). You receive the following error:

```
Tmp file too large
:
```

You need to somehow read this file to diagnose the problem.

## Solution

In this scenario, if you want to scroll through the file, you can use a tool such as more or less that allow you to view portions of the file; for example:

```
$ more TRG_m000_1489.trc
```

If you know the information you're interested in is near the end of the file, you can use tail to create a separate file containing the content you're interested in:

```
$ tail -100000 TRG_m000_1489.trc > out.txt
```

You can also use a utility such as split with the -l (lines) option to break the file into pieces:

```
$ split -l 100000 TRG_m000_1489.trc
```

The original file is still intact, but you should now see several files that begin with an x character. Each x file contains a portion of the original trace file based on the number of lines that you specified; for example:

```
$ ls x*
xaa  xab  xac  xad  xae  xaf
```

You should now be able to view these smaller files individually with the text editor. You have some control over the names of the split files; for example, the following names the split files with the string "new":

```
$ split -l 100000 TRG_m000_1489.trc new
```

A quick listing verifies this:

```
$ ls new*
newaa   newab   newac ...
```

## How It Works

Sometimes databases dump large trace files when encountering problems. If a file is too big to fit in the memory area being used by the text editor, you won't be able to directly view it; you'll have to use one of the techniques discussed in the "Solution" section to view the file.

The more, less, and tail commands operate on smaller portions of the large file, so they can present the large file in a piecemeal fashion. The split command is very useful for taking a large file and breaking it into smaller pieces.

Depending on your version of the OS, the split command may be equipped with the -n parameter, which allows you to specify the number of chunks a file is divided into. For example, to create four split files that have roughly the same size, use the following:

```
$ split -n4 TRG_m000_1489.trc
```

If the -n option isn't available, you can use the expr command and command substitution to calculate the sizes. The following example splits the trace file into four equal pieces based on line count:

```
$ split -l $(expr $(wc -l TRG_m000_1489.trc | awk '{print $1}') / 4) TRG_m000_1489.trc
```

# 5-36. Downloading Files

## Problem

You want to use a command-line tool to download a file from a remote web site.

## Solution

There are multiple tools for downloading files from the Internet; this recipe focuses on two feature-rich utilities: curl and wget. First up is curl.

### curl

The curl (transfer a URL) command is an extremely robust tool for downloading files from remote web sites using common network protocols (e.g., HTTP, HTTPS, FTP, FTPS, and so on). For example, suppose you want to download a useful DBA shell script from the github.com web site. You can do so as follows:

```
$ curl -kL github.com/ardentperf/racattack/raw/master/makeDVD/auto.sh -o auto.sh
```

The -k option is for an unsecured download, and -L signifies the location. The -o option allows you to specify the name of the file created locally. If successful, you should now have a copy of the auto.sh file.
Here's an example of downloading a file from an FTP site:

```
$ curl http://ftp.gnu.org/gnu/wget/wget-1.5.3.tar.gz -o wget-1.5.3.tar.gz
```

In this manner, you can use the command line to download files from the Internet. This section contains only a few examples of how to use curl. There are many options and features available with the robust downloading tool. Use the curl --help command to display all options.

### wget

The wget (network downloader) utility can also be used to download files from remote web sites. For example, here we download a file from the github.com web site:

```
$ wget https://github.com/ardentperf/racattack/raw/master/makeDVD/auto.sh
```

Here's another example of using wget, in which a tar file is downloaded from an FTP site:

```
$ wget http://ftp.gnu.org/gnu/wget/wget-1.5.3.tar.gz
```

If you want to rename a file, use the -O option; for example:

```
$ wget http://ftp.gnu.org/gnu/wget/wget-1.5.3.tar.gz -O my.tar.gz
```

You can also create a text file with the names of files you want to download and then use the -i option to instruct wget to download the file names within the text file. For example, suppose the file names are placed in a file named `download.txt`:

```
$ wget -i download.txt
```

In this way, you can efficiently automate file download from the Internet from the command line. We've only scratched the surface of the features available with `wget`. Use `wget --help` for a quick reference of all parameters available.

## How It Works

It's occasionally useful to be able to download files from remote servers. These files could be scripts that a DBA has posted or Oracle installation software. The `curl` and `wget` commands allow you to download remote files, provided that you have the download URL address. The basic syntax for these commands is as follows:

```
$ curl "download_url" -o file_name
$ wget "download_url" -O file_name
```

Files can be downloaded in this manner from any web site that allows downloads. For example, it is possible to download files from the My Oracle Support (MOS) web site. If you have an authenticated account, you can download files directly by using the following syntax (you must have a valid username and password to do this):

```
$ wget --http-user=user@domain.com --ask-password "file_url" -O file_name
```

Using this method to download files allows you to script and automate tasks that otherwise would require using a web browser to initiate a download. There's nothing wrong with using a web browser (indeed, this is how most files are downloaded), but if you have the need to automate a download task via the command line, `curl` and `wget` are extremely flexible and powerful utilities for this task.

# CHAPTER 6

■ ■ ■

# Archiving and Compressing Files

Most people who work with computers realize that the task of copying many files from one location to another is more efficient if the files can be bundled together and copied as a single unit. This is especially true when copying hundreds or thousands of files from one location to another. For example, in a Windows environment, if you have hundreds of files in a folder, it is fairly easy to click and drag the folder (containing the files) and copy it to a different location. This copy task would be time-consuming and error-prone if you individually copied each file within the folder.

On Linux/Solaris systems, tar, cpio, and zip are utilities that DBAs often use to group files together into one file (such as a Windows folder). Bundling a group of files together into one file is known as creating an *archive*. Archiving tools allow you to back up all files in a directory structure and preserve any file characteristics such as permissions, ownership, and contents. The archive file is used to move or copy the files as a single unit to a different location.

The tar utility was originally used to bundle (or archive) files together and write them to tape, which is why it's called *tape archive*, or tar for short. Although tar was originally used to write files to tape, its bundling capability is mainly what DBAs and developers use even today.

The cpio utility gets its name from its capability to copy files in and out of archived files. This command-line utility is also widely used by DBAs to bundle and move files.

The zip utility is another popular tool for bundling files. This utility is especially useful for moving files from one OS platform to another. For example, you can use zip to bundle and move a group of files from a Windows server to a Linux server.

Network performance can sometimes be slow when large archive files are moved from one server to another. In these situations, it is appropriate to compress large files before they are remotely transferred. Many compression programs exist, but the most commonly used are gzip, bzip2, and xz. The gzip and bzip2 utilities are widely available on most Linux/Solaris platforms. The xz utility is a newer tool and has a more efficient compression algorithm than the gzip and bzip2 compression tools.

Most of the utilities described in this chapter are frequently used by DBAs, SAs, and developers. Which utility you use for the task at hand depends on variables such as personal preference, standards defined for your environment, and features of the utility. For example, downloading installation files that are bundled with cpio means you have to be familiar with this utility. In other situations, you might use tar because the person receiving the file has requested that the file be in that format.

DBAs spend a fair amount of time moving large numbers of files to and from database servers. To do your job efficiently, it is critical to be proficient with archiving and compression techniques. In this chapter, we cover common methods that DBAs use to bundle and compress files. We also cover the basics of generating checksums, which are used to verify that bundled files are copied successfully from one server to another. First up is the tar utility.

# 6-1. Bundling Files Using tar

## Problem

You want to package several database scripts into one file using the tar utility.

## Solution

This first example uses the tar utility with the -cvf options to bundle all files ending with the string .sql that exist in the current working directory:

```
$ tar -cvf prodrel.tar *.sql
```

The -c (create) option specifies that you are creating a tar file. The -v (verbose) option instructs tar to display the names of the files included in the tar file. The -f (file) option directly precedes the name of the tar archive file. The file that is created in this example is named prodrel.tar.

---

■ **Note**    It is standard to name the tar file with the extension.tar. A file created with tar is colloquially referred to as a *tarball*.

---

If you want to include all files in a directory tree, specify the directory name from which you want the tar utility to begin bundling. The following command bundles all files in the /home/oracle/scripts directory (and any files in its subdirectories):

```
$ tar -cvf prodrel.tar scripts
```

Here is some sample output:

```
tar: Removing leading `/' from member names
/home/oracle/scripts/
/home/oracle/scripts/s2.sql
tar: /home/oracle/scripts/prodrel.tar: file is the archive; not dumped
/home/oracle/scripts/s1.sql
```

If you want to view the files that you've just bundled use the -t (table of contents) option:

```
$ tar -tvf prodrel.tar
```

Here's the corresponding output:

```
drwxr-xr-x oracle/dba         0 2015-05-10 11:19:55 home/oracle/scripts/
-rw-r--r-- oracle/dba       601 2015-05-10 11:14:30 home/oracle/scripts/s2.sql
-rw-r--r-- oracle/dba        22 2015-05-10 11:14:12 home/oracle/scripts/s1.sql
```

Note that if you retrieve files from this tarfile, the prior output shows the directories that will be created and where the scripts will be placed.

If you need to add one file to a tar archive, use the -r (append) option:

```
$ tar -rvf prodrel.tar newscript.sql
```

This example adds a directory named `scripts2` to the `tar` file:

```
$ tar -rvf prodrel.tar scripts2
```

# How It Works

DBAs, SAs, and developers often use the `tar` utility to bundle a large number of files together as one file. Once files have been packaged together, they can be easily moved as a unit to another location such as a remote server.

The `tar` command has the following basic syntax:

```
$ tar one_mandatory_option [other non-mandatory options] [tar file] [other files]
```

When running `tar`, you can specify only one mandatory option, and it must appear first on the command line (before any other options). Table 6-1 describes the most commonly used mandatory options.

***Table 6-1.*** *Mandatory* `tar` *Options*

| Option | Description |
|---|---|
| `-c, --create` | Creates a new archive file. |
| `-d, --diff, --compare` | Compares files stored in one `tar` file with other files. |
| `-r, --append` | Appends other files to `tar` file. |
| `-t, --list` | Displays the names of files in `tar` file. If other files are not listed, displays all files in `tar` file. |
| `-u, --update` | Adds new or updated files to `tar` file. |
| `-x, --extract, --get` | Extracts files from the `tar` file. If other files are not specified, extracts all files from `tar` file. |
| `-A, --catenate, --concatenate` | Appends a second `tar` file to a `tar` file. |

# Formatting Options

There are three methods for formatting options when running the `tar` command:

- Short

- Old (historic)

- Mnemonic

The *short format* uses a single hyphen (-) followed by single letters signifying the options. Most of the examples in this chapter use the short format. This format is preferred because there is minimal typing involved.

The *old format* is similar to the short format except that it doesn't use the hyphen. Most versions of `tar` still support the old syntax for backward compatibility with older Linux/Solaris distributions. We mention the old format here only so that you're aware of it; we don't use the old format in this chapter.

The *mnemonic format* uses the double-hyphen format followed by a descriptive option word. This format has the advantage that it is easier to understand which options are being used. For example, this line of code clearly shows that you're creating a tar file, using the verbose output, for all files in the /home/oracle/scripts directory (and its subdirectories):

```
$ tar --create --verbose --file prodrel.tar /home/oracle/scripts
```

The -f or --file option must come directly before the name of the tar file you want to create. You receive unexpected results if you specify the f option anywhere, but just before the name of the tar file. Look carefully at this line of code and subsequent error message:

```
$ tar -cfv prodrel.tar *.sql
tar: ora01.tar: Cannot stat: No such file or directory
```

This line of code attempts to create a file named v and put in it a file named prodrel.tar, along with files in the current working directory ending with the *.sql extension.

## Compressing

If you want to compress the files as you archive them, use the -z option (for gzip) or the -j option (for bzip2). The next example creates a compressed archive file of everything beneath the /home/oracle/scripts directory:

```
$ tar -cvzf prodrel.tar /home/oracle/scripts
```

Depending on the tar version, the previous command might not add an extension such as .gz to the name of the archive file. In that case, you can specify the file name with a .gz extension when creating the file or you can rename the file after it has been created.

If you're using a non-GNU version of tar, you might not have the z or j compression options available. In this case, you have to explicitly pipe the output of tar to a compression utility such as gzip:

```
$ tar -cvf - /home/oracle/scripts | gzip > prodrel.tar.gz
```

## Copying Directories

You can also use tar to copy a directory from one location to another on a box. This example uses tar to copy the scripts directory tree to the /home/oracle/backup directory. The /home/oracle/backup directory must be created before issuing the following command:

```
$ tar -cvf - scripts | (cd /home/oracle/backup; tar -xvf -)
```

The previous line of code needs a bit of explanation. The tar command uses standard input (signified with a hyphen [-]) as the tar file name, which is piped to the next set of commands. The cd command changes directories to /home/oracle/backup and then extracts to standard output (signified with a -). This gives you a method for copying directories from one location to another without having to create an intermediary tarball file.

---

■ **Note**    You can use the `tree` command to display a directory structure (and files contained within); for instance:

---

```
$ tree /home/oracle/scripts
```

Here is some sample output:

```
/home/oracle/scripts
|-- s1.sql
`-- s2.sql
```

You can also verify the structure of the backup directory:

```
$ tree /home/oracle/backup
```

Here's the corresponding output:

```
/home/oracle/backup
`-- scripts
    |-- s1.sql
    `-- s2.sql
```

You can also copy a directory tree from your local server to a remote box. This is a powerful one-line combination of commands that allows you to bundle a directory, copy it to a remote server, and extract it remotely:

```
$ tar -cvf - <locDir> | ssh <user@remoteNode> "cd <remoteDir>; tar -xvf -"
```

For instance, the following command copies everything in the dev_1 directory to the remote ora03 server as the oracle user to the home/oracle directory:

```
$ tar -cvf - dev_1 | ssh oracle@ora03 "cd /home/oracle; tar -xvf -"
```

You'll be prompted for the remote user password when you run the prior command. If you take out the user, `ssh` assumes that you're trying to access the remote server as your username.

# 6-2. Unbundling Files Using tar

## Problem

You want to retrieve files from a bundled `tar` file.

## Solution

Use the `-x` option to extract files from a `tar` file. It is usually a good idea to first create a new directory and extract the files in the newly created directory. This way, you don't mix up files that might already exist in a directory with files from the archive. This example creates a directory and then copies the `tar` file into the directory before extracting it:

```
$ mkdir tarball
$ cd tarball
```

At this point, it is worth viewing the files in the tar file (using the -t option). This code shows you the directories that will be created and where scripts will be restored:

```
$ tar -tvf prodrel.tar
drwxr-xr-x oracle/dba         0 2015-05-10 11:29:53 home/oracle/scripts/
-rw-r--r-- oracle/dba       601 2015-05-10 11:14:30 home/oracle/scripts/s2.sql
-rw-r--r-- oracle/dba        22 2015-05-10 11:14:12 home/oracle/scripts/s1.sql
```

The preceding output shows that the home directory will be created beneath the current working directory. It also shows that the scripts directory will be created with two SQL files.

Now copy the tar file to the current directory and extract the files from it:

```
$ cp ../prodrel.tar .
$ tar -xvf prodrel.tar
```

Here's the corresponding output that shows the directories and files that were extracted:

```
home/oracle/scripts/
home/oracle/scripts/s2.sql
home/oracle/scripts/s1.sql
```

You can also use the tree command to confirm the directory structure and files therein:

```
$ tree
.
|-- home
|    `-- oracle
|         `-- scripts
|              |-- s1.sql
|              `-- s2.sql
`-- prodrel.tar
```

## How It Works

The -x option allows you to extract files from a tar file. When extracting files, you can retrieve all files in the tar file or you can provide a list of specific files to be retrieved. The following example extracts one file from the tar file:

```
$ tar -xvf prodrel.tar scripts/s1.sql
```

You can also use pattern matching to retrieve files from a tar file. This example extracts all files that end in .sql from the tar file:

```
$ tar -xvf prodrel.tar *.sql
```

If you don't specify any files to be extracted, all files are retrieved:

```
$ tar -xvf prodrel.tar
```

---

## ABSOLUTE PATHS VS. RELATIVE PATHS

Some older, non-GNU versions of tar use absolute paths when extracting files. This line of code shows an example of specifying the absolute path when creating an archive file:

```
$ tar -cvf orahome.tar /home/oracle
```

Specifying an absolute path with non-GNU versions of tar can be dangerous. These older versions of tar restore the contents with the same directories and file names from which they were copied, so any directories and file names that previously existed on disk are overwritten.

When using older versions of tar, it is much safer to use a relative pathname. This example first changes directories to the /home directory and then creates an archive of the oracle directory (relative to the current working directory):

```
$ cd /home
$ tar -cvf orahome.tar oracle
```

This code uses the relative pathname (which is safer than using the absolute path). Having said that, you don't have to worry about absolute vs. relative paths on most Linux/Solaris systems because these systems use the GNU version of tar. This version strips off the leading / and restores files relative to where your current working directory is located.

Use the man tar command if you're not sure whether you have a GNU version of the tar utility. Near the top, you should see text such as "tar - The GNU version of the tar archiving utility". You can also use the tar -tvf <tarfile name> command to preview which directories and files will be restored to which locations.

---

# 6-3. Finding Differences in Bundled Files Using tar

## Problem

You wonder whether there have been any changes to files in a directory since you last created a tar file.

## Solution

Use the -d (difference) option of the tar command to compare files in a tar file with files in a directory tree. The following example finds any differences between the tar file prodrel.tar and the scripts directory:

```
$ tar -df prodrel.tar scripts
```

The preceding command displays any differences with the physical characteristics of any of the files. Here is some sample output:

```
scripts/s1.sql: Mod time differs
scripts/s1.sql: Size differs
```

## How It Works

Showing differences between what's in a `tar` file and the current files on disk can help you determine whether you need to create or update the `tar` file. If you find differences and want to update the `tar` file to make it current, use the `-u` option. This feature updates and appends any files that are different or have been modified since the tarball was created. This line of code updates or appends to the `tar` file any changed or new files in the `scripts` directory:

```
$ tar -uvf prodrel.tar scripts
```

This output indicates that `s1.sql` has been updated:

```
scripts/
scripts/s1.sql
```

# 6-4. Bundling Files Using cpio

## Problem

You want to use `cpio` (copy files to and from an archive) to bundle a set of files into one file.

## Solution

When using `cpio` to bundle files, specify `-o` (for out or create) and `-v` (verbose). It is customary to name a bundled `cpio` file with the extension of `.cpio`. The following command takes the output of the `ls` command and pipes it to `cpio`, which creates a file named `backup.cpio`:

```
$ ls | cpio -ov > backup.cpio
```

To list the files contained in a `cpio` file, use the `-i` (copy-in mode), `t` (table of contents), and `-v` (verbose) options:

```
$ cpio -itv < backup.cpio
```

Here's an alternate way to view the contents of a `cpio` file using the `cat` command:

```
$ cat backup.cpio | cpio -itv
```

If you want to bundle up a directory tree with all files and subdirectories, use the `find` command on the target directory. The following line of code pipes the output of the `find` command to `cpio`, which bundles all files and subdirectories in the current working directory and below:

```
$ find . -depth | cpio -ov > backup.cpio
```

If possible, don't back up a pathname starting with a / (forward slash). Our recommendation is that you navigate to the directory above the one you want to back up and initiate the cpio command from there. For example, suppose that you want to back up the /home/oracle directory (and subdirectories and files). Use the following:

```
$ cd $HOME
$ cd ..
$ find oracle -depth -print | cpio -ov > orahome.cpio
```

In this manner, the files are placed in a directory structure that starts with the directory specified in the find command.

You can also copy a directory using cpio. The following example copies the scripts directory (and any subdirectories and files) to the /home/oracle/backup directory.

```
$ find scripts -print | cpio -pdm /home/oracle/backup
```

In the preceding line of code, the -p switch invokes cpio in passthrough mode (pipes output to input). The d option instructs cpio to create leading directories, and the m option preserves the original timestamp on files.

The cpio utility can also be used to copy a directory tree from one server to another. This example copies the local orascripts directory to the remote server via ssh, in which it extracts the files into the orascripts directory on the remote server:

```
$ find orascripts -depth -print | cpio -oaV | ssh oracle@cs-xvm 'cpio -imVd'
```

It is also possible to do the reverse of the preceding code: copy a directory tree from a remote server to a local server:

```
$ ssh oracle@cs-xvm "find orascripts -depth -print | cpio -oaV" | cpio -imVd
```

# How It Works

The cpio utility is a flexible and effective tool for copying large amounts of files. The key to understanding how to package files with cpio is to know that it accepts as input a piped list of files from the output of commands such as ls or find. Here is the general syntax for using cpio to bundle files:

```
$ [ls or find command] | cpio o[other options] > filename
```

In addition to the examples shown in the solution section of this recipe, there are a few other use cases worth exploring. For example, you can specify that you want only those file names that match a certain pattern. This line of code bundles all SQL scripts in the scripts directory:

```
$ find scripts -name "*.sql" | cpio -ov > mysql.cpio
```

If you want to create a compressed file, pipe the output of cpio to a compression utility such as gzip:

```
$ find . -depth | cpio -ov | gzip > backup.cpio.gz
```

The -depth option tells the find command to print the directory contents before the directory. This behavior is especially useful when bundling files that are in directories with restricted permissions.

To add a file to a cpio bundle, use the -A (append) option. Also specify the -F option to specify the name of the existing cpio file. This example adds any files with the extension of .sql to an existing cpio archive named backup.cpio:

```
$ ls *.sql | cpio -ovAF backup.cpio
```

To add a directory to an existing cpio file, use the find command to specify the name of the directory. This line of code adds the backup directory to the backup.cpio file:

```
$ find backup | cpio -ovAF backup.cpio
```

# 6-5. Unbundling Files Using cpio

## Problem

You just downloaded some software installation files, and you notice that they are bundled as cpio files. You wonder how to retrieve files from the cpio archive.

## Solution

Use cpio with the idmv options when unbundling a file. The -i option instructs cpio to redirect input from an archive file. The -d and -m options are important because they instruct cpio to create directories and preserve file modification times, respectively. The -v option specifies that the file names should be printed as they are extracted.

The following example first creates a directory to store the scripts before unbundling the cpio file:

```
$ mkdir disk1
$ cd disk1
```

After copying the archive file to the disk1 directory, use cpio to unpack the file:

```
$ cpio -idvm < backup.cpio
```

You can also pipe the output of the cat command to cpio as an alternative way of extracting the file:

```
$ cat backup.cpio | cpio -idvm
```

You can also uncompress and unbundle files in one concatenated string of commands. This command allows you to easily uncompress and extract media distributed as compressed cpio files:

```
$ cat backup.cpio.gz | gunzip | cpio -idvm
```

## How It Works

You'll occasionally work with files that have been bundled with the cpio utility. These files might be installation software or a backup file received from another DBA. The cpio utility is used with the -i option to extract archive files. Here is the general syntax to unbundle files using cpio:

```
$ cpio -i[other options] < filename
```

You can extract all files or a single file from a cpio archive. This example uses the cpio utility to extract a single file named rman.bsh from a cpio file named dbascripts.cpio:

```
$ cpio -idvm rman.bsh < dbascripts.cpio
```

An alternative way to unpack a file is to pipe the output of cat to cpio. Here is the syntax for this technique:

```
$ cat filename | cpio -i[other options]
```

Note that you can use cpio to unbundle tar files. This example uses cpio to extract files from a script named script.tar:

```
$ cpio -idvm < script.tar
```

# 6-6. Bundling Files Using zip

## Problem

Your database design tool runs on a Windows box. After generating some schema creation scripts, you want to bundle the files on the Windows server and copy them to the Linux or Solaris box. You wonder whether there is a common archiving tool that works with both Windows and Linux/Solaris servers.

## Solution

Use the zip utility if you need to bundle and compress files and transfer them across hardware platforms. This example uses zip with the -r (recursive) option to bundle and compress all files in the /home/oracle directory tree (it includes all files and subdirectories):

```
$ zip -r ora.zip /home/oracle
```

If you want to view the files listed in the zip file, use unzip -l:

```
$ unzip -l ora.zip
```

You can also specify files that you want included in a zip file. The following command bundles and compresses all SQL files in the current working directory:

```
$ zip sql.zip *.sql
```

Use the -g (grow) option to add to an existing zip file. This example adds the file script.sql to the sql.zip file:

```
$ zip -g sql.zip script.sql
```

You can also add a directory to an existing zip archive. This line adds the directory backup to the sql.zip file:

```
$ zip -gr sql.zip backup
```

## How It Works

The zip utility is widely available on Windows and Linux/Solaris servers. Files created by zip on Windows can be copied to and extracted on a Linux or Solaris box. The zip utility both bundles and compresses files. Although the compression ratio achieved by zip is not nearly as efficient as gzip, bzip2, or xz, the zip and unzip utilities are popular because the utilities are portable across many OS platforms. If you need cross-platform portability, use zip to bundle and unzip to unbundle.

---

■ **Tip**    Run zip -h at the command line to get the help output.

---

# 6-7. Unbundling Files Using zip

## Problem

Your database-modeling tool runs on a Windows box. After generating some schema creation scripts, you want to bundle the files on the Windows server, copy them to the Linux box, and unbundle them.

## Solution

To uncompress a zipped file, first create a target directory location, move the zip file to the new directory, and finally use unzip to unbundle and uncompress all files and directories included in the zip file. The example in this solution performs the following steps:

1. Creates a directory named march

2. Changes the directory to the new directory

3. Copies the zip file to the new directory

4. Unzips the zip file

```
$ mkdir march
$ cd march
$ cp /mybackups/mvzip.zip .
$ unzip mvzip.zip
```

You should see output indicating which directories are being created and which files are being extracted. Here's a small snippet of the output for this example:

```
inflating: mscd642/perf.sql
creating: mscd642/ppt/
inflating: mscd642/ppt/chap01.ppt
inflating: mscd642/ppt/chap02.ppt
```

## How It Works

The `unzip` utility lists, tests, and extracts files from a zipped archive file. You can use this utility to unzip files, regardless of the OS platform on which the `zip` file was originally created. It is handy because it allows you to easily transfer files between servers of differing OSs (e.g., Linux, Solaris, Windows, and so on).

You can also use the `unzip` command to extract a subset of files from an existing `zip` archive. The following example extracts `upgrade.sql` from the `upgrade.zip` file:

```
$ unzip upgrade.zip upgrade.sql
```

Similarly, this example retrieves all files that end with the extension of `*.sql`:

```
$ unzip upgrade.zip *.sql
```

Sometimes you want to add only those files that exist in the source directory but don't exist in the target directory. First, recursively `zip` the source directory. In this example, the relative source directory is `scripts`:

```
$ zip -r /home/oracle/ora.zip scripts
```

Then `cd` to the target location and unzip the file with the `-n` option. In this example, there is a `scripts` directory beneath the `/backup` directory:

```
$ cd /backup
$ unzip -n /home/oracle/ora.zip
```

The `-n` option instructs the `unzip` utility to not overwrite existing files. The net effect is that you unbundle only those files that exist in the source directory but don't exist in the target directory.

# 6-8. Bundling Files Using find
## Problem

You want to find all trace files over a certain age and bundle them into an archive file. The idea is that once you bundle the files, you can remove the old trace files.

## Solution

You have to use a combination of commands to locate and compress files. This example finds all trace files that were modified more than two days ago and then bundles and compresses them:

```
$ find /ora01/admin/bdump -name "*.trc" -mtime +2 | xargs tar -czvf trc.tar.gz
```

This example uses `cpio` to achieve the same result:

```
$ find /ora01/admin/bdump -name "*.trc" -mtime +2 | cpio -ov | gzip > trc.cpio.gz
```

In this manner you can find, bundle, and compress files.

## How It Works

You often have to clean up old files on database servers. When dealing with log or trace files, it can be desirable to first find, bundle, and compress the files. At some later time, you can physically delete the files after they're not needed anymore (see Chapter 5 for examples of finding and removing files). We recommend that you encapsulate the code in this recipe in a shell script and run it regularly from a scheduling utility such as `cron` (see Chapter 10 for details on automating jobs).

# 6-9. Compressing and Uncompressing Files
## Problem

Before copying a large file over the network to a remote server, you want to compress it.

## Solution

Several utilities are available for compressing and uncompressing files. The `gzip`, `bzip2`, and `xz` utilities are widely used in Linux and Solaris environments. Each of them is briefly detailed in the following sections.

### gzip

This example uses `gzip` to compress the `dbadoc.txt` file:

```
$ gzip dbadoc.txt
```

The `gzip` utility adds an extension of `.gz` to the file after it has been compressed. To uncompress a file compressed by `gzip`, use the `gunzip` utility:

```
$ gunzip dbadoc.txt.gz
```

The `gunzip` utility uncompresses the file and removes the `.gz` extension. The uncompressed file has the original name it had before the file was compressed.

Sometimes there is a need to peer inside a compressed file without uncompressing it. The following example uses the `-c` option to send the contents of the `gunzip` command to standard output, which is then piped to `grep` to search for the string `dba_tables`:

```
$ gunzip -c dbadoc.txt.gz | grep -i dba_tables
```

You can also use the `zcat` utility to achieve the same effect. This command is identical to the previous command:

```
$ zcat dbadoc.txt.gz | grep -i dba_tables
```

# bzip2

The bzip2 utility is newer and more efficient than gzip. By default, files compressed with bzip2 are given a .bz2 extension. This example compresses a trace file:

```
$ bzip2 scrdv12_ora_19029.trc
```

To uncompress a bzip2 compressed file, use bunzip2. This utility expects a file to be uncompressed to be named with an extension of one of the following: .bz2, .bz, .tbz2, .tbz, or .bzip2. This code uncompresses a file:

```
$ bunzip2 scrdv12_ora_19029.trc.bz2
```

The bzip2 utility uncompresses the file and removes the .bz2 extension. The uncompressed file has the original name it had before the file was compressed.

Sometimes you need to view the contents of a compressed file without uncompressing it. The following example uses the -c option to send the contents of the bunzip2 command to standard output, which is then piped to grep to search for the string error:

```
$ bunzip2 -c scrdv12_ora_19029.trc.bz2 | grep -i error
```

## XZ

The xz compression utility, which is relatively new to the compression scene, creates smaller files than gzip and bzip2. Here's an example of compressing a file using xz:

```
$ xz DWREP_mmon_7629.trc
```

This code creates a file with an .xz extension. If you need extreme compression, you can use the -e and -9 options:

```
$ xz -e -9 DWREP_mmon_7629.trc
```

To list details about the compressed file, use the -l option:

```
$ xz -l DWREP_mmon_7629.trc.xz
```

Here's some sample output:

```
Strms  Blocks  Compressed Uncompressed  Ratio  Check   Filename
    1       1     72.5 KiB  1,055.2 KiB  0.069  CRC64   DWREP_mmon_7629.trc.xz
```

To uncompress a file, use the -d option:

```
$ xz -d DWREP_mmon_7629.trc.xz
```

Sometimes you need to view the contents of a compressed file without uncompressing it. The following example uses the -c option to send the contents of the xz command to standard output, which is then piped to grep to search for the string error:

```
$ xz -d -c DWREP_mmon_7629.trc.xz | grep -i error
```

## How It Works

DBAs often move files from one location to another. This action frequently includes moving files to remote servers. Compressing files before transferring them is critical to being able to copy large files. Although several compression utilities are available; the most widely used are gzip, bzip2, and xz.

The gzip utility is widely available in the Linux and Solaris environments. The bzip2 utility is a newer and more efficient compression algorithm than gzip. The bzip2 tool is CPU-intensive, but achieves high compression ratios. The xz compression tool is newer than gzip and bzip2. If you require the compressed file to be as small as possible, use xz. This tool uses more system resources, but achieves higher compression ratios.

---

■ **Note**    There is an older compression utility aptly named compress. Files compressed with this utility are given a .Z or .z extension (and can be uncompressed with the uncompress utility). This utility is less efficient than the other compression utilities mentioned in this recipe. We mention it in this chapter only because you may run into files compressed with this utility on older servers.

---

# 6-10. Validating File Contents
## Problem

You just copied a file from one server to another. You need to verify that the destination file has the same contents as the source file.

## Solution

Use a utility such as sum to compute a checksum on a file before and after the copy operation. This example uses the sum command to display the checksum and number of blocks within a file:

```
$ sum backup.tar
24092 78640
```

In the preceding output, the checksum is 24092, and the number of blocks in the file is 78640. After copying this file to a remote server, run the sum command on the destination file to ensure that it has the same checksum and number of blocks. Table 6-2 lists the common utilities used for generating checksums.

*Table 6-2.* *Common Linux Utilities Available for Generating Checksum Values*

| Checksum Utility | Description |
| --- | --- |
| sum | Calculates checksum and number of blocks |
| cksum | Computes checksum and count of bytes |
| md5sum | Generates 128-bit Message-Digest algorithm 5 (MD5) checksum and can detect file changes via --check option |
| sha1sum | Calculates 160-bit SHA1 (Secure Hash Algorithm 1) checksum and can detect file changes via --check option |

---

■ **Note**    When transferring files between different versions of the OS, the sum utility may compute a different checksum for a file, depending on the version of the OS.

---

## How It Works

When moving files between servers or compressing and uncompressing, it is prudent to verify that a file contains the same contents as it did before the copy or compress/uncompress operation. The most reliable way to do this is to compute a checksum, which allows you to verify that a file wasn't inadvertently corrupted during a transmission or compression.

A *checksum* is a value that is calculated that allows you to verify a file's contents. The simplest form of a checksum is a count of the number of bytes in a file. For example, when transferring a file to a remote destination, you can then compare the number of bytes between the source file and the destination file. This checksum algorithm is very simplistic and not entirely reliable. However, in many situations, counting bytes is the first step to determining whether a source and destination file contain the same contents. Fortunately, many standard utilities are available to calculate reliable checksum values.

DBAs also compute checksums to ensure that important files haven't been compromised or modified. For example, you can use the md5sum utility to compute and later check the checksum on a file to ensure that it hasn't been modified in any way. This example uses md5sum to calculate and store the checksums of the listener.ora, sqlnet.ora, and tnsnames.ora files:

```
$ cd $TNS_ADMIN
$ md5sum listener.ora sqlnet.ora tnsnames.ora >net.chk
```

You can then use md5sum later to verify that these files haven't been modified since the last time a checksum was computed:

```
$ md5sum --check net.chk listener.ora: OK sqlnet.ora: FAILED tnsnames.ora: OK
md5sum: WARNING: 1 of 3 computed checksums did NOT match
```

The preceding output shows that the sqlnet.ora file has been modified sometime after the checksum was computed. You can detect changes and ensure that important files have not been compromised.

# CHAPTER 7

■ ■ ■

# Shell Scripting

Shell scripting is an important skill that every professional DBA must possess. Most DBAs use this coding technique to automate many critical database administration tasks such as backups and monitoring. As part of your job, you'll be asked to maintain scripts that prior DBAs have written, and you'll also be required to write new shell scripts as required. The better you are at scripting, the better you'll be able to perform your job. To be effective at shell scripting, DBAs minimally need to be familiar with four types of tools:

- SQL

- Text editor

- Shell interface

- Shell scripting language

The most common tools that map to the previous list are SQL*Plus, the vi (or vim) editor, and the Bash shell. The Bash shell is both a shell interface and a scripting language. The previous bulleted list is a minimal list of tools that you should be familiar with. You'll be invoking a wide variety of Oracle database utilities in shell scripts such as SQL*Plus, RMAN, Data Pump, external tables, and so on.

As discussed in previous chapters, a shell is a command-line interface that allows you to interact with the Linux/Solaris kernel. Some shells that are commonly used by DBAs and developers are the Bash shell (bash), Korn shell (ksh), and C shell (csh or improved tcsh). As explained in Chapter 3, this book focuses on the Bash shell, so we won't rehash those details here.

A *shell script* is an OS file that contains one or more commands that a shell can execute. Any command that the shell can execute can be placed in a shell script file. For example, a shell script can run other shell scripts, executable binary files (such as sqlplus or rman), or any system utility (such as df, ps, and so on).

DBAs use shell scripts for critical tasks such as proactively monitoring the database and taking backups. These critical tasks need to be repeatable and reliable. DBAs typically use shell scripts to run a series of commands that accomplish the desired task. DBAs like shell scripting because they don't need to be expert programmers to write shell scripts. With a base knowledge (and a good example), it is fairly quick and easy to create a shell script that performs the desired task.

The purpose of this chapter is to provide a core set of techniques to enable you to successfully write shell scripts.

This chapter does not cover all the facets of shell scripting (that would take an entire book to accomplish). Instead, we give you the common approaches and shell scripting fundamentals that DBAs need to perform their jobs. We also provide useful real-world examples. Once you become adept at shell scripting, you'll be able to leverage these skills to automate critical database jobs. One could argue that a database administrator might exclusively use a graphical user interface (GUI) to automate database tasks. We strongly recommend you learn how to write shell scripts to automate database administration tasks. If the GUI ever becomes inaccessible or doesn't do something you need it to do, for your job's sake, you had better know how to write and debug a shell script.

The first recipe of this chapter introduces you to the basics of how to write a shell script.

# 7-1. Writing a Simple Shell Script

## Problem

You're new to shell programming, and you want to write a simple script to determine whether your database is accessible.

## Solution

Use an editor to create a new file (see Chapter 4 for details on using the vi file editor). Place the following text within the file:

```
#!/bin/bash
# Check if database is up.
ORACLE_SID=O1212
ORACLE_HOME=/orahome/app/oracle/product/12.1.0.2/db_1
PATH=$ORACLE_HOME/bin:$PATH
echo "select 'DB up' from dual;" | sqlplus -s system/foo
exit 0
```

Modify the previous code to match your ORACLE_SID and ORACLE_HOME variables and your system schema password. After you create the file, you'll also need to modify the permissions on the file to be executable. In this example, the file name is dbcheck.bsh:

```
$ chmod +x dbcheck.bsh
```

This code changes the permission of the file to executable (x). Now you should be able to successfully run the program:

```
$ dbcheck.bsh
```

If your database is up, you should receive a message like this:

```
'DBUP
-----
DB up
```

All the checking within the script is performed with one line of code:

```
echo "select 'DB up' from dual;" | sqlplus -s system/foo
```

The echo command pipes a valid SQL statement to the sqlplus executable. The sqlplus executable will then attempt to log on with the system schema and run the statement.

---

■ **Note**  Adding the file extensions .sh, .bsh, or .bash to the end of a Bash shell script is a common industry practice. Keep in mind that file extensions are meaningless in Linux/Solaris environments (other than helping you document the type of script). This is different from DOS, in which .exe, .com, and .bat indicate executable OS files.

---

# How It Works

The first line of the shell script in the "Solution" section of this recipe needs a little more explanation. We reproduced the line here for the discussion:

```
#!/bin/bash
```

The # character is normally used to comment out a line in a shell script; for example:

```
# This is a comment.
```

One exception to that rule is when #! appears as the first text in the shell script. When #! is placed on the first line, it can then be combined with a path and program name. The path and program name specify the location and name of the program that will interpret the commands within the script. This is important because it means you can have the script run with a designated shell regardless of the interactive shell you're using.

---

■ **Note**   The two-character sequence of #! is sometimes referred to as the *shebang*.

---

If you don't specify a #!/<path>/<program>, the shell you're currently logged on to will be used to interpret the commands within the script. We recommend that you specify the path and shell program on the first line of your script so that there is no ambiguity about which shell will be used to interpret the commands within the script.

On most systems, the bash interpreter is in the /bin directory. If you don't know the location of your bash executable, you can use the which or whereis command to locate it:

```
$ whereis bash
bash: /bin/bash
```

When you first attempt to run a shell script, you may receive an error similar to the following:

```
-bash: dbcheck.bsh: command not found
```

It means that your PATH variable doesn't include the current working directory. To work around this, you can reset the PATH variable to include the current working directory. This example exports the PATH variable to include the current working directory:

```
$ export PATH=$PATH:.
```

Another method for ensuring that the Bash shell can locate a script is to include the complete directory path to where the script resides. In this example, the script is located in the directory /home/oracle and is run as shown here:

```
$ /home/oracle/dbcheck.bsh
```

You can also instruct the shell to look in the current working directory to determine the location of the script. You do this by placing ./ before the script name:

```
$ ./dbcheck.bsh
```

When first running the script, you may also receive a message like this:

```
Error 6 initializing SQL*Plus
SP2-0667: Message file sp1<lang>.msb not found
```

This message most likely means that the ORACLE_HOME variable isn't set correctly. In this situation, ensure that you set the ORACLE_HOME variable to the correct location.

---

## BASH SHELL EXIT COMMAND

You can place an exit command at any location within a shell script to instruct the Bash shell to immediately terminate the program. A successful exit is normally specified with an exit or an exit 0. Exiting a shell script when a failure condition has been detected is indicated by a nonzero value, such as an exit 1. We recommend that you explicitly place an exit 0 command within your shell script to indicate a successful completion. You should also use a nonzero value such as exit 1 when an error condition has been detected.

Each Bash shell command that executes will also return an exit code. If a command executes successfully, it will terminate with a status of 0. If there has been some sort of a failure, the exit code will be nonzero. You can check the status of an exit code by inspecting the $? variable:

```
$ echo $?
0
```

The $? variable holds the exit value of the previously executed command. The nonsuccess value of an exit code will vary by each command. For example, the grep utility will return a 0 on successfully finding a match, a 1 if no matches are found, and a 2 if there has been some sort of a syntax error or missing input.

---

# 7-2. Checking Simple Conditions

## Problem

You want to check for a condition such as whether a critical database background process is running and send an e-mail if there is a problem.

## Solution

Use the if/then/else Bash control structure to check for a condition and perform an appropriate action. The following example uses an if/then/else structure to determine whether the Oracle system monitor (SMON) process is running and sends an e-mail if the process is not detected:

```
#!/bin/bash
# Check for background process.
ORACLE_SID=O1212
critProc=ora_smon
ps -ef | grep -v 'grep' | grep ${critProc}_$ORACLE_SID
```

```
if [ $? -eq 0 ]; then
  echo "SMON $ORACLE_SID is available."
else
  echo "SMON $ORACLE_SID issue." | mailx -s "issue with SMON $ORACLE_SID" dba@gmail.com
fi
exit 0
```

Place the preceding code in a file named bgcheck.bsh and make it executable:

```
$ chmod +x bgcheck.bsh
```

Then run it:

```
$ ./bgcheck.bsh
```

If the SMON process is running, you'll see output similar to the following:

```
oracle   27910    1  0 May11 ?        00:00:00 ora_smon_01212
SMON 01212 is available.
```

The previous example uses the $? variable. This variable is often used after conditional statements to evaluate the success or failure of the previous command. The $? variable contains the status of the previous command executed. If the previously executed command was successful, the $? variable will contain a 0; otherwise, it will contain a nonzero value.

## How It Works

The if/then/else control structure comes in three basic forms. The first one states that if a condition is true, execute the following commands. The syntax is as follows:

```
if condition ; then
  commands
fi
```

On the first line of code in the previous example, the keyword then is a separate command from the if keyword, so you must insert a semicolon to indicate the end line termination point of the if keyword. Another way of executing the previous bit of code is as follows:

```
if condition
then
  commands
fi
```

The next form of the if/then/else structure states if a condition is true, execute the following commands. If the first condition is false, execute a separate set of commands. Its syntax is as follows:

```
if condition ; then
  commands
else
    commands
fi
```

The third form of the if/then/else structure states that if a condition is true, execute the first set of commands; otherwise, check for the next condition. If it is true, execute the commands. This functionality is enabled with the elif keyword. You can have many elif conditions in this form. Its syntax is as follows:

```
if condition ; then
    commands
elif  condition
    commands
elif  condition
    commands
fi
```

---

■ **Tip**   You can also check for success (or not) of a command via the two conditional operators || and &&. See recipe 7-8 for more details on conditional operators.

---

# 7-3. Testing a Condition

## Problem

You want to write a script that checks for certain conditions, such as the number of parameters passed to a script. Based on the condition, you want to perform an action such as displaying an informational message or exiting the script.

## Solution

As shown in recipe 7-2, the if/then/else structure is an important programming technique. However, it is the combination of if/then/else with a condition that can be tested that gives you a much more powerful tool to automate DBA tasks. The test command enables you to check a condition within an if command. Here is the basic syntax for the test command:

```
test operand1 operator operand2
```

The test command can also be written with the [  ] syntax. This syntax uses a left square bracket to start the command and then finishes the command with a right square bracket. Its syntax is as follows:

```
[ operand1 operator operand2 ]
```

---

■ **Note**   The shell script examples in this chapter use the [  ] form of the test command.

---

For some test conditions, an operand1 isn't required. The syntax for this condition is as follows:

```
[ operator operand2 ]
```

The previous `test` conditional checks will exit with a status of 0 (true) or 1 (false), depending on the evaluation of the condition. Ensure that you have a space between the operands, operators, and brackets. The space is how the shell knows where the operator and operand are separated. If there is no space between the operator, operand, and brackets, the shell will interpret the value as one string, which will result in erroneous outcomes.

To bring `if/then/else` and `test` together, we'll write a small but useful piece of code that checks to see whether the correct number of parameters are passed to a script. The script will use the $# variable. The $# variable automatically gets assigned to the number of positional parameters typed at the command line and passed into the script. This variable is handy when you want to check for the correct number of parameters passed to a script. The script will also use the $1 variable to display the first parameter passed to the script. When parameters are passed to a script, the first parameter is automatically stored in the $1 variable, the second parameter is stored in $2, and so on.

The following bit of code uses the -ne conditional check to determine whether the number of parameters passed to the script is not equal to 1:

```
#!/bin/bash
if [ $# -ne 1 ]
then
  echo "Wrong number of parameters passed to script."
  exit 1
else
  echo "$1 passed to the script"
fi
exit 0
```

We next place this code in a script named `ss.bsh` and make it executable:

```
$ chmod +x ss.bsh
```

Now run the script with no parameters passed to it:

```
$ ./ss.bsh
```

Here is the corresponding output:

```
Wrong number of parameters passed to script.
```

Now run the script with one parameter passed to it:

```
$ ./ss.bsh testparm
```

Here is the output:

```
testparm passed to the script
```

The $0 parameter is often used in conjunction with the $# parameter to display the syntax required when invoking a script. Within a shell script, the $0 parameter contains the name of the shell script being executed. Here's a slight variation of the previous code that uses the $0 variable to display the name of the script:

```
#!/bin/bash
if [ $# -ne 1 ]
then
  echo "Wrong number of parameters passed to script."
  echo "Usage: $0 ORACLE_SID"
  exit 1
else
  echo "$1 passed to the script"
fi
exit 0
```

The -ne operator is an arithmetic operator and is used to test whether the operands are not equal. If the script (named ss.bsh) is called without passing exactly one parameter to it, the following output is displayed:

```
Wrong number of parameters passed to script.
Usage: ./ss.bsh ORACLE_SID
```

Notice the ./ in front of the script name in the previous output. To eliminate the ./ from the output, use the basename command. This utility is used to strip any directory or suffix information from file names; for example:

```
#!/bin/bash
Pgm=$(basename $0)
if [ $# -ne 1 ]
then
  echo "Wrong number of parameters passed to script."
  echo "Usage: $Pgm ORACLE_SID"
  exit 1
else
  echo "$1 passed to the script"
fi
exit 0
```

The script is executed again:

```
$ ./ss.bsh
```

Notice in the output that the name of the script is displayed without directory information:

```
Wrong number of parameters passed to script.
Usage: ss.bsh ORACLE_SID
```

One last note: the following line of code from the prior script needs a bit more explanation:

```
Pgm=$(basename $0)
```

The previous line uses a technique known as command substitution. *Command substitution* allows you to take the output of a command and populate a variable. The basic syntax for doing this is as follows:

```
variable=$(shell commands)
```

This is a powerful feature that allows you to populate variables with the output of other commands. In our example, we took the output of basename $0 and populated the Pgm variable. Be aware that in older versions of the shell you may see command substitution implemented with the back tick syntax:

```
variable=`shell commands`
```

This is an older style and won't be used in any of our examples.

## How It Works

Testing for conditions is an integral part of shell script logic. The "Solution" section provides a practical example of using the test command with the [ ] syntax. There are several additional use cases for which you'll need to test for conditions (e.g., an arithmetic condition, a string, if a file exists, and so on). Several real-world scenarios are explored in the following sections.

## Testing an Arithmetic Condition

We have occasionally been in a situation in which an abnormally high number of SQL sessions get connected to the database. It might be due to an erroneous program initiating connections to the database and never exiting. In this scenario, it is useful to have a shell script that periodically checks to see whether the number of SQL processes running on the server is less than a certain threshold.

Here's a simple script that checks to see whether the number of SQL processes is fewer than 300. If there are 300 or more processes executing, the script sends an e-mail:

```
#!/bin/bash
crit_var=$(ps -ef | grep sqlplus | wc -l)
if [ $crit_var -lt 300 ]; then
  echo $crit_var
  echo "processes running normal"
else
  echo "too many processes"
  echo $crit_var | mailx -s "too many sqlplus procs" dba@gmail.com
fi
exit 0
```

In the prior script, command substitution is used to populate the crit_var variable with the output of the ps command. The value of crit_var is then tested with the -lt (less than) arithmetic operator.

Several arithmetic operators are available with the Bash shell. Table 7-1 gives a brief description of each operator.

*Table 7-1.* *Arithmetic Operators*

| Operator | Description |
|----------|-------------|
| -eq | True if two integers are equal |
| -ne | True if two integers are not equal |
| -lt | True if operand1 is less than operand2 |
| -le | True if operand1 is less than or equal to operand2 |
| -gt | True if operand1 is greater than operand2 |
| -ge | True if operand1 is greater than or equal to operand2 |

# Testing Strings

You can use strings with test conditions, and there is a wide variety of ways to use string comparisons. For example, you may want to check to ensure that you're logged on as a certain OS user before you run commands in a script. This example checks to see whether the user running the script is oracle:

```
#!/bin/bash
checkUser=oracle
curWho=$(whoami)
if [ "$curWho" != "$checkUser" ]; then
  echo "You are currently logged on as: $curWho"
  echo "Must be logged in as $checkUser to run this script.."
  exit 1
fi
exit 0
```

In the preceding bit of code, we use command substitution to populate the curWho variable with the output of the whoami command. The curWho variable is then checked to see whether it matches the string of oracle via the != (not equal) operator. If the user doesn't match, the script displays informational messages and exits the script. Table 7-2 lists test operations for strings and their descriptions.

*Table 7-2.* *String Operators*

| String Operator | Description |
|-----------------|-------------|
| -z string | True if the string is empty |
| -n string | True if the string is not empty |
| string1 = string2 | True if string1 equals string2 |
| string1 != string2 | True if the strings are not equal |
| string1 < string2 | True if string1 sorts before string2 |
| string1 > string2 | True if string1 sorts after string2 |

## Accepting Input from the Command Line

Another useful example of a string comparison is to read user input from the keyboard and verify an operation. Suppose you want to check the current Oracle SID variable before continuing to run more commands within the script. This is useful if you work with multiple databases contained on one physical server. This script displays the value of ORACLE_SID and asks whether you want to continue running the script:

```
#!/bin/bash
keepGoing=n
echo "Current value of ORACLE_SID: $ORACLE_SID"
echo -n "Do you want to continue? y/n "
read keepGoing
if [ "$keepGoing" = "y" ]; then
  echo "Continue to run script."
else
  echo "Exiting script"
  exit 1
fi
exit 0
```

## Testing for the Existence of a File

In addition to arithmetic and string comparisons, you can also perform various tests on OS files. The test command allows you to perform checks such as the availability of a file, the file type, and so on. For example, you may want to determine whether a log file exists; if it does, you want it to send an e-mail to the appropriate support person. This script uses the -e (exists) parameter of the test command to determine this:

```
#!/bin/bash
checkFile=/home/trace/error.log
if [ -e $checkFile ]; then
  mail -s "error.log exists" dba@gmail.com <$checkFile
else
  echo "$checkFile does not exist"
fi
exit 0
```

If you want your shell script to do nothing after checking for a condition, use the colon (:) command (sometimes called *no-operation* or *null*). For example, the following bit of code does nothing if it detects that the given file exists:

```
#!/bin/bash
checkFile=/home/oracle/error.log
if [ -e $checkFile ]; then
  :
else
  echo "$checkFile does not exist"
fi
exit 0
```

Table 7-3 contains descriptions of the Bash shell tests for file operations.

*Table 7-3.* *File Operators*

| File Operator | Description |
|---|---|
| -a | True if file exists |
| -b | True if file is a block device file |
| -c | True if file is a character device file |
| -d | True if file is a directory |
| -e | True if file exists |
| -f | True if file exists and is a regular file |
| -g | True if file has set-group-id permission set |
| -h | True if file is a symbolic link |
| -L | True if file is a symbolic link |
| -k | True if file's sticky bit is set |
| -p | True if file is a named pipe |
| -r | True if the file is readable (by current user) |
| -s | True if file exists and is not empty |
| -S | True if file is socket |
| -u | True if file is set-user-id |
| -w | True if file is writable (by current user) |
| -x | True if file is executable |
| -O | True if file is effectively owned by current user |
| -G | True if file is effectively owned by current user's group |
| -N | True if file has been modified since it was last read |
| file1 -nt file2 | True if file1 is newer than file2 |
| file1 -ot file2 | True if file1 is older than file2 |
| file1 -ef file2 | True if file1 is a hard link to file2 |

▓ **Tip** The test command options will vary by OS version. For a complete listing of available test operations in your environment, use the help test command or the man test command.

# 7-4. Checking Complex Conditions

## Problem

You need to perform a sophisticated set of condition checks, such as checking for free disk space on a server. When a particular mount point reaches a certain threshold, you want to send an e-mail to the DBA team. You suspect that you'll need something more sophisticated than if/then/else checking, such as a case statement.

# Solution

In many cases, a simple if/then/else construct is all you need to check a condition. However, as soon as you are presented with many different actions to take, the if/then/else syntax can become unwieldy and nonintuitive. In these situations, use a case statement instead. The basic syntax for a case statement is as follows:

```
case expression in
  pattern1)
     commands ;;
  pattern2)
     commands ;;
esac
```

The next example in this section uses a case statement to check for free disk space. The script replies on the output of the df command. So to understand how the script works, first run df -h and view its output:

```
$ df -h
```

Here's the corresponding output for this server:

```
Filesystem         Size  Used Avail Use% Mounted on
/dev/xvda2         191G  165G   17G  91% /
/dev/xvda1         996M  136M  809M  15% /boot
```

The two mount points on this server are / and /boot. Looking ahead to the script, the mntlist variable within the script has been defined to match the mount points on this server that require monitoring for used space:

```
mntlist="/ /boot"
```

With that understanding, consider the following code, which uses a case statement to perform several checks:

```
#!/bin/bash
BOX=$(uname -a | awk '{print $2}')
mntlist="/ /boot"
for ml in $mntlist
do
echo "Mount point: $ml"
usedSpc=$(echo $(df -h $ml|awk '{print $5}'|grep -v Use|cut -d "%" -f1 -))
BOX=$(uname -a | awk '{print $2}')
case $usedSpc in
[0-9])
diskStat="relax, lots of disk space: $usedSpc"
;;
[1-7][0-9])
diskStat="disk space okay: $usedSpc"
;;
[8][0-9])
diskStat="space getting low: $usedSpc"
;;
```

169

```
[9][0-9])
diskStat="warning, running out of space: $usedSpc"
echo $diskStat $ml | mailx -s "space on: $BOX" dba@gmail.com
;;
[1][0][0])
diskStat="update resume, no space left: $usedSpc"
echo $diskStat $ml | mailx -s "space on: $BOX" dba@gmail.com
;;
*)
diskStat="huh?: $usedSpc"
esac
# end case
echo $diskStat
done
# end for
exit 0
```

Assume that the preceding code is placed in a script named `filesp.bsh` and made executable:

```
$ chmod +x filesp.bsh
```

Next the script is executed:

```
$ filesp.bsh
```

And the output is displayed:

```
Mount point: /
warning, running out of space: 91
Mount point: /boot
disk space okay: 15
```

Within the script, the `usedSpc` variable gets assigned a value that shows what percentage of disk space is used on a mount point. The `case` statement then examines `usedSpc` to determine within which range the variable falls. Finally, if a given mount point exceeds the 90% full threshold, the script e-mails the DBA a message to indicate that there could be an issue.

## How It Works

The code in the "Solution" section of this recipe uses shell commands, a `case` statement, and various coding techniques in a few lines of code. The result is a small but extremely useful script that monitors disk space. The `usedSpc` line of the script needs additional explanation. We repeat it here for convenience:

```
usedSpc=$(echo $(df -h $ml|awk '{print $5}'|grep -v Use|cut -d "%" -f1 -))
```

The `usedSpc` variable is contained within a looping structure for `ml` in `$mntlist`. The loop executes for each mount point defined in the `mntlist` variable. The `ml` variable is assigned for the current mount point being examined. The output of the `df` command is piped to the `awk` command, which extracts the fifth column. This in turn is passed to the `grep` command, which eliminates any output that contains the string `"Use"`. This output is piped to the `cut` command, which extracts the first field delimited by a % character.

Note that there's an echo command embedded into the line of code; it is used because there's extra space included in the output of the df command on some systems, and echo removes that extra space. The resultant string should be the percentage of disk space used on the mount point in question.

You may have to tweak the usedSpc line of code, depending on the output of df for your system. For example, the output of the df command might not display the string "Use" on some platforms. Case in point: on some Solaris systems, the output from the df command displays the string "Capacity" to indicate the amount of disk space used; for example:

```
$ df -h
```

Here is some sample output on a Solaris system:

```
Filesystem            Size    Used  Available Capacity  Mounted on
orapool1/ora01        350G    203G       147G      59%  /ora01
orapool2/ora02        350G    265G        85G      76%  /ora02
orapool1/ora03        350G    254G        96G      73%  /ora03
```

In this situation, you can modify the script to use grep to filter out the string "Capacity"; for example:

```
usedSpc=$(echo $(df -h $ml|awk '{print $5}'|grep -v Capacity|cut -d "%" -f1 -))
```

Here's the corresponding output when filesp.bsh is run on a Solaris system:

```
Mount point: /ora01
disk space okay: 59
Mount point: /ora02
disk space okay: 76
Mount point: /ora03
disk space okay: 73
```

Also note that for this Solaris system, the mntlist variable in the script needs to be defined as follows:

```
mntlist="/ora01 /ora02 /ora03"
```

Let's now go back to the example in the "Solution" section of this recipe: the case statement performs a sophisticated set of string comparisons on the value stored in the usedSpc variable. The case statement will check each condition until it finds a match. When a condition is met, the case statement runs any statements within the matched section and then exits.

An example will help clarify this concept. Let's look at the first condition in the case statement in the "Solution" section of this recipe:

```
[0-9])
diskStat="relax, lots of disk space: $usedSpc"
;;
```

In the preceding snippet of code, the case statement checks the value of the variable to see whether it is a one-digit string that contains a value within the range of 0 through 9. If it matches, it sets the diskStat variable to an appropriate message and exits the case statement.

Take a look at the second condition in the case statement:

```
[1-7][0-9])
diskStat="disk space okay: $usedSpc"
;;
```

In this bit of code, the case statement checks for a two-digit number. The first character it looks for must be in the range of 1 through 7. The second character can be any number from 0 to 9. If the pattern matches, the diskStat variable is set to an appropriate value, and the case statement exits.

Now examine the conditions near the end of the case statement:

```
[9][0-9])
diskStat="warning, running out of space: $usedSpc"
echo $diskStat $ml | mailx -s "space on: $BOX" dba@gmail.com
;;
[1][0][0])
diskStat="update resume, no space left: $usedSpc"
echo $diskStat $ml | mailx -s "space on: $BOX" dba@gmail.com
;;
```

The idea here is that if a mount point is 90% used or above, send an e-mail to the DBA, warning that disk space is getting low. Finally, if no match is made, the catchall clause *) will be executed, and the case statement will be exited.

The structure of the case statement allows you to perform complicated comparisons that would probably drive you crazy if you tried to code them using if/then/else statements. Table 7-4 lists some common pattern-matching characters used in case statements.

**Table 7-4.** *Common Character-Matching Patterns*

| Pattern | Description |
| --- | --- |
| a\|b | Matches either a or b |
| * | Matches any string of characters, often used for a catchall |
| [abc] | Matches any character a, b, or c |
| [a-c] | Matches any character a, b, or c |
| [0-9] | Matches any character 0 through 9 |
| "<string>" | Matches the string enclosed in the quotes |

One final note: typically we'll use the cron utility (see Chapter 10 for details) to automatically have the disk monitoring script run on a periodic basis (e.g., once every 30 minutes or once per hour). In this way, we're warned when a server is running out of space. You may be thinking, "Isn't it the system administrator's job to monitor disk space?" Yes it is, but we've been in numerous situations (too many to count) in which a mount point filled up, the database ceased working, and the production support DBA gets called. By running your own disk space-monitoring script, you'll give yourself some warning regarding disk fullness issues and save yourself a lot of headaches.

# 7-5. Repeating a Task

## Problem

You want to perform a check on several databases running on a server. You don't want to have to create a script for each database; in other words, you'd rather write one script in a flexible manner to be used for all databases.

## Solution

A for loop allows you to re-run a section of code a fixed number of times. This control construct is particularly useful because DBAs often have a known set of databases or files that need to be operated on. The for loop syntax is as follows:

```
for name [in list]
do
  commands that can use $name
done
```

The following code illustrates the power of a for loop. In this environment, there are three databases that are being monitored for a critical background process. The for loop allows you to provide an input list and have the same code re-executed for each database name in the input list:

```
#!/bin/bash
SID_LIST="dev1 dev2 dev3"
critProc=ora_smon
for curSid in $SID_LIST
do
  ps -ef | grep -v 'grep' | grep ${critProc}_$curSid
  if [ $? -eq 0 ]; then
    echo "$curSid is available."
  else
    echo "$curSid has issues." | mail -s "issue with  $curSid" dba@gmail.com
  fi
done
exit 0
```

In this manner, you can efficiently use code to repeat a task.

## How It Works

The for loop iterates through each argument passed in to the parameter list. This control structure is ideal for a fixed input list. (Depending on which shell you use, the syntax may be slightly different from the one described in the "Solution" section.)

There are a few other aspects about looping that require further analysis. For example, you can use the built-in Bash shell $@ variable to pass a parameter list to a for loop. The $@ variable contains a quoted list of arguments passed to the script. By default, a for loop will use $@ if no input list is provided. The previous code snippet can be slightly modified to take advantage of this technique, as shown here:

```
#!/bin/bash
critProc=ora_smon
for curSid in $@
do
  ps -ef | grep -v 'grep' | grep -i ${critProc}_$curSid
  if [ $? -eq 0 ]; then
    echo "$curSid is available."
  else
    echo "$curSid has issues." | mail -s "issue with  $curSid" dba@gmail.com
  fi
done
exit 0
```

Assume that the preceding bit of code is placed in a file named dbup.bsh. It can now be run from the command line to pass in a list of databases to check:

```
$ dbup.bsh dev1 dev2 dev3
```

One last note: there are many different methods to implement a for loop. For example, it is possible to iterate through a for loop based on the output of a command:

```
for a in $(ls /home/oracle)
do
    echo "$a"
done
```

You can also iterate based on a sequence of numbers:

```
for a in {1..10}
do
  echo "$a "
done
```

Here's another common method for looping through a sequence of numbers:

```
for ((a=1; a <= 10; a++))
do
  echo "$a "
done
```

The method that you choose depends on your personal preference and the task at hand.

# 7-6. Iterating Until a Condition Is Met

## Problem

You want to perform an operation an unknown number of times until a certain condition is achieved.

## Solution

The while and until flow control constructs allow a piece of code to iterate until a condition is met. In contrast with a for loop construct, the while and until loops are useful when the number of times needed to continue looping is not known beforehand. The while loop runs until a test condition has a zero exit status. The syntax for the while loop is as follows:

```
while condition ; do
   commands
done
```

A small example will demonstrate the utility of the while loop. Suppose that you want to check the sqlplus process count on a box every 15 seconds. If it exceeds a certain value, you want to send an e-mail and exit. Here's some code to do just that:

```
#/bin/bash
crit_var=0
while [ $crit_var -lt 300 ]; do
  crit_var=$(ps -ef | grep sqlplus | wc -l)
  echo "Number of sqlplus processes: $crit_var"
  sleep 15
done
echo $crit_var | mailx -s "too many sqlplus procs" dba@gmail.com
exit 0
```

The until control construct is similar to the while loop. The until loop runs until a test condition has a nonzero exit status:

```
until condition ; do
  commands
done
```

Next is a script that uses an until loop in the same fashion as the while loop example:

```
#/bin/bash
crit_var=0
until [ $crit_var -ge 300 ]; do
  crit_var=$(ps -ef | grep sqlplus | wc -l)
  echo "Number of sqlplus processes: $crit_var"
  sleep 15
done
echo $crit_var | mailx -s "too many sqlplus procs" dba@gmail.com
exit 0
```

In this way, you can continually execute a task until a condition is met.

## How It Works

The while or until constructs are useful when you need to iterate but don't know in advance the number of iterations. In other words, the requirement is to loop until a condition has been met and then exit.

Here's another useful example of using a while loop. Sometimes it is useful when debugging scripts to iterate through all arguments passed to a shell script and view the parameter values. This snippet of code uses a while loop to display all parameters passed into a script:

```
while [ $# -ne 0 ]; do
  echo $1
  shift 1
done
```

The code is placed in a shell script named test.bsh, made executable, and run as follows:

```
$ chmod +x test.bsh
$ test.bsh dev1 dev2 dev3
```

Here is the corresponding output:

```
dev1
dev2
dev3
```

In the previous code sample, the shift command is used to move the positional parameters one position to the left. You can think of the positional parameters as an array of values, and (when invoked) the shift command (destructively) moves these values left in the array by the specified number of values.

An example helps to clarify this shifty concept. Suppose that there are three parameters passed into a program: A, B, and C. The positional variable $1 will contain A, $2 will contain B, and $3 will contain C. When you issue the shift 1 command, $1 now contains B, $2 contains C, and $3 now contains nothing. Another shift will move C into $1, and $2 and $3 will now be empty, and so forth.

One last note: there are many different ways to implement a while loop. Here's a common while loop structure that C programmers will recognize:

```
((a = 1))
while (( a <= 10 ))
do
  echo "$a "
  ((a += 1))
done
```

Here's an example of using a while loop with a function (more on functions later in this chapter):

```
a=0
condition ()
{
  ((a++))
  if [ $a -lt 11 ]
  then
    return 0  # true
```

```
else
    return 1  # false
  fi
}
while condition
do
  echo "$a"
done
```

And here is yet another way to implement an until loop:

```
a=1
until (( a > 10 ))
do
  echo "$a"
  (( a++ ))
done
```

The method that you choose depends on your personal preference and the task at hand.

# 7-7. Displaying a Menu of Choices

## Problem

You want to present a menu of choices for the shell script user to pick from.

## Solution

The select command allows you to create a menu from an input list. If the input list is omitted, the positional parameters (contained in the $@ variable) are used to construct the menu. The syntax of the select command is nearly identical to that of the for command:

```
select name in [input list ]
do
  commands that use $name
done
```

Listed next is a shell script that uses the select command to query the contents of the /etc/oratab file (/var/opt/oracle/oratab in Solaris environments) and sets your Oracle OS variables, depending on which value for ORACLE_SID that you chose:

```
#!/bin/bash
# Sets Oracle environment variables.
# Setup: 1. Put oraset file in /etc (Linux), in /var/opt/oracle (Solaris)
#        2. Ensure /etc or /var/opt/oracle is in $PATH
# Usage: batch mode: . oraset <SID>
#        menu mode:  . oraset
```

```
#=======================================================
if [ -f /etc/oratab ]; then
  OTAB=/etc/oratab
elif [ -f /var/opt/oracle/oratab ]; then
  OTAB=/var/opt/oracle/oratab
else
    echo 'oratab file not found.'
    exit
fi
#
if [ -z $1 ]; then
  SIDLIST=$(egrep -v '#|\*' ${OTAB} | cut -f1 -d:)
  # PS3 indicates the prompt to be used for the Bash select command.
  PS3='SID? '
  select sid in ${SIDLIST}; do
    if [ -n $sid ]; then
      HOLD_SID=$sid
      break
    fi
  done
else
  if egrep -v '#|\*' ${OTAB} | grep -w "${1}:">/dev/null; then
    HOLD_SID=$1
  else
    echo "SID: $1 not found in $OTAB"
  fi
  shift
fi
#
export ORACLE_SID=$HOLD_SID
export ORACLE_HOME=$(egrep -v '#|\*' $OTAB|grep -w $ORACLE_SID:|cut -f2 -d:)
export ORACLE_BASE=${ORACLE_HOME%%/product*}
export TNS_ADMIN=$ORACLE_HOME/network/admin
export ADR_BASE=$ORACLE_BASE/diag
export PATH=$ORACLE_HOME/bin:/usr/ccs/bin:/opt/SENSsshc/bin/\
:/bin:/usr/bin:.:/var/opt/oracle:/usr/sbin:/etc
export LD_LIBRARY_PATH=/usr/lib:$ORACLE_HOME/lib
```

In this example, the code is placed in a file named oraset in the /etc directory on Linux (or /var/opt/
oracle on Solaris). The oraset script is made executable as follows:

```
$ chmod +x oraset
```

Before you run oraset, view the contents of the oratab file for this example:

```
ORA12CR1:/orahome/app/oracle/product/12.1.0.1/db_1:N
O1212:/orahome/app/oracle/product/12.1.0.2/db_1:N
TRG:/orahome/app/oracle/product/12.1.0.2/db_1:N
O112:/orahome/app/oracle/product/11.2.0.4/db_1:N
ORA117:/orahome/app/oracle/product/11.1.0/db_1:N
```

The names of the databases in the preceding text are ORA12Cr1, 01212, and so on. The path to each database's home directory is next in the line (separated from the database name by a : ). The last column should contain a Y or an N, which indicates whether you want the databases to automatically be restarted when the system reboots (this takes additional setup besides just the Y/N).

Now run oraset from the command line as follows:

```
$ . /etc/oraset
```

When running oraset from the command line, you should be presented with a menu such as this (derived from the database names in your oratab file):

```
1) ORA12CR1
2) 01212
3) TRG
4) 0112
5) ORA117
SID ?
```

In this example, you can now enter 1, 2, 3, 4, or 5 to set the OS variables required for whichever database you want to use. This allows you to set up required Oracle OS variables interactively, regardless of the number of database installations on the server.

## How It Works

The Bash shell built-in select command provides an easy way of presenting a menu of choices to the shell script user. The oraset script presented in the "Solution" section of this recipe is a good example of a DBA using the select command to help accurately and consistently set the required OS variables when you have multiple databases running on a server.

When running oraset, be sure to use the . (dot) notation, which instructs the shell to *source* the script. Sourcing tells your current shell process to inherit any variables set within an executed script. If you don't use the . notation, the variables set within the script are visible only within the context of the subshell that is spawned when the script is executed.

---

■ **Note**    In the Bash and C-shell shell, the source command and the . built-in are synonymous.

---

You can run the oraset script either from the command line or from a startup file (such as .profile, .bash_profile, or .bashrc). For example, place this line in your startup file:

```
. /etc/oraset
```

Now every time you log in to the server, you'll see a menu of choices that you can use to indicate the database for which you want the OS variables set. If you want the OS variables automatically set to a particular database, put an entry in your startup files such as this:

```
. /etc/oraset TRG
```

The prior line will run the oraset file for the TRG database and set the OS variables appropriately.

# 7-8. Running Commands Based on Success/Failure of the Previous Command

## Problem

You have some custom database monitoring code that you have set up. The job should be continuously running on the database server, but sometimes the job unexpectedly dies. You want to set up another job that determines whether the job isn't running; if not, it should restart the monitoring job. In other words, in one line of code, you need to run a command to see whether the process is running; if not, run another command to restart the job.

## Solution

In one line of code, use the || <space> and && control operators to conditionally execute a command based on the status of the previously run command. Here's the basic syntax for how || works:

```
<run command 1> || <run command 2 if command 1 did not succeed>
```

And here's the syntax for the && operator:

```
<run command 1> && <run command 2 if command 1 succeeded>
```

Here's a simple example illustrating how it works:

```
$ ls myfile.txt || echo "file does not exist"
```

Here's the output indicating that the echo command was executed (meaning that the ls command did not succeed in listing the myfile.txt file):

```
myfile.txt: No such file or directory
file does not exist
```

Now suppose that you create the following file:

```
$ touch myfile.txt
```

Re-run the command:

```
$ ls myfile.txt || echo "file does not exist"
```

The echo command is not executed because the ls command succeeded. The only output returned is the output of the ls command:

```
myfile.txt
```

Now that you have that background information, examine the following line of code:

```
$ ps -ef | grep dbwatch | grep -v grep || nohup /home/oracle/bin/dbwatch.bsh &
```

If the output from `ps -ef | grep dbwatch | grep -v grep` does not return a value (meaning that dbwatch is not running on the server), the following code is executed to restart the process:

```
nohup /orahome/oracle/bin/dbwatch.bsh &
```

If the `ps` command does return a value, it means the process is running, so don't execute the script to restart the job. If you want to automate this, you can place a line in `cron` as follows:

```
33 * * * * ps -ef | grep dbwatch | grep -v grep || nohup /home/oracle/bin/dbwatch.bsh &
```

The preceding code is automatically run every hour (33 minutes after the hour) and checks to see whether dbwatch is running. If not, it is restarted.

## How It Works

Sometimes it is useful (on one line of code) to have a command conditionally execute, depending on the success or failure of the previous immediately run command. The && and || operators are designed to do just that. The "Solution" section showed an example using ||; next is an example that uses &&, which means that you want a command to execute if the previous command was successful.

In this next line of code, an e-mail will be sent only if the `grep` command successfully finds the string "ORA-00600" in the `alert.log` file:

```
$ grep ORA-00600 alert*.log && echo "DB prob" | mailx -s "ORA 600 error" dba@gmail.com
```

On one line of code, you can conditionally execute commands based on the success or failure of the prior command. The examples in this recipe provide another shell-scripting tool that you can use in creative ways to monitor for various activities and alert you if there are problems.

# 7-9. Modularizing Scripts

## Problem

You want to make your scripts more modular and functional. You determine that shell functions will help accomplish this task.

## Solution

*Functions*, which are commonly used in most programming languages, are blocks of commands that perform actions. You can think of a function as a small script within another script that compartmentalizes a section of code. The idea is to define a section of code once and then call that section of code multiple times from other parts of the program. Using functions allows you to modularize your code and make it more reusable, readable, and maintainable.

Like variables, functions must be declared before you can use them. Not surprisingly, the `function` command is used to declare functions. To illustrate the use of functions, let's say you need to create a reusable bit of code that displays some debugging information. This example creates a function named showMsg:

```
function showMsg {
  echo "---------------------------------------"
  echo "You're at location: $1 in the $0 script."
  echo "---------------------------------------"
} # showMsg
```

The function can now be referenced anywhere in the script after the point at which it was declared. For example, suppose you want to use the previous function in a script. You can add it before it is called and then reference the function multiple times within the code:

```
#!/bin/bash
debug=1
function showMsg {
  echo "---------------------------------------"
  echo "You're at location: $1 in the $0 script."
  echo "---------------------------------------"
} # showMsg
#
SID_LIST="dev1 dev2 dev3"
critProc=ora_smon
#
if [[ debug -eq 1 ]]; then
showMsg 1
fi
#
for curSid in $SID_LIST
do
  ps -ef | grep -v 'grep' | grep ${critProc}_$curSid
  if [ $? -eq 0 ]; then
    echo "$curSid is available."
  else
    echo "$curSid has issues." | mail -s "issue with  $curSid" dba@gmail.com
  fi
done
#
if [[ debug -eq 1 ]]; then
showMsg 2
fi
#
exit 0
```

Assume that the preceding code is placed in a script named d.bsh. After it is executed, here is the output:

```
----------------------------------------
You're at location: 1 in the ./d.bsh script.
----------------------------------------
----------------------------------------
You're at location: 2 in the ./d.bsh script.
----------------------------------------
```

In this way, you can use a function to define the code once and execute it many times within the script.

## How It Works

Functions allow you to organize large shell scripts into modular pieces of code, allowing for easier debugging, maintenance, and reusability. Functions can also be declared and invoked directly from the OS command line. From a DBA perspective, this gives you a very powerful tool that allows you to create and use any number of useful functions that can be run as if they were OS commands. For example, create a file named dba_fcns and place it in the following commands:

```
#!/bin/bash
#-----------------------------------------------------------------------------#
# sshl : ssh with your login to remote host
  function sshl {
    echo "ssh -l $LOGNAME $*"
    ssh -l $LOGNAME $*
  } # sshl
#-----------------------------------------------------------------------------#
# ssho : ssh with the oracle userid to remote host
  function ssho {
    echo "ssh -l oracle $*"
    ssh -l oracle $*
  } # ssho
#-----------------------------------------------------------------------------#
# chkps: check for a process on the box
  function chkps {
    ps -ef | grep -i $1 | grep -v grep
  } # chkps
#-----------------------------------------------------------------------------#
```

Now source the file as shown here:

```
$ . dba_fcns
```

You now have access to the sshl, ssho, and chkps functions from the OS command line. To illustrate this, the chkps function is called while passing in the string of smon to operate on:

```
$ chkps smon
```

You'll most likely collect many functions in your DBA tool bag to alleviate having to type long, typo-prone shell commands. Yes, for the previous simple functions, you could create aliases to accomplish essentially the same task. However, functions give you the additional ability to combine several different commands, use parameters, and display useful informational messages.

# 7-10. Passing Parameters to Scripts

## Problem

You don't like hard-coding variables in your script. You want to change a script to set variables based on parameters passed to the script so your code is more reusable, flexible, and maintainable.

## Solution

First, take a look at this script with hard-coded values in it for the database SID:

```
#!/bin/bash
ORACLE_SID=brdstn
rman target / <<EOF
backup database;
EOF
```

The << characters instruct the command running (in this case, the rman utility) to receive its input from anything that appears between the first EOF and the last EOF. You don't have to use EOF for start and finish markers; you can use any text string. It simply marks the beginning and end of where the shell directs the input for the command running.

If you want to use this script as it is to back up a different database, you have to manually edit it and change the name of the database, which isn't very efficient. A better approach is to modify the script so that it can dynamically be passed the name of the database to be backed up. Assume for this example that the script name is back.bsh. The script is modified as shown to accept the database name as input:

```
#!/bin/bash
ORACLE_SID=$1
rman target / <<EOF
backup database;
EOF
```

In the previous bit of code, $1 is a built-in variable in the Bash shell. The $1 variable holds the first parameter passed to the script when invoking it. Now the script can be run by passing in a database name. In this example, pass in the name of devdb:

```
$ back.bsh devdb
```

## How It Works

Passing parameters to scripts allows for greater flexibility and reusability of a script. You can pass any number of arguments into a shell script. The first parameter is referenced inside the script as $1, the second parameter is referenced as $2, and so on. These shell variables are known as *positional parameters*, which are special variables that are set internally by the shell and are available for you to use within a script.

If you pass in more than nine positional parameters to a script, when you reference a positional variable, you will have to use braces {} to wrap the number portion of the parameter with multidigit parameters. Without braces, the variable $10 will be interpreted as the contents of $1 with a 0 concatenated to it, whereas ${10} will be interpreted as the contents of the tenth variable.

An example helps to illustrate this point. Suppose that you pass 10 parameters to a script, as shown here:

```
$ myscript.bsh a b c d e f g h i j
```

For illustration purposes, suppose that this line of code is contained within the script:

```
echo $10
```

In this case, a result of a0 is produced because it is echoing the contents of parameter 1 concatenated with a 0.

When the braces are used with the echo command, the line of code produces a j, which is the tenth parameter that was passed to the script:

```
echo ${10}
```

Remember to use the braces any time you reference a multidigit parameter within a shell script, or else you won't get the results you intended.

Note that besides positional parameters, the shell provides other special variables for you. Some of the more useful special shell variables are described in Table 7-5. Examples of using these variables are found throughout this chapter.

*Table 7-5.* *Special Shell Variables*

| Name | Description |
| --- | --- |
| $1 - $n | Positional parameters that hold values for parameters passed to the script. |
| $? | The exit status of the last command. Contains a 0 value for successfully executed commands. Contains a nonzero value for commands that failed. This nonzero value depends on what the command actually returned. |
| $0 | Within a shell script, contains the name of the shell script being executed. |
| $# | The number of positional parameters passed to a script. |
| $$ | The process number of the shell. Can be used to generate unique file names. |
| $! | The process number of the most recently executed background process. |
| $* | Contains all the positional parameters passed to the script. |

# 7-11. Processing Parameters

## Problem

When passing parameters to a shell script, you require an efficient built-in method for processing the parameters. For example, you want a simple method to test for unexpected parameters or missing parameters.

# Solution

The getopts tool is a built-in shell command that provides an efficient mechanism for validating switches and parameters passed into a shell script. The best way to understand how this works is to examine a script that uses getopts to process parameters. Suppose that you have the requirement to pass in to an RMAN backup script the database name to be backed up and whether backup compression should be enabled. You want to be able to see whether the correct parameters have been passed in and display an informative message if the parameters are incorrect. Here is a script that uses getopts to examine and act on parameters passed to an RMAN backup script:

```
#!/bin/bash
PRG=$(basename $0)
USAGE="Usage: $PRG -s SID [-c compress] [-h]"
if [ $# -eq 0 ]; then
  echo $USAGE
  exit 1
fi
#
# In the OPTSTRING variable, if the first character is a :, then surpress system
# generated messages. If a char is followed by :, then an argument is expected to be
# passed in for a given option. The OPTARG environment variable contains the
# argument passed in for a given option.
#
OPTSTRING=":s:c:h"
while getopts "$OPTSTRING" ARGS; do
  case $ARGS in
  s) ORACLE_SID=${OPTARG}
     ;;
  c) COMP_SWITCH=$(echo ${OPTARG} | tr '[A-Z]' '[a-z')
     if [ $COMP_SWITCH = "compress" ]; then
       COMP_MODE=" as compressed backupset "
     else
       echo $USAGE
       exit 1
     fi
     ;;
  h) echo $USAGE
     exit 0
     ;;
  *) echo "Error: Not a valid switch or missing argument."
     echo ${USAGE}
     exit 1
     ;;
  esac
done
#
echo rman backup
rman target / <<EOF
backup $COMP_MODE database;
EOF
#
exit 0
```

Assuming that the prior code is placed in a script named rman.bsh, ensure that the script is executable:

```
$ chmod +x rman.bsh
```

The valid parameters to this script are s (accompanied with ORACLE_SID), c (compress), and h (help). First, here's what happens when the script is run with an invalid parameter:

```
$ rman.bsh -v mydb
Error: Not a valid switch or missing argument.
Usage: rman.bsh -s SID [-c compress] [-h]
```

The usage note specifies the correct way to run the script; for example:

```
$ rman.bsh -s 01212 -c compress
connected to target database: 01212 (DBID=353735090)
RMAN>
Starting backup...
```

If you want to display help for the shell script, do so as follows:

```
$ rman.bsh -h
Usage: rman.bsh -s SID [-c compress] [-h]
```

This simple example demonstrates the flexibility and ease with which parameters are evaluated using getopts.

## How It Works

The getopts (get options) utility enables you to efficiently inspect and process command-line switches and parameters. The getopts program ensures that a standard interface is used for shell program parameter handling. The basic syntax for getopts is as follows:

```
getopts optstring name
```

The OPTSTRING variable contains the list of options expected to be passed in from the command line when the script is executed. NAME is the variable used to read the command-line options one by one. The getopts command also relies on the OPTARG environment variable. This variable contains the argument value passed in for each option.

With that understanding, the script in the "Solution" section contains the following two lines of code:

```
OPTSTRING=":s:c:h"
while getopts "$OPTSTRING" ARGS; do
```

When the first character in OPSTRING is :, it will suppress any system–generated error messages. In other words, when the first character in OPTSTRING is :, it instructs the getopts command to handle all error messages that are generated (and don't display system-generated messages).

If an option character is followed by :, an argument is expected on the command line. The s and c options are both followed by colons, so they require arguments to be passed into the script. The h option is not followed by a colon, so it does not require an argument.

---

■ **Note** There is also a getopt command (no *s* on the end). This command is used in a similar fashion to getopts. View the man getopt documentation for more information.

---

# 7-12. Running Database Commands in Scripts

## Problem

You want to run a database utility command within a shell script. For example, you want to run an RMAN backup from within a shell script.

## Solution

There are several techniques for running database commands from within shell scripts. These two techniques are commonly used:

- Running commands directly
- Capturing output in a variable

These techniques are described in the following sections.

### Running a Command Directly

Here is a script that invokes the Oracle RMAN utility and takes a backup of the database:

```
#!/bin/bash
ORACLE_SID=DEV_DB
rman target / <<EOF
backup database;
EOF
exit 0
```

The << characters instruct the command that is running (in this case, the rman utility) to receive its input from anything that appears between the first EOF and the last EOF. You don't have to use EOF for start and finish markers, you can use any text string. It simply marks the beginning and end of where the shell directs the input for the command running.

This technique applies to any Oracle utility. The following runs a SQL*Plus command within a shell script:

```
#!/bin/bash
ORACLE_SID=DEV_DB
sqlplus -s <<EOF
/ as sysdba
select sysdate from dual;
EOF
exit 0
```

## Capturing Output in a Variable

Command substitution is a technique in which you run a command and store its output in a variable. You can use command substitution to run a database utility (such as SQL*Plus). For example, you want to determine whether critical materialized views are refreshing on a daily basis. One way of doing this is to select a count from the data dictionary view USER_MVIEWS, where the last refresh date is greater than one day. This bit of code uses command substitution to run a database command and capture the output of the command in the critVar variable:

```
#/bin/bash
critVar=$(sqlplus -s <<EOF
pdb_m/abc@papd
SET HEAD OFF FEED OFF
SELECT count(*) FROM user_mviews WHERE sysdate-last_refresh_date > 1;
EXIT;
EOF)
```

The script returns a value into the variable critVar, and you can test to see whether the value is 0:

```
if [ $critVar -ne 0 ]; then
mail -s "Problem with MV refresh" dba@gmail.com <<EOF
MVs not okay.
EOF
else
  echo "MVs okay."
fi
exit 0
```

If the value in the critVar variable isn't 0, the script will send an e-mail.

## How It Works

The basic technique for running database utilities within a script is to run the utility directly (as you would from the command line) or use command substitution. The key here is that you must use the following syntax:

```
database_utility << EOF
<run database_utility commands>
EOF
```

The code instructs the shell to execute the database utility; then anything between << EOF and the next EOF are commands run by the database utility. The string "EOF" can be any string. We use EOF as our standard.

The following example uses EOF for the start and end maker. Any text between the start and end markers are commands executed by SQL*Plus. This particular script displays any database objects that have been created within the last week:

```
#!/bin/bash
newobjs=$(sqlplus -s << EOF
fbar/invqi@INVQI
select object_name
```

```
from dba_objects
where created > sysdate - 7
and owner not in ('SYS','SYSTEM');
EOF)
echo $newobjs | mailx -s "new objects" dba@gmail.com
exit 0
```

Be aware that there are two techniques for achieving command substitution in a shell script:

- $(command)

- `command`

For example, if you want to return the name of a server into a variable, you can use two techniques. The first is the following:

```
$ BOX=$(uname -a | awk '{print$2}')
```

The second is the following:

```
$ BOX=`uname -a | awk '{print$2}'`
```

The $(command) is more modern and is thus the preferred technique. Just be aware that you may see command substitution implemented with the `command` syntax.

One last note: if you're using a data dictionary view (within a shell script) that contains a $ as part of the view name, you must escape with a backslash the dollar sign within the shell script. For example, the following selects from the view V$DATAFILE the number of datafiles that have an OFFLINE status:

```
#!/bin/bash
nf=$(sqlplus -s << EOF
/ as sysdba
set head off
select count(*)
from v\$datafile
where status='OFFLINE';
EOF)
echo "offline count: $nf"  | mailx -s "# files offline" prod@supp.com
```

You must escape the $ as shown in the script (e.g., v\$datafile). If you don't escape the $, the shell script interprets the view name as a shell variable. The backslash (\) in front of the $ instructs the shell script to ignore the meaning of special characters.

# 7-13. Crafting a Robust DBA Shell Script

## Problem

You want to write a flexible and reusable shell script that incorporates the techniques used by experienced shell writers.

# Solution

Most shell scripts that DBAs use require the following functionality:

1. Sets the shell

2. Validates parameters passed to the script

3. Sets any special variables to be used in the script

4. Sets the Oracle environment variables

5. Calls the Oracle utility

6. Captures the output in a unique log file name

7. Sends an e-mail indicating the success or failure of the job

8. Exits the script

Listed next is a basic shell script that uses these techniques to determine whether a SQL*Plus connection can be made to a database. The line numbers have been included for discussion purposes; they should be deleted before you attempt to run the script:

```
1   #!/bin/bash
2   PRG=$(basename $0)
3   #
4   # Validate parameters
5   USAGE="Usage: ${PRG} <database name> "
6   if [ $# -ne 1 ]; then
7       echo "${USAGE}"
8       exit 1
9   fi
10  #
11  # Set variables used in the script
12  SID=${1}
13  CONSTR=system/foo@${SID}
14  MAILX='/bin/mailx'
15  MAIL_LIST='dba@gmail.com'
16  LOG_DIR=/home/oracle/scripts
17  DAY=$(date +%F)
18  LOG_FILE=${LOG_DIR}/${PRG}.${DAY}.$$.log
19  LOC_SID=01212
20  BOX=$(uname -a | awk '{print$2}')
21  #
22  # Source oracle variables
23  . /etc/oraset $LOC_SID
24  #
25  # Attempt to connect to database via SQL*Plus
26  crit_var=$(sqlplus -s <<EOF
27  $CONSTR
28  SET HEAD OFF FEED OFF
29  select 'success' from dual;
30  EOF)
31  #
```

```
32  # Write output to log file
33  echo ${crit_var} > $LOG_FILE
34  #
35  # Send status
36  echo $crit_var | grep success 2>&1 >/dev/null
37  if [[ $? -ne 0 ]]; then
38    $MAILX -s "Problem with ${SID} on ${BOX}" $MAIL_LIST <$LOG_FILE
39  else
40    echo "Success: ${SID} on ${BOX}" | \
41    $MAILX -s "Success: ${SID} okay on ${BOX}" $MAIL_LIST
42  fi
43  #
44  exit 0
```

■ **Tip** If you're using vi for an editor, use the set number and set nonumber commands to toggle the viewing of line numbers (see recipe 4-11 for more details).

# How It Works

The shell script in the "Solution" section of this recipe uses a wide variety of shell-programming techniques. You can use these methods to automate a diverse assortment of DBA tasks. Line numbers are included in the shell program to describe the purpose of each line. Table 7-6 contains a brief description of each line of code.

*Table 7-6. Explanation of Shell Script to Check on Database Status*

| Line Number | Explanation |
| --- | --- |
| 1 | Specifies the Bash shell command interpreter for this script. |
| 2 | Captures the name of the shell script in the PRG shell variable. The $0 variable contains the name of the program. The basename command strips off any directory text that is prepended to the program name. |
| 3–4 | Comments. |
| 5 | Constructs an information string and places it in the USAGE variable. |
| 6–9 | If the number of parameters is not equal to 1, displays the script usage string and exits the program. See recipe 7-11 for an advanced discussion of processing variables. |
| 10–11 | Comments. |
| 12 | Sets the SID variable to the parameter passed into the script. |
| 13 | Sets the CONSTR variable to contain the SQL*Plus database connection string. |
| 14 | Sets the MAILX variable to the path and name of the mail utility on the server. |
| 15 | Specifies the e-mail address of the DBA(s) to receive the job status. |
| 16 | Sets the LOG_DIR variable to the directory of the log files. |
| 17 | Sets the DAY variable to the current date string. |

(*continued*)

*Table 7-6.* (*continued*)

| Line Number | Explanation |
| --- | --- |
| 18 | Specifies the LOG_FILE to be a combination of the program name and date. The $$ variable is a unique process identifier that allows you to generate multiple log files per day. |
| 19 | Sets the LOC_SID to a local instance name on the box that the shell script is running on. |
| 20 | Sets the BOX variable to contain the name of the local database server. |
| 21–22 | Comments. |
| 23 | Use a program to set the required OS variables such as ORACLE_HOME. See recipe 7-7 for an example of a file that sets the Oracle variables. |
| 24–25 | Comments. |
| 26 | Captures in the crit_var variable the output of the SQL*Plus command. Initiates a connection to SQL*Plus. EOF specifies the starting point for the SQL*Plus commands. |
| 27 | Connects to SQL*Plus with the value in CONSTR. |
| 28–29 | Runs the SQL*Plus formatting and SQL command. |
| 30 | EOF specifies the end of the text to be interpreted as SQL. |
| 31–32 | Comments. |
| 33 | Writes the contents of the crit_var variable to the log file. |
| 34–35 | Comments. |
| 36 | Examines the contents of the crit_var variable for the string success that should have been returned from the SQL*Plus command. |
| 37 | $? contains the status of the previously run command. Checks to see whether the previous grep command found the string success. If the grep command succeeded, $? will contain a 0. The $? variable will contain a nonzero value if the grep command does not find the string success in the crit_var variable. |
| 38 | Sends an e-mail indicating there is a problem. |
| 39–41 | $? is equal to 0; therefore, the grep command found the string success in the crit_var variable. Sends an e-mail indicating that the database is up. |
| 42 | The end of the if statement. |
| 43 | Blank comment line. |
| 44 | Exits the shell script with a success status (indicated by a 0). |

---
**CREATING A LOCK FILE**

---

One common method to ensure that only one instance of a shell script is ever running at a time is to create a lock file for a script. When executing a script, if the lock file already exists, the job is currently running or previously terminated abnormally (and the lock file was not removed). Place the following code at the beginning of your script. Modify the LOCKFILE parameter to match your environment:

```
LOCKFILE=/ora01/oradata/BRDSTN/lock/rman.lock
if [ -f $LOCKFILE ]; then
  echo "lock file exists, exiting..."
  exit 1
else
  echo "DO NOT REMOVE,  RMAN LOCKFILE" > $LOCKFILE
fi
```

At the end of the script, remove the lock file:

```
if [ -f $LOCKFILE ]; then
  rm $LOCKFILE
fi
```

The use of a lock file ensures that if the script is already running and is called again, it won't start a new job.

# 7-14. Running Scripts in the Background

## Problem

You work in a distributed environment and have database servers in remote locations. You want to run a job in the background that will continue to run, even if there are network problems or after you log off the box.

## Solution

Use the & (ampersand) character to place a job in the background. This example runs the rman.bsh script in the background:

```
$ rman.bsh &
[1] 6507
```

From the previous output, [1] indicates the job number, and 6507 is the process identifier. You can verify that the program is running in the background via the jobs command:

```
$ jobs
[1]+  Running                 rman.bsh &
```

On some older systems, you may be required to use the nohup (no hangup) command to ensure that the job will still execute even if you log off the server. If using an older shell, use this syntax to place a job in the background:

```
$ nohup rman.bsh &
```

To stop a background job, use the kill command. This next line of code stops job 1:

```
$ kill %1
```

## How It Works

Sometimes you'll need to run jobs in the background. Running a job in the background has the advantage of continuing to execute even after the following situations occur:

- You logged off the box
- Network issues cause your terminal session to become disconnected
- Your session gets disconnected due to a server session timeout setting

For long-running jobs, you can run them in the background and not have to worry about restarting the job just because you become disconnected from the server.

## Explaining & and nohup

By default, when you run a shell script from the command line, it will run in the foreground. To execute a job in the background, place an ampersand character at the end of the command string. Here is the general syntax:

```
$ <command>  &
```

Using & ensures that a command will continue to run, even if you log off the box. On some older systems, you may be required to use the nohup command to achieve this functionality. In this example, the nohup command is used to run a shell script in the background:

```
$ nohup export_db.bsh &
```

By default, the output from a nohup command is written to a file named nohup.out. You can monitor the job by continuously viewing the output file:

```
$ tail -f nohup.out
```

You can redirect the output to the file of your choice as follows:

```
$ nohup export_db.bash >exp.out &
```

You can interactively monitor the output of the previous job by viewing it with the tail -f command:

```
$ tail -f exp.out
```

---

▓ **Note**   If you want a job to consistently run in the background at a specified time, use a scheduling utility such as `cron`. See Chapter 10 for details on automating jobs.

---

## Using screen to Detach and Reattach to a Session

Using the & and nohup commands is the traditional way of keeping a job running in the background. You can also use the Linux `screen` command to achieve the same result with significantly more functionality. The `screen` command starts a terminal session on your server that will persist for you even if there is an unexpected network disruption.

To start a `screen` session, issue the following command:

```
$ screen
```

If you receive an error message such as "Cannot open terminal */dev/pts/1*," change the permissions on that file as `root`:

```
# chmod a+rw /dev/pts/1
```

When you invoke `screen`, you see a terminal from which you can type commands and run scripts. The difference between a `screen` session and a normal terminal session is that the `screen` session will continue to run even after you are detached.

For example, suppose that you are at your work location and you log on to a database server and start a `screen` session. You then start a long-running backup job in your `screen` session. After the job is started, you detach from the screen session by pressing Ctrl+A and then the D key (press the Ctrl and the A key at the same time, release them, and then press the D key). You can then drive home, remotely log on to the database server, and reattach to the `screen` session you started while you were at work. You can monitor the backup job as if you were looking at the same terminal you started at work.

Here's a simple example of how this works. Type `screen`, as shown here:

```
$ screen
```

Print the current working directory so that you have some output on the screen that you can recognize when you attach to this `screen` session from another terminal:

```
$ pwd
/home/oracle
```

Now press Ctrl+A and then the D key, which detaches you from the `screen` session. You should see the following message:

```
[detatched]
```

Now start a different terminal session and log on to the database server. Issue the following command to display any detached `screen` sessions:

```
$ screen -ls
There is a screen on:
        31334.pts-1.rmougprd2    (Detached)
1 Socket in /tmp/uscreens/S-oracle.
```

You can reattach to any screen session using the -r (reattach) option followed by [[pid.]tty[.host]]. For this particular example, you can re-establish the screen connection by typing this:

```
$ screen -r 31334.pts-1.rmougprd2
```

You should now see the output of the previously entered pwd command. It is as if you never left the screen terminal session. This is a *very* powerful utility that can be used to start jobs and then monitor them from another remote terminal session. You can even share a screen session with other users.

To display screen online help, press Ctrl+A and then the ? key. To leave a screen session, use the exit command, which will stop your screen session.

# 7-15. Monitoring the Progress of a Script

## Problem

You're executing a shell script and want to monitor its progress.

## Solution

Sometimes you have to monitor the progress of a long-running shell script. You can use the Linux tail command with the f (follow) switch to display the output of a job as it is written to a log file. In this example, the output of a backup job is redirected to an output file named rmanback.out:

```
$ rmanback.bash >rmanback.out 2>&1
```

From another session, the output being written to the log file is interactively viewed with the tail -f command:

```
$ tail -f rmanback.out
```

Here is a snippet of typical output that might be displayed to the screen:

```
channel ORA_DISK_2: starting archive log backupset
channel ORA_DISK_2: specifying archive log(s) in backup set
input archive log thread=1 sequence=868 recid=859 stamp=628426116
...
```

## How It Works

DBAs often used the tail command to monitor things like alert logs and view potential issues with the database as they are happening. In this example, you continuously follow the display of what's being written to an Oracle database alert.log file:

```
$ tail -f alert_BRDSTN.log
```

Here's a snippet of typical output written to the alert.log file:

```
Completed: ALTER DATABASE BACKUP CONTROLFILE TO TRACE
DBID: 2917656785
Thread 1 advanced to log sequence 71
Current  log# 2 seq# 71 mem# 0: /ora01/oradata/BRDSTN/oradata/redo02a.log
```

When you want to discontinue viewing the contents of a log file, press Ctrl+C to break out of the tail command.

# 7-16. Debugging a Script

## Problem

Your script isn't doing what you expected. You want to debug the script.

## Solution

The Bash shell has several features that are useful for debugging and troubleshooting problems in scripts. The -n (no execution) switch allows you to check the syntax of a script before you run it. To check a Bash shell script for syntax errors, use -n as shown here:

```
$ bash -n db.bash
```

If the script contains any errors, it will display a message such as this:

```
db.bsh: line 10: syntax error: unexpected end of file
```

Another useful debugging feature is the -o xtrace option, which instructs the Bash shell to display every command before it is executed. This option also shows any variable substitutions and expansions, so you can view the actual variable values used when the shell script executes. You can invoke the -o xtrace feature from the command line as follows:

```
$ bash -o xtrace <script name>
```

Notice that the output contains lines that don't seem to have anything to do with your code:

```
+ alias 'rm=rm -i'
+ alias 'cp=cp -i'
+ alias 'mv=mv -i'
+ '[' -f /etc/bashrc ']'
+ . /etc/bashrc
+++ id -gn
+++ id -un
+++ id -u
++ '[' root = root -a 0 -gt 99 ']'
++ umask 022
++ '[' '' ']'
+ export JAVA_HOME=/opt/java
```

That's because the first several lines in the output are from code-executed startup scripts. Also of note: the plus signs in the output indicate the level of nesting of a command within the script.

## How It Works

As shell scripts become longer and more complex, it can sometimes be problematic to squash the source of bugs within a script. This problem can be especially acute when you maintain code that somebody else wrote.

If you just want to see the tracing for specific commands within the script, embed set-o xtrace directly within your code at the desired location. In this example, tracing is turned on before the if statement and then turned off at the end:

```
set -o xtrace
if [ $? -eq 0 ]; then
  echo "$critProc is available."
else
  echo "$critProc has issues." | mail -s "problem with  $critProc" bbill@gmail.com
fi
set +o xtrace
```

Here is what the output looks like when the prior script is run with tracing enabled:

```
++ '[' 0 -eq 0 ']'
++ echo ' is available.'
 is available.
++ set +o xtrace
```

To enable a set command feature, you must use the minus (-) sign, which may seem counterintuitive. Equally counterintuitive, use a plus (+) sign to disable a set command feature.

---

■ **Note** You can also use the set -x command to print each command's parameter assignments before they are executed; to turn off tracing, use set +x, which is identical to the set -o xtrace and set +o xtrace commands.

---

# CHAPTER 8

■ ■ ■

# Analyzing Server Performance

The separation of tasks between a SA and a DBA is often blurred. This blurring of roles can be especially true in small shops in which you wear multiple hats. Even in large organizations with established roles and responsibilities, you'll still experience an occasional "all-hands-on-deck" fire drill in which you're expected to troubleshoot server issues. In these scenarios, you must be familiar with the OS commands used to extract information from the server. An expert DBA does not diagnose database problems in a vacuum; you have to be server-savvy.

Whenever there are application-performance issues or availability problems, the first question asked from the DBA's perspective is usually this one: "What's wrong with the database?" Regardless of the source of the problem, the burden is often on the DBA to verify whether the database is behaving well. This process sometimes includes identifying server bottlenecks. The database and server have an interdependent relationship. DBAs need to be well-versed in techniques to monitor server activity.

When you have a server that houses dozens of databases, and you experience performance issues, you have to determine whether the bottleneck is related to CPU, memory, I/O, or the network. Furthermore, you have to pinpoint which processes on the box are consuming the most resources. In these scenarios, it is more productive to diagnose issues with OS tools to lead you to the process that is consuming the most server resources. After you identify the process, you can determine whether it is associated with a database and then further identify the type of process (SQL*Plus, RMAN, Data Pump, and so on).

This chapter covers techniques used to analyze the server's CPU, memory, I/O, and network performance. Take some time to become familiar with the relevant commands covered in each section. Being able to quickly survey system activity will vastly broaden your DBA skill set.

Table 8-1 summarizes the OS utilities commonly used by DBAs and SAs. This table lists the recipe in which the tool is discussed and what aspect of performance the tool covers (note that some tools are covered in other chapters). Being familiar with these OS commands and how to interpret the output will allow you to work as a team with SAs, storage administrators, network engineers, and developers when diagnosing server performance issues.

**Table 8-1.** *Performance and Monitoring Utilities*

| Tool | Description | Recipe(s) | Process | CPU | Memory | I/O | Network | Tracing |
|------|-------------|-----------|---------|-----|--------|-----|---------|---------|
| vmstat | Processes CPU, memory, and IO consumption | 8-1, 8-6 | X | X | X | X | | |
| sar | Current and historical resource usage | 8-2, 8-9 | | X | X | X | X | |
| top | Identifies sessions consuming CPU and memory | 8-3, 8-5 | X | X | X | | | |
| ps | Processes memory and CPU consumption | 8-3, 8-5 | X | X | X | | | |
| prstat | Solaris active process statistics | 8-3 | X | X | X | | | |
| mpstat | CPU statistics | 8-4 | | X | | | | |
| uptime | System uptime and load | 3-6 | | X | X | | | |
| w | Users and processes on a machine | 3-6 | X | X | X | | | |
| ipcs | Shared memory and semaphores | 9-8 | | | X | | | |
| sysresv | Oracle instance memory and semaphores | 9-9 | | | X | | | |
| free | Free and used memory | 8-6 | | | X | | | |
| iotop | Process I/O usage | 8-7 | X | | | X | | |
| iostat | Disk I/O statistics | 8-8 | | | | X | | |
| df | Free disk space | 7-4, 8-12 | | | | X | | |
| du | Disk usage | 5-30 | | | | X | | |
| dd | File copy and formatting | 8-1, 8-8 | | | | X | | |
| netstat | Network statistics | 8-9 | | | | | X | |
| traceroute | Tracks route packet takes from one server to another | 8-9 | | | | | X | |
| ping | Connectivity between servers | 8-10 | | | | | X | |

*(continued)*

*Table 8-1.* (*continued*)

| Tool | Description | Recipe(s) | Process | CPU | Memory | I/O | Network | Tracing |
|------|-------------|-----------|---------|-----|--------|-----|---------|---------|
| tnsping | Oracle database connectivity | 8-10, 8-11 | | | | | X | |
| strace | Linux process tracing | 8-11 | | | | | | X |
| truss | Solaris process tracing | 8-11 | | | | | | X |
| lsof | Linux files currently opened by processes | 8-12 | X | | | | | |
| pfiles | Solaris files currently opened by processes | 8-12 | X | | | | | |

When diagnosing server issues, start with utilities such as vmstat, sar, top, and ps. These tools give you a quick overview of overall system performance. Then you can use other tools to drill down into CPU, memory, I/O, and network details.

# 8-1. Identifying System Bottlenecks

## Problem

Application users are reporting that the database seems slow. You want to determine whether there are any system resource bottlenecks on the database server.

## Solution

The vmstat (virtual memory statistics) tool is intended to help you quickly identify bottlenecks on your server. The vmstat command displays real-time performance information about processes, memory, paging, disk I/O, and CPU usage. This example shows using vmstat on a Linux server (the output is slightly different on Solaris) to display the default output with no options specified:

```
$ vmstat
procs -----------memory------------ --swap-- ----io---- --system-- -------cpu-------
 r  b   swpd    free     buff   cache  si   so   bi    bo    in   cs   us sy  id wa st
 0  0      0 1185336 10615632  991736   0    0    5     9     9   12    0  0 100  0  0
```

Here are some general heuristics you can use when interpreting the output of vmstat:

- If b (processes sleeping) is consistently greater than 0, you may not have enough CPU processing power.

- If so (memory swapped out to disk) and si (memory swapped in from disk) are consistently greater than 0, you may have a memory bottleneck. On some systems, these columns may be labeled pi and po.

- If the wa (time waiting for I/O) column is high, it is usually an indication that the storage subsystem is overloaded.

By default, only one line of server statistics is displayed when running vmstat (without supplying any options). This one line of output displays average statistics calculated from the last time the system was rebooted. Although it is fine for a quick snapshot, use vmstat with this syntax if you want to gather metrics over a period of time:

```
$ vmstat <interval in seconds> <number of intervals>
```

In this mode, vmstat reports statistics sampling from one interval to the next. For example, if you want to report system statistics every 2 seconds for 10 intervals, issue this command:

```
$ vmstat 2 10
```

The default unit of measure for the memory columns of vmstat is in kilobytes. If you want to view memory statistics in megabytes, use the -S m (statistics in megabytes) option:

```
$ vmstat -S m
```

## How It Works

If your database server seems sluggish, analyze the vmstat output to determine where the resources are being consumed. Table 8-2 details the meanings of the columns displayed in the default output of vmstat.

*Table 8-2.* Column Descriptions of vmstat Output

| Column | Description |
| --- | --- |
| R | Number of processes waiting for runtime |
| b | Number of processes in uninterruptible sleep |
| swpd | Total virtual memory (swap) in use (KB) |
| free | Total idle memory (KB) |
| buff | Total memory used as buffers (KB) |
| cache | Total memory used as cache (KB) |
| si | Memory swapped in from disk (KB/s) |
| so | Memory swapped out to disk (KB/s) |
| bi | Blocks read in (blocks/s) from block device |
| bo | Blocks written out (blocks/s) per second to block device |
| in | Interrupts per second |
| cs | Context switches per second |
| us | User-level code time as a percentage of total CPU time |
| sy | System-level code time as a percentage of total CPU time |
| id | Idle time as a percentage of total CPU time |
| wa | Time waiting for I/O completion |
| st | Time stolen from virtual machine |

You can also send the vmstat output to a file, which is useful for analyzing historical performance over a period of time. This example samples statistics every 5 seconds for a total of 60 reports and then records the output in a file:

```
$ vmstat 5 60 > vmout.perf
```

Another useful way to use vmstat is with the watch tool. The watch command is used to execute another program on a periodic basis. This example uses watch to run the vmstat command every 5 seconds and to highlight any differences between each snapshot onscreen:

```
$ watch -n 5 -d vmstat
```

When running vmstat in watch -d (differences) mode, you see changes onscreen as they alter from snapshot to snapshot. To exit from watch, press Ctrl+C.

You can obtain a better idea of how vmstat operates by viewing the output while simulating some server activity. First, inspect the output of vmstat while there is little system activity:

```
$ vmstat 2 10
procs -----------memory----------- ---swap-- ----io---- --system-- -----cpu-------
 r  b   swpd    free   buff   cache   si   so   bi    bo    in   cs us sy id wa st
 0  0  44588 3170020 184644 5222292    0    0    2    68     1    0  5  1 94  0  0
 0  0  44588 3169392 184644 5222336    0    0    0     8   497  864  2  0 98  0  0
 0  0  44588 3169400 184644 5222396    0    0    0   220   448  746  0  0 100 0  0
```

Now simulate server activity by creating a large randomly populated 1GB file with the dd command:

```
$ dd if=/dev/urandom of=GIGtestfile bs=1M count=1024 oflag=direct &
```

This should have the effect of increasing the CPU usage as the random numbers are generated. Additionally, there should be I/O activity generated as the file is populated. While the prior command is running in the background (via the & operator), you can run vmstat:

```
$ vmstat 2 10
```

Here are a few lines of the output indicating that the CPU is less idle (more busy) and the I/O blocks written out (bo column in the output) parameter has increased:

```
procs -----------memory----------- --swap-- ----io---- --system-- -----cpu------
 r  b   swpd    free   buff   cache   si   so   bi    bo    in   cs us sy id wa st
 1  0  44588 3128704 184664 5256092    0    0    0   912   743  920  1 25 74  0  0
 1  0  44588 3108500 184664 5274432    0    0    0   400   664  934  1 25 74  0  0
 5  0  44588 3070472 184664 5311608    0    0    0   366   647  882  1 25 73  0  0
```

---

| OSWATCHER |
| --- |

Oracle provides a collection of scripts that gather and store metrics for CPU, memory, disk, and network usage. The OSWatcher tool suite automates the gathering of statistics using tools such as top, vmstat, iostat, mpstat, netstat, and traceroute.

You can obtain OSWatcher from the Oracle MOS web site. Search for document ID 301137.1 or for the document titled "OSWatcher User Guides." Navigate to the Contents page and search for the Download link.

This utility also has an optional graphical component for visually displaying performance metrics. The OSWatcher utility is currently supported on the following platforms: Linux, Solaris, AIX, and HP-UX. For Windows, Oracle recommends using the Cluster Health Monitor (see document ID 736752.1).

---

# 8-2. Analyzing Current and Past System Performance

## Problem

Users are reporting that the database application seems sluggish every morning at 10:00 a.m. To troubleshoot the issue, you want to view the current CPU, memory, and I/O load on the server; and display resource activity at 10:00 a.m. for previous days in the week.

## Solution

The sar (system activity reporter) utility is unique in that it allows you to view current CPU, memory, and I/O resource usage; as well as server activity for a point in time in the past (e.g., an hour ago, yesterday, and so on).

## Displaying CPU Use

To show real-time CPU statistics, use the -u (CPU utilization) option and specify a snapshot interval (in seconds) and the number of reports. The following displays current processor activity with a snapshot interval of 2 seconds for a total of 10 reports:

```
$ sar -u 2 10
```

Here is some sample output:

| 12:50:42 | CPU | %user | %nice | %system | %iowait | %steal | %idle |
|---|---|---|---|---|---|---|---|
| 12:50:44 | all | 0.00 | 0.00 | 0.00 | 0.00 | 0.00 | 100.00 |
| 12:50:46 | all | 2.49 | 0.00 | 0.37 | 0.12 | 0.00 | 97.01 |
| 12:50:48 | all | 0.37 | 0.00 | 0.37 | 0.00 | 0.12 | 99.13 |

The most important column in the output is %idle. A low %idle could be an indication that the CPUs are underpowered or indicative of a high application load. The %iowait column displays the time waiting for I/O. It follows that a high %iowait time indicates that the I/O subsystem is a potential bottleneck.

If you have multiple CPUs, you can view the output per CPU with the -P ALL options. You should now see one line per CPU in the output:

```
$ sar -u -P ALL
```

To report on the current day's CPU activity, use the -u option without an interval:

```
$ sar -u
```

To view a previous day's statistics, use sar with the -f (file) option. On Linux systems, the files that sar uses to report on statistics for different days of the month are logged in the /var/log/sa directory (on Solaris systems, look in the /var/adm/sa directory). These files have the naming convention of saNN, where NN is the two-digit day of the month. So if today is the ninth day of the month, and you want to report on CPU activity for the eighth day, use the following:

```
$ sar -u -f /var/log/sa/sa08
```

Keep in mind that sar keeps only the last 7 days of history files by default. See the "How It Works" section of this recipe if you need to increase the retention period.

The output of using the -f option can be quite long. You can report on a time range via the -s (start time) and -e (end time) options. For example, to report on memory load starting at 10:00 a.m. and ending at 11:00 a.m., do so as follows:

```
$ sar -r -f /var/log/sa/sa08 -s 10:00:00 -e 11:00:00
```

Some older versions of sar don't provide an ending time option. You can creatively use commands such as grep to filter the output for the desired times; for example:

```
$ sar -r -f /var/log/sa/sa08 | grep ^10 | grep AM
```

In this manner, you can narrow down the range of activity you want to display.

## Displaying Memory Activity

Use sar with the -r (report memory) option to report on memory statistics. To show real-time memory statistics, specify a snapshot interval (in seconds) and the number of reports. The following displays current memory activity with a snapshot interval of 2 seconds for a total of 10 reports:

```
$ sar -r 2 10
```

Here is a small snippet of output:

```
08:44:45 AM kbmemfree kbmemused  %memused kbbuffers  kbcached kbswpfree kbswpused  %swpused
kbswpcad
08:44:47 AM   2616532  13005612     83.25    200668   5705848  10243940     44500      0.43
836
...
```

The output shows the total memory free and used, and the amount of swap space used. A high degree of swapping indicates that you may need more memory. When run in this mode, the output can be wide and lengthy; it doesn't quite fit within the limits of this physical page.

To report on real-time swapping statistics, specify the -W option. This example generates current swapping statistics snapshots every 3 seconds for a total of 10 reports:

```
$ sar -W 3 10
```

Here is some sample output indicating that little or no swapping is occurring:

```
08:54:01 AM   pswpin/s pswpout/s
08:54:04 AM      0.00      0.00
08:54:07 AM      0.00      0.00
```

To report on the current day's memory activity, use the -r option without an interval:

```
$ sar -r
```

To view historical memory statistics, use sar with the -f (file) option. For example, to have sar display memory paging statistics for the first day of the month, run it with the -B (report paging statistics) and -f (file) options, as follows:

```
$ sar -B -f /var/log/sa/sa01
```

Here is a partial listing of the report:

```
11:10:01 AM   pgpgin/s pgpgout/s   fault/s  majflt/s
11:20:01 AM      0.02     16.17     18.37      0.00
11:30:01 AM      3.49     21.68     74.15      0.04
11:40:01 AM   4182.58    439.44    320.94      0.68
11:50:02 AM   4960.03   1027.79   4384.73      0.51
```

The previous output shows that there was a substantial increase in paging in from disk (pgpgin/s), pages paged out to disk (pgpgout/s), and page faults per second (fault/s) at approximately 11:40 a.m.

## Displaying I/O Load

Use sar with the -b (report I/O) option to report on I/O statistics. To show real-time I/O statistics, specify a snapshot interval (in seconds) and the number of reports. On Linux systems, the following displays current I/O activity with a snapshot interval of 2 seconds for a total of 10 reports:

```
$ sar -b 2 10
```

Here's a partial snippet of the output (this output may vary depending on your version of Linux and the sar command):

```
09:01:19 AM        tps      rtps      wtps   bread/s   bwrtn/s
09:01:21 AM      19.39      0.00     19.39      0.00    448.98
09:01:23 AM      13.93      0.00     13.93      0.00    366.17
...
```

The tps column shows the I/O transfers per second to the device. The rtps indicates read requests per second, and the wtps shows write requests per second.

■ **Note**   On Solaris systems, use sar with the -d (disk) option to report on disk activity. The -d option may be available on Linux, depending on the version.

To report on the current day's I/O activity, specify the -b option with no time interval:

```
$ sar -b
```

To report on I/O statistics for a previous day in the month, use -b with the -f option. For example, to have sar display disk statistics for the tenth day of the month, run it as follows:

```
$ sar -b -f /var/log/sa/sa10
```

## How It Works

The sar utility is used to generate current load metrics as well as report on system resource usage for a point in time in the past. If you have the requirement of troubleshooting performance issues that have occurred in the past, sar is the utility to use.

You can think of sar as an AWR or Statspack for the OS. The AWR or Statspack tools allow you to view database activity for a range of time in the past. The sar utility is similar in that it allows you to report on historical server activity for CPUs, memory, and I/O. The AWR or Statspack reports depend on scheduled database jobs that periodically populate permanent database tables with information containing historical database activity. Whereas the sar utility uses cron jobs to periodically populate OS files that can be used for historical reporting regarding server activity.

With that in mind, let's look more closely at the sar cron jobs, the resource usage history files, and how to manually create a sar file.

## Understanding sar cron jobs

This sar utility is configured when you install the sysstat system package. You can check for its existence as follows:

```
$ sar -V
sysstat version ...
```

If sysstat isn't installed, and if you have root access, you can install it with the yum utility (or whatever utility is your standard for installing packages) as follows:

```
# yum install sysstat
```

When you install the sysstat package, sar will be installed along with two cron jobs. These cron jobs will be instantiated to create files used by the sar utility to report on historical server statistics. On Linux systems, you can view these cron jobs by looking in the /etc/cron.d/sysstat file; for example, here's a sample cron entry:

```
# run system activity accounting tool every 10 minutes
*/10 * * * * root /usr/lib64/sa/sa1 1 1
# generate a daily summary of process accounting at 23:53
53 23 * * * root /usr/lib64/sa/sa2 -A
```

Once the cron jobs have been running for a few days, to report on a previous day's CPU statistics, use the -f option to specify the file that corresponds to the day of interest.

On Solaris systems, you can view the sar-related cron jobs by viewing the /var/spool/cron/crontabs/sys file. Here's a sample entry:

```
0 * * * 0-6 /usr/lib/sa/sa1
20,40 8-17 * * 1-5 /usr/lib/sa/sa1
5 18 * * 1-5 /usr/lib/sa/sa2 -s 8:00 -e 18:01 -i 1200 -A
```

## Changing sar File Retention Period

On Linux systems, the files that sar uses to report statistics for different days of the month are located in the /var/log/sa directory. On Solaris systems, the sar files are located in the /var/adm/sa directory.

These files have the naming convention of saNN, where NN is the two-digit day of the month. Typically only the last week or so of files will be retained. A quick listing of the /var/adm/sa directory helps to clarify this:

```
$ cd /var/log/sa
$ ls -la sa[0-9]*
```

Here is some sample output:

```
-rw-r--r-- 1 root root 332016 Jun  1 16:50 sa01
-rw-r--r-- 1 root root 332016 Jun  2 16:50 sa02
-rw-r--r-- 1 root root 332016 Jun  3 16:50 sa03
-rw-r--r-- 1 root root 332016 Jun  4 16:50 sa04
-rw-r--r-- 1 root root 332016 Jun  5 16:50 sa05
-rw-r--r-- 1 root root 332016 Jun  6 16:50 sa06
-rw-r--r-- 1 root root 255984 Jun  7 11:20 sa07
-rw-r--r-- 1 root root 332016 May 30 16:50 sa30
-rw-r--r-- 1 root root 332016 May 31 16:50 sa31
```

From the prior output, the last 9 days of files are retained. These files are created and populated by the sar cron jobs. The sar utility uses the information contained therein to report on historical performance metrics.

On Linux systems, you can control the number of files retained by modifying the HISTORY parameter in the /etc/sysconfig/sysstat file. The location of the sysstat file varies by OS.

On Solaris systems, the old sar files are removed by the /usr/lib/sa/sa2 utility. The last line of the sa2 script finds the oldest sar files and removes them; for example:

```
/usr/bin/find /var/adm/sa \( -name 'sar*' -o -name 'sa*' \) -mtime +7 -exec /usr/bin/rm {} \;
```

As root, you can manually adjust the -mtime parameter as required. Usually the default of 7 days is sufficient.

## Creating a `sar` File

While reporting on real-time statistics, use the `-o` (out) option to send output to a file:

```
$ sar -b 2 10 -o saroutJun1.perf
```

This code creates a binary output file that can later be used to analyze disk I/O metrics. At some later point, you can use `sar` with the `-f` option to report on the contents of that file; for example:

```
$ sar -b -f saroutJun1.perf
```

This code provides a way of indefinitely saving the `sar` metrics for a given point in time. During a quiet period, you might want to do this to establish a baseline of metrics or during a heavy load to capture specific metrics that you want to analyze at some later point (and not worry about the file being automatically deleted).

# 8-3. Identifying CPU-Intensive Processes

## Problem

You want to identify which Oracle session is consuming the most CPU on the database server. If it is an Oracle session running a SQL query, you want to display the associated SQL.

## Solution

There are two tools that are useful for quickly identifying top CPU-consuming processes: `top` and `ps`. First, let's discuss `top`.

## Using `top`

The `top` utility is one of the first tools a DBA or SA will use to view server resource usage. This utility provides a dynamic report that refreshes every few seconds and displays the top resource-consuming processes; for example:

```
$ top
```

Here is a partial listing of the output:

```
top - 15:31:27 up 7 days,  5:17,  2 users,  load average: 0.17, 0.35, 0.37
Tasks: 222 total,   2 running, 220 sleeping,   0 stopped,   0 zombie
Cpu(s):  8.2%us, 16.3%sy,  0.0%ni, 75.4%id,  0.0%wa,  0.0%hi,  0.0%si,  0.1%st
Mem:  15622144k total, 15524472k used,    97672k free,  9085000k buffers
Swap: 10288440k total,        0k used, 10288440k free,  3160848k cached

  PID USER      PR  NI  VIRT  RES  SHR S %CPU %MEM    TIME+  COMMAND
 9156 oracle    25   0 2595m 366m 184m R 99.9  2.4 13:51.84 oracle_9156_o12
    1 root      15   0 10368  676  572 S  0.0  0.0  0:00.17 init
    2 root      RT  -5     0    0    0 S  0.0  0.0  0:00.38 migration/0
    3 root      34  19     0    0    0 S  0.0  0.0  0:00.05 ksoftirqd/0
...
```

The first five lines show system load, summary of processes running, CPU load, memory load, and swap statistics. The lines after that show individual processes and corresponding resource consumption. For this particular example, the Oracle process 9156 is consuming a great deal of CPU. The output will refresh every few seconds. To exit top, press Ctrl+C.

## Using ps

Now compare the use of top with the ps command. The ps command (in combination with the pcpu option) is used to identify the PIDs of sessions consuming the most CPU on the server; for example:

```
$ ps -e -o pcpu,pid,user,tty,args | sort -n -k 1 -r | head
```

Here is a partial listing of the output:

```
31.0  9156 oracle   ?        oracle01212 (DESCRIPTION=(LOCAL=YES)(ADDRESS=(PROTOCOL=beq)))
1.0   9155 oracle   pts/2    sqlplus   as sysdba
...
```

The first column is the percentage of CPU being consumed. The second column shows the PID (process 9156 is consuming the most CPU on this server). The third column shows that the oracle user is running this process and we can derive the database name from the fifth column to be 01212.

We recommend that you create an alias for the ps command; for example:

```
$ alias topcpu='ps -e -o pcpu,pid,user,tty,args | sort -n -k 1 -r | head'
```

This example allows you to quickly run the command without having to remember the syntax:

```
$ topcpu
```

## Retrieving Oracle Process Information

The main takeaway from the prior sections using top and ps is that process 9156 is consuming a great deal of CPU on the server and that it is an Oracle process associated with the 01212 database. Now you can use the PID from the output as an input to the following query to show information about the Oracle session responsible for the high consumption of CPU resources:

```
SET LINES 200 PAGES 0 HEAD OFF LONG 100000
COL dummy_value NOPRINT
--
SELECT 'dummy_value' dummy_value,
  'USERNAME    : ' || s.username    || CHR(10) ||
  'SCHEMA      : ' || s.schemaname  || CHR(10) ||
  'OSUSER      : ' || s.osuser      || CHR(10) ||
  'MODULE      : ' || s.program     || CHR(10) ||
  'ACTION      : ' || s.schemaname  || CHR(10) ||
  'CLIENT INFO : ' || s.osuser      || CHR(10) ||
  'PROGRAM     : ' || s.program     || CHR(10) ||
  'SPID        : ' || p.spid        || CHR(10) ||
  'SID         : ' || s.sid         || CHR(10) ||
  'SERIAL#     : ' || s.serial#     || CHR(10) ||
```

```
'KILL STRING : ' || '''' || s.sid || ',' || s.serial# || ''''   || CHR(10) ||
'MACHINE     : ' || s.machine      || CHR(10) ||
'TYPE        : ' || s.type         || CHR(10) ||
'TERMINAL    : ' || s.terminal     || CHR(10) ||
'CPU         : ' || q.cpu_time/1000000      || CHR(10) ||
'ELAPSED_TIME: ' || q.elapsed_time/1000000  || CHR(10) ||
'BUFFER_GETS : ' || q.buffer_gets  || CHR(10) ||
'SQL_ID      : ' || q.sql_id       || CHR(10) ||
'CHILD_NUM   : ' || q.child_number || CHR(10) ||
'START_TIME  : ' || TO_CHAR(s.sql_exec_start,'dd-mon-yy hh24:mi') || CHR(10) ||
'STATUS      : ' || s.status       || CHR(10) ||
'SQL_TEXT    : ' || q.sql_fulltext
FROM            v$session s
JOIN            v$process p ON (s.paddr  = p.addr)
LEFT OUTER JOIN v$sql     q ON (s.sql_id = q.sql_id)
WHERE s.username IS NOT NULL -- eliminates background procs
AND NVL(q.sql_text,'x') NOT LIKE '%dummy_value%' -- eliminates this query from output
AND    p.spid           = '&PID_FROM_OS'
ORDER BY q.cpu_time;
```

For this example, when you run the prior query and supply to it the PID of 9156, you get the following output:

```
USERNAME     : SYS
SCHEMA       : SYS
OSUSER       : oracle
MODULE       : sqlplus@dtc07dsg (TNS V1-V3)
ACTION       : SYS
CLIENT INFO  : oracle
PROGRAM      : sqlplus@dtc07dsg (TNS V1-V3)
SPID         : 9156
SID          : 91
SERIAL#      : 60916
KILL STRING  : '91,60916'
MACHINE      : dtc07dsg
TYPE         : USER
TERMINAL     : pts/2
CPU          : 275.473216
ELAPSED_TIME : 279.805467
BUFFER_GETS  : 64650
SQL_ID       : 1z4xyfmw1rpqy
CHILD_NUM    : 0
START_TIME   : 02-may-15 15:09
STATUS       : ACTIVE
SQL_TEXT     : select a.table_name from dba_tables a, dba_indexes, dba_extents, ...
```

From the prior output, you see that a SQL*Plus session is consuming a great deal of CPU time. You can also determine when the query started, the username, the kill string, and the SQL identifier from the output.

Once you identify information regarding the process, you can drill down further to display the execution plan and the resources the process is waiting for. For example, you can view the SQL execution plan with the SQL ID and child number:

```
SQL> SELECT * FROM table(DBMS_XPLAN.DISPLAY_CURSOR('&sql_id',&child_num));
```

Here's another useful query that uses the SID and serial number to display the state of a session and whether it is working or waiting for a resource:

```
SELECT sid,
DECODE(state, 'WAITING','Waiting', 'Working') state,
DECODE(state, 'WAITING', 'So far '||seconds_in_wait,
'Last waited '|| wait_time/100)|| ' seconds for '||event
FROM v$session
WHERE sid = '&&session_id'
AND serial# = '&&serial';
```

This information is very useful when diagnosing performance issues related to Oracle processes running on the server.

## How It Works

When you run multiple databases on one server and are experiencing server-performance issues, it can be difficult to identify which database and session are consuming the most system resources. In these situations, use the top utility or the ps command to identify the highest-consuming processes. The top utility provides a dynamic interface that periodically refreshes to give you the current snapshot of resource consumption, whereas the ps command provides a quick one time snapshot of top resource usage.

You may be wondering whether it is better to use top or ps to identify resource-consuming processes. If your server has top installed, top will probably be your first choice; its ease of use and interactive output is hard to beat. Having said that, the ps command is universally available, so you may have to use ps if the top command is not available. Also the ps command may show you a more descriptive program name associated with the process.

Once you have a process identified, if it's an Oracle process use the SQL query in the "Solution" section to further identify the type of Oracle process. You then have the option of trying to tune the operation (whether it be SQL, RMAN, and so on), or you might want to terminate the process (see recipe 3-2 for details on how to kill a process and/or stop a SQL session).

## Explaining top

The top command deserves a little more explanation than what was shown in the "Solution" section of this recipe. By default, top will repetitively refresh (every 3 seconds) information regarding the most CPU-intensive processes. While top is running, you can interactively change its output. For example, if you type >, the column that top is sorting moves one position to the right.

Table 8-3 lists some key features that you can use to alter the top display to the desired format.

*Table 8-3.* *Commands to Interactively Change the* top *Output*

| Command | Function |
|---|---|
| Spacebar | Immediately refreshes the output. |
| < or > | Moves the sort column one position to the left or to the right. By default, top sorts on the CPU column. |
| d | Changes the refresh time. |
| R | Reverses the sort order. |
| z | Toggles the color output. |
| h | Displays the help menu. |
| F or O | Chooses a sort column. |

Type q or press Ctrl+C to exit top. Table 8-4 describes several of the columns displayed in the default output of top.

*Table 8-4.* *Column Descriptions of the* top *Output*

| Column | Description |
|---|---|
| PID | Unique process identifier. |
| USER | OS username running the process. |
| PR | Priority of the process. |
| NI | Nice value or process. Negative value means high priority. Positive value means low priority. |
| VIRT | Total virtual memory used by the process. |
| RES | Nonswapped physical memory used. |
| SHR | Shared memory used by the process. |
| S | Process status. |
| %CPU | Processes percent of CPU consumption since last screen refresh. |
| %MEM | Percent of physical memory the process is consuming. |
| TIME | Total CPU time used by the process. |
| TIME+ | Total CPU time, showing hundredths of seconds. |
| COMMAND | Command line used to start a process. |

You can also run top using the -b (batch mode) option and send the output to a file for later analysis:

```
$ top -b > tophat.out
```

While in batch mode, the top command will run until you kill it (by pressing Ctrl+C) or until it reaches a specified number of iterations. You could run the previous top command in batch mode with a combination of nohup and & to keep it running, regardless of whether you were logged on to the system. The danger there is that you might forget about it and eventually create a very large output file (and an angry SA).

If you have a particular process that you're interested in monitoring, use the -p option to monitor a PID or the -U option to monitor a specific username. You can also specify a delay and number of iterations by using the -d and -n options. The following example monitors the oracle user with a delay of 5 seconds for 25 iterations:

```
$ top -U oracle -d 5 -n 25
```

---

■ **Tip** Use the man top or top --help commands to list all the options available with your OS version.

---

## Solaris `prstat`

Note that on Solaris systems, the prstat utility can also be used to identify which processes are consuming the most CPU resources. For example, you can instruct the prstat to report system statistics every 5 seconds:

```
$ prstat 5
```

Here is some sample output:

```
   PID USERNAME  SIZE   RSS STATE  PRI NICE     TIME  CPU PROCESS/NLWP
  7601 oracle   8430M 4081M sleep  101    -   3:51:47 2.0% oracle/1
  1614 oracle   6382M 4093M sleep  101    -  48:07:20 0.0% oracle/1
 20071 oracle   8431M 7746M sleep   54    0   0:00:00 0.0% oracle/1
```

Type q or press Ctrl+C to exit prstat. After identifying a top resource-consuming process, you can determine which database the process is associated with by using the ps command. This example reports on process information associated with the PID of 7601:

```
$ ps -ef | grep 7601 | grep -v grep
  oracle  7601    1  0   Apr 10 ?            231:47 ora_vktm_DWREP
```

---

### USING THE /PROC/<PID> FILES TO MONITOR PROCESS ACTIVITY

For every Linux process that is running, a directory is created in the /proc virtual filesystem. For example, if you want to view details regarding the operating PID of 9156, you can navigate to the virtual /proc/9156 directory and do a long listing. There you will see several informational files and directories related to this running process:

```
$ cd /proc/9156
$ ls -l
```

Here is a partial listing of the output:

```
-r-------- 1 oracle dba 0 May  2 15:42 auxv
-r--r--r-- 1 oracle dba 0 May  2 15:02 cmdline
-rw-r--r-- 1 oracle dba 0 May  2 15:42 coredump_filter
-r--r--r-- 1 oracle dba 0 May  2 15:42 cpuset
lrwxrwxrwx 1 oracle dba 0 May  2 15:42 cwd -> /u01/app/oracle/product/12.1.0.2/db_1/dbs
-r-------- 1 oracle dba 0 May  2 15:29 environ
lrwxrwxrwx 1 oracle dba 0 May  2 15:42 exe -> /u01/app/oracle/product/12.1.0.2/db_1/
bin/oracle
```

The output indicates this is an `oracle` process, and now you can analyze it further by looking at the memory usage `maps` file or the `status` file. Because these files don't exist on disk, use a utility such as `cat` to display their contents:

```
$ cat /proc/<PID>/maps
$ cat /proc/<PID>/status
```

# 8-4. Identifying CPU Bottlenecks

## Problem

You want to monitor the system load on your CPUs.

## Solution

As a DBA, you also need to periodically examine the load on CPUs to determine system bottlenecks. The `mpstat` (multiple processor statistics) utility displays statistics for processors on the server:

```
$ mpstat
```

Here's a snippet of the output:

```
Linux 2.6.18-308.4.1.0.1.el5xen (rmougserv)      05/02/2015
04:53:12 PM  CPU   %user   %nice   %sys %iowait    %irq   %soft  %steal   %idle    intr/s
04:53:12 PM  all    0.10    0.00    0.10    0.10    0.00    0.00    0.01   99.70    179.01
```

The default output of `mpstat` shows only one line of aggregated statistics for all CPUs on the server. You can also view snapshots that report statistics accumulated between intervals. The following example uses the -P option to report only on processor 0; it displays output every 2 seconds for a total of 10 different reports:

```
$ mpstat -P 0 2 10
```

Here are a few lines of the output:

```
04:54:22 PM  CPU   %user   %nice   %sys %iowait    %irq   %soft  %steal   %idle    intr/s
04:54:24 PM    0    0.00    0.00    0.00    0.00    0.00    0.00    0.00  100.00     93.94
04:54:26 PM    0    0.00    0.00    0.00    0.00    0.00    0.00    0.00  100.00     92.61
04:54:28 PM    0    0.00    0.00    0.00    0.00    0.00    0.00    0.00  100.00    135.68
```

The amount of idle time is the most important statistic. If the CPUs have a low idle percentage, it is indicative of a high load. See Table 8-5 for an interpretation of the `mpstat` output.

**Table 8-5.** *Column Definitions for* mpstat *Processor Statistics*

| Column | Description |
|--------|-------------|
| CPU | Processor number. Starts at 0. The all row reports average statistics for all processors. |
| %user | Percentage of CPU utilization while executing at user level. |
| %nice | Percentage of CPU utilization while executing at user level with nice priority. |
| %sys | Percentage of CPU utilization while executing at kernel level. |
| %iowait | Percentage of time CPUs were idle during an outstanding disk I/O operation. |
| %irq | Percentage of time spent by CPUs servicing interrupts. |
| %soft | Percentage of time spent by CPUs to service software interrupts. |
| %steal | Percentage of time CPUs waiting while the hypervisor servicing another virtual processor. |
| %idle | Percentage of time that CPUs were idle without outstanding disk I/O operations. |
| intr/s | Total number of interrupts received per second by CPUs. |

On Solaris systems, the output of mpstat is slightly different; for example:

```
$ mpstat -P 0 2 20
 CPU minf mjf xcal  intr ithr  csw icsw migr smtx  srw syscl  usr sys  wt idl
   0    8   0 358   795  266  645    5   68  195    3   497    3   3   0  94
   1    8   0 235   477  133  677    5   68  177    3   515    4   3   0  94
   2    7   0 328   609  257  705    5   70  197    3   511    3   3   0  94
```

The amount of idle time is the most telling statistic. A low idle time is indicative of high processer load.

# How It Works

The mpstat utility is useful for specifically analyzing the CPU load. Here are some general guidelines for interpreting its output:

- If %idle is high, your CPUs are most likely not overburdened.

- If the %iowait output is a nonzero number, you may have some disk I/O contention.

On multiprocessor servers, you can use the -P ALL options of the mpstat command to print each CPU's statistics on separate lines:

```
$ mpstat -P ALL
```

Here's a partial listing of the output:

```
05:07:53 PM  CPU  %user  %nice  %sys %iowait  %irq  %soft  %steal  %idle  intr/s
05:07:53 PM  all   0.11   0.00  0.12    0.10  0.00   0.00    0.01  99.67  179.26
05:07:53 PM    0   0.18   0.01  0.21    0.36  0.00   0.00    0.01  99.23  117.26
05:07:53 PM    1   0.11   0.00  0.12    0.01  0.00   0.00    0.00  99.76   18.92
05:07:53 PM    2   0.06   0.00  0.04    0.01  0.00   0.00    0.00  99.89   21.05
05:07:53 PM    3   0.09   0.00  0.10    0.01  0.00   0.00    0.00  99.80   22.04
```

The prior output shows that this server has four CPUs (indicated by a line for CPUs 0, 1, 2, and 3). The %idle column is in the 99% range, indicating that there is little load on the CPUs on this box.

You can also save the output of mpstat to a file. This example saves to a file all CPU activity reported every 10 seconds for 100 times:

```
$ mpstat -P ALL 10 100 > mpperf.perf
```

This code allows you to save performance statistics so that you can analyze and contrast performance for different time periods.

# 8-5. Identifying Memory-Intensive Processes

## Problem

You want to identify which Oracle session is consuming the most memory on the database server. If it is an Oracle session running a SQL query, you want to display the associated SQL.

## Solution

You can use either the top utility or the ps command to display top memory using processes. Let's look at top first.

### Using top

The easiest way to run top is as follows:

```
$ top
```

By default, top displays the output sorted by CPU usage. To shift the output to sort by memory usage, use the > key to shift the reporting output one column to the right (%MEM). Here is some sample output:

```
Tasks: 223 total,   1 running, 222 sleeping,   0 stopped,   0 zombie
Cpu(s):  0.0%us,  0.0%sy,  0.0%ni,100.0%id,  0.0%wa,  0.0%hi,  0.0%si,  0.0%st
Mem:  15622144k total, 15369420k used,   252724k free,  8759664k buffers
Swap: 10288440k total,        0k used, 10288440k free,  3505156k cached

  PID USER      PR  NI  VIRT  RES  SHR S %CPU %MEM    TIME+  COMMAND
 3217 cloudera  19   0 2770m 1.0g  17m S  0.0  6.9  0:52.84 java
  637 oracle    15   0 2409m 404m 394m S  0.0  2.7  0:00.65 ora_dbw0_o1212
 4204 emcadm    16   0  671m 249m  12m S  0.0  1.6  1:02.31 java
 2525 oracle    25   0 2462m 193m 186m S  0.0  1.3  0:15.40 oracle_2525_o12
```

## Using ps

You can also use the ps command with the pmem option to identify the top memory-consuming processes and their associated PIDs. We recommend that you search specifically for Oracle processes because the ps output can be quite lengthy; for example:

```
$ ps -e -o pmem,pid,user,tty,args | grep -i oracle | sort -n -k 1 -r | head
```

Here is some sample output:

```
1.2   625 oracle   ?       ora_mman_01212
0.7   655 oracle   ?       ora_mmon_01212
0.4   691 oracle   ?       ora_cjq0_01212
```

From the second column in the previous output, the process with the ID of 625 is consuming 1.2 percent of the memory. Now that you have the PID, you can use the query from the "Solution" section of recipe 8-2 to further identify the type of Oracle process (e.g., RMAN, SQL*Plus, Data Pump, and so forth).

## How It Works

If you're experiencing performance issues, determining which processes are consuming the most memory will give you another piece of information to troubleshoot the issue. The top and ps commands are quite useful in this regard. The top command provides an interactive way to dynamically view memory usage patterns, whereas the ps command is more useful as a one-line command to get a snapshot of memory activity. We recommend that you create an alias for the ps command; for example:

```
$ alias topmem='ps -e -o pmem,pid,user,tty,args | grep -i oracle | sort -n -k 1 -r | head'
```

This code will allow you to quickly run the command without having to remember the syntax:

```
$ topmem
```

You should use the memory usage information along with the CPU usage (see recipe 8-2) to determine which processes are consuming the most resources and then further investigate those processes.

# 8-6. Identifying Memory Bottlenecks

## Problem

You want to view the current usage of memory on your database server.

## Solution

Paging and swapping activity is an indicator of the efficiency of memory usage on your sever. In general, high amounts of paging and swapping indicate an inadequate amount of memory. Numerous utilities are available to monitor paging and swapping. For example, you can use vmstat (virtual memory statistics) to monitor the current memory usage. In this line of code, vmstat reports are generated every 2 seconds for a total of 3 reports:

```
$ vmstat 2 3
```

Here is some sample output:

```
procs -----------memory----------- --swap-- ----io---- --system-- ------cpu------
 r  b   swpd    free    buff   cache  si   so   bi    bo    in   cs  us sy  id wa st
 0  0      0 358448 8753168 3539596   0    0    4    10     8    1   1  1  98  0  0
 0  0      0 358424 8753168 3539596   0    0    0    16   416  637   0  0 100  0  0
 0  0      0 358424 8753168 3539596   0    0    0   378   484  631   0  0 100  0  0
```

If you have a fairly recent version of Linux, you can also use the -a option, which displays active and inactive memory. Here is an example of running vmstat with the -a option:

```
$ vmstat -a 2 3
```

Here's what the output looks like with the additional columns:

```
procs -----------memory----------- ---swap-- -----io--- --system-- ------cpu-------
 r  b   swpd    free   inact  active  si   so   bi    bo    in   cs  us sy  id wa st
 0  0      0 358812 9180892 4841900   0    0    4    10     8    1   1  1  98  0  0
 0  0      0 358812 9180892 4841912   0    0    0    62   427  637   0  0 100  0  0
 0  0      0 358812 9180892 4841912   0    0    0     0   421  629   0  0 100  0  0
```

If your server shows high amounts of memory swapped in from disk (si column) or the amount of memory swapped out to disk (so column), you may have a memory bottleneck.

The output of vmstat on Solaris reports the same type of information as Linux systems; for example:

```
$ vmstat 2 3
kthr      memory            page            disk          faults      cpu
 r b w     swap    free  re  mf pi po fr de sr vc  vc  vc -- in   sy    cs us sy  id
 0 0 0 18541480 2994160  20 119  0  0  0  0  2 184 146  0 9203 8216 10930  3  3  94
 0 0 0 18463736 3091248 138 335  0  0  0  0  2   6   5  0 5188 3617  5081  0  0  99
 0 0 0 18464824 3090824   0   3  0  0  0  0  0  2  38   0 4792 2256  4600  0  0 100
```

In this output, the page section reports on swapping, and I/O is reported under disk.

## How It Works

One of the main indicators of memory health is the amount of paging and swapping that is occurring. If you read five different Linux performance-tuning white papers, you'll get five slightly different definitions of paging and swapping. We do not split hairs about the exact definitions of those terms; our statement is that in general, paging and swapping are the movement of the contents of memory to and from disk.

*Paging* and *swapping* occur when there isn't enough physical memory to accommodate all the memory needs of the processes on the server. When paging and swapping take place, performance usually suffers because the process of copying memory contents to and from disk is an inherently slow activity. A tool such as vmstat can help you identify excessive swapping.

## Using free

You can also use the free command to display current memory used, both physical and virtual (swap):

```
$ free
               total        used        free      shared     buffers      cached
Mem:        15622144    15269820      352324           0     8753168     3539596
-/+ buffers/cache:       2977056    12645088
Swap:       10288440           0    10288440
```

From the previous output, you see that this system has 15GB of RAM, almost all of it being used. It has about 10GB of swap space, almost none of which is used. Don't be too alarmed if your Linux system is using most of its physical memory; that's typical on many Linux servers.

---

■ **Note**    See Chapter 9 for details on using ipcs to view the memory and semaphores used by your database.

---

You can use the -s option to have the free command report output on a repeating interval. This example uses free to display memory usage in two-second snapshots and sends the output to a file:

```
$ free -s 2 > freemem.perf
```

Press Ctrl+C to exit from free when using the -s option. By default, the free output reports memory usage in kilobytes. Use -m to print in megabytes or -g to display the output of free in gigabytes.

## Using watch

An effective way to use free is in combination with the watch command. The watch command is used to execute another program on a periodic basis. This example uses watch to run the free utility every 3 seconds via the -n (interval) option. The -d (differences) option is used to have the output highlighted onscreen when there is a change in value from snapshot to snapshot:

```
$ watch -n 3 -d free
Every 3.0s: free                                Sun May  3 17:42:33 2015
               total        used        free      shared     buffers      cached
Mem:        15622144    15264004      358140           0     8753168     3539700
-/+ buffers/cache:       2971136    12651008
Swap:       10288440           0    10288440
```

You should be able to visually see any changes in memory activity onscreen when running in this mode. To exit from watch, press Ctrl+C.

You can also view the current characteristics of memory by viewing the /proc/meminfo file. You can use the file to display the current physical memory and swap space being used. This example uses the cat utility to display the current memory usage:

```
$ watch -d cat /proc/meminfo
```

By default, the watch command will refresh the screen every 2 seconds. You should visually see differences highlighted from interval to interval:

```
Every 2.0s: cat /proc/meminfo              Sun May  3 17:44:38 2015

MemTotal:      15622144 kB
MemFree:         358044 kB
Buffers:        8753168 kB
Cached:         3539912 kB
SwapCached:           0 kB
Active:         4842728 kB
SwapTotal:     10288440 kB
SwapFree:      10243872 kB
...
```

If you see an unusual amount of swap space being used (low SwapFree), it is an indication that your server needs more memory. To exit from watch, press Ctrl+C.

# 8-7. Identifying I/O-Intensive Processes

## Problem

You want to determine which processes are generating the most I/O.

## Solution

Use the iotop utility to display the top I/O-generating processes. On most systems, running iotop requires root access (signified in this example by the # character command prompt). Here's the simplest way to invoke it:

```
# iotop
```

Here is some sample output:

```
  TID  PRIO   USER     DISK READ    DISK WRITE    SWAPIN   IO>       COMMAND
21553  be/4  oracle    0.00 B/s     0.00 B/s     -5.02 %  99.99 %  [oracle_21553_o1]
24423  be/4  oracle    0.00 B/s     0.00 B/s      0.00 %   1.99 %  ora_p003_01212
24348  be/4  oracle    0.00 B/s     0.00 B/s      0.00 %   1.36 %  ora_lgwr_01212
24331  be/4  oracle    0.00 B/s     0.00 B/s      0.00 %   0.72 %  ora_gen0_01212
24401  be/4  oracle    0.00 B/s     0.00 B/s      0.00 %   0.64 %  ora_arc3_01212
24427  be/4  oracle    0.00 B/s     0.00 B/s      1.99 %   0.56 %  ora_p005_01212
```

This output displays the overall disk read and disk write rates, along with the PID, user, and command. If it's an Oracle process, you can use the SQL query from the "Solution" section of recipe 8-2 to retrieve further details regarding the process from the data dictionary.

## How It Works

The iotop utility is a top-like utility that displays processes and associated I/O. There are many different modes you can use. For example, if you want to display I/O associated with one user, you can do so as follows:

```
# iotop -user oracle
```

If you want to change the refresh rate (in seconds), you can specify the interval with the -d switch. The following instructs iotop to refresh the screen every 5 seconds:

```
# iotop -d 5
```

The iotop is an effective utility that displays top I/O-consuming processes on a server. When you're experiencing disk I/O bottlenecks, this tool provides a quick method for identifying processes that may need further investigation.

# 8-8. Identifying I/O Bottlenecks

## Problem

You want to determine whether your disk storage is a bottleneck.

## Solution

The iostat command can help you determine whether disk I/O is potentially a source of performance problems. Using the -x (extended) option with the -d (device) option is a useful way to generate I/O statistics. This example uses the -x and -d options to display extended device statistics every 10 seconds:

```
$ iostat -xd 10
```

You need a really wide screen to view this output; here's a partial listing:

```
Device:     rrqm/s wrqm/s   r/s   w/s  rsec/s  wsec/s    rkB/s    wkB/s avgrq-sz
avgqu-sz    await  svctm  %util
sda          0.01   3.31  0.11  0.31    5.32   28.97     2.66    14.49    83.13
0.06  138.44   1.89   0.08
```

---

■ **Note**  On Solaris systems, the iostat output may report the disk utilization as %b (percent busy). Also on Solaris systems, use iostat -Mnxz <n> to display output using megabytes, list descriptive names, show extended statistics, and remove lines with all zeros.

---

This periodic extended output allows you to view which devices are experiencing spikes in read and write activity in real time. To exit from the previous iostat command, press Ctrl+C.

When trying to determine whether device I/O is the bottleneck, here are some general guidelines when examining the iostat output:

- Look for devices with abnormally high blocks read or written per second.

- If any device is near 100% utilization, it is a strong indicator that I/O is a bottleneck.

Once you have determined that you have a disk I/O–contention issue, you can use utilities such as AWR (if licensed), Statspack (no license required) or the V$ views to determine whether your database is I/O stressed. For example, the AWR report contains an I/O statistics section with the following subsections:

- IOStat by Function Summary

- IOStat by Filétype Summary

- IOStat by Function/Filetype Summary

- Tablespace IO Stats

- File IO Stats

If you want to display current database sessions that are waiting for I/O resources, you can query the data dictionary as follows:

```
SELECT a.username, a.sql_id, b.object_name, b.object_type, a.event
FROM v$session a
    ,dba_objects b
    ,v$event_name c
WHERE b.object_id = a.row_wait_obj#
AND    a.event = c.name
AND    c.wait_class = 'User I/O';
```

## How It Works

The iostat command can help you determine whether disk I/O is potentially a source of performance problems. If you execute iostat without any options, you'll get a default report that displays averages since the system was last started:

```
$ iostat
avg-cpu:  %user   %nice   %sys %iowait   %idle
          18.91    0.04    1.20    0.15   79.70

Device:             tps   Blk_read/s   Blk_wrtn/s   Blk_read   Blk_wrtn
sda                7.14       398.01       409.52  164484368  169239542
sda1               0.00         0.00         0.00       1538        166
sda2              54.15       396.92       407.74  164032098  168505032
sda3               0.35         1.04         1.77     429820     733168
```

Notice that there are two sections in the iostat output. The first section is the CPU Utilization Report. The second section relates to disk I/O and is referred to as the Device Utilization Report.

Table 8-6 describes the columns used for disk I/O. (Use the -d option of iostat to display only device statistics.)

**Table 8-6.** *Column Descriptions of iostat Disk I/O Output*

| Column | Description |
|---|---|
| Device | Device or partition name |
| tps | I/O transfers per second to the device |
| Blk_read/s | Blocks per second read from the device |
| Blk_wrtn/s | Blocks written per second to the device |
| Blk_read | Number of blocks read |
| Blk_wrtn | Number of blocks written |
| rrqm/s | Number of read requests merged per second that were queued to device |
| wrqm/s | Number of write requests merged per second that were queued to device |
| r/s | Read requests per second |
| w/s | Write requests per second |
| rsec/s | Sectors read per second |
| wsec/s | Sectors written per second |
| rkB/s | Kilobytes read per second |
| wkB/s | Kilobytes written per second |
| avgrq-sz | Average size of requests in sectors |
| avgqu-sz | Average queue length of requests |
| await | Average time in milliseconds for I/O requests sent to the device to be served |
| svctm | Average service time in milliseconds |
| %util | Percentage of CPU time during which I/O requests were issued to the device; near 100% indicates device saturation |

You can also instruct iostat to display reports at a specified interval. The first report displayed reports averages since the last server reboot; each subsequent report shows statistics since the previously generated snapshot. The following example displays a device statistic report every 3 seconds:

```
$ iostat -d 3
```

To exit from the previous iostat command, press Ctrl+C. You can also specify a finite number of reports that you want generated, which is useful for gathering metrics to be analyzed over a period of time. This example instructs iostat to report every 2 seconds for a total of 15 reports:

```
$ iostat 2 15
```

When you work with locally attached disks, the output of the iostat command clearly shows you where the I/O is occurring. However, it is not that clear-cut in environments that use external arrays for storage. What you are presented with at the filesystem layer is some sort of a virtual disk that might also have been configured by a volume manager. Virtual disks are often referred to as *volumes* or *logical units* (*LUNs*).

A LUN is a logical disk that physically comprises one or more physical disks. The LUN represents the virtualization layer between the physical disks and the applications running on the database server. Figure 8-1 illustrates at a high level the abstraction involved with virtual disks.

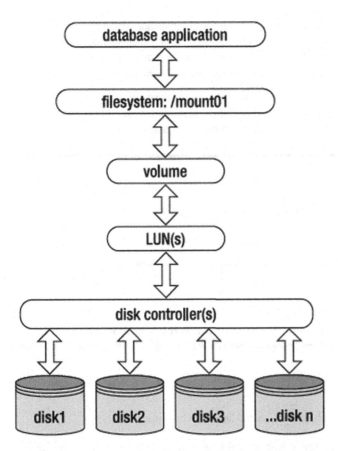

***Figure 8-1.*** *Abstraction layers between database application and physical disks*

When you work with virtual disks, the output from iostat reports on read/write activity at the virtual disk level, not the underlying physical disks. In these situations, there may be many layers of abstraction between the database application and physical disks, which can make it difficult to isolate the exact source of an I/O bottleneck. We recommend that you work closely with your storage administrator to determine whether a particular set of LUNs and underlying physical disks are a source of poor I/O performance.

## DETERMINING I/O RATES

To get an estimate of the I/O rate of your storage system, use the dd command in combination with the time command. On Linux systems, use the ofile and ifile parameters to simulate direct I/O; otherwise, you're reading and writing to memory and will receive misleading results. For example, use the following to estimate writes:

```
$ time dd if=/dev/zero of=testfile bs=8k count=1000 oflag=direct
```

The following estimates reads:

```
$ time dd of=/dev/null if=testfile bs=8k count=1000 iflag=direct
```

These metrics are helpful for determining the speed at which the OS can write and read a file. Keep in mind that it will provide estimates for sequential writes/reads. You would have to consider something more sophisticated to simulate database I/O activity (random writes/reads and multiple processes). Having said that, this approach is still a good starting point for diagnosing I/O issues.

On Solaris systems, the dd command doesn't have the oflag and iflag options. If the storage is ZFS, use the zfs utility to set caching to metatdata via zfs set primarycache=metadata <filesystem>. You will most likely have to contact your storage administrator to run the prior command with the appropriate filesystem.

# 8-9. Monitoring Network Traffic

## Problem

You suspect that the network might be a bottleneck. You want to view network statistics.

## Solution

Use the netstat (network statistics) command to display network traffic. Perhaps the most useful way to view netstat output is with the -ptc options. These options display the PID and TCP connections, and they continuously update the output:

```
$ netstat -ptc
```

Press Ctrl+C to exit the previous command. Here's a partial listing of the output:

```
(Not all processes could be identified, non-owned process info will not be shown, you would
have to be root to see it all.) Active Internet connections (w/o servers)
Proto Recv-Q Send-Q Local Address  Foreign Address  State       PID/Program name
tcp        0      0 rmug.com:62386 rmug.com:1521    ESTABLISHED 22864/ora_pmon_RMDB
tcp        0      0 rmug.com:53930 rmug.com:1521    ESTABLISHED 6091/sqlplus
tcp        0      0 rmug.com:1521  rmug.com:53930   ESTABLISHED 6093/oracleRMDB1
tcp        0      0 rmug.com:1521  rmug.com:62386   ESTABLISHED 10718/tnslsnr
```

If the Send-Q (bytes not acknowledged by remote host) column has an unusually high value for a process, it may indicate an overloaded network. The useful aspect about the previous output is that you can determine the OS PID associated with a network connection. If you suspect that the connection in question is an oracle session, you can use the techniques described in the "Solution" section of recipe 8-2 to map an OS PID to an oracle process or SQL statement.

■ **Note** On Linux systems, the /proc/net directory stores information about current network settings and activity.

## How It Works

When performance issues occur, the network is usually not the cause. Most likely you'll determine that bad performance is related to a poorly constructed SQL statement, inadequate disk I/O, or not enough CPU or memory resources. However, as a DBA, you need to be aware of all sources of performance bottlenecks and how to diagnose them. In today's highly interconnected world, you must possess network troubleshooting and monitoring skills. The netstat utility is a good starting place for monitoring server network connections.

On Linux systems, you can also use the sar command with the -n option to report on network statistics. The -n option takes one of the following as an argument: DEV (network devices), EDEV (error count), SOCK (sockets), or FULL (all). The following command displays the current day's network device statistics:

```
$ sar -n DEV
```

Here's a limited listing of the output:

```
12:00:01 AM   IFACE   rxpck/s txpck/s  rxbyt/s  txbyt/s  rxcmp/s  txcmp/s  rxmcst/s
12:10:01 AM     lo      0.00    0.00     0.00     0.00     0.00     0.00     0.00
12:10:01 AM    eth0     0.34    0.11    39.17    10.22     0.00     0.00     0.04
12:10:01 AM    eth1     0.00    0.00     0.00     0.00     0.00     0.00     0.00
12:10:01 AM    sit0     0.00    0.00     0.00     0.00     0.00     0.00     0.00
```

The previous output shows the number of packets transmitted and received per second, as well as the bytes and compressed packets (snapshots taken in 10-minute intervals).

If you experience performance issues when connecting to remote servers, sometimes it is useful to see the route that a packet takes to get from one server to another. To use traceroute, log on to the server and then trace the route to the remote server:

```
$ traceroute <remote_server_name>
```

This information is meaningful to a network engineer and can troubleshoot network performance issues.

# 8-10. Troubleshooting Database Connectivity

## Problem

You're attempting to connect to a database and are receiving the following error:

```
ERROR:
ORA-12154: TNS:could not resolve the connect identifier specified
```

You want to determine the root cause of this issue.

## Solution

To diagnose database connectivity issues, first use the OS ping utility to determine whether the remote box is accessible; for example:

```
$ ping dwdb
dwdb is alive
```

If ping doesn't work, work with your SA or network administrator to ensure that you have server-to-server connectivity in place.

Next, use telnet to see whether you can connect to the remote server and port (that the listener is listening on); for example:

```
$ telnet dwdb 1521
Trying 127.0.0.1...
Connected to dwdb.
Escape character is '^]'.
```

This output indicates that connectivity to a server and port is okay. If it doesn't work (you don't see "Connected to" in the output), contact your SA or network administrator for further assistance.

Now use tnsping to determine whether Oracle Net is working. This utility will verify that the Oracle Net listener is running on the remote server; for example:

```
$ tnsping dwrep
..........
Used TNSNAMES adapter to resolve the alias
Attempting to contact (DESCRIPTION = (ADDRESS = (PROTOCOL = TCP)
(HOST = dwdb.us.farm.com)(PORT = 1521))
(CONNECT_DATA = (SERVER = DEDICATED) (SERVICE_NAME = DWREP)))
OK (500 msec)
```

What's sometimes confusing is that the prior output indicates only that the listener is up and receiving requests; it doesn't necessarily indicate that there actually is a service (DWREP in this example) registered with the listener on the remote host. To further verify that the actual service is registered with the listener, you have to log on to the remote server and run the lsnrctl utility to verify the services registered with the listener:

```
$ lsnrctl services <listener_name>
```

If you don't provide a listener name, the default name of LISTENER is assumed. You can also use the lsnrctl status <listener_name> command to verify that the listener is up and which services are registered with the listener. If you're not sure what the listener name is, use the ps command to identify it:

```
$ ps -ef | grep tns
```

Here is some sample output that indicates that the default listener name (LISTENER) is used on this server:

```
oracle   27480     1  0 10:09 ?        00:00:00
/u01/app/oracle/product/12.1.0.2/db_1/bin/tnslsnr LISTENER -inherit
```

Also verify that the remote database is available by establishing a local connection as a non-SYS account (SYS can often connect to a troubled database when other schemas can't); for example:

```
$ sqlplus system/manager
```

If you can't connect via this command, verify that a critical mount point hasn't filled up via the df command:

```
$ df -h
```

If Oracle can't write to files in the ORACLE_HOME/dbs directory, or if archiving is enabled and the archive location is full, the database will hang and not accept new connections.

If everything looks good to this point, verify that the TNS information is correct. If the remote listener and database are working, ensure that the mechanism for determining TNS information (such as the tnsnames.ora file) contains the correct information. Sometimes the client machine will have multiple TNS_ADMIN locations and tnsnames.ora files. One way to verify whether a particular tnsnames.ora file is being used is to rename it and see whether you get a different error when you attempt to connect to the remote database.

## How It Works

Diagnosing database connectivity issues can be quite frustrating. If you've followed all the suggestions in the "Solution" section of this recipe and are still having issues, examine the client sqlnet.log file and/or the server listener.log file. Sometimes these log files show additional information that will pinpoint the issue. The locations of these files can vary by the Oracle release and how a DBA has implemented Oracle Net. Usually the Oracle Net files are in the following directory:

```
$ORACLE_BASE/diag/tnslsnr/instance_name/listener/trace
```

If you can't find the files, use the find command; for example:

```
$ cd $ORACLE_BASE
$ find . -name listener.log
```

Here is some sample output:

```
./diag/tnslsnr/dwrep/listener/trace/listener.log
```

If all else fails, you can enable higher levels of output to the Oracle Net logging files. See the *Oracle Database Net Services Administrator's Guide* for details (freely available for download on the docs.oracle.com web site).

# 8-11. Tracing a Process

## Problem

You're troubleshooting database network connectivity issues and want to trace the tnsping process to determine which tnsnames.ora file is being used. In other words, you want to determine the directory locations and the order in which tnsping looks for tnsnames.ora files.

## Solution

This solution has two sections: one for using strace on Linux and one for using truss on Solaris.

## Using strace

To reiterate, the task at hand is to determine what order and in which directories the tnsping utility is looking for tnsnames.ora files. You know that tnsping looks in multiple locations, but aren't sure of the order. The strace tool can provide this information. First, run strace to trace tnsping without any options:

```
$ strace tnsping bogus_service
```

This code generates a great deal of output; here's a small snippet:

```
access("/u01/app/oracle/product/12.1.0.2/db_1/network/admin/tnsnames.ora", F_OK)
= -1 ENOENT (No such file or directory)
mmap(NULL, 143360, PROT_READ|PROT_WRITE, MAP_PRIVATE|MAP_ANONYMOUS, -1, 0)
= 0x2ac9aa003000
munmap(0x2ac9aa003000, 143360)         = 0
stat("/u01/app/oracle/product/12.1.0.2/db_1/ldap/admin/ldap.ora", 0x7fffba717a30) = -1
ENOENT (No such file or directory)
brk(0x126ff000)                        = 0x126ff000
...
```

Most of the output isn't useful. To extract the relevant lines, pipe the output to grep and cut the field (delimited by double quotes) of interest:

```
$ strace tnsping bogus_sid 2>&1 >/dev/null|grep '\.ora'|cut -f2 -d\"|cut -f1 -d\"|uniq
```

Here is the useful output showing the directory locations and order in which tnsping is looking for tnsnames.ora files:

```
/u01/app/oracle/product/12.1.0.2/db_1/network/admin/sqlnet.ora
/home/oracle/.tnsnames.ora
/u01/app/oracle/product/12.1.0.2/db_1/network/admin/tnsnames.ora
/var/yp/binding/us.oracle.com.2
/u01/app/oracle/product/12.1.0.2/db_1/ldap/admin/fips.ora
/u01/app/oracle/product/12.1.0.2/db_1/ldap/admin/ldap.ora
/u01/app/oracle/product/12.1.0.2/db_1/network/admin/ldap.ora
```

This output shows the order, location, and file names that the tnsping process searches for when attempting to connect to a service registered with a listener.

## Using truss

On a Solaris system, you can use truss to trace a process. First, use truss to trace tnsping without any options:

```
$ truss tnsping bogus_service
```

Here's a small section of a large amount of output:

```
stat("/orahome/app/oracle/product/12.1.0.2/db_1/network/admin/ldap.ora", 0xFFFFFFFF7FFF5EB0)
Err#2 ENOENT
stat("/etc/resolv.conf", 0xFFFFFFFF7FFF6540)    = 0
open("/etc/resolv.conf", O_RDONLY)              = 7
```

Most of that output isn't useful. To extract the relevant lines, pipe the output to grep and cut the relevant field (delimited by double quote marks):

```
$ truss tnsping bogus_service 2>&1 | grep '\.ora' | cut -f2 -d\" | cut -f1 -d\" | uniq
```

Here's the information showing the order and location of the files that tnsping is accessing:

```
/orahome/app/oracle/product/12.1.0.2/db_1/network/admin/sqlnet.ora
/orahome/oracle/.tnsnames.ora
/orahome/app/oracle/product/12.1.0.2/db_1/network/admin/tnsnames.ora
/orahome/app/oracle/product/12.1.0.2/db_1/ldap/admin/fips.ora
/orahome/app/oracle/product/12.1.0.2/db_1/ldap/admin/ldap.ora
/orahome/app/oracle/product/12.1.0.2/db_1/network/admin/ldap.ora
```

So by tracing the process, you can glean more insight on its inner workings.

# How It Works

Tracing utilities gives you a window into internal system calls (and parameters) initiated by a process. On rare occasions, you may need to trace a process. In our experience, DBAs rarely use tracing facilities. However as the "Solution" section demonstrates, tracing a process is an effective troubleshooting technique in certain situations. The strace (Linux) and truss (Solaris) utilities provide the capability to trace a process.

The "Solution" section showed examples of initiating a trace on a process as the command is interactively executed. It is also possible to trace a process that is already running. Suppose that you want to trace an Oracle background process. First determine its PID:

```
$ ps -ef | grep smon
oracle   24354     1  0 09:46 ?        00:00:00 ora_smon_01212
```

On Linux, run strace and provide the PID to it:

```
$ strace -p 24354
```

To send the output to a file, use the -o option:

```
$ strace -o smon.txt  -p 24354
```

On Solaris, run truss with the appropriate PID. First, use ps to determine the PID of the process:

```
$ ps -ef | grep smon
  oracle 18618     1  0   Jun 12 ?          1:04 ora_smon_TRG
```

Now use truss to trace the process:

```
$ truss -p 18618
```

Here the output is sent to a file while tracing:

```
$ truss -o smon.txt -p 18618
```

Note that the `dtrace` utility is available for Linux and Solaris. This utility is an entire framework that has its own scripting language that provides insight into all aspects of the OS. Using `dtrace` can be quite involved but critical if you require extensive tracing capabilities. The `strace` and `truss` tools are better suited to trace a single process.

# 8-12. Listing Files Opened by Processes

## Problem

You've logged on to a database server and want to help diagnose a problem. After logging on to the server, you realize there's no mechanism to automatically set the `oracle` OS variables, so the standard variables (`ORACLE_HOME`, `ORACLE_SID`, and so on) haven't been set for your user. You want to determine the location of `ORACLE_HOME`.

## Solution

Identify the Oracle instances running on the server. Use the `ps` and `grep` commands to isolate any Oracle SMON background processes:

```
$ ps -ef | grep smon
```

The output indicates that the PID of 25128 is associated with the SMON background process:

```
oraus    25128    1  0 Mar18 ?        00:02:23 ora_smon_semgc1
```

Now use the `lsof` (list open files) command to identify files opened by that process. The following line of code searches for the string "oracle" in the output:

```
$ lsof -p 25128 | grep 'bin\/oracle' | awk '{ print $9 }'
```

Here is some sample output:

```
/orahome/app/oracle/product/12.1.0.1/db_1/bin/oracle
```

In this way, you can quickly determine the location of `ORACLE_HOME`, even when the standard variables haven't been set for your current user logon.

## How It Works

The `lsof` command is ideal for identifying processes and associated open files. This command is quite flexible and has many options. For example, if you want to view processes that have opened a particular file, you can do so by passing the file name to the command; for example:

```
$ lsof /u01/dbfile/O1212/system01.dbf
```

Here are a few lines of the output:

```
COMMAND      PID    USER    FD    TYPE DEVICE   SIZE/OFF       NODE NAME
ora_dbrm_  16201 oracle   256u    REG  202,2 524296192   14065848 /u01/dbfile/01212/system01.dbf
ora_dbw0_  16207 oracle   258uW   REG  202,2 524296192   14065848 /u01/dbfile/01212/system01.dbf
ora_lgwr_  16209 oracle   260u    REG  202,2 524296192   14065848 /u01/dbfile/01212/system01.dbf
...
```

If you want to view processes that have opened files under a specific directory, you can do so with the +D option:

```
$ lsof +D /u01/dbfile/01212
```

To report on files opened by a particular user, use the -u option:

```
$ lsof -u oracle
```

On Solaris systems, the lsof command may not be available. Instead, use the pfiles command to list open files. For example, if you want to identify ORACLE_HOME in a Solaris environment, first identify the SMON processes running on the server:

```
$ ps -ef | grep smon
oracle 22184     1    0    Mar 13 ?            5:15 ora_smon_EMREP
```

To identify files opened by the prior process, use the pfiles command, pass it the PID, and then search for any helpful keywords such as the string "dbs":

```
$ pfiles 22184 | grep dbs
```

Here is some output:

```
/orahome/app/oracle/product/12.1.0.2/db_1/dbs/hc_EMREP.dat
```

In this way, you can determine the location of files used by Oracle processes.

# CHAPTER 9

■ ■ ■

# Viewing and Configuring System Resources

As part of normal operations, Oracle database processes constantly coordinate and communicate with system server processes. In Linux or Solaris, this type of process-to-process coordination is referred to as *interprocess communication* (IPC). OSs typically support three types of interprocess communication mechanisms: semaphores, shared memory, and message queues. Oracle database applications typically require significant amounts of semaphore and shared memory resources to function properly.

A *semaphore* is a construct used by the OS to control which processes can have access to other server resources such as shared memory. The number of OS resources that a database application can consume is governed by several kernel parameters. Maintaining these values is described in detail in this chapter.

---

■ **Note**    The *kernel* is the core program of the OS that manages access to OS resources required by other processes on the system. The kernel is typically responsible for process, CPU, memory, disk management, and network activities.

---

Nowadays, almost any medium-to-large database can quickly exceed the default kernel settings for system resource limits. Therefore, most database vendors (Oracle, MySQL, DB2, PostgreSQL, and so on) have their own set of recommended values for the kernel parameters that govern the various required OS resources.

Before you can install a database on a server, it prudent to first ensure that that the kernel parameters are configured correctly. An incorrectly configured kernel usually results in either a nonfunctioning or poorly performing database. For example, if enough shared memory can't be allocated when Oracle starts, an error message like this will be thrown:

```
ORA-27123: unable to attach to shared memory segment
```

To avoid these problems, a knowledgeable DBA must know how to view and set kernel parameters that affect database availability and performance. This chapter begins with a high-level overview of how to examine and modify kernel parameters, and then dives into specific details for settings most critical for database applications.

One last note before you start: many of the recipes in this section have slightly different solutions, depending on whether you're using Linux or Solaris. The differences are noted where applicable.

# 9-1. Displaying Server Hardware and the Operating System

## Problem

You have the task of installing the Oracle database software (binaries). Before you download and install the software, you need to verify the system architecture and OS version of the target host.

## Solution

This "Solution" section contains two sections: one for Linux and the other for Solaris. First, let's discuss viewing server information on Linux.

### Linux

Use the uname (print system information) utility with the -a option to display system details. Here's the output for a typical Linux system:

```
$ uname  -a
Linux dv3.rmug.org 2.6.18-308.4.1.0.1.el5xen #1 SMP
Tue Apr 17 16:41:30 EDT 2012 x86_64 x86_64 x86_64 GNU/Linux
```

You can also produce the previous output piecemeal via the following options: -s (kernel name), -n (nodename), -r (kernel release), -v (kernel version), -m (machine), -p (processor), -i (hardware platform), and -o (operating system). For example, to print the hardware platform, use the following:

```
$ uname -p
x86_64
```

Use uname with the --help parameter to display all choices available in your environment.

### Solaris

For Solaris systems, you can use the uname command to print out hardware details:

```
$ uname -a
SunOS devz1 5.11 11.1 sun4v sparc sun4v
```

This output indicates that the OS release is 5.11, the platform is sun4v, and the hardware class is sparc. You can also print out the server details in a columnar format using the -X option:

```
$ uname -X
System = SunOS
Node = devz1
Release = 5.11
KernelID = 11.1
Machine = sun4v
BusType = <unknown>
Serial = <unknown>
Users = <unknown>
```

```
OEM# = 0
Origin# = 1
NumCPU = 16
```

Here's how to confirm the release level:

```
$ cat /etc/release
Oracle Solaris 11.1 SPARC
...
```

You can show the architecture via the isainfo command:

```
$ isainfo -kv
64-bit sparcv9 kernel modules
```

# How It Works

In today's global environment, you'll often connect remotely to database servers located in dispersed data centers. In these situations, you'll frequently use the uname command with the -a option to verify which machine you're logged on to.

In a Linux environment, you can also view server information by querying the virtual files in the /proc directory. For example, you can view the current version of the server by viewing the /proc/version file:

```
$ cat /proc/version
Linux version 2.6.18-308.4.1.0.1.el5xen (mq@ca-build56.us.rmug.com)
(gcc version 4.1.2 20080704 (Red Hat 4.1.2-50)) #1 SMP Tue Apr 17 16:41:30 EDT 2012
```

The Linux /proc virtual filesystem acts as an interface for viewing and configuring kernel parameters. The /proc directory is a hierarchy of files and subdirectories that contain the current settings of kernel values. It is appropriately named /proc because this virtual filesystem sends information to other system processes. This filesystem is virtual because its files don't actually reside on disk. Note that most files beneath the /proc directory have a 0-byte size. The /proc virtual files are created dynamically in memory from kernel data when you access them.

For your convenience, the /proc filesystem is subdivided into directories that contain related parameters. For example, the /proc/sys subdirectory contains many of the parameters used to configure the kernel. Use the man proc command to view documentation on the /proc virtual filesystem for your server.

Some utilities, such as top and free, extract information from the /proc virtual files and present it in a human-readable formatted fashion.

Table 9-1 describes some of the virtual files in the /proc directory. Use your favorite file-viewing utility (cat, more, less, view, grep, and so on) to inspect these virtual files.

*Table 9-1.* *Descriptions of Linux Virtual Files in the* /proc *Directory*

| File Name | Contains Information Regarding |
|---|---|
| /proc/cpuinfo | CPU and system architecture. |
| /proc/meminfo | Free and used memory for both physical RAM and swap. |
| /proc/net | Directory containing network information. |
| /proc/mounts | All mounted filesystems. |
| /proc/diskstats | Disk I/O statistics for each disk. |
| /proc/devices | PCI devices. |
| /proc/filesystems | Filesystems compiled into the kernel. |
| /proc/sys | Contains subdirectories and files pertaining to kernel variables. Some variables can be configured with the sysctl command. |
| /proc/cmdline | Parameters passed to the kernel at boot time. |
| /proc/version | Version of the OS. |

# 9-2. Listing CPUs

## Problem

The Oracle installation documentation recommends installing the binaries on a server with CPUs that meet certain requirements. You want to display the CPU characteristics on your server.

## Solution

This "Solution" section contains two sections: one for Linux and the other for Solaris. First let's cover viewing CPU information on Linux.

## Linux

You can quickly obtain in-depth information about the physical characteristics of the CPU(s) on a Linux server by viewing the virtual /proc/cpuinfo file:

```
$ cat /proc/cpuinfo
```

For multiple processor boxes, there is a section in the output for each CPU. The first CPU on the box is identified as 0, the next one as 1, and so on. Here's a partial listing of some typical output from /proc/cpuinfo:

```
processor     : 0
vendor_id     : GenuineIntel
cpu family    : 6
model         : 45
model name    : Intel(R) Xeon(R) CPU E5-2690 0 @ 2.90GHz
stepping      : 7
cpu MHz       : 2893.100
cache size    : 20480 KB
```

```
physical id   : 0
siblings      : 1
core id       : 0
cpu cores     : 1
...
```

## Solaris

For Solaris systems, use the prtdiag utility to display CPU information:

```
$ prtdiag
```

Here's a partial listing of the output:

```
================================= Virtual CPUs ==========

CPU ID Frequency Implementation       Status
------ --------- --------------------- -------
0      2848 MHz  SPARC-T4             on-line
1      2848 MHz  SPARC-T4             on-line
2      2848 MHz  SPARC-T4             on-line
3      2848 MHz  SPARC-T4             on-line
...
```

### How It Works

Sometimes you need to know whether the CPUs on your box are powerful enough to handle the database software being installed. If you have multiple CPUs on your server, you'll see a listing for each CPU. On Linux systems, use the information in the /proc/cpuinfo file to determine whether your server meets Oracle's prerequisites for CPU minimum megahertz speed, which is usually the cpu MHz line in the /proc/cpuinfo file. On Solaris systems, use the prtdiag utility to view CPU information.

# 9-3. Displaying Physical Memory

## Problem

Oracle's installation documentation recommends that you have a certain minimal amount of memory installed on the server. You want to verify that you have enough memory on a box before you do a database installation.

## Solution

This "Solution" section contains two sections: one for Linux and the other for Solaris. First up is Linux.

## Linux

With Linux, you can view the contents of the /proc/meminfo file with grep to check the total physical memory amount:

```
$ grep MemTotal /proc/meminfo
MemTotal:     15622144 kB
```

On Linux systems, issue the following grep command to view the total amount of swap memory:

```
$ grep SwapTotal /proc/meminfo
SwapTotal:    10288440 kB
```

---

■ **Tip**   See Oracle's MOS notes 233753.1 and 269426.1 for a detailed discussion of /proc/meminfo.

---

## Solaris

On Solaris systems, use the prtconf utility to display installed memory:

```
$ prtconf | grep "Memory size"
```

Here's a snippet of the output:

```
Memory size: 32768 Megabytes
```

On Solaris systems, run the following command to view the swap size:

```
$ swap -l
swapfile                dev    swaplo   blocks      free
/dev/zvol/dsk/rpool/swap 196,2     16 67108848 67108848
```

## How It Works

When dealing with database servers, you have to be aware of two types of memory: physical RAM and virtual (swap). Depending on the software you install on a box, you are sometimes required to check to see whether there is sufficient RAM and swap memory on the target server. If you don't have enough physical or swap memory, usually the Oracle Universal Installer will alert you to any inadequacies when you attempt to perform the installation.

You can also view physical and swap memory by issuing the free command with no options. This command gives you a view of the currently free and consumed memory on the box:

```
$ free
            total        used        free      shared     buffers      cached
Mem:      2074904     2050512       24392           0       84704     1759792
-/+ buffers/cache:    206016     1868888
Swap:     4184924       74652     4110272
```

On Linux systems, if you want to view per-process memory consumption, use the following cat commands:

```
$ cat  /proc/<PID>/maps
$ cat  /proc/<PID>/status
```

On Solaris systems, use the pmap command to see process-to-memory mappings. First use the ps command to identify the process of interest:

```
$ ps -ef | grep smon | grep -v grep
oracle  7625    1   0   Apr 10 ?            9:29 ora_smon_DWREP
```

Then use the PID as input to the pmap command:

```
$ pmap -x 7625
```

Here's a partial listing of the output:

```
7625:    ora_smon_DWREP
          Address       Kbytes       RSS       Anon    Locked Mode   Mapped File
0000000100000000       214912    197232          -         - r-x--  oracle
000000010D2DE000         1584       1144        320         - rwx--  oracle
000000010D46A000           24          -          -         - rwx--  oracle
...
```

---

## TEMPOARARILY ADDING SWAP SPACE

If you're short on swap space, you can temporarily add a swap file to your server. As the root user, run the following commands to add approximately 1GB of swap space:

```
# dd if=/dev/zero of=tempswap bs=1k count=1000000
# chmod   600 tempswap
# mkswap   tempswap
# swapon   tempswap
```

Verify that the swap space was added with the -s option of the swapon command:

```
# swapon -s
```

To remove the temporary swap file, as root run the following commands:

```
# swapoff   tempswap
# rm tempswap
```

After disabling the swap file, you should see the swap space in /proc/meminfo return to its original value.

---

# 9-4. Viewing Kernel Parameters

## Problem

You're installing database binaries on a new server and need to modify kernel parameters per the installation documentation. Before you make the change, you first want to view all kernel parameters.

## Solution

The solution varies by OS. First let's view Linux kernel parameters:

### Linux

Run the following grep command as root to view the current kernel settings in the /proc/sys/kernel directory:

```
# grep . /proc/sys/kernel/*
```

The previous command instructs grep to print all strings contained in files located in the /proc/sys/ kernel directory. Here is a partial listing of the output:

```
/proc/sys/kernel/sem:250          32000    100     128
/proc/sys/kernel/shmall:2097152
/proc/sys/kernel/shmmax:1073741824
/proc/sys/kernel/shmmni:4096
```

---

■ **Note**  You can view many files in the /proc virtual filesystem as a non-root account. However, you will need root access to view all virtual files.

---

You can also use grep to filter for a particular setting. The example searches for the string sem in any files in the /proc/sys/kernel directory:

```
# grep . /proc/sys/kernel/* | grep  sem
/proc/sys/kernel/sem:250          32000 100     128
```

If you want to save all the current kernel values in a file, pipe the output of the grep command to a file:

```
# grep  . /proc/sys/kernel/* >jul11_kernel_parms.txt
```

### Solaris

Solaris 10 and above no longer use the /etc/system file to manage shared memory. Solaris uses the resource control facility for memory management. The /etc/project file is where project settings are stored. To verify the project settings, first use the id command to determine the project identifier:

```
$ id -p
uid=2000(oracle) gid=200(dba) projid=200(group.dba)
```

Now use the `prctl` command to view the maximum shared memory allowed for a project:

```
$ prctl -n project.max-shm-memory -i project group.dba
project: 200: group.dba
NAME    PRIVILEGE       VALUE    FLAG   ACTION                      RECIPIENT
project.max-shm-memory
        privileged      24.0GB    -     deny                            -
        system          16.0EB   max    deny                            -
```

And you can also view the maximum number of semaphore IDs for a project:

```
$ prctl -n project.max-sem-ids -i project group.dba
NAME    PRIVILEGE       VALUE    FLAG   ACTION                      RECIPIENT
project.max-sem-ids
        privileged       128      -     deny                            -
        system          16.8M    max    deny
```

If you're logged on as the `oracle` user, you can also verify parameters for the current process as follows:

```
$ prctl -n project.max-shm-memory -i process $$
process: 20506: bash
NAME    PRIVILEGE       VALUE    FLAG   ACTION                      RECIPIENT
project.max-shm-memory
        privileged      24.0GB    -     deny                            -
        system          16.0EB   max    deny                            -
```

---

■ **Tip**   On Solaris systems, if you receive the "ORA-27102: out of memory" message when creating a database, see MOS note 1370537.1.

---

# How It Works

Occasionally, you'll need to verify kernel parameter settings when you're troubleshooting issues. On Linux systems, you can view settings in the `/proc/sys/kernel` directory. On Solaris systems, use the `prctl` utility to view kernel parameters.

# Using `sysctl`

On Linux systems, another way to display all kernel parameters is via the `sysctl` utility, which allows you to view and modify the kernel files found in the `/proc/sys` directory. Use the `-a` option of `sysctl` to view all kernel parameters:

```
# sysctl -a
```

Here is a small snippet of the large output of the previous command:

```
kernel.msgmnb = 16384
kernel.msgmni = 16
kernel.msgmax = 8192
kernel.shmmni = 4096
kernel.shmall = 2097152
kernel.shmmax = 1073741824
```

You can save the output of the sysctl -a command to a text file, as shown here:

```
# sysctl -a > /root/kernelsysctl.txt
```

Inspect the output of the sysctl -a command. Note that the kernel values are either a single value or an array of values. When just a single value is involved, it is fairly easy to determine the parameter setting. For example, from the output of sysctl -a, the maximum setting for shared memory (shmmax) is 1,073,741,824 bytes:

```
kernel.shmmax  = 1073741824
```

When the kernel settings are stored as an array, it becomes a bit more difficult to determine a particular value. For example, this array of four values shows the current kernel settings for sem (semaphores):

```
kernel.sem  = 250        32000    100      128
```

When you work with array values, it is important to know which element of the array maps to which kernel setting. In the previous output, the values of the semaphore array 250 32000 100 128 map to the following kernel parameters: semmsl, semmns, semopm, and semmni, respectively. For example, semmsl is set to 250 and defines the maximum number of semaphores in a semaphore array. The meanings of these semaphore parameters are discussed in detail in recipe 9-6.

## Viewing Shared Memory

On Linux systems, all the shared memory parameters appropriately begin with the string shm. Use the ls (list) command with the -1 (that's a number one) option to display which shared memory parameters are available on your Linux system:

```
$ ls -1 /proc/sys/kernel/shm*
```

You should see output similar to this:

```
/proc/sys/kernel/shmall
/proc/sys/kernel/shmmax
/proc/sys/kernel/shmmni
```

Next, use the cat command to view individual shared memory settings. This example shows how to view the maximum size (in bytes) of a shared memory segment (shmmax) that can be created:

```
$ cat  /proc/sys/kernel/shmmax
2147483648
```

Table 9-2 describes the shared memory parameters. Some of these parameters may not be updatable on your particular Linux system.

***Table 9-2.*** *Shared Memory Kernel Parameter Descriptions*

| IPC Shared Memory Parameter | Description |
|---|---|
| shmmax | Maximum size (in bytes) for shared memory segment |
| shmmin | Minimum size (in bytes) of shared memory segment |
| shmall | Total amount of shared memory (in bytes or pages) that can be used at any time |
| shmseg | Maximum number of shared memory segments per process |
| shmmni | Maximum number of shared memory segments for the entire system |

# 9-5. Modifying Kernel Parameters

## Problem

You're performing a database installation. The Oracle documentation specifies the recommended settings for several kernel parameters, but you want to modify these kernel parameters.

## Solution

This solution is split into two sections: one for Linux and one for Solaris. Let's look at Linux first.

## Linux

On Linux systems, there are several valid techniques for changing kernel parameters: running sysctl, editing sysctl.conf, adding entries with echo, and adding entries with cat. This section focuses on using sysctl and editing the sysctl.conf file directly. See the "How It Works" section for details on using echo and cat to modify kernel parameters.

Use the sysctl command with the -w option to dynamically modify kernel parameters. The following command changes the kernel semaphore settings in the /proc/sys/kernel/sem virtual file:

```
# sysctl  -w kernel.sem="250   32000 100 128"
```

Notice that there are no spaces around the = sign. If you attempt to run the sysctl command with spaces around the = sign, you will receive an error like the following:

```
error: 'kernel.sem'  must  be of  the  form  name=value
error: Malformed setting '='
error: '250  32000 100 128'  must  be of  the  form  name=value
```

To make changes persist across system reboots, use your favorite editor (such as vi) to add the parameters to the /etc/sysctl.conf file.

---

■ **Tip**  Use the man  sysctl or sysctl --help command for all options available in your environment.

---

You can also directly modify the /etc/sysctl.conf file and then use the sysctl -p command to make desired kernel parameter changes. This example uses vi to first edit the /etc/ sysctl.conf file:

```
# vi /etc/sysctl.conf
# Add changes and then exit...
```

After you modify the /etc/sysctl.conf file, you can use the sysctl -p command to make the entries in the /etc/sysctl.conf file instantiated as the current values used by the Linux kernel:

```
# sysctl -p
```

The previous command loads into memory the values found in the /etc/sysctl.conf file. You can verify that the values were changed by using cat to view the corresponding virtual file.

When you edit the sysctl.conf file, we recommend that you first make a copy of the file with the date embedded into the file name. For example, before making any changes, create a copy of the file, as shown here:

```
# cp /etc/sysctl.conf    /etc/sysctl.conf.01_jan_08
```

Making a copy serves two purposes. First, it provides you with a copy of the parameters as they were before the change, which comes in handy if you want to revert to the previous settings for any reason. Second, this also gives you an audit trail of all kernel changes made via this file. You can then use commands such as diff to display differences in file versions (see recipe 5-14 for details).

## Solaris

To modify kernel parameters on Solaris systems, use the prctl command. The following modifies the max-shm-memory parameter to 8GB:

```
# prctl -n project.max-shm-memory -v 8gb -r -i project group.dba
```

The following command modifies the max-sem-ids parameter to 256:

```
# prctl -n project.max-sem-ids -v 256 -r -i project group.dba
```

When you use the prctl command, you don't have to reboot the system to instantiate the parameters. However, you do need to use the projmod command to ensure that the parameters are added to the /etc/ project file, so that the parameters persist across system reboots. This example updates the /etc/project for the max-shm-memory parameter:

```
# projmod -sK "project.max-shm-memory=(privileged,8G,deny)" group.dba
```

## How It Works

One advantageous feature of both Linux and Solaris is that you can dynamically change many of the kernel settings while the system is running. The parameters take effect as soon as you change them, and you are not required to reboot the system. This is different from many other OSs that require a server reboot for kernel changes to become instantiated.

On Linux systems, the /proc/sys directory contains virtual files that correspond to kernel settings. You can change the /proc/sys files to dynamically configure kernel values. Hundreds of parameters exist that you can modify. Run the following find command to give you a rough idea of how many kernel files there are with your version of Linux:

```
# find /proc/sys -type f | wc -l
598
```

Not all virtual files in the /proc/sys directory can be modified. One quick way to determine whether a /proc/sys file can be altered is to check the permissions. Any file that shows the writable permission can be changed. This example uses the ls -altr command to view the /proc/sys/kernel file permissions:

```
# ls -altr /proc/sys/kernel
```

Here is a partial listing of the output. Notice that the first two files are not modifiable, but the last three can be modified (signified by the w write permission):

```
-r--r--r--    1 root   root   0 Sep    4 16:32  version
-r--r--r--    1 root   root   0 Sep    4 16:32  tainted
-rw-r--r--    1 root   root   0 Sep    4 16:32  shmmni
-rw-r--r--    1 root   root   0 Sep    4 16:32  shmmax
-rw-r--r--    1 root   root   0 Sep    4 16:32  shmall
```

The shmmax parameter can have a significant impact on database performance. With Oracle databases, this parameter should be set to a value higher than the SGA size. If the shmmax value is too small, you may not be able to start your Oracle instance. Correctly sizing and configuring shared memory are important DBA tasks when building a new database server.

Databases use shared memory as a holding area for data read from disk. Database processes read and modify the data held in shared memory. The shared memory area uses semaphores to control exclusive access to memory segments. A database will fail to start if there isn't enough shared memory available to be allocated. Therefore, it is paramount that DBAs know how to manage shared memory because it has a direct impact on database availability and performance.

---

■ **Caution**    Be careful when modifying kernel values. Modifying a kernel parameter to an unusable value can cause the system to become unstable and require a restart with the boot disk.

---

## Adding sysctl.conf Entries with echo

You can use the echo command to modify kernel parameters by writing the desired output to the specified virtual file. This example writes the values 250 32000 100 128 to the virtual /proc/sys/kernel/sem file using the echo command:

```
# echo 250 32000 100 128 > /proc/sys/kernel/sem
```

This command immediately changes the kernel settings for the sem (semaphores) parameter. If you want the change to persist across system reboots, you also need to add an entry to the /etc/sysctl.conf file. This file is read when the system boots to determine the settings for kernel parameters. You can edit the /etc/sysctl.conf file directly (with an editor such as vi) and add the following line:

```
kernel.sem  = 250 32000 100 128
```

Alternatively, you can use the echo command to add the desired parameters to the end of the /etc/sysctl.conf file, as shown here:

```
# echo "kernel.sem  = 250 32000 100 128"  >> /etc/sysctl.conf
```

Notice that the previous command uses >> to concatenate the desired entry to the bottom of the /etc/sysctl.conf file. Don't use just a single right arrow > because it would overwrite the contents of /etc/sysctl.conf.

When you use echo and >> to write to the contents of the /etc/sysctl.conf file, no checks are performed to determine whether the kernel parameters you are writing to the file already exist. The echo and >> techniques simply add the values to the bottom of the file.

If two entries in the /etc/sysctl.conf file configure the same kernel parameter, the value that appears nearest to the bottom of the file will be the one that gets set because the parameters are processed from top to bottom. For example, suppose that you have the following two lines in the /etc/sysctl.conf file:

```
kernel.sem  = 500 64000 200 500
kernel.sem  = 250 32000 100 128
```

The bottom line in the previous listing will be set last, so it will dictate the kernel setting for the kernel.sem value.

After you use echo to write to the /etc/sysctl.conf file, you can use the sysctl -p command to make the entries in the /etc/sysctl.conf file instantiated as the current values used by the Linux kernel:

```
# sysctl  -p
```

# Adding `sysctl.conf` entries with `cat`

The technique shown here is handy for adding several entries to the /etc/sysctl.conf file at the same time. First, use the cat command to add entries to the /etc/sysctl.conf file. This example shows how to use cat to write typical kernel parameter settings for an Oracle database:

```
# cat  >> /etc/sysctl.conf  <<EOF
kernel.shmall  = 2097152
kernel.shmmax  = 536870912
kernel.shmmni  = 4096
kernel.sem  = 250 32000 100 128
fs.file-max  = 65536
net.ipv4.ip_local_port_range  =  1024 65000
net.core.rmem_default  = 262144
net.core.rmem_max  = 262144
net.core.wmem_default  = 262144
net.core.wmem_max  = 262144
EOF
```

This command uses cat to write all the values encapsulated between the two EOF markers to the /etc/sysctl.conf file, which allows you to add several parameters simultaneously to the /etc/sysctl.conf file. When using cat and >> to write parameters to the /etc/sysctl.conf file, there is no automatic checking to determine whether the parameters already exist in the file. Using cat and >> will simply write to the bottom of the file.

After the desired changes are made, use the `sysctl -p` command to make the entries in the /etc/sysctl.conf file the current values used by the Linux kernel, as shown here:

```
# sysctl -p
```

# 9-6. Displaying Semaphores

## Problem

The Oracle installation documentation recommends configuring the system semaphores to certain minimal values. Before you modify the settings, you want to view the semaphore parameters.

## Solution

This "Solution" section contains two sections: one for Linux and the other for Solaris. First, let's discuss displaying semaphores on Linux.

### Linux

On Linux systems, you can view semaphore information by displaying the contents of the /proc/sys/kernel/sem file. This example uses the `cat` command to view semaphore data (you don't have to be root to view these values):

```
$ cat /proc/sys/kernel/sem
250         32000    100        128
```

Notice that there are four values listed for semaphores in the previous output. The numbers represent the value for the following semaphore kernel parameters: `semmsl`, `semmns`, `semopm`, and `semmni`, respectively. For example, the `semmsl` value is currently 250, `semmns` is 32000, and so forth.

### Solaris

On Solaris, first view the project for the current user:

```
$ id -p
uid=2000(oracle) gid=200(dba) projid=200(group.dba)
```

Use the `prctl` command to show various semaphore settings for the currently logged-on user. For example, the following shows the maximum number of semaphores per set:

```
$ prctl -n process.max-sem-nsems $$
```

Here is some sample output:

```
process: 10033: -ksh
NAME    PRIVILEGE       VALUE    FLAG   ACTION                    RECIPIENT
process.max-sem-nsems
        privileged       512      -     deny                          -
        system          32.8K    max    deny                          -
```

The line of code shows the maximum number of semaphore IDs allowed for the project:

```
$ prctl -n  project.max-sem-ids $$
```

This shows the maximum number of semaphore operations allowed per semop call:

```
$ prctl -n process.max-sem-ops $$
```

# How It Works

Before making changes to any kernel information, prudent to first view the current values. Table 9-3 details the meanings of the relevant Linux semaphore variables. Notice that all semaphore variable names aptly begin with the letters sem. These semaphore names may vary slightly, depending on which version of the OS you're using.

*Table 9-3.* *Semaphore Kernel Parameters and Descriptions*

| IPC Semaphore Parameter | Description |
| --- | --- |
| semmsl | Maximum number of semaphores per set (array) |
| semmns | Maximum number of semaphores on entire system |
| semopm | Maximum operations for semop system call |
| semmni | Maximum number of semaphore arrays on entire system |
| semvmx | Maximum value of a semaphore |

Semaphores are locking mechanisms that coordinate mutually exclusive access to sharable system resources. Semaphores act as gatekeepers to ensure that particular shared system resources are not accessed by multiple processes at the same time. Databases use semaphores to manage access to OS resources such as shared memory.

Database background processes require semaphores to manage mutually exclusive access to shared resources. If there aren't enough semaphores available for all database processes, the database might not start or a runtime failure might occur. For semaphore-related problems, it is critical that DBAs know how to view and configure these kernel parameters.

| RAILROAD SEMAPHORES |
| --- |

In the early days of the railroad, engineers quickly discovered the need for communicating the status of railway lines over long distances. Knowing in advance whether a railway line was in use had a direct impact on survivability. To minimize collisions, railroad engineers devised techniques of signaling via signs visible over long distances.

The signs that the railways used consisted of moving mechanical arms or multicolored lights. These mechanical signs and lights—colloquially called *semaphores*—were used to communicate in advance whether a set of tracks was free from an obstruction (such as an oncoming train). In this way, the railway engineers ensured that only one train at a time used a single section of tracks.

Semaphores in computers function much like their railway counterparts. Semaphores signify whether a resource is busy. These constructs are typically used to manage exclusive access to segments of shared memory. A database process that needs access to a shared memory segment must first check the status of the corresponding semaphore variable to guarantee that the section is not already in use. In this way, semaphores ensure that only one process at a time operates on a particular shared memory area.

# 9-7. Configuring Semaphores

## Problem

You're installing Oracle software on a database server and need to modify the semaphore settings.

## Solution

This "Solution" section contains two sections: one for Linux and the other for Solaris. First, let's discuss configuring semaphores on Linux.

## Linux

On Linux systems, first check the current values in case they need to be referenced later. To view the current semaphore settings, use the cat command:

```
# cat /proc/sys/kernel/sem
250     32000    128    128
```

The values in the previous output represent the settings for the following semaphore parameters in this order: semmsl, semmns, semopm, and semmni.

This example uses the echo command to increase the maximum number of semaphore arrays (semmni) from 128 to 256:

```
# echo 250 32000 100 256 > /proc/sys/kernel/sem
```

---

■ **Note**    See recipe 9-5 for alternate ways of changing Linux kernel parameters.

---

## Solaris

To modify kernel parameters on Solaris systems, use the `prctl` command. The following command modifies the `max-sem-ids` parameter to 256:

```
# prctl -n project.max-sem-ids -v 256 -r -i project group.dba
```

When using the `prctl` command, you don't need to reboot the system to instantiate the parameters, but you do need to use the `projmod` command to ensure that the parameters are added to the /etc/project file. This process ensures that the parameters persist across system reboots. Here are some examples of using `projmod` to make settings permanent across system reboots:

```
# projmod -sK "project.max-sem-ids=(privileged,256,deny)" group.dba
# projmod -sK "project.max-shm-ids=(privileged,100,deny)" group.dba
# projmod -sK "project.max-sem-nsems=(privileged,256,deny)" group.db
```

## How It Works

After you change the semaphore settings, it is a good idea to use the `cat` command to verify that the changes took place:

```
# cat   /proc/sys/kernel/sem
250      32000    100    256
```

If you want the changes to persist across a system reboot, ensure that you modify the /etc/sysctl.conf file appropriately. In this example, an editor (such as `vi`) is used to add the following entry to the /etc/sysctl.conf file:

```
kernel.sem   = 250 32000 100 256
```

---

■ **Note**    Refer to Oracle's installation documentation for recommended semaphore settings for your version of Oracle and OS.

---

# 9-8. Viewing Memory Structures

## Problem

Your database has experienced a hard. You want to see whether any database-related memory structures are still physically allocated on the server.

## Solution

For both Linux and Solaris, use the `ipcs` (interprocess communication status) command without any options to view the current allocated physical memory, semaphores, and message queues:

```
$ ipcs
```

Here is some typical output:

```
------ Shared Memory  Segments  --------
Key          shmid      owner      perms      bytes        nattch      status
0xb3e36378  131072      oracle     640        421527552    17
------ Semaphore  Arrays  --------
Key          semid      owner    perms    nsems
0x288e2800 1146880      oracle   640      126
0x288e2801 1179649      oracle   640      126
0x288e2802 1212418      oracle   640      126
0x288e2803 1245187      oracle   640      126
0x288e2804 1277956      oracle   640      126
------ Message  Queues  --------
Key     msqid    owner    perms    used-bytes    messages
```

The prior output has three sections. The oracle user has 421,527,552 bytes of shared memory allocated. There are five semaphore arrays allocated with 126 semaphores per array. There are no message queues allocated.

## How It Works

The "Solution" section of this recipe demonstrates how to view in-memory structures that are currently allocated. On Linux systems, to view the system limits imposed on memory and semaphores, use the -lms options of the ipcs command:

```
$ ipcs -lms
------ Shared Memory Limits --------
max number of segments = 4096
max seg size (kbytes) = 1048576
max total shared memory (kbytes) = 8388608
min seg size (bytes) = 1

------ Semaphore Limits --------
max number of arrays = 128
max semaphores per array = 250
max semaphores system wide = 32000
max ops per semop call = 100
semaphore max value = 32767
```

Compare the maximum memory values to the settings in the /proc/sys/kernel directory:

```
$ cat /proc/sys/kernel/shmall
2097152
$ cat /proc/sys/kernel/shmmax
1073741824
$ cat /proc/sys/kernel/shmmni
4096
```

To view all the options available with the ipcs command, use the -h (help) option.

# 9-9. Removing In-Memory Structures

## Problem

Your database unexpectedly crashed, and for some reason the semaphores and shared memory have not been released. Other databases are running on the server, so you can't reboot the system to release the shared memory objects. You want to manually remove these orphaned memory structures.

## Solution

On both Linux and Solaris systems, first view the structures to be removed with the `ipcs -sm` command:

```
$ ipcs -sm
```

On this server, there are two instances of Oracle running, each with one allocated shared memory segment and five sets of semaphore arrays:

```
------ Shared Memory  Segments  --------
Key          shmid     owner   perms       bytes  nattch     status
0xb3e36378 32768      oracle    640    421527552      16
0x34525e84 65537      oracle    640    421527552      11

------ Semaphore  Arrays  --------
key          semid      owner    perms  nsems
0x288e2800 360448      oracle     640    126
0x288e2801 393217      oracle     640    126
0x288e2802 425986      oracle     640    126
0x288e2803 458755      oracle     640    126
0x288e2804 491524      oracle     640    126
0x3239d0e4 622597      oracle     640    126
0x3239d0e5 655366      oracle     640    126
0x3239d0e6 688135      oracle     640    126
0x3239d0e7 720904      oracle     640    126
0x3239d0e8 753673      oracle     640    126
```

■ **Caution**    If you're working on a server that has multiple Oracle instances running, ensure that you remove the correct memory structure. If you remove the wrong structure, you will inadvertently crash another database.

If you have multiple databases on one server, first verify which memory structures belong to the orphaned instance by running the Oracle `sysresv` utility (located in the `ORACLE_HOME/bin` directory). This command reports on memory structures that correspond to your current instance setting of `ORACLE_SID`. Run this command as the owner of the Oracle binaries (usually `oracle`):

```
$ sysresv
```

Here is the pertinent output:

```
IPC  Resources  for ORACLE_SID  "RMDB2"  :
Shared  Memory:
ID      KEY
65537     0x34525e84
Semaphores:
ID      KEY
622597    0x3239d0e4
655366    0x3239d0e5
688135    0x3239d0e6
720904    0x3239d0e7
753673    0x3239d0e8

Total /dev/shm size: 14168080384 bytes, used: 1828995072 bytes
Shared Memory:
ID          KEY
1397653516    0x00000000
1397686285    0x00000000
1397719054    0x00000000
1397620747    0x00000000
1397751823    0x6ecd05d4
Semaphores:
ID          KEY
4718634     0xaee7d96c
```

You can remove memory objects either by key or ID. This example uses the -m option to remove a shared memory segment by its ID:

```
$ ipcrm -m 622597
```

This example uses the -s option to remove a semaphore array using an ID:

```
$ ipcrm  -s  4718634
```

You can verify that the memory structures have been removed by running sysresv again.

## How It Works

The ipcrm command uses either the key or the ID as its input for identifying which IPC object to remove. The basic syntax for using ipcrm is as follows:

```
$ ipcrm  [ -M key |  -m  id  | -Q key | -q  id |  -S  key |  -s  id ]
```

In the previous syntax description, -M is used with a shared memory key, -m is used with a shared memory ID, -S is used with a semaphore key, and -s is used with a semaphore ID.

Occasionally, you might have a database crash and for some reason the database semaphores or shared memory structures haven't been released properly by the OS. In these rare situations, if you don't have the luxury of rebooting the server, you have to first identify the unreleased memory object with the ipcs and sysresv commands and then remove it with the appropriate ipcrm command.

# 9-10. Viewing Network Configuration Settings

## Problem

The Oracle documentation recommends setting some network parameters on Linux systems to minimal values. You first want to inspect the current network settings.

---

■ **Note**  This recipe applies only to Linux systems.

---

## Solution

The virtual /proc network files are usually located either in /proc/sys/net/core or in /proc/ sys/net/ipv4. By using the ls -altr command, you can see that most of the virtual network files in /proc/sys/net/core are updatable:

```
# ls -altr /proc/sys/net/core
```

Here's a partial listing of the output:

```
total 0
-rw-r--r-- 1 root root 0 Jun 12 22:02 xfrm_larval_drop
-rw-r--r-- 1 root root 0 Jun 12 22:02 xfrm_aevent_rseqth
-rw-r--r-- 1 root root 0 Jun 12 22:02 xfrm_aevent_etime
-rw-r--r-- 1 root root 0 Jun 12 22:02 xfrm_acq_expires
-rw-r--r-- 1 root root 0 Jun 12 22:02 wmem_max
-rw-r--r-- 1 root root 0 Jun 12 22:02 wmem_default
...
```

Use the cat command to view a particular virtual network file. This example uses cat to display the current setting for the rmem_default kernel parameter:

```
# cat /proc/sys/net/core/rmem_default
524288
```

## How It Works

To view a complete listing of network settings, use the sysctl command and grep for the string net:

```
# sysctl -a | grep -i net
```

You'll be presented with a great deal of output. Table 9-4 lists some of the network kernel parameters that you may have to modify for database servers.

**Table 9-4.** *Network Kernel Parameter Descriptions*

| Network Kernel Parameter | Location | Description |
| --- | --- | --- |
| rmem_default | /proc/sys/net/core | Default socket receive buffer size |
| wmem_default | /proc/sys/net/core | Default socket send buffer size (in bytes) |
| rmem_max | /proc/sys/net/core | Maximum socket receive buffer size (in bytes) |
| wmem_max | /proc/sys/net/core | Maximum socket send buffer size (in bytes) |
| tcp_keepalive_time | /proc/sys/net/ipv4 | Number of seconds a connection is idle before TCP starts sending keepalive probes |
| tcp_keepalive_intvl | /proc/sys/net/ipv4 | Interval (in seconds) between keep-alive probes |
| tcp_keepalive_probes | /proc/sys/net/ipv4 | Number of unacknowledged probes sent before connection is terminated |
| tcp_retries1 | /proc/sys/net/ipv4 | Number of times TCP will attempt to normally transmit packet |
| tcp_retries2 | /proc/sys/net/ipv4 | Maximum number of times a TCP will attempt to transmit a packet |
| tcp_syn_retries | /proc/sys/net/ipv4 | Maximum number of SYNs attempts to transmit |
| ip_local_port_range | /proc/sys/net/ipv4 | Ports allowed for TCP and UDP traffic |

# VIEWING IP INFORMATION

You'll occasionally need to view aspects about your network, such as the server's Internet Protocol (IP) address. Look in the /etc/hosts file to view your hostname and IP information. The /etc/hosts file contains a cross-reference between IP addresses and server names. This example uses cat to display the contents of the /etc/hosts file:

```
$ cat /etc/hosts
```

Here's a sample of what you might find:

```
127.0.0.1      localhost.localdomain  localhost
177.22.33.89   db123.cent.com    db123
```

You can also use the hostname -i command to view your server IP address and hostname -d to display domain information.

# 9-11. Configuring Network Settings

## Problem

You're installing database software on a Linux server, and the Oracle documentation indicates that you need to configure some network parameters.

---

■ **Note** This recipe applies only to Linux systems.

---

## Solution

Use the echo command to update the /proc/sys/net/ipv4/ip_local_port_range file. This example uses the echo command to change the first local port allowed for TCP and UPD traffic to 1024 and the last local port to 65000:

```
# echo 1024 65000 > /proc/sys/net/ipv4/ip_local_port_range
```

You can verify the changes with the cat command:

```
# cat /proc/sys/net/ipv4/ip_local_port_range
1024    65000
```

You need to add these entries to the /etc/sysctl.conf file to have the changes persist across system reboots. Here's a sample entry in the /etc/sysctl.conf file:

```
net.ipv4.ip_local_port_range=1024 65000
```

## How It Works

Before changing any network kernel parameters, make sure that you first save a copy of the original values somewhere so that you can change back to the old values if the new values cause undesirable results. In the example, the value of the ip_local_port_range is first viewed with the cat command:

```
$ cat /proc/sys/net/ipv4/ip_local_port_range
32768    61000
```

---

■ **Note** Refer to the Oracle installation documentation for recommended settings for network kernel parameters for your version of Oracle and OS.

---

# 9-12. Modifying System Open File Limits

## Problem

The Oracle installation documentation for Linux recommends setting the system-wide open file limit for the server. You want to enable this restriction.

---

■ **Note**    This solution applies only to Linux systems.

---

## Solution

Use the echo command or the sysctl command to dynamically modify the /proc/sys/fs/file-max value. This example uses the echo command to change the file-max value on the fly to 65536:

```
# echo 65536 > /proc/sys/fs/file-max
```

Use the cat command to verify that the change took place:

```
# cat /proc/sys/fs/file-max
65536
```

Here's an example of using sysctl  -w to modify the maximum open file limit:

```
# sysctl -w fs.file-max=65536
```

Remember to add an entry to the /etc/sysctl.conf file to make the changes persist across system reboots.

## How It Works

Linux imposes a limit on the overall number of files that can simultaneously be open on the server. Servers that host database applications tend to have many simultaneously open files. If the default value for the maximum number of open files is too low, you most likely will have to increase it. You'll know that you've hit the maximum limit on the number of open files if you start seeing errors pertaining to "running out of file handles."

This maximum open file limit is governed by the Linux kernel /proc/sys/fs/file-max virtual file. You can also view the maximum number of file handles by viewing the contents of the /proc/sys/fs/file-nr virtual file:

```
# cat /proc/sys/fs/file-nr
885 0 65536
```

This output shows the current number of allocated file handles, the number of free file handles, and the maximum number of file handles, respectively.

# 9-13. Showing Shell Limits

## Problem

You want to view system resource limits instantiated by your logon shell.

## Solution

This solution applies to both Linux and Solaris systems. Use the -a (all) option of the ulimit command to print the current soft limits for a process:

```
$ ulimit -a
core  file size          (blocks, -c) 0
data  seg size           (kbytes, -d) unlimited
file size                (blocks, -f) unlimited
pending  signals               (-i) 1024
max  locked  memory      (kbytes,  -l) 32
max  memory  size        (kbytes,  -m) unlimited
open files                     (-n) 10000
pipe  size         (512  bytes, -p) 8
POSIX  message  queues     (bytes, -q) 819200
stack  size              (kbytes,  -s) 10240
cpu time    ▪           (seconds, -t) unlimited
max  user  processes           (-u) 16375
virtual memory           (kbytes,  -v) unlimited
file  locks                    (-x) unlimited
```

This output displays the parameter, units of measurement, option used to manipulate the parameter, and its current setting. To view the hard limit resources, use the ulimit -aH command. If you want to view a soft or hard limit for a particular setting, specify its option. For example, to display the hard limit for the number of open files, use the -Hn option:

```
$ ulimit -Hn
20000
```

## How It Works

Your logon shell will impose default maximum limits on various resources that a process can use, such as the number of open files, processes per user, amount of memory allocated, and so on. These shell limits are defined by the ulimit command. Each resource has a soft limit setting and a hard limit setting. The soft limit setting establishes the default resource limit when a user logs on to the system. If the user process exceeds the soft limit setting for a resource, an error will be thrown. The user can manually increase the setting of the soft limit setting for a resource up to (but not exceeding) the value defined by the hard limit.

A user can modify the hard limit down, but cannot modify the hard limit up. So if you set a hard limit to a lower value, you can't reset it to its original value. Only the root user can modify a hard limit to a higher value.

On Linux systems, the default values for soft and hard limits on the server are established by adding entries into the /etc/security/limits.conf file. On Solaris systems, use the prctl and projmod commands if you need to modify resource limits. Database processes tend to consume more resources than the default shell limits allow. Therefore, it's important that you're familiar with viewing and modifying shell resource limits.

■ **Note** The Bash, Bourne, and Korn shells use the `ulimit` command to view and modify shell resource limits. If you are using the C shell, use the `limit` command.

# 9-14. Changing Shell Limits

## Problem

You're performing an Oracle installation on a new server and need to modify the shell limits per the installation instructions.

■ **Note** This recipe applies only to Linux systems. Solaris systems use the `prctl` and `projmod` utilities to maintain shell limits; typically, the default configuration is adequate.

## Solution

To alter the default shell limits for a user on Linux systems, edit the `/etc/security/limits.conf` file as root. This example shows how to change the number of processes and number of open files defined for the `oracle` user:

```
oracle   soft   nproc   2047
oracle   hard   nproc   16384
oracle   soft   nofile 1024
oracle   hard   nofile 65536
```

In this output, the first line defines the soft limit for the number of processes for the `oracle` user to 2047, and the second line sets the hard limit for the number of processes to 16384. The third and fourth lines set the soft and hard limits for the number of open files for the `oracle` user, respectively. These limits will be imposed on the `oracle` user when logging on to the server.

■ **Caution** Do not set the hard limit for a user resource to be higher than the system-wide limit. In particular, don't set the hard limit for the number of open files to be higher than the value defined in the `/proc/sys/fs/file-max` virtual file. If a process can open the maximum number of files that reaches the system-wide setting, the system can run out of open files, and the system can become unstable.

## How It Works

The `ulimit` command provides a way to view and limit resources used by a shell and the resources of subprocesses started by a shell. As a non-root user, you can change your soft limits up to the value defined by the hard limit. As the root user, you can modify hard limits to higher values.

For example, to adjust the soft limit of the number of open files to 15000, issue the following:

```
$ ulimit -Sn 15000
```

To view the change, issue the command without a value:

```
$ ulimit -Sn
15000
```

If you exceed the value defined by the hard limit, you'll receive an error such as the following:

```
-bash: ulimit: open files: cannot modify limit: Invalid argument
```

When you add entries to the /etc/security/limits.conf file on Linux systems, the default shell limit is set for the user process when users log on to the system. Table 9-5 shows the values and their meaning when changing the /etc/security/limits.conf file.

*Table 9-5. Description of Limits Set via /etc/security/limits.conf Virtual File*

| Parameter | Limits |
| --- | --- |
| core | Core file size (in KB) |
| data | Maximum data size (in KB) |
| fsize | Maximum file size (in KB) |
| memlock | Maximum locked in memory address space (in KB) |
| nofile | Maximum number of open files |
| rss | Maximum resident set size (in KB) |
| stack | Maximum stack size (in KB) |
| cpu | Maximum CPU time (in minutes) |
| nproc | Maximum number of processes |
| as | Address space limit |
| maxlogins | Maximum number of logins for user |
| priority | Priority at which to run user process |
| Locks | Maximum number of locks for user |

When working with database applications, you might not ever want to have a database process constrained by a soft limit. Instead, you might want only the hard limit to govern the amount of resources a database process uses. In this case, you can set the soft limit equal to the hard limit in the database user login profile file. For example, if the oracle user on your Linux box uses the Bash shell, you would modify the .bash_profile logon file (see recipe 2-5 for further details).

The following entries are added to the oracle user's .bash_profile file to establish the soft limits equal to the hard limits:

```
ulimit -u  16384
ulimit -n  65536
```

When you use the ulimit command, if you don't denote a -S (soft) or -H (hard) option, both the soft and hard limits are set to the value specified. Whenever the oracle user logs on, the soft and hard limits for the number of processes will be 16384, and the soft and hard limits for the number of open files will be 65536.

If you write an entry into the logon file that exceeds the hard limit, the user will receive an error such as this at logon time:

```
-bash: ulimit:  open files: cannot modify limit: Operation not permitted
```

---

■ **Note**    The Bourne and Korn shells use the `.profile` initialization file for setting parameters on logon. The C shell uses the `.login` or `.cshrc` file.

---

# CHAPTER 10

# Automating Jobs with cron

In almost every type of Linux/Solaris environment—from development to production—DBAs rely heavily on automating tasks such as database backups, monitoring, and maintenance jobs. Automating routine tasks allows DBAs to be much more effective and productive. Automated environments inherently run more smoothly and efficiently than manually administered systems.

This chapter focuses on showing you how to leverage the cron job scheduler. The cron scheduling tool, which is universally available on Linux/Solaris systems, is accessible and easy to use. For these reasons, this utility is frequently chosen by DBAs to automate database jobs. Because cron is heavily used by DBAs, developers, and SAs, it is mandatory to have a working knowledge of this tool.

This chapter builds on your knowledge of Linux/Solaris OS commands, editing files, and shell scripting. You'll need this skill set to automate your database surroundings. You should be able to extend the following recipes to meet the automation requirements of your environment.

## 10-1. Enabling Access to Schedule Jobs

### Problem

As the oracle OS user, you're attempting to add an entry to the cron table and you receive the following error message:

```
You (oracle) are not allowed to use this program (crontab)
```

You want to grant access to the oracle user to use the crontab utility.

### Solution

As the root user, add oracle to the /etc/cron.allow file with the echo command:

```
# echo oracle >> /etc/cron.allow
```

Once the oracle entry is added to the /etc/cron.allow file, you can use the crontab utility to schedule a job.

---

■ **Note**   You can also use an editing utility (such as vi) to add an entry to this file.

---

## How It Works

The root user can always schedule jobs with the crontab utility, but other users must be listed in the /etc/cron.allow file. If the /etc/cron.allow file does not exist, the OS user must not appear in the /etc/cron.deny file. If neither the /etc/cron.allow nor the /etc/ cron.deny file exists, only the root user can access the crontab utility.

---

■ **Note**    On Solaris systems, the cron.allow and cron.deny files are located in the /etc/cron.d directory.

---

The cron program is a job-scheduling utility that is ubiquitous in Linux/UNIX environments. This tool derives its name from *chronos* (the Greek word for time). The cron (the geek word for *scheduler*) tool allows you to schedule scripts or commands to run at a specified time and repeat at a designated frequency.

When your server boots up, a cron background process is automatically started that manages all cron jobs on the system. On Linux systems, the cron background process is also known as the cron daemon. This process is started on system startup by the /etc/init.d/crond script. You can check to see whether the cron daemon process is running with the ps command:

```
$ ps -ef | grep crond | grep -v grep
root     3049     1 0 Aug02 ?     00:00:00 crond
```

On Linux systems, you can verify the status of the cron daemon using the service command:

```
$ /sbin/service crond status
crond (pid 3049) is running...
```

On Solaris systems, you can verify that a cron service is running via the svcs (service status) command. This line of code prints out the services and filters the output via grep:

```
$ svcs -a | grep cron
online         Aug_13   svc:/system/cron:default
```

On Linux systems, the root user uses several files and directories when executing system cron jobs. The /etc/crontab file contains commands to run system cron jobs. Here's a typical listing of the contents of the /etc/crontab file:

```
SHELL=/bin/bash
PATH=/sbin:/bin:/usr/sbin:/usr/bin
MAILTO=root
HOME=/
# run-parts
01 * * * * root run-parts /etc/cron.hourly
02 4 * * * root run-parts /etc/cron.daily
22 4 * * 0 root run-parts /etc/cron.weekly
42 4 1 * * root run-parts /etc/cron.monthly
```

This /etc/crontab file uses the run-parts utility to run scripts located in the following directories: /etc/cron.hourly, /etc/cron.daily, /etc/cron.weekly, and /etc/cron.monthly. If there is a system utility that has to run other than on an hourly, daily, weekly, or monthly basis, it can be placed in the /etc/cron.d directory.

Each user can create a crontab (also known as a cron table) file, which contains the list of programs that you want to run at a specific time and interval. This file is usually located in the /var/spool/cron directory (on Solaris systems, look in /var/spool/cron/crontabs). For every user who creates a cron table, there is a file in the /var/spool/cron directory named after that user.

The cron background process is somewhat idle. It wakes up once every minute and checks /etc/crontab, /etc/cron.d, and the user cron table files; and determines whether there are any jobs that have to be executed.

# 10-2. Editing the cron Table

## Problem

You have the following RMAN backup code stored in a file named rmanback.bsh in the /home/oracle/bin directory:

```
#!/bin/bash
ORACLE_SID=TRG
ORACLE_HOME=/orahome/app/oracle/product/12.1.0.2/db_1
PATH=$PATH:$ORACLE_HOME/bin
#
rman target / <<EOF
backup database;
EOF
exit 0
```

You want to have a database backup script run automatically at 11:05 p.m. every night.

## Solution

To schedule a job, you must add a line in your cron table that specifies the time you want the job to execute. You can edit your cron table directly with the -e (editor) option of the crontab command:

```
$ crontab -e
```

If you're presented with a random number and a blank prompt when you first edit your cron table, your default editor is probably ed, not vi or vim. If you are in ed rather than vi, set your EDITOR OS variable to be vi:

```
$ export EDITOR=vi
```

When issuing the crontab -e command, you will be presented with a file to edit: cron table (or crontab). To schedule a script named rmanback.bsh (located in the /home/oracle/bin directory) to run daily at 11:05 p.m., enter the following line into your cron table (more on the cron syntax coming in recipe 10-3):

```
5 23 * * * /home/oracle/bin/rmanback.bsh
```

Exit the cron table file. If your default editor is vi, type :wq to exit. When you exit crontab, your cron table is saved for you. To view your cron entries, use the -l (list) option of the crontab command:

```
$ crontab -l
```

You should see this line:

```
5 23 * * * /home/oracle/bin/rmanback.bsh
```

The prior line indicates that you have successfully scheduled the file rmanback.bsh (located in /home/oracle/bin) to run daily at 23:05 (in 24-hour clock time/military time).

## How It Works

Ensure that you become comfortable editing the cron table because you'll modify it quite often as your automation requirements change. The most common way to modify the cron table is with the crontab -e command.

## Loading the cron Table from a File

Another method for modifying your cron table is to load it directly with a file name using the following syntax:

```
$ crontab <filename>
```

With the previous line of code, the crontab utility will load the contents of the specified file into your cron table. We recommend that you perform the following steps when modifying your cron table with this method:

1.  Create a file with the contents of your existing cron table:

    ```
    $ crontab -l > mycron.txt
    ```

2.  Make an additional copy of your cron table before you edit it so that you can revert to the original if you introduce errors and can't readily figure out what's incorrect. It also provides an audit trail of changes to your cron table:

    ```
    $ cp mycron.txt mycron.jul29.txt
    ```

3.  You can now edit the mycron.txt file with your favorite text editor:

    ```
    $ vi mycron.txt
    ```

4.  To schedule a script named rmanback.bsh to run daily at 11:05 p.m., enter the following into the file:

    ```
    5 23 * * * /home/oracle/bin/rmanback.bsh
    ```

5.  When you finish making edits, load the crontab back, as shown here:

    ```
    $ crontab mycron.txt
    ```

If your file doesn't conform to the cron syntax, you'll receive an error such as the following:

```
"mycron.txt":6: bad day-of-week
errors in crontab file, can't install.
```

In this situation, either correct the syntax error or reload the original copy of the cron table.

## Removing the cron Table

You can completely remove your cron table with the -r option, although you'll rarely (if ever) use it. Having said that, note that the following will completely remove your cron table:

```
$ crontab -r
```

Just to emphasize this point, the -r option is for *remove*, not *read*. Don't make the mistake of accidentally removing an entire cron table when you simply want to edit it. Before using the -r option, save your cron table in a text file:

```
$ crontab -l > cron.june10.txt
```

That way, you can refer to the saved file if you didn't intend to delete your cron table. It's a best practice to save the cron table before you edit it. We've worked in numerous environments in which a DBA or developer accidentally removed a cron table or erroneously removed entries. Without a backup, you'll probably have a hard time remembering exactly what was in the cron table before the change was made.

## Automating the cron Table Backup

As mentioned in the previous section, consider making a backup of the contents of the cron table before you edit it. Some DBAs have cron automatically create a backup of the contents of the cron table. Consider adding this line to your cron table (the cron syntax is described next in recipe 10-3):

```
* * 1 * * crontab -l > /home/oracle/scripts/crontab.$(date +\%m).txt
```

For the prior entry to work, the directory of /home/oracle/scripts must exist. The crontab -l command will save the contents of the cron table into a text file. The name of the file will contain a numeric number that corresponds to the current month (e.g., crontab.01.txt, ..., crontab.12.txt). It will create a copy of the contents of your cron table on the first of each month (see recipe 10-6 for more details on redirecting cron output to a file).

# 10-3. Understanding cron Table Entries

## Problem

You've seen an example of a cron table entry such as the following:

```
5 23 * * * /home/oracle/bin/rmanback.bsh
```

Before you add your own entries, you want some background information about how to interpret the preceding line.

# Solution

Your cron table is a list of numbers and commands that the cron background process will run at a specified time and schedule. The crontab utility expects entries to follow a well-defined format. Each entry in the crontab is a single line composed of six fields (it is never split into multiple lines). The first five fields specify the execution time and frequency, and the sixth field consists of OS commands or scripts to be executed. Here's a sample of the format:

```
min hr dayOfMonth monthOfYear dayOfWeek commandsOrScripts
```

Table 10-1 describes each field in further detail.

***Table 10-1.*** *cron Table Column Descriptions and Allowed Values*

| Field | Description | Allowed Values |
| --- | --- | --- |
| Min | Minute of the hour | 0-59, or * |
| Hr | Hour of the day (in 24-hour format) | 0-23, or * |
| dayOfMonth | Day of the month | 1-31, or * |
| monthOfYear | Month of the year | 1-12, or * |
| dayOfWeek | Day of the week | 0-6, or *; depending on version, a 0 can also be specified by a 7 |
| commandsOrScripts | OS commands or scripts | Any combination of commands or scripts |

Each entry, which is usually specified with a number, can also be an asterisk (*), which indicates that all possible values are in effect. For example, the following line of code instructs cron to send an email saying "wake up" at 12:05 p.m. every day of the month, each month, and each day of the week:

```
05 12 * * * echo "wake up" | mailx -s "wake up" dba@gmail.com
```

Each of the first five entries can be separated by commas or hyphens. A comma indicates multiple values for an entry, whereas a hyphen indicates a range of values. For example, the following entry sends an email saying "wake up" every half hour, from 8 a.m. to 4:30 p.m., Monday through Friday:

```
0,30 8-16 * * 1-5 echo "wake up" | mailx -s "wake up" dba@gmail.com
```

The fourth column (month of the year) and fifth column (day of the week) can be represented with numeric values or by three-letter abbreviations. For example, the following entry in the crontab uses three-letter abbreviations for months and days:

```
0,30 8-16 * Jan-Dec Mon-Fri echo "wake up" | mailx -s "wake up" dba@gmail.com
```

On some OS versions, you can skip a value within a range by following the entry with /<integer>. For example, if you want to run a job every other minute, use 0-59/2 in the minute column. You can also use a slash (/) with an asterisk to skip values. For example, to run a job every fourth minute, use */4 in the minute column. You can do similarly for every fourth hour */4 (00, 04, 08, 12, 16, 20).

The sixth field in the cron table entry can be a combination of commands or shell scripts. For example, the following cron entry runs the rmanback.bsh shell script (located in the /home/oracle/bin directory) daily at 4:00 a.m.:

```
0 4 * * * /home/oracle/bin/rmanback.bsh
```

Lines that start with a # are comments in the cron table. In other words, any text entered after # is ignored by cron. For example, the following comment is usually added as the first line of the cron table to provide a quick syntax guide of the required format for subsequent entries:

```
# min(0-59) hr(0-23) dayofMonth(1-31) monthofYear(1-12) dayofWeek(0/7-6) commandsOrScripts
```

Here's another popular way to provide a quick syntax guide using the first two lines of the cron table:

```
# Minute   Hour   Day of Month   Month of Year       Day of Week      Commands or Scripts
# (0-59)   (0-23)    (1-31)      (1-12 or Jan-Dec)   (0-6 or Sun-Sat)
```

# How It Works

Interpreting a cron table entry can seem cryptic at first. The key is to understand that the first five columns specify a time and frequency, and the sixth column contains OS commands or scripts being executed.

Having said that, the cron utility has a few quirks that need further explanation. For example, the fifth column is the day of the week. Sunday is usually designated by a 0 (with some OSs, Sunday can also be designated by a 7); Monday by a 1; Tuesday by a 2; and so on, to Saturday, which is indicated with a 6.

There also appear to be overlapping columns, such as the third column (day of the month) and the fifth column (day of the week). These columns allow you to create flexible schedules for jobs that have to run on schedules such as the 1st and 15th day of the month, or on a certain day of the week. Put an asterisk in the column that you're not using. For example, to run a backup job on the 1st and 15th (at 4:00 a.m.), do so as follows:

```
0 4 1,15 * * /home/oracle/bin/rmanback.bsh
```

Or if you need a job to run on every Tuesday (at 4:00 a.m.), do so as follows:

```
0 4 * * 2 /home/oracle/bin/rmanback.bsh
```

If you have to run a job on the 1st and 15th and every Tuesday, fill in both columns:

```
0 4 1,15 * 2 /home/oracle/bin/rmanback.bsh
```

## Running a Job Every Minute

Suppose that you want a job to check once per minute to see whether a database server is available. You can do so by putting the following in your cron table (you have to modify the IP address for your server):

```
* * * * * ping 11.214.402.51
```

A * in every column instructs cron to run the command once per minute. If the ping command is successful, nothing happens. If an error is thrown by a command run from cron, cron will by default send an email to the email account of the OS owner of the cron table (see recipe 10-6 for details on how to modify locations where email is sent). This is a simple but effective method for monitoring the availability of a database server.

## Running a Job Every *N* Seconds

The cron utility can be scheduled to run with a granularity as small as minutes. Although you can't schedule a cron at the granularity of seconds, it is possible to creatively run a script from cron every *N* many seconds. For example, suppose that you want to run a script every 30 seconds from cron. You can simulate it as follows:

```
* * * * * /home/oracle/bin/commands.sh
* * * * *  sleep 30; /home/oracle/bin/commands.sh
```

In this manner, you can enable commands or jobs that have to run more frequently than 1 minute. It is probably a rare requirement, but sometimes necessary.

## Using Keywords to Run Jobs

Note that on some of the modern versions of cron, you can specify keywords to indicate a time and frequency for a job to start. For example, the following instructs cron to run a job daily at midnight:

```
@daily /home/oracle/bin/rmanback.bsh
```

Table 10-2 shows the mapping of frequency keywords to the standard syntax.

*Table 10-2. Frequency Keyword and Equivalent Standard Syntax*

| Keyword | Standard Syntax | Translation |
| --- | --- | --- |
| hourly | 0 * * * * | Run at the top of every hour |
| daily | 0 0 * * * | Run daily at midnight |
| weekly | 0 0 * * 0 | Run weekly first day of week at midnight |
| monthly | 0 0 1 * * | Run monthly on the first day of month at midnight |
| yearly | 0 0 1 1 * | Run yearly on first month of the year at midnight |
| reboot | Execute when system reboots | |
| midnight | Same as daily | |
| annually | Same as yearly | |

Specifying a keyword is syntactically easier, but has less flexibility as to what minute, hour, or day the job will execute. Keep in mind that you probably won't have several cron jobs to execute at the same time (overloading the system), so don't overuse keywords such as hourly and daily.

| USING THE AT SCHEDULER |
| --- |

You can use the `at` command to schedule a job to run once at a specified point in the future. Here's an example:

```
$ echo "'go home' | mailx -s 'time to go' dba@gmail.com"  | at 23:00
```

The prior command schedules an `at` job to send an email at 23:00 (11:00 p.m.), reminding the DBA that it is time to go home. You can use the `atq` (at queue) command to verify that the job is scheduled:

```
$ atq
111     2015-06-14 23:00 a oracle
```

If you want to remove the job, use the `-r` option:

```
$ at -r 111
```

In this manner, the `at` scheduler is a simple but effective way to create a scheduled job.

# 10-4. Setting Operating System Variables

## Problem

You have this simple shell script that contains a SQL*Plus command:

```
#!/bin/bash
sqlplus -s <<EOF
system/manager
select username from dba_users;
EOF
```

You notice that a script executes well when you run it manually from the command line:

```
$ sqltest.bsh
USERNAME
--------------------
SYS
SYSTEM
...
```

However, when the script runs from `cron`, it throws errors reporting that commands can't be found:

```
sqlplus: command not found
```

You want to determine the cause of the issue and ensure that the script runs successfully from `cron`.

## Solution

When cron executes a script, it doesn't run the OS user's startup or login files (such as .bashrc or .bash_profile), so the variables set in the startup scripts aren't available when cron executes. When a shell script running from cron can't find a command, it usually means that a required directory path has not been defined. Therefore, any script executed from cron has to explicitly set any required variables such as ORACLE_HOME, ORACLE_SID, and PATH. In this situation, one solution is to set any required variables directly within the shell script. Here's an example:

```
#/bin/bash
export ORACLE_HOME=/u01/app/oracle/product/12.1.0.2/db_1
export ORACLE_SID=O1212
export PATH=$PATH:$ORACLE_HOME/bin
#
sqlplus -s <<EOF
system/foo
select username from dba_users;
EOF
```

In this way, the shell script has the required variables available when it executes from cron.

## How It Works

When running a shell script from cron, you should explicitly define any variables the shell script requires. Don't rely on startup scripts because they will not get executed.

The solution section showed how to directly place the variables within the shell script. In many scenarios, however, DBAs prefer to keep a separate script that contains required variable definitions and execute them from any other shell scripts that require the variables to be set.

An example will demonstrate this. Suppose that you have two shell scripts. The first one, .bash_profile, contains commands to set OS variables:

```
export ORACLE_HOME=/u01/app/oracle/product/12.1.0.2/db_1
export ORACLE_SID=O1212
export PATH=$PATH:$ORACLE_HOME/bin
```

And suppose you also have a shell script named sqltest.bsh that contains the following code:

```
#!/bin/bash
sqlplus -s <<EOF
system/manager
select username from dba_users;
EOF
```

You can instruct cron to first run the script to set the oracle user's environment variables and then run the script containing database commands. You specify multiple scripts separated by a semicolon. Here's an example:

```
0 4 * * * . /home/oracle/.bash_profile; /home/oracle/bin/sqltest.bsh
```

Notice that the first script is run with the dot notation to source the environment variables so that the variables are visible to any subsequent scripts or commands that are executed.

276

# 10-5. Specifying the Execution Shell

## Problem

Suppose that the following script is running from cron:

```
export ORACLE_HOME=/u01/app/oracle/product/12.1.0.2/db_1
export ORACLE_SID=O1212
export PATH=$PATH:$ORACLE_HOME/bin
#
sqlplus -s <<EOF
system/foo
select username from dba_users;
EOF
```

When a cron job executes, the script is throwing an error, saying it can't find the export command:

```
export: Command not found.
```

You want to determine why this standard Bash shell command (export, in this case) isn't functioning properly.

## Solution

A script is run from cron, it will run the script using the default shell defined for a user. Therefore, if your default shell is defined to be the C shell the OS will execute any commands/scripts running from cron using the C shell (unless otherwise noted), so commands unique to the Bash shell will not be interpreted correctly. For example, suppose that the default shell is the C shell; an error is returned when the following Bash shell export command runs because the C shell doesn't have an export command:

```
export ORACLE_SID=O1212
export: Command not found.
```

To work around this, ensure that all scripts specify in the first line which shell should be used to interpret the commands. Here's an example:

```
#!/bin/bash
```

Another method to ensure that the correct shell is used is to specify the shell to execute the script. For example, the following cron entry instructs cron to execute the script using the Bash shell:

```
0 4 * * * /bin/bash /home/oracle/bin/sqltest.bsh
```

On Linux systems, you can also use the cron SHELL variable to instruct cron to run commands within the cron table using a specific shell:

```
SHELL=/bin/bash
0 4 * * * /home/oracle/bin/sqltest.bsh
```

## How It Works

The solution section outlined three techniques to ensure that the correct shell is used when commands or scripts are executed. Any of these methods is fine, and DBAs use all three. The technique used usually boils down to a personal preference or a standard that a group has adopted.

# 10-6. Redirecting `cron` Output

## Problem

You're trying to troubleshoot issues with a `cron` job and want to ensure that you have a log file that captures the output when `cron` executes.

## Solution

You can specify that any output generated by a `cron` entry be redirected to a file. This example writes standard output to a file named `rmanback.log` (for this example to work, the `/home/oracle/bin/log` directory must exist):

```
0 0 * * * /home/oracle/bin/rmanback.bsh >/home/oracle/bin/log/rmanback.log
```

Keep in mind that > is synonymous with 1>, so the following line is equivalent to the prior line:

```
0 0 * * * /home/oracle/bin/rmanback.bsh 1>/home/oracle/bin/log/rmanback.log
```

If you want standard error to be redirected to the same place as standard output, do so as follows:

```
0 0 * * * /home/oracle/bin/rmanback.bsh 1>/home/oracle/bin/log/rmanback.log 2>&1
```

In the previous line, 1> redirects standard output, and 2>&1 specifies that the standard error should go to the same location in which the standard output is located (refer to recipe 2-9 for more details on redirecting output).

If the log file already exists, > instructs the OS to overwrite the file and create a new file. If you want to append to an existing log file, use the >> syntax:

```
0 0 * * * /home/oracle/bin/backup.bsh 1>>/home/oracle/bin/log/bck.log 2>&1
```

This code appends any relevant messages (both regular and error messages) to the existing log file. Sometimes you'll want to append if you have to capture the output from multiple runs of a job. For example, it is hard to troubleshoot something that happened a few days ago if you have a daily job that overwrites the existing log file.

## How It Works

In most scenarios, you should save the output of your `cron` job in a log file, which provides a troubleshooting mechanism when there are issues. In addition to capturing the `cron` job output in a file, you can have the output emailed to you (a unique file name for the log file might be required). These topics are discussed next.

## Mailing Output

If you don't redirect the output for a cron job, any output from the job will be emailed to the user who owns the cron job. On Linux systems, you can override it by specifying the MAILTO variable directly within the cron table. Here's an example:

```
MAILTO=dba@gmail.com
0 0 * * * /home/oracle/bin/rmanback.bsh
```

If you don't want the output to go anywhere, redirect output to the proverbial bit bucket. The following entry sends the standard output and standard error to the /dev/null device:

```
0 0 * * * /home/oracle/bin/rmanback.bsh 1>/dev/null 2>&1
```

Solaris systems do not support the MAILTO feature. To work around it, pipe the cron job to an email address as follows:

```
0 0 * * * /home/oracle/bin/rmanback.bsh | mail -s "backup" dba@gmail.com
```

## Generating Unique Log File Names

If you have to generate a unique name for the log file each time it runs, use the date command. The following generates a unique daily log file name:

```
0 0 * * * /home/oracle/bin/rmanback.bsh
1>/home/oracle/bin/log/rmanback.$(/bin/date +\%Y\%m\%d).log
```

---

■ **Note**  The two preceding lines of code were on one line in the cron table, but didn't fit on this page. The line was broken into two lines (but should be just one line in the cron table). There is no way to split a single cron command line onto multiple lines with the backslash (\) character (as you can do when operating in the shell).

---

The percent (%) character is escaped with the backslash (\) character. The % character has to be escaped; otherwise, cron will interpret % as a newline character, and all code after the first % will be sent to the command as standard input.

You can creatively modify the date command per your requirements. For example, if you want to keep only the last 7 days of log files, specify the date command to return only the day of the week (not the year, month, or day):

```
0 0 * * * /home/oracle/bin/rmanback.bsh 1>/home/oracle/bin/log/rmanback.$(/bin/date +\%u).log
```

The date +%u command will return an integer 0 through 6, depending on the day of the week. After 7 days, you'll end up with 7 log files: rmanback.0.log through rmanback.6.log. As each new week rolls around, the old log files will be overwritten.

---

## ATTACHING FILES TO AN EMAIL

If you're working with a log file or binary file that you want sent as an attachment (not as the message body), use the `uuencode` command or the `mutt` utility to accomplish this task. The basic syntax for `uuencode` is as follows:

```
uuencode [INFILE] REMOTEFILE
```

For example, to attach a file named `prodAWR.html` to an email, do so as follows:

```
$ uuencode prodAWR.html prodAWR.html | mail -s "prod AWR report" dba@gmail.com
```

You may be thinking that you could just send the email like this:

```
$ mail -s "prod AWR report" dba@gmail.com <prodAWR.html
```

You can do so if the output contains only ASCII text. If the file isn't an ASCII file, however, the output will not be interpreted as an attachment and will arrive as indecipherable text. In this situation, you must attach the file to the email so that it won't be interpreted as the message body.

If available, you can also use the `mutt` utility to attach files to email. Here's an example:

```
$ echo "AWR rpt" | mutt -a "/home/oracle/prodAWR.html" -s "AWR rpt" -- dba@gmail.com
```

In this way, you can attach files (log files, binary files, backup files, and so on) to an email.

---

# 10-7. Embedding Conditional Logic

## Problem

You want to automate a job that checks for a condition.

## Solution

The solution is to realize that you can use standard Bash shell operators directly from within cron. For example, to test whether the output from the ps command returned a value, use the && or || operators (refer to Chapter 7 for details on conditional operators).

Here's a sample cron entry that will check once per hour for a background process (smon in this situation); if the background process isn't running, an email is sent:

```
01 * * * * ps -ef | grep smon>/dev/null || echo "problem" | mailx -s "issue" dba@gmail.com
```

In the preceding line of code, the || operator is interpreted this way: "If the command to the left of the || operator is not successful (ps does not return a value), run the code to the right of the || operator."

Suppose that you want an automated job to run once per hour to check for the existence of an error file, and to send an email if it exists. You can do so as follows:

```
01 * * * * [ -f /home/oracle/err.txt ] && mailx -s "exists" dba@gmail.com </home/oracle/err.txt
```

In the prior line of code, the && is interpreted as follows: "If the command to the left of the && operator is successful (the file exists), run the code to the right of the && operator."

DBAs and SAs use `test` instead of `[ ]` to accomplish the same task. The following line of code is equivalent to the prior line of code:

```
01 * * * * test -f /home/oracle/err.txt && mailx -s "exists" dba@gmail.com
</home/oracle/err.txt
```

In this manner, you can automate tasks depending on a condition existing (or not).

# How It Works

Once you understand that you can use standard Bash shell features directly from within `cron`, you can creatively schedule jobs as required in your environment. To that point, it's worth repeating this example from Chapter 7:

```
33 * * * * ps -ef | grep dbwatch | grep -v grep || nohup /home/oracle/bin/dbwatch.bsh &
```

The prior line of code checks for the existence of a process; if it isn't present, the job is restarted in the background.

You can separate commands within `cron` by using a semicolon, and you can also execute code in a subshell by enclosing it in parentheses. For example, at 2 minutes after the top of the hour, execute the following:

```
02 * * * * cd /home/oracle/err ; (tail -100 err.txt) | grep ORA-00600 && echo "found error"
```

---

■ **Caution** Don't embed overly complex logic into a `cron` table; it makes the logic hard to understand and results in less-maintainable code. If you find the logic is getting complicated, put the code into a shell script and execute the script instead.

---

Table 10-3 summarizes special shell features that are often used to embed logic into `cron` jobs.

*Table 10-3. Shell Operators and Meanings*

| Operator | Meaning |
|---|---|
| & | Run the command in the background. |
| ; | Run the command to the left of ; and run the command to the right of ; (e.g., separate the two commands). |
| && | If command to the left of && is successful, run the command to the right of &&. |
| \|\| | If the command to the left of \|\| fails, run the command to the right of \|\|. |
| ( ) | Execute the command within the parentheses in a subshell. |
| [ ] | Test a condition (can also use the `test` command). |

# 10-8. Troubleshooting `cron`

## Problem

Your `cron` job doesn't appear to be running. You want to do some troubleshooting to determine the cause of the issue.

## Solution

If you have a `cron` job that isn't running correctly, follow these steps to troubleshoot the issue:

1. Copy your `cron` entry, paste it to the OS command line, and manually run the command. A small typo in a directory or file name can often be the source of the problem. Manually running the command highlights errors like these.

2. If the script runs Oracle utilities, ensure that you source (set) the required OS variables within the script (such as ORACLE_HOME, ORACLE_SID, and PATH). These variables are often set by startup scripts (such as HOME/.bashrc) when you log on. Because `cron` doesn't run a user's startup scripts, any required variables must be set explicitly within the script.

3. Ensure that the first line of any shell scripts invoked from `cron` specifies the name of the program that will be used to interpret the commands within the script. For example, #!/bin/bash should be the first entry in a Bash shell script. Because `cron` doesn't run a user's startup scripts (such as HOME/.bashrc), you can't assume that your OS user's default shell will be used to run a command or script evoked from `cron`.

4. If you execute a script, check the permissions on the script file and ensure that it is set to executable for the user running the script.

5. Ensure that the `cron` background process or service is running.

6. Check your email on the server. The `cron` utility will usually send an email to the OS account when there are issues with a misbehaving `cron` job.

7. Inspect the contents of the /var/log/cron file for any errors. Sometimes this file has relevant information regarding a `cron` job that has failed to run.

We've found that any issues with `cron` are usually related to one of the previously listed items. The prior list is a good place to start when experiencing chronic issues.

## How It Works

Troubleshooting `cron` is necessary when the job doesn't execute as expected, which often can be due to environment variables not being set. If you want to explicitly view the environment settings as `cron` is using them, put this line in your `cron` table:

```
* * * * * env > /tmp/env.txt
```

After the command executes and populates the env.txt file, remove the line from the `cron` table. The env.txt file will show the environment variables and values that `cron` is using. In this manner, you can quickly determine what `cron` is using for variables such as PATH and HOME; they may not be what you were expecting. Therefore, it is always better to explicitly set any required variables.

Additionally, cron will execute commands using the default shell of the OS user that owns the cron table. This means if your default shell is the C shell, any commands exclusive to the Bash shell will not be correctly interpreted when running a cron job. As a best practice, explicitly instruct cron which shell to use when executing commands and scripts.

If you suspect that something is wrong with the cron service or background daemon, you can verify that it is working via the wall (write all users) command by adding this entry to your cron table:

```
* * * * * wall "cron is working"
```

If all is well, all users logged on to the server will see a message at the top of the minute, indicating that cron is working. Because all users logged on to the server will see the message, remember to remove this cron entry as soon as you're done testing. If you don't want to send the message to all users, use the write command with a specified terminal (use the who command to list logged-in users and terminal information).

## ORACLE SCHEDULER VERSUS CRON

Oracle Scheduler is a tool that provides a way to automate job scheduling. Implemented via the DBMS_SCHEDULER internal PL/SQL package, Oracle Scheduler offers a sophisticated set of features for scheduling jobs. There are currently more than 70 procedures and functions available within the DBMS_SCHEDULER package.

You may be wondering whether to use Oracle Scheduler or the Linux/Solaris cron utility for scheduling and automating tasks. Here are some of the benefits that Oracle Scheduler has over cron:

- Makes the execution of a job dependent on the completion of another job

- Robust resource balancing and flexible scheduling features

- Runs jobs based on an event (such as the completion of another job)

- DBMS_SCHEDULER PL/SQL package syntax works the same, regardless of the OS

- Runs status reports using the data dictionary

- In a clustered environment, no need to worry about synchronizing multiple cron tables for each node in the cluster

- Is implemented, maintained, and monitored via Enterprise Manager

Regardless of Oracle Scheduler's benefits, many DBAs prefer to use a scheduling utility such as cron. Here are some of the advantages of cron:

- Easy to use; simple, tried and true; takes only seconds to create or modify jobs

- Almost universally available on all Linux/Solaris boxes; for the most part, runs nearly identically, regardless of the Linux/Solaris platform (yes, there are minor differences)

- Database agnostic; operates independently of the database and works the same way regardless of the database vendor or version

- Works even when the database is not available

These lists aren't comprehensive, but they give you an idea of the uses of each scheduling tool. If you require something more sophisticated than cron, consider using Oracle Scheduler. Note that cron and Oracle Scheduler aren't mutually exclusive; for a given task, use whichever tool meets your requirements.

■ ■ ■

# CHAPTER 11

# Managing Server Software

Fortune 500 companies have embraced Oracle and Red Hat Enterprise Linux, and Linux has become a dominant force in the server industry. More and more Fortune 500 companies have adopted Linux as a corporate standard. With Oracle's presence over the server space with its engineered systems, Linux has become a norm for DBAs. In the world of engineered systems and virtualized infrastructures, DBAs often perform or share system administration responsibilities. The greatest Real Application Cluster (RAC) DBAs know Linux intimately and know the best practices for tuning it. For larger companies, a true delineation of roles and responsibilities still exists. This chapter is for DBAs who perform software management roles in the Linux world—in particular, Red Hat and Oracle Enterprise Linux (Oracle Linux).

This chapter takes a bare-bones Red Hat Enterprise Linux installation and registers the Red Hat server to Oracle's Unbreakable Linux Network, leverages Oracle's RDBMS PreInstall RPM for Oracle Database 11g Release 2 and Oracle Database 12c to preconfigure a Linux server for Oracle installation, performs a silent installation of Oracle Database *11g/12c* software, clones a fully patched Oracle installation, performs a silent database creation, and completes the server build by setting up a silent network configuration. Silent mode installations are the foundations of creating an automated server installation procedure.

This chapter demonstrates how to install RPMs, switch to Oracle's Unbreakable Linux Network from the Red Hat Network, list the contents of an RPM package, correlate OS executables to RPMs, download RPMs, automate with Oracle's validated install, and remove RPMs.

The database software management portion of this chapter concentrates exclusively on silent installations. While learning how to set up a database server from a soup-to-nuts implementation, you'll also learn about RPM and YUM package management.

## 11-1. Installing Packages
### Problem

You want to install software components on the Linux server.

### Solution #1

By far the easiest way to manage software on the Linux server is with the yum command, as shown in this example:

```
# yum install screen -y
Loaded plugins: product-id, subscription-manager
This system is not registered to Red Hat Subscription Management. You can use
subscription-manager to register.
Setting up Install Process
```

```
Resolving Dependencies
--> Running transaction check
---> Package screen.x86_64 0:4.0.3-16.el6 will be installed
--> Finished Dependency Resolution

Dependencies Resolved

================================================================================
 Package          Arch         Version                 Repository          Size
================================================================================
Installing:
 screen           x86_64       4.0.3-16.el6            viscosity          494 k

Transaction Summary
================================================================================
Install      1 Package(s)

Total download size: 494 k
Installed size: 795 k
Downloading Packages:
Running rpm_check_debug
Running Transaction Test
Transaction Test Succeeded
Running Transaction
  Installing : screen-4.0.3-16.el6.x86_64                                    1/1
  Verifying  : screen-4.0.3-16.el6.x86_64                                    1/1

Installed:
  screen.x86_64 0:4.0.3-16.el6

Complete!
```

## Solution #2

Another way to manage software on the Linux server is by executing the rpm command with the -i option (or --install) to install the package.

Here's an example of installing the screen executable:

```
# rpm -ihv screen-4.0.3-1.el5.i386.rpm
Preparing...                    ######################################### [100%]
   1:screen                     ######################################### [100%]
```

The -h option displays hash marks during the installation. The -v option provides verbose output that reports the progress of the installation. The rpm executable can install packages from the local filesystem, CD, or remote server accessible by HTTP or FTP.

## How It Works

Yellowdog Updater, Modified (YUM) is a command-line, open-source package management utility for Linux dependent on the RPM Package Manager. YUM is a modified version of the original update command developed for Yellow Dog Linux that relies heavily on package headers. On the header of each package, forward and reverse dependency information is available for installation and rollback of the package. With this information in databases known as repositories, YUM can simplify package installation by determining other packages required to satisfy dependencies.

In a nutshell, RPM is a package management system. *RPM* originally stood for Red Hat Package Manager because it was designed by Red Hat for Red Hat distributions. Because RPM was intended for Linux distributions and used by many Linux distributions, RPM now stands for *RPM Package Manager*. The RPM system is composed of a local database, the rpm executable, and the RPM package files. The local RPM database, which is stored in the /var/lib/rpm directory, houses metadata information about installed packages, including package prerequisites and file attributes. Because the local RPM database tracks all the packages and file attributes, removing a package becomes a relatively simple operation.

The RPM package file is composed of compressed archive files and dependency information. The package name or label contains the following attributes:

```
<name>-<version>-<release>.<architecture>.rpm
```

Here's an example of the package label:

```
unixODBC-2.2.11-7.1.i386.rpm
```

The unixODBC RPM is a required RPM for Oracle Database 11g. For this example, the RPM version is 2.2.11, and the release of the RPM is 7.1. This particular RPM is designed for a 32-bit Intel IA32 (x86) CPU. The AMD64/Intel em64t RPM has the architecture name x86_64.

RPMs that contain source code show .src before the .rpm suffix. Although you might not find binary RPMs associated with your architecture and flavor of Linux, an equivalent source code RPM may be available for another type of Linux. You can download the source and compile the RPM.

Notice that certain RPMs have the .noarch extension in the file names to denote that the RPM doesn't have a dependency on your system's architecture.

---

■ **Note**    Starting in Red Hat Enterprise Linux (RHEL) 5 and Oracle Linux (OL) 5, YUM has become the de facto standard for most companies when it comes to installing software on Linux servers. Starting with RHEL 5/OL and higher, up2date is no longer the tool of choice.

---

# 11-2. Switching to the Oracle Unbreakable Linux Network
## Problem

You installed RHEL 6 or 7, but want to leverage Oracle's Unbreakable Linux Network (ULN). You want to start performing updates from ULN instead of Red Hat Network (RHN).

## Solution

Before you can start taking advantage of ULN, you must download and upgrade to the new version of the up2date and up2date-gnome packages from https://linux.oracle.com/switch.html for your version of Red Hat and server architecture. In addition, you must have a valid CSI and license for Oracle Linux (OL).

You can download the files from the `http://linux-update.oracle.com/rpms/` web site. For Red Hat Linux 7 64-bit architecture, download two files: `uln_register_ol7.tgz` and `uln_register-gnome_ol7.tgz`. For Red Hat Linux 6 (both 32-bit and 64-bit architectures), download two files: `uln_register.tgz` and `uln_register-gnome.tgz`. For updates to switching instructions, please review the steps from the Oracle web site: `https://linux.oracle.com/switch.html`.

## Installing Oracle up2date for Older Releases

Once you download the up2date and up2date-gnome packages, you can upgrade the existing packages as the root user on your Red Hat system using the `rpm -Uhv` command, as shown here:

```
# rpm -Uhv up2date-5.10.1-40.8.el5.i386.rpm \
                              up2date-gnome-5.10.1-40.8.el5.i386.rpm
warning: up2date-5.10.1-40.8.el5.i386.rpm: Header V3 DSA signature: NOKEY, key ID
1e5e0159
Preparing...                ########################################### [100%]
   1:up2date                ########################################### [ 50%]
   2:up2date-gnome          ########################################### [100%]
```

If you don't have up2date-gnome installed, you can exclude that RPM. If you're running on OS versions prior to Red Hat Linux (RHEL) 6, you must import Oracle's GPG keys by executing the `import` option:

```
rpm --import /usr/share/rhn/RPM-GPG-KEY
```

## Registering with ULN

Now you are ready to register the Red Hat server with ULN. Once you register the Red Hat server, you can start using the up2date command to automatically download and install/upgrade packages on the Linux server. The single greatest feature of up2date is that all the dependencies are automatically resolved without the administrator's intervention.

The biggest frustration with RPM management is dealing with a colloquialism referred to as *dependency hell*. For example, suppose that RPM X has a dependency on RPMs A, B, and C. RPM B has another dependency on L, M, and N. Not realizing the RPM dependencies, when you try to install RPM N, you encounter another dependency for RPM N that requires RPMs H and I. You simply want to install RPM X, but you stumble into a multitude of other RPM requirements, and the dependency requirements stack on top of each other. You'll encounter situations in which up2date can significantly simplify the management of a Linux server.

To start the registration process if you are on RHEL 3, RHEL 4, or RHEL 5, you can execute the following command:

```
up2date --register
```

You can execute the command `up2date --register --nox` to launch up2date in non-GUI mode. Without the `--nox` option, your `DISPLAY` parameter must be set to a valid X server or the VNC server. Initially, you'll see the Welcome to ULN Update Agent screen. Click the Forward button to be directed to the ULN Login screen. Because this is the first time you are logging in to up2date, you must provide all the credentials onscreen, including a login ID, a password (twice for verification), and a licensed CSI number.

For RHEL 6 and RHEL 7, execute the `uln_register` command to switch from RHN to ULN. Carefully follow the onscreen instructions and enter the requested information. The `uln_register` process also collects machine information and uploads it to the Oracle server. System should be subscribed to the latest OL 7 channel on ULN to perform the YUM update in the case of RHEL 7.

## How It Works

Switching from RHN to Oracle's ULN is straightforward. Once you purchase a license of OL, you can start receiving support from Oracle Support instead of Red Hat. You can start to receive support from a single front end for both the OS and the database from Oracle Support.

Once you have successfully registered your Red Hat server with ULN, you can access the ULN portal via https://linux.oracle.com. In the Login and Password fields, you can provide the login and password credentials that you supplied while registering your Red Hat server.

Whether you are on OL or RHEL, you can leverage Oracle's public YUM server for package management. Everyone knows that if you are on OL, you can take advantage of Oracle's public YUM server for Oracle RDBMS PreInstall RPMs. However, few realize that even Red Hat customers can take advantage of Oracle's public YUM server. To configure the Red Hat for Oracle public YUM server, first download the repository configuration file. Repositories are set up in the /etc/yum.repos.d directories. You can set up more than one YUM repository for a Linux server.

To obtain a listing of available repositories for your server, execute the yum command with the `repolist` argument:

```
# yum repolist
```

Because you're working with RHEL 6.6, download Oracle's public YUM repository configuration files for OL 6 and place the file in the /etc/yum.repos.d directory:

```
# wget http://public-yum.oracle.com/public-yum-ol6.repo
--2015-05-18 15:26:52--  http://public-yum.oracle.com/public-yum-ol6.repo
Resolving public-yum.oracle.com... 67.200.133.11, 67.200.133.9
Connecting to public-yum.oracle.com|67.200.133.11|:80... connected.
HTTP request sent, awaiting response... 200 OK
Length: 5046 (4.9K) [text/plain]
Saving to: "public-yum-ol6.repo"

100%[===================================================================================>]
5,046       --.-K/s   in 0.002s

2015-05-18 15:26:52 (2.16 MB/s) - "public-yum-ol6.repo" saved [5046/5046]
```

You have to download the OL GPG key with the same wget command and place the file in the /etc/pki/rpm-gpg directory:

```
wget http://public-yum.oracle.com/RPM-GPG-KEY-oracle-ol6 -O /etc/pki/rpm-gpg/
RPM-GPG-KEY-oracle
```

If you don't download this GPG key, you'll encounter the following error during any kind of YUM package maintenance:

```
GPG key retrieval failed: [Errno 14] Could not open/read file:///etc/pki/rpm-gpg/
RPM-GPG-KEY-oracle
```

Once you download the Oracle GPG key, you can verify the GPG key with the gpg command. A public key fingerprint is a short sequence of bytes used to authenticate a longer public key. You create fingerprints by applying a cryptographic hash function to a public key. With the –with-fingerprint parameter, you can verify the fingerprint associated with the GPG key:

```
# gpg --quiet --with-fingerprint /etc/pki/rpm-gpg/RPM-GPG-KEY-oracle
pub  2048R/EC551F03 2010-07-01 Oracle OSS group (Open Source Software group) <build@oss.
oracle.com>
      Key fingerprint = 4214 4123 FECF C55B 9086  313D 72F9 7B74 EC55 1F03
```

---

■ **Note**    Another advantage of registering a server with Oracle's ULN or leveraging the public YUM server is that you can execute up2date or yum to download and install ASM-related RPMs. You don't have to investigate which ASM-specific RPMs have to be downloaded based on the kernel level of your Linux server; yum automatically determines which packages need to be downloaded for you.

---

# 11-3. Associating Linux Files with RPM Packages
## Problem

One of the servers has an executable you need, but another server doesn't. You want to identify the RPM package to install on the server.

## Solution #1

Look at the yum provides command with the fully qualified path to the pkill executable to see which RPM delivers the executable:

```
$ yum provides /usr/bin/pkill
Loaded plugins: downloadonly
procps-3.2.8-21.el6.x86_64 : System and process monitoring utilities
Repo        : public_ol6_latest
Matched from:
Filename    : /usr/bin/pkill
...
...
```

## Solution #2

Look for the gedit executable, but this time by passing the –qf parameters to the rpm command:

```
[root@rac5 bin]# rpm -qf /usr/bin/gedit
gedit-2.16.0-5.el5
```

The -qf option also works for shared objects. If you happen to be curious about which package the libc.so file came from, you can issue the -qf option, as demonstrated here:

```
[root@rac5 lib]# rpm -qf libc.so
glibc-devel-2.5-18
```

## How It Works

The yum command has the provides option, which returns the package name if you specify the path of the executable or shared library. The provides option also accepts a wildcard parameter (*) for the path enclosed by double quotes, as shown here:

```
# yum provides "*bin/gedit"
Loaded plugins: downloadonly
public_ol6_UEKR3_latest/filelists
| 8.2 MB      00:21
1:gedit-2.28.4-3.el6.x86_64 : Text editor for the GNOME desktop
Repo         : public_ol6_latest
Matched from:
Filename     : /usr/bin/gedit
```

rpm provides features to query the RPM database to extract the owning package. You can correlate an executable or library from the OS to an RPM. You can execute rpm with the -qf (-q for -query and -f for -file) option to determine which RPMs are associated with a specified file or executable.

# 11-4. Listing the Contents of an RPM Package
## Problem

You want to look inside the .rpm file to view the contents of the package and peek at the destination in which the files will be extracted.

## Solution #1

The repoquery executable provides the capability to view the destination location of files for a package. The repoquery comes with the yum-utils RPM and has to be installed with yum:

```
# yum install yum-utils
```

Once the yum-utils package is installed, leverage the repoquery executable with the –l option (or –listing option) against the screen rpm:

```
# repoquery -l screen
/etc/pam.d/screen
/etc/screenrc
/usr/bin/screen
/usr/share/doc/screen-4.0.3
/usr/share/doc/screen-4.0.3/COPYING
/usr/share/doc/screen-4.0.3/FAQ
/usr/share/doc/screen-4.0.3/NEWS
```

```
/usr/share/doc/screen-4.0.3/README
/usr/share/doc/screen-4.0.3/README.DOTSCREEN
/usr/share/info/screen.info.gz
/usr/share/man/man1/screen.1.gz
/usr/share/screen
/usr/share/screen/utf8encodings
/usr/share/screen/utf8encodings/01
/usr/share/screen/utf8encodings/02
/usr/share/screen/utf8encodings/03
/usr/share/screen/utf8encodings/04
/usr/share/screen/utf8encodings/18
/usr/share/screen/utf8encodings/19
/usr/share/screen/utf8encodings/a1
/usr/share/screen/utf8encodings/bf
/usr/share/screen/utf8encodings/c2
/usr/share/screen/utf8encodings/c3
/usr/share/screen/utf8encodings/c4
/usr/share/screen/utf8encodings/c6
/usr/share/screen/utf8encodings/c7
/usr/share/screen/utf8encodings/c8
/usr/share/screen/utf8encodings/cc
/usr/share/screen/utf8encodings/cd
/usr/share/screen/utf8encodings/d6
/var/run/screen
```

## Solution #2

You can execute rpm with the -qlp option to list the destination location for files in a package. Here's an example in which the contents of the openmotif21 RPM are examined with HTTP:

```
[root@rac5 up2date]# rpm -qlp http://dbaexpert.com/rpms/openmotif21-2.1.30-
11.RHEL4.6.i386.rpm
warning: http://dbaexpert.com/rpms/openmotif21-2.1.30-11.RHEL4.6.i386.rpm: Header
V3 DSA signature: NOKEY, key ID b38a8516
/usr/X11R6/lib/libMrm.so.2
/usr/X11R6/lib/libMrm.so.2.1
/usr/X11R6/lib/libUil.so.2
/usr/X11R6/lib/libUil.so.2.1
/usr/X11R6/lib/libXm.so.2
/usr/X11R6/lib/libXm.so.2.1
/usr/share/doc/openmotif21-2.1.30
/usr/share/doc/openmotif21-2.1.30/COPYRIGHT.MOTIF
/usr/share/doc/openmotif21-2.1.30/README
/usr/share/doc/openmotif21-2.1.30/RELEASE
/usr/share/doc/openmotif21-2.1.30/RELNOTES
```

As mentioned in Recipe 11-1, you can execute the previous rpm command against a file on the local filesystem, CD, or remote server with HTTP or FTP access.

# How It Works

You can use the repoquery command to list package contents. It will work with installed packages as well as packages not yet installed. The repoquery has numerous options. The -l option lists files in the package in question. The -i option (--info) lists descriptive information from the package.

Here's an example using the -i option to obtain informative description about the screen package:

```
# repoquery -i screen

Name         : screen
Version      : 4.0.3
Release      : 16.el6
Architecture : x86_64
Size         : 814092
Packager     : None
Group        : Applications/System
URL          : http://www.gnu.org/software/screen
Repository   : public_ol6_latest
Summary      : A screen manager that supports multiple logins on one terminal
Source       : screen-4.0.3-16.el6.src.rpm
Description :
The screen utility allows you to have multiple logins on just one
terminal. Screen is useful for users who telnet into a machine or are
connected via a dumb terminal, but want to use more than just one
login.

Install the screen package if you need a screen manager that can
support multiple logins on one terminal.
```

The rpm command has a myriad of options, and the -p option allows you to view information directly from the package. The two commonly executed options with -p are -qip and -qlp. The -qlp option lists all the files that make up the package.

The -qip option provides detailed information about the package. Here, the same command is executing as previously, except with the -qip option:

```
# rpm -qip http://dbaexpert.com/rpms/openmotif21-2.1.30-
11.RHEL4.6.i386.rpm
warning: http://dbaexpert.com/rpms/openmotif21-2.1.30-11.RHEL4.6.i386.rpm: Header
V3 DSA signature: NOKEY, key ID b38a8516
Name         : openmotif21              Relocations: /usr/X11R6
Version      : 2.1.30                        Vendor: (none)
Release      : 11.RHEL4.6               Build Date: Sat 07 Oct 2006 08:45:00
AM CDT
Install Date: (not installed)          Build Host: ca-build10.us.oracle.com
Group        : System Environment/Libraries   Source RPM: openmotif21-2.1.30-
11.RHEL4.6.src.rpm
Size         : 2249149                    License: Open Group Public License
Signature    : DSA/SHA1, Mon 09 Oct 2006 08:24:28 PM CDT, Key ID 2e2bcdbcb38a8516
URL          : http://www.opengroup.org/openmotif/
Summary      : Compatibility libraries for Open Motif 2.1.
Description :
This package contains the compatibility libraries for running Open Motif 2.1
applications.
```

Notice that the -qip option provides additional details about the packages, such as when the package was built, from which machines, the source RPM, the size, the signature, and even a description of what the package is about. You can also combine these options as -qlip, which shows both detailed information about the package and the list of all files in the package.

# 11-5. Downloading Packages

## Problem

You want to download RPMs from the Linux terminal.

## Solution

By installing a package called yum-plugin-downloadonly on RHEL 6, you can start downloading RPMs:

```
# yum install yum-plugin-downloadonly
```

After installing the yum-plugin-downloadonly package, you can execute the yum command as if you were actually installing the software, but provide it two additional parameters: --downloadonly and --downloaddir. Here's the syntax to download the screen package to the /tmp directory:

```
[root@ika82 ~]# yum install --downloadonly --downloaddir=/tmp screen
Loaded plugins: downloadonly
Setting up Install Process
Resolving Dependencies
--> Running transaction check
---> Package screen.x86_64 0:4.0.3-16.el6 will be installed
--> Finished Dependency Resolution

Dependencies Resolved

================================================================================
 Package         Arch         Version        Repository                   Size
================================================================================
Installing:      screen       x86_64         4.0.3-16.el6   public_ol6_latest   494 k

Transaction Summary
================================================================================
Install      1 Package(s)

Total download size: 494 k
Installed size: 795 k
Is this ok [y/N]: y
Downloading Packages:
screen-4.0.3-16.el6.x86_64.rpm                               | 494 kB     00:01

exiting because --downloadonly specified
```

You can confirm that the screen package successfully downloaded the screen RPMs to the /tmp directory by performing a directory listing:

```
[root@ika82 ~]# ls -ltr /tmp/*.rpm
-rw-r--r--. 1 root root 505732 Apr 22  2011 /tmp/screen-4.0.3-16.el6.x86_64.rpm
```

## How It Works

By default, the yum-plugin-downloadonly RPM is not installed; you have to install the RPM manually. The greatest benefit of downloading the RPMs with yum is that all dependent packages are automatically downloaded together. For example, the perl RPM has many dependent packages, and all the perl and dependent RPMS can be downloaded with a single command.

# 11-6. Automating Server Builds with Oracle RDBMS Server PreInstall RPM
## Problem

You don't want to spend time researching RPM requirements to install Oracle Database 11g/12c. You want to take advantage of Oracle's preconfigured validated installation process.

## Solution

If you are running on OL or RHEL (a rebuild from the source RPM is required), you can fully leverage Oracle's automated preinstallation processes. Oracle's validated install automates the download of all the required RPMs; the installation of RPMs, including dependency requirements; the setup of the Linux kernel parameters; the creation of the oracle user in the /etc/passwd file; and the creation of entries in the /etc/group file for dba and oinstall. You simply execute the yum command with the following options:

```
# yum install oracle-rdbms-server-12cR1-preinstall
...
...
Transaction Summary
================================================================================
Install      13 Package(s)

Total download size: 7.5 M
Installed size: 23 M
Is this ok [y/N]: y
Downloading Packages:
(1/13): compat-libcap1-1.10-1.x86_64.rpm                      |  17 kB     00:00
...
(13/13): xorg-x11-xauth-1.0.2-7.1.el6.x86_64.rpm              |  34 kB     00:00
--------------------------------------------------------------------------------
Total                                            1.7 MB/s | 7.5 MB     00:04
```

```
..
Running Transaction
  Installing : libstdc++-devel-4.4.7-11.el6.x86_64                          1/13
..
  Installing : oracle-rdbms-server-12cR1-preinstall-1.0-13.el6.x86_64      13/13
  Verifying  : compat-libcap1-1.10-1.x86_64                                 1/13
..
  Verifying  : libXmu-1.1.1-2.el6.x86_64                                   13/13

Installed:
  oracle-rdbms-server-12cR1-preinstall.x86_64 0:1.0-13.el6

Dependency Installed:
  compat-libcap1.x86_64 0:1.10-1          compat-libstdc++-33.x86_64 0:3.2.3-69.el6
  gcc-c++.x86_64 0:4.4.7-11.el6
  ksh.x86_64 0:20120801-21.el6_6.3        libXmu.x86_64 0:1.1.1-2.el6
  libXxf86dga.x86_64 0:1.1.4-2.1.el6
  libXxf86misc.x86_64 0:1.0.3-4.el6       libaio-devel.x86_64 0:0.3.107-10.el6
  libdmx.x86_64 0:1.1.3-3.el6
  libstdc++-devel.x86_64 0:4.4.7-11.el6 xorg-x11-utils.x86_64 0:7.5-6.el6
  xorg-x11-xauth.x86_64 1:1.0.2-7.1.el6

Complete!
```

The output for this RPM installation spans pages of output. For the complete output, visit the following URL: http://www.dbaexpert.com/blog/oracle-rdbms-server-12cr1-preinstall/. For Linux servers that house Oracle Database 11g Release 2 on RHEL (a recompile from the source RPM is required) or OL, you should leverage the oracle-rdbms-server-11gR2-preinstall RPM:

```
# yum install oracle-rdbms-server-11gR2-preinstall
```

Starting from Oracle Database 11g Release 2, you no longer use the Oracle-validated install; leverage the new oracle-rdbms-server-11gR2-preinstall instead. The Oracle 12c RDBMS PreInstall RPM also modifies the kernel parameters in the /etc/sysctl.conf kernel configuration file. The following entries are added:

```
# oracle-rdbms-server-12cR1-preinstall setting for fs.file-max is 6815744
fs.file-max = 6815744

# oracle-rdbms-server-12cR1-preinstall setting for kernel.sem is '250 32000 100 128'
kernel.sem = 250 32000 100 128

# oracle-rdbms-server-12cR1-preinstall setting for kernel.shmmni is 4096
kernel.shmmni = 4096

# oracle-rdbms-server-12cR1-preinstall setting for kernel.shmall is 1073741824 on x86_64

# oracle-rdbms-server-12cR1-preinstall setting for kernel.shmmax is 4398046511104 on x86_64
kernel.shmmax = 4398046511104
```

```
# oracle-rdbms-server-12cR1-preinstall setting for kernel.panic_on_oops is 1 per Orabug
19642132
kernel.panic_on_oops = 1

# oracle-rdbms-server-12cR1-preinstall setting for net.core.rmem_default is 262144
net.core.rmem_default = 262144

# oracle-rdbms-server-12cR1-preinstall setting for net.core.rmem_max is 4194304
net.core.rmem_max = 4194304

# oracle-rdbms-server-12cR1-preinstall setting for net.core.wmem_default is 262144
net.core.wmem_default = 262144

# oracle-rdbms-server-12cR1-preinstall setting for net.core.wmem_max is 1048576
net.core.wmem_max = 1048576

# oracle-rdbms-server-12cR1-preinstall setting for fs.aio-max-nr is 1048576
fs.aio-max-nr = 1048576

# oracle-rdbms-server-12cR1-preinstall setting for net.ipv4.ip_local_port_range is 9000
65500
net.ipv4.ip_local_port_range = 9000 65500
```

In addition, the preinstall RPM process adjusts the /etc/passwd file to include the oracle user and creates the /home/oracle directory:

```
oracle:x:54321:54321::/home/oracle:/bin/bash
```

Furthermore, entries for dba and oinstall are added to the /etc/group file:

```
oinstall:x:54321:
dba:x:54322:oracle
```

## How It Works

After Linux is installed and the system is released to the DBAs, you have to quickly configure the Linux server for database software provisioning. If the server is installed with OL 6, you can leverage the oracle-rdbms-server-12cR1-preinstall RPM directly from the public YUM repository. Many DBAs don't realize that the Oracle RDBMS 11g/12c PreInstall RPM installation option exists. With the oracle-rdbms-server-12cR1-preinstall RPM, you can install required packages required by the Oracle Universal Installer with a single command. Executing the command can prepare a majority of your Linux server requirements to install Oracle Database Server, such as the following:

- The user oracle and the groups oinstall (software owner) and dba (for OSDBA), which are used during database installation, are created
- Kernel parameters are modified in /etc/sysctl.conf for shared memory such as semaphores, the maximum number of file descriptors, and so on

- Settings for hard and soft shell resource limits are made in `./etc/security/limits.conf` such as the locked-in memory address space, the number of open files, the number of processes, and core file size

- Non-Uniform Memory Access (NUMA) and Transparent Huge Pages (THP) are also disabled in the `/etc/grub.conf` configuration file

---

■ **Note**    For detailed information about NUMA, THP, and kernel parameters, please see Chapter 13.

---

Having Oracle RDBMS Server PreInstall RPM for OL is one the biggest benefits of adopting OL from RHEL or other Linux distributions. With a single command, you can preconfigure the OL environment for OEM 12c Agent, EBS R12, and Oracle Database 11gR2/12c installations. Not only does Oracle configure the Linux environment but many of the best practices are also incorporated in the process.

For Oracle RDBMS Server PreInstall RPMs for Oracle Database 11g Release 2 and Oracle Database 12c Release 1, you can download them from the latest channel of the `public-yum` repository: `http://public-yum.oracle.com/repo/OracleLinux/OL6/latest/x86_64/`. You have to scroll down quite a bit; the RPMs that start with capital letters are listed above RPMs that have lowercase letters.

You can also download PreInstall RPMs for Oracle EBS R12 and OEM Agent 12c from the addons channel from the `public-yum` repository. Oracle provides a separate RPM for each release of OEM 12c. Please visit the following URL for the latest versions of `oracle-ebs-server-R12-preinstall-1.0-7.el6.x86_64.rpm` and `oracle-em-agent-12cR4-preinstall-1.0-7.el6.x86_64.rpm` RPMs: `http://public-yum.oracle.com/repo/OracleLinux/OL6/addons/x86_64/`.

Lots of DBAs aren't aware that Oracle also provides the source RPMs for each of the preinstall RPMs. For example, you can download the source RPM for the `oracle-rdbms-server-12cR1-preinstall.rpm` file. The file will be called `oracle-rdbms-server-12cR1-preinstall.src.rpm` and will exist in the same URL location as other RPMS.

---

■ **Note**    For step-by-step instructions on taking an OL source RPM and rebuilding it for RHEL, download the following white paper: `http://www.dbaexpert.com/blog/collaborate-2014-extreme-oracle-db-infrastructure-as-a-service-paper/`. This white paper goes through the process of performing an installation with the `oracle-rdbms-server-12cR1-preinstall` source RPM with the `rpm -ihv` command and manipulating the manifest that is created. After you modify the specification file, the paper reveals the process to generate a RPM file with the `rpmbuild` command so that you can leverage and provision Oracle's preinstallation RPM on RHEL. You can repeat the same procedures against the OEM Agent preinstall RPM and the Oracle E-Business Suite preinstall RPM and leverage them on RHEL.

---

# 11-7. Upgrading Packages
## Problem

You realize that you have older versions of software components. You want to upgrade some of the older packages to the newest release.

## Solution #1

To upgrade an existing package and all the dependent packages, you can execute the yum command with the update option:

```
# yum update perl
```

## Solution #2

To upgrade an existing package, you can execute rpm with the -Uhv option (or --upgrade). For this particular solution, you'll upgrade the perl RPM. Execute the rpm executable with the -Uhv option to upgrade the perl package:

```
# rpm -Uhv perl-5.8.8-10.0.1.el5_2.3.i386.rpm
Preparing...              ########################################### [100%]
   1:perl                 ########################################### [100%]
```

## How It Works

The yum command with the update option is the best option for upgrading packages on the Linux server. The update option installs the latest version of a package or group of packages. If you don't provide the package name(s), yum will attempt to upgrade all the packages. To remove and replace just the obsoleted packages, provide the --obsoletes option.

Optionally, you can upgrade an existing package with the -Uhv option. Behind the scenes, the original package will be removed, and the new package will be installed. The original configuration file will remain but will be renamed with the .rpmsave extension. Because the -U option removes and installs the package(s), you can also use the -U option to install packages. If the package doesn't exist, the package(s) will be installed.

---

▦ **Tip** If you have a requirement to upgrade a large quantity of packages (or even apply upgrades to all the existing packages), you can use the -F option (or --freshen). The -F option will not install packages if the packages don't already exist.

---

# 11-8. Removing Packages
## Problem

You want to remove a package from the Linux server.

# Solution #1

The preferred method of removing a package is by leveraging the yum command with the erase option. To remove the screen package without a prompt, you can execute the following syntax:

```
# yum -y erase screen
Loaded plugins: product-id, subscription-manager
This system is not registered to Red Hat Subscription Management. You can use
subscription-manager to register.
Setting up Remove Process
Resolving Dependencies
--> Running transaction check
---> Package screen.x86_64 0:4.0.3-16.el6 will be erased
--> Finished Dependency Resolution

Dependencies Resolved

=================================================================================
 Package          Arch            Version              Repository          Size
=================================================================================
Removing:
 screen           x86_64          4.0.3-16.el6         @viscosity          795 k

Transaction Summary
=================================================================================
Remove          1 Package(s)

Installed size: 795 k
Downloading Packages:
Running rpm_check_debug
Running Transaction Test
Transaction Test Succeeded
Running Transaction
  Erasing     : screen-4.0.3-16.el6.x86_64                                1/1
  Verifying   : screen-4.0.3-16.el6.x86_64                                1/1

Removed:
  screen.x86_64 0:4.0.3-16.el6

Complete!
```

# Solution #2

Another way to remove a package is to execute the rpm command with the -e option (or --erase). To remove the screen package, you can execute the following syntax:

```
rpm -e screen
```

## How It Works

Similar to package installation, software can be removed from the server with the yum command using the erase option. The remove option is an alias to the erase option. The yum erase command will uninstall any packages as well as dependent packages. You can also uninstall a package group such as a Web Server or X Window System with the yum remove command.

Software can also be removed from the server with the rpm command with the -e option. You must provide the installed package name as the second parameter; don't provide the package file name. The example in the solution removes the screen package from the system. You'll often not be able to remove an RPM because of dependency requirements; you have to know the dependency order to remove the designated RPM. Although we don't recommend it, you can avoid the dependency check with the --nodeps option.

# 11-9. Checking RPM Requirements to Install Oracle Database

## Problem

Make sure that your database software installation goes as smoothly as possible. Check to see whether the Linux server has the required list of packages specified by Oracle to install Oracle Database 12c.

## Solution

You can execute the following short code snippets called rpm6.ksh (for RHEL/OL 6) and rpm7.ksh (for RHEL/OL 7) to quickly see whether the Linux server complies with the package requirements required to install and configure a database:

```
$ cat rpm6.ksh
rpm -q --queryformat "%{NAME}-%{VERSION}.%{RELEASE} (%{ARCH})\n" \
binutils compat-libcap1 compat-libstdc++-33 gcc gcc-c++ glibc glibc-devel \
ksh libgcc libstdc++ libstdc++-devel libaio libaio-devel \
libXext libXtst libX11 libXau libxcb libXi make sysstat  \
unixODBC unixODBC-devel

$ cat rpm7.ksh
rpm -q --queryformat "%{NAME}-%{VERSION}.%{RELEASE} (%{ARCH})\n" \
binutils compat-libcap1 gcc gcc-c++ glibc glibc-devel ksh \
libaio libaio-devel libgcc libstdc++ libstdc++-devel libXi libXtst \
make sysstat unixODBC unixODBC-devel
```

We recommend that the screen RPM be included in every Oracle server, just as Oracle ASMLIB libraries should be part of every server installation. Executing an RPM check with the rpm6.ksh script against an OL 6.6 server yields the following results:

```
$ ./rpm6.ksh
binutils-2.20.51.0.2.5.42.el6 (x86_64)
compat-libcap1-1.10.1 (x86_64)
compat-libstdc++-33-3.2.3.69.el6 (x86_64)
gcc-4.4.7.11.el6 (x86_64)
```

```
gcc-c++-4.4.7.11.el6 (x86_64)
glibc-2.12.1.149.el6 (x86_64)
glibc-devel-2.12.1.149.el6 (x86_64)
ksh-20120801.21.el6_6.3 (x86_64)
libgcc-4.4.7.11.el6 (x86_64)
libstdc++-4.4.7.11.el6 (x86_64)
libstdc++-devel-4.4.7.11.el6 (x86_64)
libaio-0.3.107.10.el6 (x86_64)
libaio-devel-0.3.107.10.el6 (x86_64)
libXext-1.3.2.2.1.el6 (x86_64)
libXtst-1.2.2.2.1.el6 (x86_64)
libX11-1.6.0.2.2.el6 (x86_64)
libXau-1.0.6.4.el6 (x86_64)
libxcb-1.9.1.2.el6 (x86_64)
libXi-1.7.2.2.2.el6 (x86_64)
make-3.81.20.el6 (x86_64)
sysstat-9.0.4.27.el6 (x86_64)
package unixODBC is not installed
package unixODBC-devel is not installed
```

## How It Works

Because you plan to run Oracle databases on a 64-bit Linux OS, check for both 32-bit and 64-bit packages. For example, you have to install both 32-bit and 64-bit components of the compat-db package. You can specify the -qf option (or --queryformat) followed by format options to manipulate the output display. The query string format consists of static strings similar to the printf syntax.

In this solution, the "%{NAME}-%{VERSION}.%{RELEASE} (%{ARCH})\n" format is specified to display the architecture. If the output displays (x86_64), you can confirm that the 64-bit package is installed. If the output displays (i386), you have confirmation that the 32-bit version of the package is installed. Here's the complete RPM requirement for Oracle Database 12c on RHEL and OL 6 and 7: http://www.dbaexpert.com/blog/rpm-requirement-on-red-hat-and-oracle-linux-6-and-7-for-oracle-database-12c-release-1/.

You still have to review the output from the provided scripts to ensure that the output meets or exceeds the level of the package expected. The primary purpose of this script is to provide a single consolidated output to review the RPMs, compared with what is required by Oracle to successfully install Oracle Database 12c.

# 11-10. Performing Initial Silent Oracle Software Installation with Response Files
## Problem

You want to perform an initial install of the Oracle binaries on a new server. You suspect that the network bandwidth will cause issues when trying to run the graphical installer. You want to do a silent install of the Oracle binaries with a response file.

On another note, you want to reduce the amount of time needed to install Oracle Database 12c. You want to automate the installation procedures by performing the installation with the silent option.

# Solution #1

In this solution, only Oracle software binaries are installed to the designated target Oracle Home directory. This solution assumes that you have successfully downloaded, copied, and unbundled the Oracle installation software on your database server. After unbundling the installation software, you should see a directory named response in the database directory.

First, change the directory to the response directory and list the files. You should see several response files:

```
dbca.rsp  db_install.rsp  netca.rsp
```

For this solution, you're interested in the db_install.rsp response file to perform a silent installation of the Oracle Database 12c software stack. Before you manipulate this response file, make a backup copy of the file. Open the db_install.rsp response file with an editor such as vi and provide valid values for your environment for various variables within the response file. In this example, the response file is called 12c_db.rsp and is placed in the /tmp directory. Little over a dozen parameters were modified because you're interested only in installing the software; you don't want to create a database with the installation. In a typical new implementation, you'll install Oracle Database 12c and apply the latest PSU. You'll want to create the database after the PSU is applied.

Let's review the contents of the response file to install the Oracle Database Software. You'll filter out all comments and blank lines of the response file with the egrep command. Then you'll perform another level of filtering and look only at lines that have a value associated after the equal sign. Using the following one-liner code example, you can review all the pertinent variables to the db_install.rsp response file:

```
$ egrep -v "^#|^$" db_install.rsp |awk -F"=" '{if ($2)print $1"=" $2}'
oracle.install.responseFileVersion=/oracle/install/rspfmt_dbinstall_response_schema_v12.1.0
oracle.install.option=INSTALL_DB_SWONLY
ORACLE_HOSTNAME=dal66a
UNIX_GROUP_NAME=oinstall
INVENTORY_LOCATION=/u01/app/oraInventory
SELECTED_LANGUAGES=en
ORACLE_HOME=/u01/app/oracle/product/12.1.0.2/dbhome_1
ORACLE_BASE=/u01/app/oracle
oracle.install.db.InstallEdition=EE
oracle.install.db.DBA_GROUP=dba
oracle.install.db.OPER_GROUP=dba
oracle.install.db.BACKUPDBA_GROUP=dba
oracle.install.db.DGDBA_GROUP=dba
oracle.install.db.KMDBA_GROUP=dba
SECURITY_UPDATES_VIA_MYORACLESUPPORT=false
DECLINE_SECURITY_UPDATES=true
```

The first parameter to review is the oracle.install_ option. This parameter accepts three values: INSTALL_DB_SWONLY, INSTALL_DB_AND_CONFIG, and UPGRADE_DB. You'll look at INSTALL_DB_SWONLY in this solution to install only the software.

UNIX_GROUP_NAME is usually either dba or oinstall. Depending on the level of delineation you want among various support organizations, you can opt to have different groups. For example, you can create a special Linux group in the /etc/group file have the backup team assigned to this group, and assign this group to the BACKUPDBA_GROUP.

ORACLE_HOSTNAME should be the local hostname on which the installation will occur. The ORACLE_HOME directory must point to the directory location in which you want the Oracle software to be installed, and it should be a directory in which the oracle account has write access. The ORACLE_HOME variable will match the value in the oratab file (usually located in the /etc directory) for your installation. The oratab file contains entries for databases that run locally on the server.

Each line of the oratab file consists of three parameters: database name, database software location (also known as ORACLE_HOME), and startup flag. The last parameter plays a significant role in automating database startups. If the value of the last parameter is set to Y, the dbstart shell script located in the $ORACLE_HOME/bin directory will include the database to start when the server reboots. The ORACLE_HOME_NAME is a unique name for the software home of this installation.

The oracle.install.db.InstallEdition has an option only for the Enterprise Edition (EE). In previous releases, you can specify whether the installation was for the Standard Editor or EE, but because you downloaded the EE software, the response file has this parameter prepopulated with the value of EE.

Set your directory to the database directory (the directory to which the downloaded zip files will extract). In this directory, you'll find the runInstaller executable. The response directory is a subdirectory of this directory. Now you can install the binaries by executing the runInstaller with the following command-line syntax:

```
$ ./runInstaller -silent -responseFile /tmp/db_install.rsp
Starting Oracle Universal Installer...

Checking Temp space: must be greater than 500 MB.   Actual 3674 MB    Passed
Checking swap space: must be greater than 150 MB.   Actual 4095 MB    Passed
Preparing to launch Oracle Universal Installer from /tmp/OraInstall2015-05-16_12-53-14PM.
Please wait ...[oracle@dal66a database]$ You can find the log of this install session at:
 /u01/app/oraInventory/logs/installActions2015-05-16_12-53-14PM.log
The installation of Oracle Database 12c was successful.
Please check '/u01/app/oraInventory/logs/silentInstall2015-05-16_12-53-14PM.log' for more
details.

As a root user, execute the following script(s):
        1. /u01/app/oraInventory/orainstRoot.sh
        2. /u01/app/oracle/product/12.1.0.2/dbhome_1/root.sh

Successfully Setup Software.
```

Once the installation completes successfully, as root execute both the orainstRoot.sh and root.sh scripts. In this example, the orainstRoot.sh script resides in the /u01/app/oraInventory directory, and the root.sh script resides in the /u01/app/oracle/product/12.1.0/dbhome_1 directory:

```
$ sudo /u01/app/oraInventory/orainstRoot.sh

Changing permissions of /u01/app/oraInventory.
Adding read,write permissions for group.
Removing read,write,execute permissions for world.

Changing groupname of /u01/app/oraInventory to oinstall.
The execution of the script is complete.

$ sudo /u01/app/oracle/product/12.1.0.2/dbhome_1/root.sh
Check /u01/app/oracle/product/12.1.0.2/dbhome_1/install/root_dal66a_2015-05-16_13-22-19.log
for the output of root script
```

You can now start using this new installation of the Oracle software and create a database.

# Solution #2

In this solution, you'll install the Oracle software binaries to the designated target Oracle Home directory and also create a database so that you can get a kick start into Oracle development and deployment. This solution assumes that you have successfully uploaded and unbundled the Oracle install software on your database server.

You'll manipulate the same db_install.rsp response file as in Solution #1, except you'll also input values for the Database Configuration Options section and change the oracle.install.option to INSTALL_DB_AND_CONFIG from INSTALL_DB_SWONLY. All the parameters needed to create the database in the Database Configuration Options start with oracle.install.db.xxxxxx.

Let's review a sample response file that was manipulated to install Oracle Database 12c software and to create a database called DBATOOLS to the /oradata1 filesystem:

```
$ egrep -v "^#|^$" 12c_db_with_database.rsp |awk -F"=" '{if ($2)print $1"=" $2}'
oracle.install.responseFileVersion=/oracle/install/rspfmt_dbinstall_response_schema_v12.1.0
oracle.install.option=INSTALL_DB_AND_CONFIG
ORACLE_HOSTNAME=dal66a
UNIX_GROUP_NAME=oinstall
INVENTORY_LOCATION=/u01/app/oraInventory
SELECTED_LANGUAGES=en
ORACLE_HOME=/u01/app/oracle/product/12.1.0/dbhome_2
ORACLE_BASE=/u01/app/oracle
oracle.install.db.InstallEdition=EE
oracle.install.db.DBA_GROUP=dba
oracle.install.db.OPER_GROUP=dba
oracle.install.db.BACKUPDBA_GROUP=dba
oracle.install.db.DGDBA_GROUP=dba
oracle.install.db.KMDBA_GROUP=dba
oracle.install.db.config.starterdb.type=GENERAL_PURPOSE
oracle.install.db.config.starterdb.globalDBName=DBATOOLS
oracle.install.db.config.starterdb.SID=DBATOOLS
oracle.install.db.ConfigureAsContainerDB=true
oracle.install.db.config.PDBName=vna01
oracle.install.db.config.starterdb.characterSet=WE8MSWIN1252
oracle.install.db.config.starterdb.memoryOption=false
oracle.install.db.config.starterdb.memoryLimit=1024
oracle.install.db.config.starterdb.installExampleSchemas=false
oracle.install.db.config.starterdb.password.ALL=oracle123
oracle.install.db.config.starterdb.password.SYS=oracle123
oracle.install.db.config.starterdb.password.SYSTEM=oracle123
oracle.install.db.config.starterdb.password.DBSNMP=oracle123
oracle.install.db.config.starterdb.password.PDBADMIN=oracle123
oracle.install.db.config.starterdb.managementOption=DEFAULT
oracle.install.db.config.starterdb.enableRecovery=true
oracle.install.db.config.starterdb.storageType=FILE_SYSTEM_STORAGE
oracle.install.db.config.starterdb.fileSystemStorage.dataLocation=/oradata1
oracle.install.db.config.starterdb.fileSystemStorage.recoveryLocation=/oradata1
SECURITY_UPDATES_VIA_MYORACLESUPPORT=false
DECLINE_SECURITY_UPDATES=true
```

Invoking the runInstaller command in silent mode and providing the configuration file mentioned previously produce the following results:

```
$ ./runInstaller -silent -responseFile /tmp/12c_db_with_database.rsp
Starting Oracle Universal Installer...

Checking Temp space: must be greater than 500 MB.   Actual 3665 MB     Passed
Checking swap space: must be greater than 150 MB.   Actual 4095 MB     Passed
Preparing to launch Oracle Universal Installer from /tmp/OraInstall2015-05-16_01-44-57PM.
Please wait ...[oracle@dal66a database]$ [WARNING] [INS-30011] The ADMIN password entered
does not conform to the Oracle recommended standards.
   CAUSE: Oracle recommends that the password entered should be at least 8 characters in
length, contain at least 1 uppercase character, 1 lower case character and 1 digit [0-9].
   ACTION: Provide a password that conforms to the Oracle recommended standards.
You can find the log of this install session at:
 /u01/app/oraInventory/logs/installActions2015-05-16_01-44-57PM.log
The installation of Oracle Database 12c was successful.
Please check '/u01/app/oraInventory/logs/silentInstall2015-05-16_01-44-57PM.log' for more
details.

As a root user, execute the following script(s):
        1. /u01/app/oraInventory/orainstRoot.sh
        2. /u01/app/oracle/product/12.1.0/dbhome_2/root.sh

Successfully Setup Software.
As install user, execute the following script to complete the configuration.
        1. /u01/app/oracle/product/12.1.0/dbhome_2/cfgtoollogs/configToolAllCommands
           RESPONSE_FILE=<response_file>

        Note:
        1. This script must be run on the same host from where installer was run.
        2. This script needs a small password properties file for configuration assistants
           that require passwords (refer to install guide documentation).
```

As you can see, the output looks very similar to the output in Solution #1. The primary difference in this output is that you are prompted to execute the $ORACLE_HOME/cfgtoollogs/configToolsAllCommands script with the response file name as an input parameter. The response file that is being requested is not the same as the response file used for the software installation; it is a small password properties file. The db_install.rsp response file doesn't store any passwords, but the actual installation does prompt you for passwords for SYS, SYSTEM, DBSNMP, PDBADMIN, EMADMIN, and ASMSNMP users to configure the database.

Here's a sample password properties file needed to configure the database deployment with passwords for the SYS, SYSTEM, DBSNMP, PDBADMIN, EMADMIN, and ASMSNMP accounts:

```
$ cat cfgrsp.properties
oracle.assistants.server|S_SYSPASSWORD=oracle123
oracle.assistants.server|S_SYSTEMPASSWORD=oracle123
oracle.assistants.server|S_DBSNMPPASSWORD=oracle123
oracle.assistants.server|S_PDBADMINPASSWORD=oracle123
oracle.assistants.server|S_EMADMINPASSWORD=oracle123
oracle.assistants.server|S_ASMSNMPPASSWORD=oracle123
```

■ **Note**    Once you are finished with the installation, please remember to discard the password properties file or change the passwords. For installation purposes, please set the file permission to 600.

The output to the configToolAllCommands with the password property file is rather verbose and lengthy. Here's a section of the generated output:

```
$ /u01/app/oracle/product/12.1.0/dbhome_2/cfgtoollogs/configToolAllCommands RESPONSE_FILE=/
home/oracle/cfgrsp.properties
Setting the invPtrLoc to /u01/app/oracle/product/12.1.0/dbhome_2/oraInst.loc

perform - mode is starting for action: configure

May 16, 2015 1:51:21 PM oracle.install.config.common.NetCAInternalPlugIn invoke
INFO: NetCAInternalPlugIn: ... adding </ouiinternal>
May 16, 2015 1:51:21 PM oracle.install.driver.oui.config.GenericInternalPlugIn invoke
INFO: Executing NETCA
May 16, 2015 1:51:21 PM oracle.install.driver.oui.config.GenericInternalPlugIn invoke
INFO: Command /u01/app/oracle/product/12.1.0/dbhome_2/bin/netca /orahome /u01/app/oracle/
product/12.1.0/dbhome_2 /orahnam OraDB12Home1 /instype typical /inscomp client,oraclenet,
javavm,server,ano /insprtcl tcp /cfg local /authadp NO_VALUE /responseFile /u01/app/oracle/
product/12.1.0/dbhome_2/network/install/netca_typ.rsp /silent  /silent   /ouiinternal May
16, 2015 1:51:21 PM
...
...
...

oracle.install.driver.oui.config.GenericInternalPlugIn handleProcess
INFO: Read: 78% complete
May 16, 2015 2:00:17 PM oracle.install.driver.oui.config.GenericInternalPlugIn handleProcess
WARNING: Skipping line: 78% complete
May 16, 2015 2:00:17 PM oracle.install.driver.oui.config.GenericInternalPlugIn handleProcess
INFO: Read: 100% complete
May 16, 2015 2:00:17 PM oracle.install.driver.oui.config.GenericInternalPlugIn handleProcess
WARNING: Skipping line: 100% complete
May 16, 2015 2:00:17 PM oracle.install.driver.oui.config.GenericInternalPlugIn handleProcess
INFO: Read: Look at the log file "/u01/app/oracle/cfgtoollogs/dbca/DBATOOLS/DBATOOLS.log"
for further details.
May 16, 2015 2:00:17 PM oracle.install.driver.oui.config.GenericInternalPlugIn handleProcess
WARNING: Skipping line: Look at the log file "/u01/app/oracle/cfgtoollogs/dbca/DBATOOLS/
DBATOOLS.log" for further details.

perform - mode finished for action: configure

You can see the log file: /u01/app/oracle/product/12.1.0/dbhome_2/cfgtoollogs/oui/
configActions2015-05-16_01-51-20-PM.log
```

As a final validation, you have to review the log file and check to see whether the database is running. First, review the configuration tools log file to confirm that you have reached 100% progress for DBCA:

```
$ cat /u01/app/oracle/cfgtoollogs/dbca/DBATOOLS/DBATOOLS.log

Unique database identifier check passed.

/oradata1/ has enough space. Required space is 7665 MB , available space is 61030 MB.
File Validations Successful.
Copying database files
DBCA_PROGRESS : 1%
DBCA_PROGRESS : 2%
DBCA_PROGRESS : 27%
Creating and starting Oracle instance
..
Completing Database Creation
..
Creating Pluggable Databases
DBCA_PROGRESS : 78%
DBCA_PROGRESS : 100%
Database creation complete. For details check the logfiles at:
 /u01/app/oracle/cfgtoollogs/dbca/DBATOOLS.
Database Information:
Global Database Name:DBATOOLS
System Identifier(SID):DBATOOLS
```

You can perform a couple of basic health checks to validate that the DBATOOLS database is running and the database listener is up by checking on the PMON process and the database listener process. With the ps command, you can filter on the process listing for the keywords pmon and tns, separated by a pipe to denote that you're looking for both conditions with the egrep command.

You can also introduce a grep command with a -v option to ignore output that has the word grep in the list, as shown here:

```
$ ps -ef |egrep "pmon|tns" |grep -v grep
oracle    8357    1  0 13:59 ?        00:00:00 ora_pmon_DBATOOLS
root        15    2  0 13:27 ?        00:00:00 [netns]
oracle    7486    1  0 13:51 ?        00:00:00 /u01/app/oracle/product/12.1.0/dbhome_2/bin/
                                               tnslsnr LISTENER -inherit
```

# How It Works

Using a response file allows you to fully automate the installation and configuration of Oracle software. The Oracle Universal Installer reads the values you specify in the response file to perform the installation. This technique is desirable in several scenarios. For example, if you often perform remote installs across a WAN with limited bandwidth, using the graphical installer may not be an option (because of extremely slow response times and network hangups).

You can easily customize the response file for database options required for your environment. You can then reuse the same response file for future installations. The silent installation technique allows you to perform repeatable and standardized Oracle installations and even upgrades. You can document the exact steps required and have junior DBAs and/or SAs install the oracle binaries using a response file.

As a surprise to some DBAs, you can create your own custom response file with the runInstaller program and the -record option. In essence, your selections during the runInstaller session will be recorded into the specified response file name. The syntax to create a custom response file looks like this:

```
./runInstaller -record -destinationFile /tmp/custom_db_install.rsp
```

The -destinationFile option specifies the location of the target response file. You don't have to actually perform an install to create a response file. As long as you navigate to the Summary screen of the installation process, the response file will be created.

Make sure that the value you specify for ORACLE_HOME doesn't conflict with an already existing home in the oraInst.loc file. This file is usually located in the /etc directory. For ORACLE_HOME_NAME, review the contents of the inventory.xml file located in the OraInventory subdirectory, which is usually located in the $ORACLE_BASE/../oraInventory/ContentsXML directory (i.e., /u01/app/oraInventory/ContentsXML directory).

# 11-11. Creating a Database with a Response File

## Problem

You can't launch the DBCA in GUI mode because your network connectivity is extremely slow or because you are behind multiple firewalls in an extremely secure data center. You want to create a database with the DBCA in silent mode.

You want to automate your database builds and to build databases with consistent configurations and initialization parameters.

## Solution

The good news is that you can create a database in silent mode after you modify the dbca.rsp response file to your desired configuration. This particular solution demonstrates the simplicity of creating a database after modifying a minimal number of parameters in the dbca.rsp response file. At a minimum, the parameters OPERATION_TYPE, GDBNAME, SID, TEMPLATE_NAME, SYSPASSWORD, SYSTEMPASSWORD, DATAFILEDESTINATION, STORAGETYPE, CHARACTERSET, and NATIONALCHARACTERSET should be modified.

Oracle Database 12c has the multitenancy option to create pluggable databases (PDBs). You can enable PDBs by setting the CREATEASCONTAINERDATABASES to yes and then specifying the NUMBEROFPDBS, PDBPREFIX, and PDBADMINPASSWORD parameters. In this example, all the previously mentioned parameters in the dbca.rsp file were modified after the original file was backed up to dbca.rsp.BKUP.

Here's a sample dbca.rsp response file in the /tmp directory that has been manipulated to create a database called TOOLSDEV with two pluggable databases. To reveal just the modified responses, leverage the egrep command with the –v option to ignore all lines that start with a comment and blank lines:

```
$ cat /tmp/dbca.rsp |egrep -v "^#|^$"
[GENERAL]
RESPONSEFILE_VERSION = "12.1.0"
OPERATION_TYPE = "createDatabase"
[CREATEDATABASE]
GDBNAME = "TOOLSDEV"
SID = "TOOLSDEV"
CREATEASCONTAINERDATABASE =yes
NUMBEROFPDBS =2
PDBNAME =vna
```

```
PDBADMINPASSWORD = "oracle123"
TEMPLATENAME = "General_Purpose.dbc"
SYSPASSWORD = "oracle123"
SYSTEMPASSWORD = "oracle123"
EMCONFIGURATION = "NONE"
DATAFILEDESTINATION =/oradata1
RECOVERYAREADESTINATION=/oradata1
STORAGETYPE=FS
CHARACTERSET = "AL32UTF8"
NATIONALCHARACTERSET= "AL16UTF16"
DATABASETYPE = "MULTIPURPOSE"
AUTOMATICMEMORYMANAGEMENT = "FALSE"
TOTALMEMORY = "1024"
```

Because the software is already installed, you have to launch dbca in silent mode from $ORACLE_HOME/ bin directory. In this solution, dbca is launched with the -silent parameter and the -responseFile parameter, followed by the location of the response file:

```
$ dbca -silent -responseFile /tmp/dbca.rsp
Cleaning up failed steps
5% complete
Copying database files
7% complete
9% complete
41% complete
Creating and starting Oracle instance
43% complete
48% complete
53% complete
57% complete
58% complete
59% complete
62% complete
64% complete
Completing Database Creation
68% complete
71% complete
75% complete
85% complete
96% complete
100% complete
Look at the log file "/u01/app/oracle/cfgtoollogs/dbca/TOOLSDEV/TOOLSDEV0.log"
for further details.
```

In silent mode, dbca provides a progress status to notify you where it is in the database-creation process. During the initial phase, RMAN performs a restore of the data files. Once the restore is complete, dbca creates and starts the instance. Finally, post–database configuration steps are executed.

After the database is created, you can view the log file in the $ORACLE_BASE/cfgtoollogs/ dbca/$ORACLE_SID directory. You'll also notice an entry in the /etc/oratab file for the new database named TOOLSDEV:

```
TOOLSDEV:/apps/oracle/product/11.1.0/DB:N
```

# How It Works

Nowadays, creating databases with the DBCA is standard in many organizations. Many DBAs launch the DBCA and configure databases in GUI mode, but a few exploit the options available to them using the response file. By effectively leveraging DBCA with the silent option, you can automate database creation and create databases consistently across the organization. You can modify the dbca.rsp file to build databases on ASM and even create RAC databases. You can control almost every aspect of the response file similar to launching the DBCA in GUI mode. Your DBA organization should seriously consider standardizing on creating databases in silent mode using the dbca.rsp response file.

You can also leverage DBCA without a response file and fully supply all the parameters to create databases. The following dbca code example creates a general-purpose database called oraprod on the /oradata01 filesystem with the recovery area destination to the /fra01 filesystem. We're also creating redo logs that are 500MB in size and multiplexing the redo logs across the /oradata01 and /fra01 filesystems. We have disabled Enterprise Manager Express configuration in favor of the Oracle Enterprise Manager Cloud Control 12c configuration to be done in the future. We have set pertinent initialization parameters with the initparams parameters.

Here's the dbca code example that creates a database, including setting pertinent initialization parameters:

```
./dbca -silent \
-createDatabase \
-templateName General_Purpose.dbc \
-gdbName oraprod \
-createAsContainerDatabase false \
-emConfiguration none \
-datafileDestination '/oradata01' \
-recoveryAreaDestination '/fra01' \
-storageType FS \
-sid oraprod \
-SysPassword oracle123 \
-SystemPassword oracle123 \
-emConfiguration none \
-redoLogFileSize 500 \
-listeners LISTENER \
-registerWithDirService false \
-characterSet WE8ISO8859P1 \
-nationalCharacterSet AL16UTF16 \
-databaseType MULTIPURPOSE \
-initparams audit_file_dest='/app/oracle/admin/oraprod/adump' \
-initparams compatible='12.1.0.2' \
-initparams db_create_file_dest='/oradata01' \
-initparams db_create_online_log_dest_1='/oradata01' \
-initparams db_create_online_log_dest_2='/fra01' \
-initparams db_recovery_file_dest='/fra01' \
-initparams pga_aggregate_target=1024 \
-initparams diagnostic_dest='/app/oracle' \
-initparams parallel_max_servers=20 \
-initparams processes=500 \
-initparams sga_target=10240 \
-initparams control_files='/oradata01/oraprod/control01.ctl' \
-initparams db_recovery_file_dest_size=25000
```

---

■ **Note**    The backslash (\) is needed because DBCA expects a single-line command with all the parameters. In a nutshell, the backslash escape character tells the shell to ignore the next character. In this example, the backslash tells the shell to ignore the newline character, thus making the entire script appear as a single line to DBCA.

---

# 11-12. Creating a Network Configuration with a Response File
## Problem

You struggle to launch Oracle Network Configuration Assistant (NETCA) in GUI mode because your network connectivity is extremely slow or because you are behind multiple firewalls in an extremely secure data center. You want to create a database listener with NETCA in silent mode.

## Solution

You can launch NETCA in silent mode by using a response file. Here's a sample response file with modifications called netca.rsp:

```
$ cat /tmp/net.rsp
[GENERAL]
RESPONSEFILE_VERSION="12.1"
CREATE_TYPE= "CUSTOM"
LOG_FILE=""/tmp/netca.log""
[Session]
ORACLE_HOME="/u01/app/oracle/product/12.1.0/dbhome_2"
[oracle.net.ca]
INSTALLED_COMPONENTS={"server","net8","javavm"}
INSTALL_TYPE=""custom""
LISTENER_NUMBER=1
LISTENER_NAMES={"LISTENER"}
LISTENER_PROTOCOLS={"TCP;1521"}
LISTENER_START=""
NAMING_METHODS={"LDAP","TNSNAMES","HOSTNAME"}
NSN_PROTOCOLS={"TCP;HOSTNAME;1521"}
NSN_NUMBER=3
NSN_NAMES={"DEV","DBATOOLS","RMANPROD"}
NSN_SERVICE = {"DEV","DBATOOLS","RMANPROD"}
NSN_PROTOCOLS={"TCP;rac5.dbaexpert.com;1521","TCP;rac6.dbaexpert.com;1521","TCP;rac7.
dbaexpert.com;1521"}
```

Executing NETCA in silent mode and passing the modified response file /tmp/net.rsp yields the following output:

```
$ netca -silent -responseFile /tmp/net.rsp

Sun May 17 07:20:03 CDT 2015 Oracle Net Configuration Assistant
Parsing command line arguments:
    Parameter "silent" = true
    Parameter "responsefile" = /tmp/net.rsp
    Parameter "log" = /tmp/netca.log
Done parsing command line arguments.
Oracle Net Services Configuration:
Configuring Listener:LISTENER
Listener configuration complete.
Oracle Net Listener Startup:
    Running Listener Control:
      /u01/app/oracle/product/12.1.0/dbhome_2/bin/lsnrctl start LISTENER
    Listener Control complete.
    Listener started successfully.
Default local naming configuration complete.
    Created net service name: DEV
Default local naming configuration complete.
    Created net service name: DBATOOLS
Default local naming configuration complete.
    Created net service name: RMANPROD
Profile configuration complete.
Oracle Net Services configuration successful. The exit code is 0
```

Behind the scenes, NETCA created three files in the $ORACLE_HOME/network/admin directory: sqlnet.ora, tnsnames.ora, and listener.ora. The output to NETCA is logged in the /tmp/netca.log file.

## How It Works

Although DBAs often don't realize the potential of automation through response files, they can configure Oracle's network topology in a single command by launching NETCA. With the proper standardization in directory structures and naming conventions, DBAs can script and manipulate the network configuration response files by leveraging executables such as awk and sed.

You can specify an alternate location for the netca log file by modifying the LOG_FILE parameter. Similar to the other silent installations, you must specify a valid ORACLE_HOME directory. The other portions of the netca response file that require explanation are the NSN_ parameters (*NSN* stands for number of service names). The parameter NSN_PROTOCOLS defines the protocol and associated parameters for each service name. The parameter NSN_NUMBER defines the number of service names to create. For this particular solution, the response file defines three service names to create in the tnsnames.ora file. The names of the TNSNAMES connect strings are defined to be DEV, RMANPROD, and DBATOOLS. All three of the TNSNAMES connect strings leverage service names. For this solution, you want every server to have entries for DBATOOLS and RMANPROD.

Here's the contents of the tnsnames.ora file:

```
$ cat tnsnames.ora
# tnsnames.ora Network Configuration File: /u01/app/oracle/product/12.1.0/dbhome_2/network/
admin/tnsnames.ora
# Generated by Oracle configuration tools.

RMANPROD =
  (DESCRIPTION =
    (ADDRESS_LIST =
      (ADDRESS = (PROTOCOL = TCP)(HOST = rac7.dbaexpert.com)(PORT = 1521))
    )
    (CONNECT_DATA =
      (SERVICE_NAME = RMANPROD)
    )
  )

DEV =
  (DESCRIPTION =
    (ADDRESS_LIST =
      (ADDRESS = (PROTOCOL = TCP)(HOST = rac5.dbaexpert.com)(PORT = 1521))
    )
    (CONNECT_DATA =
      (SERVICE_NAME = DEV)
    )
  )

DBATOOLS =
  (DESCRIPTION =
    (ADDRESS_LIST =
      (ADDRESS = (PROTOCOL = TCP)(HOST = rac6.dbaexpert.com)(PORT = 1521))
    )
    (CONNECT_DATA =
      (SERVICE_NAME = DBATOOLS)
    )
  )
```

Likewise, NETCA generated the following entries in the listener.ora file:

```
$ cat listener.ora
# listener.ora Network Configuration File: /u01/app/oracle/product/12.1.0/dbhome_2/network/
admin/listener.ora
# Generated by Oracle configuration tools.

LISTENER =
  (DESCRIPTION_LIST =
    (DESCRIPTION =
      (ADDRESS = (PROTOCOL = TCP)(HOST = dal66a)(PORT = 1521))
      (ADDRESS = (PROTOCOL = IPC)(KEY = EXTPROC1521))
    )
  )
```

Finally, NETCA produces the sqlnet.ora file, which contains this single entry to define the directory path:

```
NAMES.DIRECTORY_PATH= (LDAP, TNSNAMES, HOSTNAME)
```

# 11-13. Applying Patch Set Updates (PSUs) and Interim Patches
## Problem

You have to apply a patch set update (PSU) or interim patches to resolve a database issue or eradicate a bug you encountered in your database.

## Solution

Most of the time, applying a patch is simple with the opatch command-line interface, which accepts numerous arguments. The syntax for opatch is as follows:

```
$ ./opatch -help
Oracle Interim Patch Installer version 12.1.0.1.7
Copyright (c) 2015, Oracle Corporation. All rights reserved.

 Usage: opatch [ -help ] [ -report ] [ command ]

           command := apply
                   compare
                        lsinventory
                        lspatches
                        napply
                        nrollback
                        rollback
                        query
                        version
                        prereq
                        util
```

The most common supplied opatch arguments are these:

- apply
- lsinventory
- rollback
- version

Let's take, for example, the April 2015 Patch 20299023—Database Patch Set Update 12.1.0.2.3 (includes CPUApr2015). You can download the patch file p20299023_121020_Linux-x86-64.zip to your download directory and extract the compressed archived file with the unzip command. If you want to see the contents of the .zip file without extracting the file, pass the -l argument to the unzip command. The unzip command will create a directory called 20299023 and extract all the files into the directory.

If this is the first PSU going on the Oracle Home, or if you have not patched in a while, you also have to download and apply patch 6880880, which happens to be the patch update for OPatch. You have to download patch 6880880 from support.oracle.com or follow the download link from https://updates. oracle.com/download/6880880.html.

This patch is extremely simple to apply. Simply download the patch, upload the zip file to your server, unzip the contents of the patch, and replace the contents of the $ORACLE_HOME/OPatch directory with the OPatch unzipped directory from this patch. If you are applying this patch for the Grid Infrastructure (GI) home, you must replace the contents of the OPatch directory as root.

For most patches, you can read the README.txt file located in the base directory of the patch, which has explicit directions on how to apply the patch. Although the majority of patches require a simple apply parameter, some patches have prerequisite and postpatch steps. Some patches may even require multiple dependent patches to be executed.

The README.txt file for PSUs will indicate that you have to read the README.html file. As a general rule, prior to applying any patch, the database must be shut down. Oracle does provide what is known as an *online patch* for which the database doesn't have to be shut down for high availability considerations. You must examine the README.txt (or in this case, the README.html file) to see whether a particular patch qualifies as an online patch. Because this particular PSU requires the database to be shut down, you'll incur an outage window to apply the patch.

The opatch executable is located in the $ORACLE_HOME/OPatch directory. The easiest way to apply a patch is to include the opatch executable to your PATH environment variable. To do so, simply export your PATH environment variable as $ORACLE_HOME/OPatch:$PATH.

---

■ **Note** Make sure to run the command opatch apply as the oracle account from the uncompressed patch subdirectory. Also, the OS environment variable ORACLE_HOME has to be set accordingly before running opatch.

---

The directory is already changed to 20299023. Based on the README.html file, you can apply this patch with the command opatch apply.

Here's the OPatch process in action to apply this PSU:

```
$ opatch apply
Oracle Interim Patch Installer version 12.1.0.1.7
Copyright (c) 2015, Oracle Corporation.  All rights reserved.

Oracle Home       : /u01/app/oracle/product/12.1.0/dbhome_2
Central Inventory : /u01/app/oraInventory
   from           : /u01/app/oracle/product/12.1.0/dbhome_2/oraInst.loc
OPatch version    : 12.1.0.1.7
OUI version       : 12.1.0.2.0
Log file location : /u01/app/oracle/product/12.1.0/dbhome_2/cfgtoollogs/opatch/opatch2015-
                    05-16_17-48-29PM_1.log

Verifying environment and performing prerequisite checks...
OPatch continues with these patches:   19769480  20299023

Do you want to proceed? [y|n]
y
User Responded with: Y
All checks passed.
Provide your email address to be informed of security issues, install and
```

initiate Oracle Configuration Manager. Easier for you if you use your My
Oracle Support Email address/User Name.
Visit http://www.oracle.com/support/policies.html for details.
Email address/User Name:

You have not provided an email address for notification of security issues.
Do you wish to remain uninformed of security issues ([Y]es, [N]o) [N]:   Y

Please shutdown Oracle instances running out of this ORACLE_HOME on the local system.
(Oracle Home = '/u01/app/oracle/product/12.1.0/dbhome_2')

Is the local system ready for patching? [y|n]
y
User Responded with: Y
Backing up files...
Applying sub-patch '19769480' to OH '/u01/app/oracle/product/12.1.0/dbhome_2'

Patching component oracle.rdbms.deconfig, 12.1.0.2.0...
Patching component oracle.xdk, 12.1.0.2.0...
Patching component oracle.tfa, 12.1.0.2.0...
Patching component oracle.rdbms.util, 12.1.0.2.0...
Patching component oracle.rdbms, 12.1.0.2.0...
Patching component oracle.rdbms.dbscripts, 12.1.0.2.0...
Patching component oracle.xdk.parser.java, 12.1.0.2.0...
Patching component oracle.oraolap, 12.1.0.2.0...
Patching component oracle.xdk.rsf, 12.1.0.2.0...
Patching component oracle.rdbms.rsf, 12.1.0.2.0...
Patching component oracle.rdbms.rman, 12.1.0.2.0...
Patching component oracle.ldap.rsf, 12.1.0.2.0...
Patching component oracle.ldap.rsf.ic, 12.1.0.2.0...

Verifying the update...
Applying sub-patch '20299023' to OH '/u01/app/oracle/product/12.1.0/dbhome_2'
ApplySession: Optional component(s) [ oracle.has.crs, 12.1.0.2.0 ]  not present in the
Oracle Home or a higher version is found.

Patching component oracle.tfa, 12.1.0.2.0...
Patching component oracle.rdbms.deconfig, 12.1.0.2.0...
Patching component oracle.rdbms.rsf, 12.1.0.2.0...
Patching component oracle.rdbms, 12.1.0.2.0...
Patching component oracle.rdbms.dbscripts, 12.1.0.2.0...
Patching component oracle.rdbms.rsf.ic, 12.1.0.2.0...
Patching component oracle.ldap.rsf, 12.1.0.2.0...
Patching component oracle.ldap.rsf.ic, 12.1.0.2.0...

Verifying the update...
Composite patch 20299023 successfully applied.
Log file location: /u01/app/oracle/product/12.1.0/dbhome_2/cfgtoollogs/opatch/opatch2015-05-
16_17-48-29PM_1.log

OPatch succeeded.

Now check the inventory to see whether the patch exists. To view the patch list, pass the lsinventory argument to the opatch command, as shown here:

```
[oracle@dal66a 20299023]$ opatch lsinventory |grep ^Patch
Patch  20299023  : applied on Sat May 16 17:49:12 CDT 2015
Patch description:  "Database Patch Set Update : 12.1.0.2.3 (20299023)"
```

In this inventory listing, you are filtering on the output and are looking for a line that starts with the word Patch to determine applied patches.

---

■ **Note**    The ^ (caret) sign, designated by pressing Shift+6, represents the metacharacter for the beginning of the line. By filtering on ^Patch from the output of the opatch inventory command, you are looking for the first letter of the line that starts with Patch to retrieve a high-level summary of just the patches that have been successfully applied to the Oracle Home.

---

You can see from the output that 12.0.1.2.3 PSU is applied to the Oracle Home. You can execute the command opatch lsinventory -detail to produce a detailed output of all the patches.

You are not quite finished. You still have to perform the postpatch operations against each database that leverages this Oracle Home. In Oracle Database 11g with the PSU, the database is patched by executing the catbundle.sql SQL script:

```
SQL> @catbundle.sql psu apply
```

Starting in Oracle Database 12c, you have to execute the datapatch script from the $ORACLE_HOME/OPatch directory:

```
$ cd $ORACLE_HOME/OPatch
$ ./datapatch -verbose
```

datapatch replaces the need to execute the catbundle.sql script to apply the database portion of the database.

## How It Works

OPatch is a collection of Perl scripts and Java classes providing the capability to apply and roll back PSUs and interim (one-off) patches to an Oracle database environment. opatch is the primary driver that calls the Perl modules and Java classes. Although the minimum perl requirement is 5.005_03, Oracle recommends the perl version to be at least 5.6 or greater. You can download OPatch from MetaLink from the Patches & Updates tab by performing a simple search on *patchset 6880880*. For additional information, please review MetaLink Note 224346.1.

OPatch requires a Java Runtime Environment (JRE) to be available on the Linux server. In addition, it has requirements for system commands such as jar, fuser, ar, and make on the Linux servers. Patch information and backups reside in the $ORACLE_HOME/.patch_storage/{patch_file} directory.

Just as you can install a patch with the apply parameter, you can uninstall a patch with the rollback parameter. The rollback parameter accepts an additional parameter, -id, to specify the patch number to roll back.

In this example, you roll back the same patch that was applied in the solution:

```
$ opatch rollback -id 20299023
```

Oracle offers a cumulative quarterly patch of the most critical fixes of known bugs and issues in PSUs. Customers are encouraged to apply PSUs to avoid many of the known problems. We recommend that customers apply N-1 on PSUs. For the month of April, customers should apply January's PSUs. If your go-live date is far in the future, you can apply the most recent PSU.

Oracle provides its quarterly security patch updates (SPUs)—formerly known as critical patch updates (CPUs)—to address security vulnerabilities to the database and application server products. Nonsecurity patches are often included in the CPU because they are dependent patches. You probably receive e-mail updates telling you when they are available for download. We recommend that you closely scrutinize the quarterly SPUs and apply them in a timely manner.

---

■ **Note**    If you have the GI stack and Oracle Database Software, the GI stack must always be at a higher version, higher patch set, and higher PSU than the Oracle Database Software.

---

# 11-14. Cloning an Oracle Home
## Problem
You want to easily clone a fully patched Oracle software installation from one database server to another database server. You want the cloning process to be a simple zip and unzip of the software to a new server and to fully benefit from all the patches that were applied on the original server.

## Solution
If you happen to be a DBA who still creates tar archives of the Oracle binaries, you can continue to, as the saying goes, have your cake and eat it too. It is much easier to copy the Oracle binaries than it is to install the software from the CD or unzipped media software, especially if the source Oracle software is fully patched with the latest release of Oracle PSUs/one-off patches or with a set of patches that has been fully vetted by the quality assurance (QA) team.

You can accomplish in one command what can take hours if you have slow WAN connectivity between your desktop and the Linux server. With one command, you can provide an Oracle software stack that is fully patched that might take you days to deliver if your Oracle Home has lots of patches installed. If you are not comfortable with the silent installation option, you also have to find an X server or VNC server to which you set the DISPLAY environment variable.

In this solution, you see how to clone an Oracle Home after you transfer the binaries from another server using the rcp/scp, tar, zip/unzip, or rsh/ssh command. First, set the ORACLE_HOME environment variable to the new directory you just copied over. For example, the ORACLE_HOME environment variable for this solution is set to /app/oracle/product/12.1.0.2/db. From the $ORACLE_HOME/clone/bin directory, execute the perl command as shown here to clone the Oracle Database Software to the new database server:

```
$ perl clone.pl ORACLE_HOME=/app/oracle/product/12.1.0.2/db ORACLE_HOME_NAME=12102_home_base
ORACLE_BASE=/app/oracle/product -ignoreSysPrereqs -invPtrLoc /etc/oraInst.loc
./runInstaller -clone -waitForCompletion  "ORACLE_HOME=/app/oracle/product/12.1.0.2/db"
"ORACLE_HOME_NAME=12102_home_base" "ORACLE_BASE=/app/oracle/product" -ignoreSysPrereqs
```

```
-invPtrLoc  /etc/oraInst.loc  -silent -paramFile /app/oracle/product/12.1.0.2/db/clone/
clone_oraparam.ini
Starting Oracle Universal Installer...

Checking Temp space: must be greater than 500 MB.    Actual 29399 MB    Passed
Checking swap space: must be greater than 500 MB.    Actual 3967 MB     Passed
Preparing to launch Oracle Universal Installer from /tmp/OraInstall2015-02-12_02-57-31PM.
Please wait ...You can find the log of this install session at:
 /app/oracle/oraInventory/logs/cloneActions2015-02-12_02-57-31PM.log
..............................................  5% Done.
..............................................  10% Done.
..............................................  15% Done.
..............................................  20% Done.
..............................................  25% Done.
..............................................  30% Done.
..............................................  35% Done.
..............................................  40% Done.
..............................................  45% Done.
..............................................  50% Done.
..............................................  55% Done.
..............................................  60% Done.
..............................................  65% Done.
..............................................  70% Done.
..............................................  75% Done.
..............................................  80% Done.
..............................................  85% Done.
..........
Copy files in progress.

Copy files successful.

Link binaries in progress.

Link binaries successful.

Setup files in progress.

Setup files successful.

Setup Inventory in progress.

Setup Inventory successful.

Finish Setup successful.
The cloning of 12102_home_base was successful.
Please check '/app/oracle/oraInventory/logs/cloneActions2015-02-12_02-57-31PM.log' for more
details.

Setup Oracle Base in progress.

Setup Oracle Base successful.
```

```
.................................................  95% Done.
```

As a root user, execute the following script(s):
        1. /app/oracle/product/12.1.0.2/db/root.sh

```
.................................................  100% Done.
```

As part of the prerequisite checks, the cloning process will determine whether you have enough space in the /tmp directory and sufficient swap space is available for Oracle. The cloning process will reset various shell scripts and modify metadata information with the local host information.

invPtrLoc is an optional parameter that specifies the fully qualified file name that contains the location of the oraInventory. The invPtrLoc parameter should not be used in a RAC environment. The oraInst.loc file, by default, is located in the /etc directory in the Linux OS and looks like this:

```
inventory_loc=/u01/app/oraInventory
inst_group=oinstall
```

By default, inventory_loc will point one level below the $ORACLE_BASE directory of the oracle user account (/u01/app/oraInventory when ORACLE_BASE is /u01/app/oracle). As a precautionary measure, you should back up the oraInventory directory prior to attaching an Oracle Home. When you execute root. sh, it will also execute root.sh in silent mode.

## How It Works

DBAs still continue to tar and un-tar the Oracle binaries from one server to another. In some companies, especially in non-RAC environments, DBAs copy the binaries from development database servers to QA and production database servers with a command such as tar piped to ssh.

Here's a popular one-liner script that you can leverage to copy Oracle binaries from one directory level above the Oracle Home to the target node:

```
tar cvf - {DIR_NAME} |ssh {target_node} "cd /apps/oracle/product/12.1.0.2; tar xvf -"
```

---

■ **Note**    There is no requirement to shut down databases or listeners prior to copying the Oracle Database Software from the source database server to the target database server. For the GI software, you must unlock the GI software stack, which will shut down the cluster.

---

The tar command piped to ssh ensures that symbolic links get copied over as symbolic links. The best thing about this approach is that you don't have to incur double storage to store a local and remote copy of the tar archive.

Perl version 5.6 or higher is required when cloning Oracle Database 12c. When cloning Oracle software to a new server, make sure that all the prerequisite requirements are met as the perl clone.pl process doesn't validate them.

Starting from Oracle Database 10g, Oracle supports cloning of Oracle Homes from source and target servers. The target server has to have all the Linux prerequisites and packages installed to ensure that the cloning process will be successful. You can clone the production Oracle Home to the lower environments, such as QA or DEV environments, to ensure that all the patches are identical from source and target Oracle Homes. You can strategically position the cloning process to upgrade a database from the current release to a higher release. For example, you can clone a newer version of the Oracle Home to the production database server. During the cutover window, you can simply switch Oracle Homes to the newer version and execute the post installation scripts to upgrade the database catalog.

# 11-15. Attaching an Oracle Home
## Problem

You want to merge multiple Oracle inventories or rebuild/re-create the central inventory of all the Oracle Homes because the inventory is corrupt.

## Solution

From the $ORACLE_HOME/oui/bin directory, you can execute the attachHome.sh shell script. Oracle provides a shell script to attach the Oracle Home to the oraInventory. The attachHome.sh script has the following content:

```
$ cat attachHome.sh
#!/bin/sh
OHOME=/u01/app/oracle/product/12.1.0/dbhome_2
OHOMENAME=OraDB12Home1
CUR_DIR=`pwd`
cd $OHOME/oui/bin
./runInstaller -detachhome ORACLE_HOME=$OHOME ORACLE_HOME_NAME=$OHOMENAME $* >
/dev/null 2>&1
./runInstaller -attachhome ORACLE_HOME=$OHOME ORACLE_HOME_NAME=$OHOMENAME $*
cd $CUR_DIR
```

Executing the attachHome.sh script yields the following results:

```
$ ./attachHome.sh
Starting Oracle Universal Installer...

Checking swap space: must be greater than 500 MB.   Actual 4095 MB    Passed
The inventory pointer is located at /etc/oraInst.loc
'AttachHome' was successful.
```

According to the attachHome.sh shell script, the script first detaches the Oracle Home from the oraInventory prior to attaching the new Oracle Home. In previous releases of Oracle, the runInstaller program was executed with the –attachHome option and provided the Oracle Home location and the Oracle Home name, as shown here:

```
$ ./runInstaller -silent -attachHome ORACLE_HOME="/u01/app/oracle/product/12.1.0/dbhome_2"
ORACLE_HOME_NAME=" OraDB12Home1"
Starting Oracle Universal Installer...

Checking swap space: must be greater than 500 MB.   Actual 8174 MB    Passed
The inventory pointer is located at /etc/oraInst.loc
'AttachHome' was successful.
```

You can even attach RAC Oracle Homes by specifying an additional parameter called `CLUSTER_NODES`, which has to be enclosed in curly brackets, as shown here:

```
CLUSTER_NODES={rac3,rac4}
```

## How It Works

Execute the `attachHome.sh` shell script to attach the Oracle Home to the central Oracle inventory. You have to execute the `attachHome.sh` script from each of the Oracle Homes. Once you have successfully attached the new Oracle Home, you can view the contents of the `inventory.xml` file to confirm that the new Oracle Home is listed.

As stated earlier, the oraInventory directory location resides one level below $ORACLE_BASE. Here's what the `inventory.xml` file looks like:

```
$ cat $ORACLE_BASE/../oraInventory/ContentsXML/inventory.xml
<?xml version="1.0" standalone="yes" ?>
<!-- Copyright (c) 1999, 2014, Oracle and/or its affiliates.
All rights reserved. -->
<!-- Do not modify the contents of this file by hand. -->
<INVENTORY>
<VERSION_INFO>
    <SAVED_WITH>12.1.0.2.0</SAVED_WITH>
    <MINIMUM_VER>2.1.0.6.0</MINIMUM_VER>
</VERSION_INFO>
<HOME_LIST>
<HOME NAME="OraDB12Home1" LOC="/u01/app/oracle/product/12.1.0/dbhome_2" TYPE="O" IDX="1"/>
</HOME_LIST>
<COMPOSITEHOME_LIST>
</COMPOSITEHOME_LIST>
</INVENTORY>
```

You can see that the `ORACLE_HOME_NAME` of `OraDB12Home1` is listed as a member in the XML inventory file.

■ ■ ■

# CHAPTER 12

# VirtualBox for Oracle

Oracle VM VirtualBox, formerly known as Sun VirtualBox or Sun xVM VirtualBox, is a hypervisor for x86 computers from Oracle Corporation. Oracle VM VirtualBox is a cross–platform virtualization software that allows you to run multiple OSs at the same time on Windows, Mac OS X, Linux, and Oracle Solaris OSs. Many IT professionals heavily leverage VirtualBox to learn new and emerging technologies. VirtualBox allows IT professionals to test, develop, demo, and deploy their applications and databases on virtual machines (VMs) on their local desktops or laptops.

There are two types of hypervisors: type 1 (native or bare-metal) and type 2 (hosted). A type 1 hypervisor runs directly on a physical server with no software layer between the hypervisor and the physical hardware, which is why it is often referred to as a bare metal hypervisor. This hypervisor is designed to be extremely fast for enterprise environments. VMware ESXi, Oracle VM, Linux KVM, Hyper-V, and Citrix XenServer are all examples of type 1 hypervisors. Hypervisors are very different in their functionality and features. Hypervisors VMware, Hyper-V, OVM, and KVM have a lot of similarities, but they are also very different. Just as Oracle, SQL Server, and MySQL are relational databases, there are significant differences in how they do things, as well as the environments and ecosystems in which they run.

A type 2 hypervisor runs on top of an OS such as Windows (VMWare Workstation) or a Mac (VMware Fusion), and VirtualBox (which runs on the following platforms: Linux, Solaris, Windows, and Mac). With a type 2 hypervisor, the VM has to go through the hypervisor software as well as the OS, thus inducing additional overhead. A type 2 hypervisor is great for running multiple VMs on laptops and PCs. VMware Workstation, Parallels, and VirtualBox are additional examples of type 2 hypervisors.

This chapter focuses on installing and configuring Oracle VM VirtualBox to set up a VM to host Oracle databases. You'll proceed with creating additional virtual disks for Oracle ASM virtual disks and presenting the virtual disks to other VMs as shared storage. The chapter also briefly mentions the network infrastructure available for VirtualBox.

You'll dive in to the details of creating and maintaining Linux templates, cloning new Linux VMs ready for instant deployment from golden image templates, and managing snapshots.

## 12-1. Installing Oracle VM VirtualBox

### Problem

You want to install Oracle VM VirtualBox to get started on the virtualization journey.

### Solution

You can download and install Oracle VM VirtualBox from `http://www.oracle.com/technetwork/ server-storage/virtualbox/downloads/index.html#vbox`. Oracle VM VirtualBox software is available for Windows, Mac OS X, Solaris 10+, and Linux platforms. Installing VirtualBox is simple and straightforward, and can be completed in minutes.

This example shows what the installation on a Mac OS looks like. If you downloaded the VirtualBox for the Mac, you have a file name that resembles VirtualBox-4.3.26-98988-OSX.dmg. You see the installer shown in Figure 12-1 when you double-click the .dmg file.

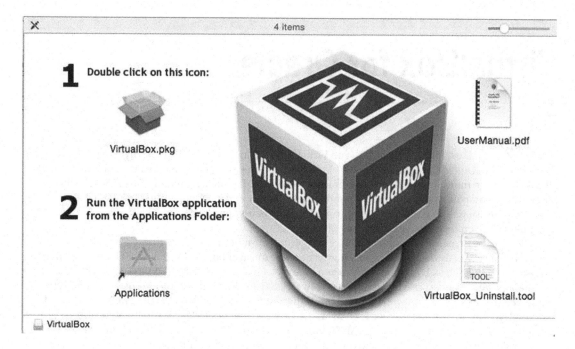

*Figure 12-1.* *VirtualBox installer software*

Double-click the Virtualbox.pkg icon to start the installation. On the Mac, you are directed to a window that specifies that the package needs to run a program to determine whether the software can be installed. Confirm that you agree by clicking the Continue button to proceed to the Welcome screen. From the Welcome screen, you can click the Continue button to proceed with the installation.

On the Standard install screen, you can change the default installation location of the binaries. By clicking the Install button, you'll be prompted to enter the Username and Password for an administrative account that has privileges to install software on the machine to continue. When the installation completes, you'll see a success window indicating that the software was installed without issues.

As you can see from the installation procedures, VirtualBox is extremely simple to install and use.

## How It Works

By learning to implement VirtualBox, you are beginning the steps of creating a virtual infrastructure on your Windows, Mac, or Linux machine. VirtualBox is the perfect vehicle for DBAs and developers to learn about virtualization, Linux, and various Oracle technologies. Lots of professionals learn new technologies by installing VirtualBox on their laptops to create VMs of various OSs. VirtualBox is the perfect virtualization technology because it is easily accessible and completely free to deploy. VirtualBox is the preferred type 2 hypervisor for Oracle professionals running Oracle databases on OL.

Oracle announced recent addition of guest platforms, including the following:

- OL 6
- Ubuntu Linux and Fedora distributions
- Mac OS X 10.9 "Mavericks"
- Windows 8.1 and Windows Server 2012 R2

---

■ **Note** Oracle provides downloadable Oracle virtual appliances (packaged VMs) for VirtualBox so that you can get started with a particular Oracle technology right away. Navigating your way around a new software stack is challenging enough without having to spend multiple cycles on the install process. Instead, you can download prebuilt Oracle VM VirtualBox appliances from Oracle's web site. Deployment of the packaged virtual appliances is as easy as 1-2-3: download, assemble the files, and import into VirtualBox. For more information about virtual appliances, please see recipe 12-7.

---

# 12-2. Setting Up VirtualBox Virtual Machine (VM)

## Problem

You want to create your first VM to instantiate a Linux server and install Oracle Database 12c.

## Solution

You'll focus on configuring VirtualBox to create a new VM for OL 6/7 and installing OL 6/7 from the ISO image as a guest OS. The OL 6/7 ISO image can be downloaded from edelivery.oracle.com—Oracle Software Delivery Cloud. You must have a (free) valid Oracle Account to download the Linux ISO.

To create a VM, click the New button in the top-left corner of the Oracle VM VirtualBox Manager and provide a descriptive name for the VM, location of the VM, and the OS type. The name that is specified will be used to identify the VM configuration. Specify a descriptive name and select the guest OS type and version. In this example, you want to select Linux for the type and Oracle (64-bit) for the version. You can choose Red Hat (64-bit) if your infrastructure is still running Red Hat.

Here's the list of Linux flavors supported by VirtualBox:

- Linux 2.2
- Linux 2.4 (32-bit/64-bit)
- Linux 2.6 (32-bit/64-bit)
- Arch Linux (32-bit/64-bit)
- Debian Linux (32-bit/64-bit)
- openSUSE (32-bit/64-bit)
- Fedora (32-bit/64-bit)
- Gentoo (32-bit/64-bit)
- Mandriva (32-bit/64-bit)

- Red Hat (32-bit/64-bit)

- TurboLinux (32-bit/64-bit)

- Ubuntu (32-bit/64-bit)

- Xandros (32-bit/64-bit)

- OL (32-bit/64-bit)

- Other Linux (32-bit/64-bit)

In the same screen, you have to configure the amount of memory allocated for this VM (see Figure 12-2). Please be aware that the memory that you allocate in the memory size screen will not be available while the guest VM is running. Do not overallocate memory if you are leveraging your machine for other applications such as Microsoft Word, Microsoft Excel, or Microsoft PowerPoint. Microsoft products are notorious for draining memory on the machine when they are being used. To effectively run any Oracle Database 12c, you should allocate a minimum of 4GB of memory and two virtual CPUs (vCPUs). Allocate 4GB for this VM, take the default option to Create a Virtual Hard Drive Now, and click the Create button.

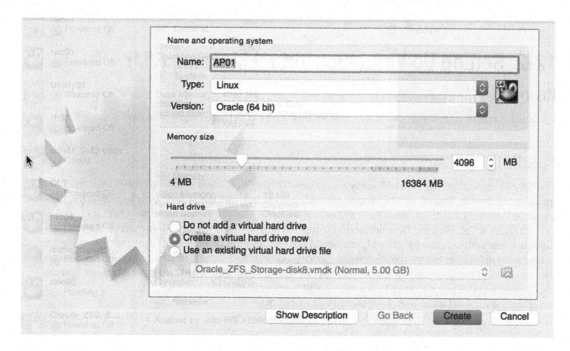

*Figure 12-2.* *Creating a new VM*

In the next screen, provide some basic information about the virtual hard drive you are creating for the VM. This virtual hard drive will be where you'll place the Linux OS. Unless you're planning for this virtual disk to be compatible with VMware or other virtualization technology, choose the default VDI (VirtualBox Disk Image). For VMware-compatible disks, select VMDK (Virtual Machine Disk). Figure 12-3 shows the options for location and size of the virtual disk.

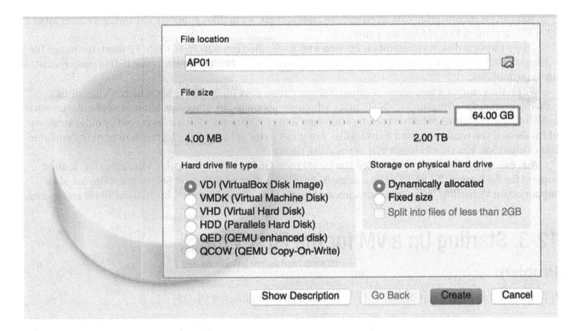

*Figure 12-3. File location and size for virtual disk for new VM*

Select the Dynamically Allocated option to choose a thinly provisioned virtual disk. If you want better performance, you can choose the Fixed Size option. For a fixed size disk, VirtualBox preallocates all the space up front; the dynamically allocated disk allocates disk space only as your usage consumption grows.

For VMDK virtual disks, you also have the option to split the files into 2GB files. This example creates a 64GB disk; if you choose the option to split the files of less than 2GB, you'll have approximately 32 files. For this VM instantiation, you'll allocate 64GB for the root and /u01 filesystems. You may opt to create multiple virtual disks: one for the root filesystem and another one for the /u01 filesystem. Click the Create button to create the VM.

---

■ **Note** If you chose fixed size virtual disk(s), you'll be waiting for a while when you click the Create button. The fixed size disk will consume the entire disk size, even if only a fraction of the disk space is being consumed. A fixed size disk will occupy lots more disk space, but it will incur less overhead.

---

Once the VDI disk is created with the specified size (thin for dynamically allocated or thick for fixed size provisioned), you'll be directed back to the Oracle VM VirtualBox Manager screen. You should also notice the newly created VM on the left side of the screen.

## How It Works

You just created a VM with one vCPU, 4GB of memory, and a 64GB virtual disk. You should allocate at least two vCPUs for any VM running an Oracle database. You can change the number of vCPUs by clicking the Settings button for the VM and then clicking the Processor button in the middle of the screen. You can increase the number of vCPUs from one to two or even higher.

You can create powerful VMs on enterprise class servers. VirtualBox supports VM configurations up to 32 vCPUs and up to 1TB of RAM for a guest VM.

Like a physical disk, a virtual disk is created with a specified capacity in MB/GB/TB when the image file is created. Unlike a physical disk, a virtual disk can be expanded after it is created, even if data already exists on the virtual disk.

VirtualBox supports four types of virtual disks: a Virtual Disk Image (VDI) file, which is VirtualBox's native container for virtual disks; VMDK disks, which are leveraged by other virtualization technologies such as VMware; VHD format, which is used by Microsoft; and HDD format, which is leveraged by older versions of Parallels. If you want to expand a virtual disk to a greater size or have all the feature functionality available from VirtualBox, you should select VDI as your disk choice.

You can create Linux guest VMs: Red Hat (5/6/7) and OL (5/6/7) in particular. VirtualBox has limited support for 2.4 kernels; 2.6 and 3.x Linux kernels are fully supported. 32/64-bit Solaris guest OSs are also supported on VirtualBox. Supported versions are Solaris 11, Solaris 11 Express, and Solaris 10 U6 and higher.

# 12-3. Starting Up a VM for the First Time

## Problem

Now that you have created your first VM you want to start installing the OL OS.

## Solution

You can configure the VM (in particular, the CD/DVD drive) so that the VM can be started from a bootable ISO image. Click the Settings button in the top-left corner next to the New button to view the general settings for the VM.

A window that looks like Figure 12-4 displays. Click the Storage button in the top middle of the row.

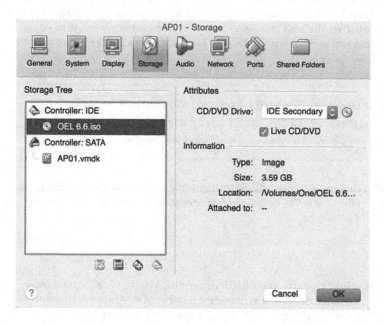

*Figure 12-4.* *Storage settings for the VM*

On the left side of the screen, choose the IDE controller and click the empty CD icon. On the right side of the screen, click the CD image icon for the CD/DVD drive in the Attributes section (next to the IDE Secondary drop list) and click the Choose a Virtual CD/DVD Disk File option. Find your ISO image for OL 6 from the browser and select OL 6.6 ISO. As a final step, make sure to click the Live CD/DVD check box option.

From the Storage screen, you can click the OK button to go back to the main Oracle VM VirtualBox Manager screen. From the Oracle VM VirtualBox Manager screen, select the VM that you just created and click the green Start icon on the top of the screen. Because you specified the OL 6.6 ISO image to be the virtual CD/DVD disk file, the VM will boot off the OL 6.6 ISO image and start the Linux installation on the VM. For complete step-by-step installation steps of OL 6.6, please visit the DBAExpert.com/blog site and search on Oracle Linux installation.

## How It Works

You'll focus on configuring VirtualBox to create a new VM for OL 6 and installing OL 6 from the ISO image as a guest OS. Oracle 6.7 is the latest and greatest release of OL at the time of writing this book. The OL 6 Update 7 ISO image can be downloaded from edelivery.oracle.com, Oracle's Software Delivery Cloud. You must have a valid (free) Oracle Account to download the Linux ISO.

Once the Oracle 6 ISO image is set up with the virtual CD/DVD player, click the Start button on the top portion of the Oracle VM VirtualBox Manager ( ) or right-click the VM and select the Start option. If you selected the Live CD/DVD option, the installation process starts instantly.

# 12-4. Creating Additional Virtual Disks

## Problem

You want to create additional virtual disks for ASM. You want to create additional disks for the DATA and FRA disk groups.

## Solution

To create another virtual disk for the guest VM, you have two options from the Oracle VM VirtualBox Manager. You can either click the storage section of the VM, or click the Setting button next to the New button on the top-left corner and click the Storage button on the middle-top portion of the General screen. From the Storage screen, look for the Serial ATA (SATA) controller and click the Controller: SATA line. A CDROM icon and a disk icon with a plus sign will appear. Click the disk icon with a plus sign, and you'll see the buttons Choose Existing Disk and Create New Disk (see Figure 12-5).

*Figure 12-5.* *Adding a virtual hard disk*

Because this is a new virtual hard disk, click the Create New Disk button. You'll now see the same Hard Drive File Type screen that displays in Figure 12-6.

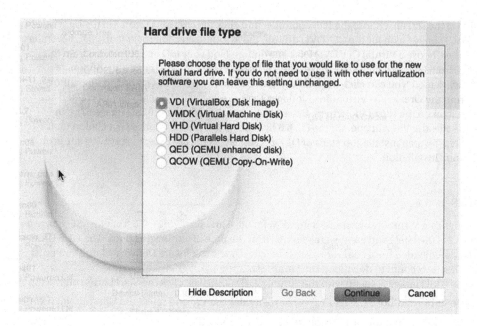

*Figure 12-6. Hard drive file type screen for the VM*

Choose the VDI (VirtualBox Disk Image) option and click Continue. As you continue with the disk creation process, you'll be directed to the Storage on Physical Hard Drive screen, in which you have to choose between creating a dynamically allocated disk or a fixed size disk. Choose the Dynamically Allocated option and click the Continue button to proceed to the File Location and Size screen, as displayed in Figure 12-7.

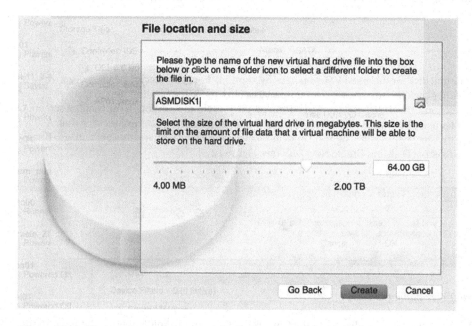

*Figure 12-7. File location and size screen for the VM*

Finally you have to specify the name and size of the virtual disk. For this example, you'll create a 64GB disk called ASMDISK1. VirtualBox will create a file called ASMDISK1.vdi. Once you click the Create button, you'll see your virtual disk on the Storage Tree (left side) of the Storage screen, as seen in Figure 12-8.

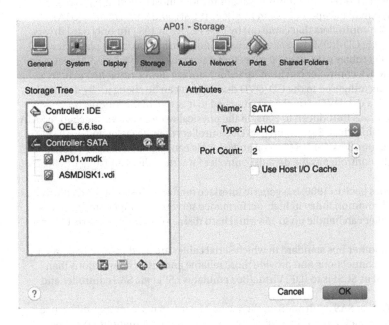

*Figure 12-8. Storage tree*

You have to repeat these steps for each virtual disk for the ASM disk groups.

---

▪ **Note** Alternatively, you'll see a disk icon with a plus sign on it under the Storage Tree section of the screen. Clicking the disk icon enables you to either create a CD/DVD device or a hard disk.

---

So far, you have gone through the process of creating virtual disks from the Oracle VM VirtualBox Manager. Now let's look at creating virtual disks with the command-line interface (CLI). Here's the command to create a VMDK to provision disks to run Oracle ASM on a Linux VMs:

```
$ VBoxManage createhd --filename asm1.vmdk --size 4096 --format VMDK --variant Fixed
0%...10%...20%...30%...40%...50%...60%...70%...80%...90%...100%
Disk image created. UUID: 1e2ab785-7687-42a5-bfd9-28962820f0eb
```

In this example, you created VMDK format disks so that you can port them to VMware later. To create a VDI disk, simply replace the --format option to be VDI. You should always create a VDI disk if you don't plan to migrate to another virtualization platform.

# How It Works

You want to provision four disks for each of the DATA and FRA disk groups. The differences between VMDK, VDI, VHD, and HDD disks was briefly covered. VirtualBox emulates the four most common types of hard disk controllers: IDE, SATA (AHCI), Small Computer System Interface (SCSI), and SAS. The IDE (ATA) controllers are backward-compatible controllers that came out by IBM PC/AT in 1984 for only hard drives. Later, the support expanded to include CD-ROM drivers and other removable media. In the physical world, IDE standard uses flat ribbon parallel cables with 40 or 80 wires that can connect 2 devices. A VM may have one IDE controller enabled, and an IDE controller can have up to four storage devices attached to it. By default, one of the four devices is preconfigured to the CD/DVD drive, but it can be changed. By default, a new VM has one IDE controller with a CD/DVD virtual drive attached to it as one of the four ports.

SATA is the newer standard that was introduced in 2003. In the physical world, devices attached to SATA controllers can be added/removed while the OS is running. SATA controllers operate faster and are less CPU-resource intensive than IDE controllers. With SATA controllers, VMs can also handle up to 30 virtual disks. VirtualBox leverages the SATA controller as the default controller for virtual disks and attaches the first virtual disk to the SATA controller.

SCSI, another standard that goes back to 1986, is a generic interface for data transfer between all kinds of devices. SCSI controllers are still common today in high-performance servers for connecting hard disks and tape devices. Each SCSI controller can handle up to 15 virtual hard disks. VirtualBox supports LSI and BugLogic SCSI controllers.

Serial Attached SCSI (SAS) is another bus standard in which serial cables are used instead of parallel cables. Serial cables simplify device connections and provide more reliable and faster connections than SATA. You can think of SAS is to SCSI as SCSI is to IDE. VirtualBox emulates LSI Logic SAS controller and supports up to eight devices.

Whether you choose SATA, SCSI, or SAS in VirtualBox, there won't be much performance difference in your personal desktop. All the controller support by VirtualBox is provided for compatibility with legacy hardware and hypervisors.

# 12-5. Provisioning/Sharing a Disk with Another VM

## Problem

You want to make the virtual disks to be shared disks. Disks created for RAC must be created as shared disks.

## Solution

One of the caveats about a shareable disk is that the virtual disk must be created as a fixed size disk in which the disk file fully consumes the allocated space at the time of creation. Once you create virtual disks for ASM disk groups, you can designate them to be shareable with one of the two options: using the VBoxManage (Oracle VM VirtualBox Command Line Management Interface Version) executable or leveraging the Virtual Media Manager.

With VBoxManage modifyhd, you can change the characteristic of a virtual disk and make them shareable, as shown here:

```
$ VBoxManage modifyhd asm1.vmdk --type shareable
```

For other options with the modifyhd parameter, issue this command:

```
$ VBoxManage --help modifyhd
```

To leverage the Virtual Media Manager, click the File menu from the top-left part of the screen and choose the menu option for Virtual Media Manager. From the Virtual Media Manager, locate your disk, right-click the disk, select the Sharable radio button option, and click the OK button.

After you make the virtual disks shareable, you have to assign them to the second or third or fourth RAC VM. You have to add virtual disks (refer to recipe 12-4), but select the option to choose existing disks (as shown in Figure 12-5) and select the shared disk from the file browser to complete the process for each disk.

## How It Works

Shared disks are required for Oracle RAC. Making a virtual disk shareable can be accomplished via the command line with the VBoxManage command or with the VirtualBox Media Manager. For shared disks, you should place the shared disks in a different folder from the VM. We also recommend the following folder topology and virtual disk placement for a RAC configuration:

```
dallasrac01
dallasrac02
dallasrac_shared_disk
            ov01_disk.vdi
            ov02_disk.vdi
            ov03_disk.vdi
            data01_disk.vdi
            data02_disk.vdi
            data03_disk.vdi
            data04_disk.vdi
            fra01_disk.vdi
            fra02_disk.vdi
            fra03_disk.vdi
            fra04_disk.vdi
```

You should create separate folders for each node and a dedicated folder for the shared disks. Disks for Oracle Cluster Registry (OCR) and voting files be a minimum of 8GB in size, and we also recommend 3 disks with normal redundancy for the OCR and Vote (OV) disk group. Each OCR file is 400MB in size and each voting file is 300MB in size in Oracle Database 12c. The Grid Infrastructure Management Repository (GIMR) consumes approximately 3.3GB in size and is by default in the same location as the OV files. Starting in Oracle version 12.1.0.2, there are options to move the GIMR to another disk group.

In this example, all the shared disks were intentionally created in a separate folder. You can create a dallasrac03 VM folder from a copy of the dallasrac01 VM folder. As a separate task, you can add the shared disks and easily provision another RAC node into the configuration.

# 12-6. Configuring the Virtual Network

## Problem

You want to configure the virtual network for both private and public network access.

## Solution

To create a virtual network within VirtualBox, navigate to the Oracle VM VirtualBox Manager, click the VM for which you want to create a virtual network, and click the Settings button ( ⚙ ) on the top-left corner next to the New button. You'll see a window with the title - [VM NAME] - General. This screen has eight buttons: General, System, Display, Storage, Audio, Network, Ports, and Shared Folders. Navigate your mouse to the top of the screen and click the Network button on the top of the screen. Figure 12-9 shows four adapters in the Network screen.

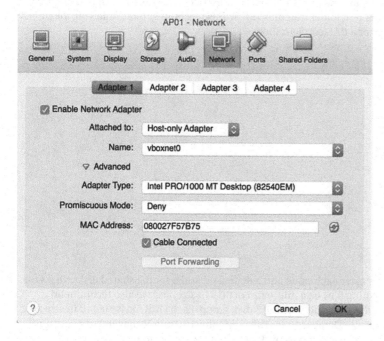

*Figure 12-9.* *Oracle VM VirtualBox Manager Network screen*

You'll leverage Adapter 1 to be the private network and Adapter 2 to be the public network. The default settings for Adapter 1 are Enabled and NAT.

Click the Attached To: field drop-down list; you'll see that Oracle VM VirtualBox Manager offers seven different networking offerings: Not Attached, NAT, NAT Network, Bridged Adapter, Internal Network, Host-only Adapter, and Generic Driver. Figure 12-10 displays all the network offerings from the Oracle VM VirtualBox Manager.

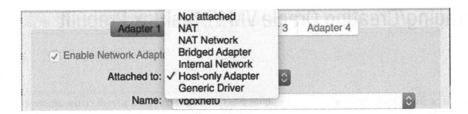

***Figure 12-10.*** *Oracle VM VirtualBox Manager network adapter options*

Choose Host-only Adapter for the private network (Adapter 1) and select vboxnet0 for the name. Next, configure the second adapter for the public network interface. Click the Adapter 2 folder, and (for simplicity's sake), choose Internal Network for the "Attached To:" drop-down list. Click the Enable Network Adapter check box. You'll see the name of the Internal Network (intnet) displayed.

## How It Works

The networking portion of VirtualBox is problematic for lots of DBAs. But with a little explanation, understanding the networking component can be simplified. This section concentrates on four common networking options: Network Address Translation (NAT), Host-only Adapter, Internal Network, and Bridged Adapter. There is also the Not Attached option, but this type is commonly leveraged for troubleshooting. The Not Attached mode implies that there is a network card but no network connectivity. You can think of it as having an Ethernet cable that is not plugged into the network interface card.

NAT, which is the default networking mode for VirtualBox, provides the simplest way to access an external network. NAT is popular because it typically doesn't require any changes to the host or guest OS. With NAT, you can surf the Web, check e-mail, and download files from the guest VM, but the outside world can't communicate with the guest VM. NAT enables the guest VM to reach the Internet via a private IP address that can't be seen from the host or the rest of the network. When the guest VM sends an IP packet to a remote server, the NAT service does the following:

- Intercepts the packet

- Extracts the TCP/IP segments

- Manipulates the IP address to the IP address of the host machine

- Sends the packet to the remote server

To the outside world, only the IP address of the host machine is revealed. Reply packets are received by the host and sent on to the guest VM.

With the Host-only Adapter, you can create a virtual network between the host and a set of VMs. Similar to a loopback interface, you can establish connectivity between the VMs and the host.

With the Bridged Adapter, VirtualBox interfaces directly to the network interface and exchanges packets directly, bypassing the host OS's network layer. You can connect to the same switch/router that the host OS is connected to and obtain an IP address that is on the same subnet as the host. The guest VM can act like an equal citizen as the host and be presented like any other server on the network.

Internal Networking (or isolated network) is similar to the bridged networking in the sense that the VM can communicate with the outside world. With Internal Networking, the outside world can see only the other VMs on the host that are connected to the same internal network, so it is considered more secure. Internal networks are created automatically and identified by name.

# 12-7. Leveraging/Creating Oracle VM VirtualBox Prebuilt Templates

## Problem

You want to leverage the prebuilt Oracle VM VirtualBox templates that Oracle has created and reduce the amount of time to stand up an environment. You want to create an Oracle VM VirtualBox template to share with another DBA or to another organization. You also want to share the Oracle VM VirtualBox template with VMware folks.

## Solution #1: Leveraging Oracle's Prebuilt Template

This solution looks into leveraging an Oracle template for the OL 6 Admin. Start by downloading the OL 6 Admin VM (OracleLinux65.ova) file from the Oracle web site: http://www.oracle.com/technetwork/community/developer-vm/index.html.

---

■ **Note** You can download numerous prebuilt templates from Oracle. Be careful: some of the templates are only for Oracle VM, not for VirtualBox.

---

Once the download of the .ova file completes, navigate to the File menu and select the Import Appliance option. You'll see an Appliance Settings window, in which you specify what to import. Click the file browser, find the .ova file that you downloaded, and click the Continue button.

From the Appliance Settings screen (see Figure 12-11), you can review the specifications of the VM and modify components such as the name of the VM or whether you want to enable the CD/DVD player or the sound card. You also have the option to reinitialize the MAC address of all the network cards.

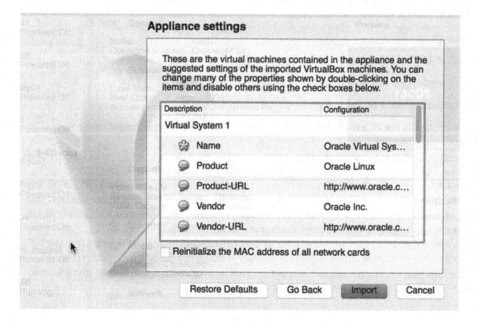

*Figure 12-11.* Import Appliance: Appliance Settings screen

Click the Import button to start the import process. You'll be immediately directed to the terms and conditions and software license agreement screen. You must agree to the terms and license agreements before the process starts. Once you click the Import button, it should take less than couple of minutes for the import of the OL 6 Admin VM to complete. You'll see Oracle Virtual Sysadmin Days (Powered Off) when the import is complete.

## Solution #2: Creating Your Own OVA Template

You can create your own template in the form of an .ova file. Choose the VM that you want to create an Open Virtualization Archive or Application (OVA) template for, go to the File menu, and select the Export Appliance option. Choose the location and version of the Open Virtualization Format (OVF) file that you want to create and click the Continue button. By default, VirtualBox defaults to OVF 1.0 format. You have the option to select the Write Manifest File check box.

In the Appliance Settings screen, review the VM that you are about to export. After you make the changes that you want and review the configuration specification, click the Export button to start the OVA creation process. The amount of time that it takes depends on how many virtual disks you have, the size of the virtual disks, and how much data are in the virtual disks.

## How It Works

Oracle provides numerous prebuilt templates for various Oracle products, including OL and Oracle Solaris 10/11. You can save hours and days by leveraging the prebuilt templates for instant VM provisioning. Oracle recommends using its prebuilt templates for development and education purposes, but they should never be used for production environments. For the OL 6 Admin VM, you need at least 2GB of RAM and 10GB of free disk space. You also have to know the password for the root and oracle accounts: 'oracle' (without the single quotes).

OVF is a packaging standard designed to address the portability and deployment of a VM or appliance so that it can be imported and be leveraged with other virtualization technologies. With the OVF standard, you can create a VM package that can be deployed between VMware Player and VirtualBox. The OVF package can be stored in an OVA, a single file distribution using the TAR format. You can think of an OVA as a single compressed and "installable" version of a VM.

You can take an OVA file, rename it to a .tar file and execute a tar command with the -tvf options (t=list contents to standard out; v=verbose; f=read the archive from the specified file) to list the contents of the original .ova file:

```
$ mv OracleLinux65.ova OracleLinux65.tar
$ tar -tvf OracleLinux65.tar
-rw------- 0 someone 46184 Dec 6 2013 OracleLinux65.ovf
-rw------- 0 someone someone 2189755904 Dec 6 2013 OracleLinux65-disk1.vmdk
-rw------- 0 someone someone   68096 Dec 6 2013 OracleLinux65-disk2.vmdk
-rw------- 0 someone someone   68096 Dec 6 2013 OracleLinux65-disk3.vmdk
```

The OVF format has two standards that you have to be concerned with. The OVF 1.0 standard provided the standardized virtualization format that solved the critical business need for software vendors and cloud providers. OVF 1.0 was widely adopted and became an international standard adopted by ISO/IEC in 2011.

The OVF 2.0 standard provides additional capabilities over the 1.0 format for improved network configurations, shared disks, more flexible scaling/deployment options, and basic placement policies such as affinity rules and encryption capabilities.

# 12-8. Cloning a VM

## Problem

You want to clone a VM to create another VM.

## Solution

To clone an existing VM from the Oracle VM VirtualBox Manager, right-click the VM and select the Clone option, as displayed in Figure 12-12.

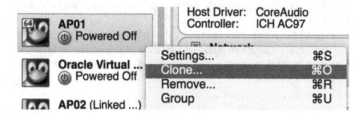

*Figure 12-12.* *Cloning a VM*

You'll see the option to clone a VM only if the VM is powered off. In the first screen of the cloning process, you must provide a name for the new VM that you are about to create from the clone. You also have the option to reinitialize the MAC address of all the network cards during the cloning process. After you supply the name of the cloned VM, click Continue to proceed. You'll be directed to the Clone Type screen, as shown in Figure 12-13.

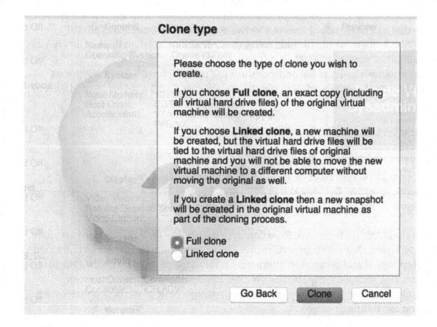

*Figure 12-13.* *Clone Type screen*

The Clone Type screen shows two options: Full Clone and Linked Clone. In this example, choose the Full Clone option and click the Clone button. Depending on the size of the virtual disks, you'll see a status window indicating progress of the copy of virtual disks and such. Once the cloning process is complete, you'll land back at the Oracle VM VirtualBox Manager screen.

For the Linked Clone option, you'll see on the name of the VM (Linked Base for AP02) on the VM library on the left of the screen.

## How It Works

As you have seen in this solution, cloning a powered-off VM is extremely simple. The full clone represents an exact copy of the source VM, including all the virtual disks. Alternatively, you can create a linked clone in which the virtual disks will be tied to the virtual hard drives files of the original VM. With linked clones, a new snapshot will be created for the original VM as part of the cloning process. Only changes to the cloned VM will be written to disk.

In this example, choose the option to fully clone the source VM. With the full clone type, the amount of time it takes to create a clone VM is directly correlated to the size of the virtual disks of the source VM. For larger files, it will take longer to perform a full clone. For linked clones, the cloning process is almost instantaneous. You can create linked clones in minutes from the source VM. For linked clone types, it operates in the copy-on-write technology.

# 12-9. Working with Snapshots

## Problem

You want to create a snapshot of the VM to revert back to in the event of a catastrophic situation such as a failed OS upgrade or failed database upgrades.

## Solution

To create a VM snapshot, you have to be in the Oracle VM VirtualBox manager. From there, you can click the Snapshots button on the top-right corner of the screen. The Snapshots button has a little camera on the left of the button label and also has the number of snapshots taken in parentheses.

Figure 12-14 shows that three snapshots already exist for the current VM called den00. If you look at the left side of the Oracle VM VirtualBox Manager, you'll see that next to the VM den00 is the snapshot name of the latest snapshot taken: (My Snapshot).

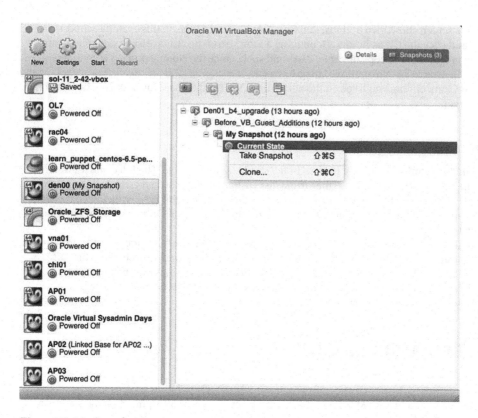

*Figure 12-14. Snapshot inventory*

You can perform a snapshot from the Current State. You can also start the clone process from the Current State or any of the previous snapshots that were taken. If you navigate to previous snapshots and right-click a snapshot name, you can also restore the VM from that specific snapshot or even delete the snapshot to clean up space.

Figure 12-15 reveals the options available for a snapshot. You can also look at detailed information about the snapshot by choosing the Show Details option.

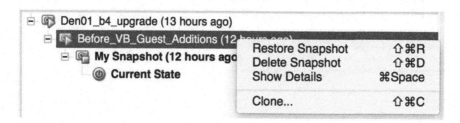

*Figure 12-15. Snapshot options*

You can revert the VM back to a previous snapshot by choosing the Restore Snapshot option. You'll see a warning window that asks whether you're sure you want to restore the snapshot. If you click the Restore button, your VM will be restored to the point-in-time snapshot that was taken.

## How It Works

The VM can be online or be powered off to take a point-in-time snapshot. For Oracle databases, you should always create a snapshot of the VM from the powered-off state. This way, all the Oracle header files are consistent because the database should also be offline, and you have a cold backup of the database. If you're working on an application server or web server, you may opt to take a snapshot while the VM is online.

To perform a live snapshot, navigate to the Machine menu option on top of the screen and choose the Take Snapshot option, as displayed in Figure 12-16.

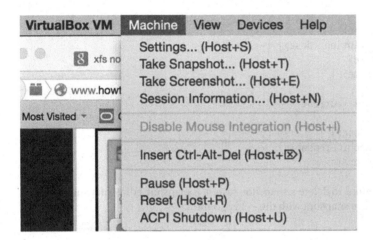

***Figure 12-16.*** *Taking an online snapshot*

Figure 12-14 shows five buttons on the right pane window. The first camera button creates a snapshot. The second button, with the semicircle arrow on the camera, restores a snapshot. The third button, with an X on the camera, removes a snapshot. The fourth button has a little circle at the bottom-right corner of the camera. You can look at the details of the snapshot such as when the snapshot was taken and additional documentation for the snapshot. The fifth button, which looks like a paste icon, is the cloning button. With this button, you can clone any snapshot to create a new VM.

This example demonstrates how to leverage the CLI to perform snapshots. You can perform a snapshot with the snapshot option and pass additional parameters to create a snapshot (the take option of the CLI) and provide a name and description for the snapshot:

```
$ vboxmanage snapshot den00 take "CLI Snapshot" --description "Snapshot was taken via CLI"
0%...10%...20%...30%...40%...50%...60%...70%...80%...90%...100%
```

You can list all the snapshots that were taken with the snapshot [VM Name] list parameters:

```
$ vboxmanage snapshot den00 list
  Name: Den01_b4_upgrade (UUID: fa8c8efc-6c29-49cd-81a0-7339da706bc0)
  Description:
Before our 12.1.0.2.2 upgrade
    Name: Before_VB_Guest_Additions (UUID: f0d88500-e06c-460e-93df-9fb31608fe30)
      Name: My Snapshot (UUID: e18a1bb0-a31d-4301-9184-a3f35fb3d53a)
      Name: CLI Snapshot (UUID: a692d5bd-b0bc-43de-91f6-582045ddf8ab) *
      Description:
Snapshot was taken via CLI
```

343

If you want to review all the options for managing snapshots with the vboxmanage CLI, provide the -help option followed by the keyword snapshot, as shown here:

```
$ vboxmanage --help snapshot
Oracle VM VirtualBox Command Line Management Interface Version 4.3.26
(C) 2005-2015 Oracle Corporation
All rights reserved.

Usage:

VBoxManage snapshot      <uuid|vmname>
              take <name> [--description <desc>] [--live] |
              delete <uuid|snapname> |
              restore <uuid|snapname> |
              restorecurrent |
              edit <uuid|snapname>|--current
                 [--name <name>]
                 [--description <desc>] |
              list [--details|--machinereadable]
              showvminfo <uuid|snapname>
```

As you can see, you have other options to delete a snapshot, restore a snapshot, edit a snapshot, show details for a snapshot, and even take a live snapshot with the --live option.

■ ■ ■

# CHAPTER 13

# Optimizing Linux for Oracle Databases

Companies are migrating away from large IBM, HP, or Sun hardware to commodity hardware running Linux. With the readily available 18-core Intel chips at affordable prices, companies can run massive Linux compute nodes at a fraction of the cost of enterprise UNIX servers on IBM, HP, and Sun. Linux is proven to have rock-solid OSs that provide extreme reliability similar to its counterpart UNIX OSs such as IBM AIX, HP/UX, and Sun Solaris. With proper optimizations, Linux can scale like its counterparts and run Oracle databases even faster. Think about a single compute node on an Exadata X5-2 configuration. It comes with 36 CPU cores and up to 768GB of physical memory. If you run a 2-node RAC for a Quarter Rack, you can harness 72 cores of processing power and approximately 1.5TB of memory.

Optimizing the Linux OS is an integral part of the Oracle database server. Having a well-tuned Linux engine is crucial to database performance. Companies incorporate best practices and optimizations into a reference architecture for Linux builds. You will focus on creating a lean and secure Linux infrastructure for Oracle that will perform consistently with each build.

Laying out a well-designed Linux architecture for an Oracle database is a critical factor for success. This chapter will lay out the optimal foundation for Linux reference architecture for an Oracle database. You will learn how to optimize Linux from a memory perspective, tweak kernel parameters for additional throughput, choose the right I/O scheduler, and increase network bandwidth for Oracle.

## 13-1. Minimalizing the Linux Environment for Performance and Security

### Problem

You want to install only the required packages that are needed to install and configure Oracle Database 12c.

### Solution

During the installation of Oracle or Red Hat Linux, you want to choose the minimal installation option. You can select the Minimal Install option from the top-left corner of the Software Selection screen (see Figure 13-1).

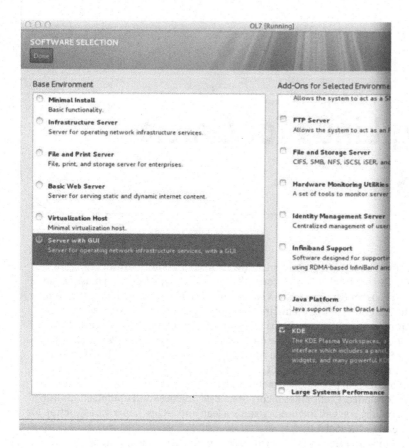

*Figure 13-1.* *Software selection for Linux installation*

With the Minimal Install method, you get only the basic functionality of the Linux OS. You will follow up after the minimal Linux installation and leverage the Oracle 12c RDBMS Server PreInstall RPM to continue to the next level. The Oracle RDBMS PreInstall RPM installs only the required set of RPMS needed to install Oracle. A majority of the Linux database servers don't need much more RPMS beyond what is installed by the Oracle RDBMS PreInstall RPM.

---

■ **Note** For information on leveraging the Oracle 12c RDBMS Server PreInstall RPM for automating Linux server configurations for Oracle databases, please review Chapter 11.

---

You can then build additional infrastructure—such as hugepages, I/O optimizations, network optimizations, and kernel optimizations—to take the Linux optimizations to another level.

## How It Works

You want to install just the minimum packages to effectively limit the amount of miscellaneous processes running on the database server and to run only database-related processes on the database server. Lots of customers make the mistake of installing the full GUI desktop on the Linux server. Although this method is great for educational purposes, you should never install the GUI desktop on a production database server. From a performance perspective, minimal installation helps by keeping the server "lean and mean." In addition, the less you have on the server, the less you have to secure. When it comes to patching the Linux server, the less you have installed, the fewer times you have to patch the server with updates.

A leaner server with less software usually runs faster than a server with all the software installed on it. For example, X-Server or VNC Server is not installed with the minimal installation, and you don't see X-Server processes running on a database server. At the same time, if you execute the chkconfig --list command to review all the services with run level settings, a majority of the non-Oracle related services should be turned off. You should also disable services such as http on the database server. A good rule to follow for optimal database performance is to separate out database-server processes from application-server processes.

On database servers, you should run in run level 3 (Multiuser mode with networking) and never run a database server in run level 5, which is GUI Desktop mode (the same as run level 3 + display manager). The default run level is controlled in the /etc/inittab file. In general, the fewer processes you have running in the background, the better off you will be. The parameter to control the run level looks like this:

```
id:3:initdefault:
```

# 13-2. Configuring Hugepages

## Problem

You want to configure hugepages to save memory and increase the performance of Oracle running on the Linux server.

## Solution

Setting up hugePages requires one kernel parameter change and modifications to two entries to the /etc/securities/limits.conf file. The kernel parameter that has to be modified is vm.nr_hugepages in the /etc/sysctl.conf file.

The /etc/security/limits.conf file has to be adjusted to account for soft and hard limits for Oracle, respectively, to increase the max locked memory limit:

```
oracle      soft    memlock      50331648
oracle      hard    memlock      50331648
```

After the kernel parameters are set, it is highly recommended that you reboot the server.

## How It Works

Leveraging hugepages provides great advantages on the Linux server. You will recognize performance through increased Translation Lookaside Buffer (TLB) hits. Hugepages ensure that System Global Area (SGA) components are locked in memory and are never swapped out. Hugepages also reduce the overhead associated with bookkeeping work for the kernel to manage kernel pages.

Suppose that the default kernel page is 4KB. By increasing the kernel page to 2M, you effectively reduce the number of kernel pages that you have to manage by a factor of 500x. The kernel parameters are typically set in granules of 2MB. For example, if you are allocating 48GB as your hugepage size, you have to set your kernel parameter to 24576 (48*1024/2) in the /etc/sysctl.conf file.

There is no such thing as a free meal: you can't use the automatic memory management (AMM) feature of Oracle when you implement hugepages. More specifically, the MEMORY_TARGET initialization parameter of the Oracle database can't be used. The Program Global Area (PGA), which is also part of AMM, can't be automatically changed, so when hugepages are used, the SGA_TARGET and SGA_MAX_SIZE parameters have to be used. The good news is that the PGA_AGGREGATE_TARGET is a dynamic parameter and can be adjusted as needed. You can view the dynamic view associated with the PGA and set this parameter intelligently, as suggested by Oracle's advisor view: V$PGA_TARGET_ADVICE.

Settings for hugepages should be set based on the amount of physical memory and total amount of SGA of each database on the Linux server. As a standard, you can determine default settings for hugepages for servers, depending on the amount of physical memory on the server. The default settings will just be a standard for new server builds as a starting point. The amount of memory to allocate for hugepages varies with different databases and applications. Some applications may need more PGA memory allocation. For example, you can specify the following set of guidelines for your company:

- =<20GB of physical memory and below; 1/2 of the physical memory will be configured for hugepages

- >20GB of physical memory, 3/4 of the physical memory will be configured for hugepages

## Automating Hugepages Server Configuration

Here's a handy script to add to your arsenal, which will one day save you tons of valuable time. Whether you are setting hugepages on a new server or an existing server with multiple databases, you can set up hugepages for the server with a single shell script. This script, set_hugepages.ksh, accepts a single command-line option for the amount of memory in MB that you want to allocate for hugepages. If you don't specify the amount of memory to allocate for hugepages, the script will determine the total physical memory from the server and take a majority percentage of the memory specified by the DEFAULT_HP_PERCENTAGE variable. The current script is set to 60% of the physical memory.

The goal of the following script is to determine the values for the vm.nr_hugepages kernel parameter and the soft and hard memlock parameters for the security limits configuration files:

```
# cat set_hugepages.ksh
#!/bin/ksh
export HP_SIZE_MB=$1
DEFAULT_HP_PERCENTAGE=60

if [ "$HP_SIZE_MB" = "" ]; then
  echo "HugePage Value not specified in the command-line options."
  echo "We will set the HugePages value based on $DEFAULT_HP_PERCENTAGE % of physical memory"
  SERVER_MEMORY_KB=$(grep ^MemTotal /proc/meminfo |sed -e 's/[^0-9]*//g' -e 's/ //g')
  let SERVER_MEMORY_MB=$SERVER_MEMORY_KB/1024
  echo "Server Memory: $SERVER_MEMORY_MB"

  let DEFAULT_HP_SIZE=$SERVER_MEMORY_MB*$DEFAULT_HP_PERCENTAGE/100
  echo "Default HugePage size based on $DEFAULT_HP_PERCENTAGE %: $DEFAULT_HP_SIZE"

  export HP_SIZE_MB=$DEFAULT_HP_SIZE
fi
```

```
LINUX_VER=$(cat /etc/redhat-release |sed -e 's/[^0-9]*//g' -e 's/ //g')
echo "Linux Version is: $LINUX_VER"
echo ""

echo "Checking to see if HugePages is already set"
grep -i vm.nr_hugepages /etc/sysctl.conf
RC=$?
echo ""

function calc_hp {
let HP_KB=$HP_SIZE_MB*1024
echo "HugePages KB = $HP_KB"
let HP_PRESETTING=$HP_KB/2048
let HP_SETTING=$HP_PRESETTING+6
echo "HP Settings:  $HP_PRESETTING $HP_SETTING"
echo "New HugePage Setting for /etc/sysctl.conf"
echo "vm.nr_hugepages=$HP_SETTING"
}
calc_hp

export TMP_SYSCTL=/tmp/sysctl.conf.tmp
if [ "$RC" -eq 1 ]; then
  echo "Return Code for HugePages: $RC"
  echo "HugePages is not set!"
  echo "# -- HugePage Setting for Oracle Databases -- #" >>/etc/sysctl.conf
  echo "vm.nr_hugepages=$HP_SETTING" >>/etc/sysctl.conf

elif [ "$RC" -eq 0 ]; then
  echo "HugePages is set..."
  cp /etc/sysctl.conf /tmp/sysctl.conf.$$
  cat /etc/sysctl.conf |grep -v "vm.nr_hugepages" >$TMP_SYSCTL
  echo "vm.nr_hugepages=$HP_SETTING" >>$TMP_SYSCTL
  cp $TMP_SYSCTL /etc/sysctl.conf
fi

let MEMLOCK_VALUE=$HP_SETTING*2048
cat /etc/security/limits.conf |grep -v ^# |grep -i memlock |grep -v grep 2>/dev/null
export MEMLOCK_RC=$?
if [ "$MEMLOCK_RC" -eq 0 ]; then
  export SECURITY_LIMITS_FILE=/etc/security/limits.conf
else
  export SECURITY_LIMITS_FILE=$(grep -il memlock /etc/security/limits.d/*.conf)
fi

# -- MEMLOCK has never been set so we need to find the limits.conf file
cat /etc/security/limits.conf |egrep -v "^#" |grep nproc
export NPROC_RC=$?
if [ "$SECURITY_LIMITS_FILE" = "" ]; then
  if [ "$NPROC_RC" -eq 0 ]; then
    export SECURITY_LIMITS_FILE=/etc/security/limits.conf
```

```
  else
    # -- We need to find the limits file for RHEL 6 directory structure
    export SECURITY_LIMITS_FILE=$(grep -i nproc /etc/security/limits.d/* |awk -F ":"
    {'print $1'} |tail -1)
    [ "$SECURITY_LIMITS_FILE" = "" ] && export SECURITY_LIMITS_FILE=/etc/security/
    limits.d/90-memlock.conf
  fi
fi

  export TMP_LIMITS_FILE=/tmp/limits.conf.tmp
  #echo "Security Limits File:  $SECURITY_LIMITS_FILE"
  cp $SECURITY_LIMITS_FILE /tmp/limits.conf.$$
  cat $SECURITY_LIMITS_FILE |egrep -v "memlock" >$TMP_LIMITS_FILE

  echo ""
  echo "# -- HugePage Setting for Oracle Databases -- #" >>$TMP_LIMITS_FILE
  echo "# -- Here's the changes that were made to the $SECURITY_LIMITS_FILE"
  echo "oracle soft memlock $MEMLOCK_VALUE" >>$TMP_LIMITS_FILE
  echo "oracle hard memlock $MEMLOCK_VALUE" >>$TMP_LIMITS_FILE
  cp $TMP_LIMITS_FILE $SECURITY_LIMITS_FILE
  grep -i memlock $SECURITY_LIMITS_FILE

echo ""
echo "# ------------------------------------------------------- #"
echo "# Your system has been set for hugepages.   "
echo "# Please reboot your server to see the changes!"
echo ""
```

Before you make changes to the current kernel parameters and configuration file, back up the files by copying them to the /tmp directory. Also create a temporary file in the /tmp directory with the .tmp extension to massage before overlaying the original files. You can download this script from the DBAExpert.com web site. This script is evolving and will be improved upon with each release of Oracle and Red Hat Linux.

Executing the previous set_hugepages.ksh script produces the following output:

```
# ./set_hugepages.ksh
HugePage Value not specified in the command-line options.
We will set the HugePages value based on 60 % of physical memory
Server Memory: 3587
Default HugePage size based on 60 %: 2152
Linux Version is: 66

Checking to see if HugePages is already set
vm.nr_hugepages=15006

HugePages KB = 2203648
HP Settings:  1076 1082
New HugePage Setting for /etc/sysctl.conf
vm.nr_hugepages=1082
HugePages is set...
```

```
# -- Here's the changes that were made to the /etc/security/limits.d/oracle-rdbms-server-
12cR1-preinstall.conf
oracle soft memlock 2215936
oracle hard memlock 2215936


# ----------------------------------------------------------- #
# Your system has been set for hugepages.
# Please reboot your server to see the changes!
```

To specify an exact value for hugepages, pass in a parameter into the script with a value in megabytes:

```
# ./set_hugepages.ksh 64000
```

You must reboot the server to recognize hugepage changes. If you log in as the Oracle Linux account owner, you can confirm the hugepage settings by typing the ulimit command with the -l option. The -l option reports the maximum size that can be locked into memory:

```
# su - oracle
[oracle@dal66a ~]$ ulimit -l
30732288
```

Notice that the value of ulimit -l matches the soft and hard memlock values from the security limits configuration files.

## Computing the Value of Huge Pages on an Existing Linux Server

Oracle Support provides a nifty shell script that calculates the total hugepages for a server that has one or more Oracle databases running. In a nutshell, the script will compute recommended values for HugePages/HugeTLB configuration for the current database server by rolling up all the shared memory segments. Please review the shell script to calculate the recommended for Linux Huge Pages/HugeTLB Configuration (Doc ID 401749.1).

You can copy and paste the script called hugepages_settings.sh and execute on a server that has existing databases already running on it. The script is dependent on the fact that the database is running, and the database has allocated shared memory that is visible with the ipcs -m command. The script also assumes that the database is not running in AMM mode. Here's a sample output of the hugepages_settings.sh script:

```
$ ./hugepages_setting.sh

This script is provided by Doc ID 401749.1 from My Oracle Support
(http://support.oracle.com) where it is intended to compute values for
the recommended HugePages/HugeTLB configuration for the current shared
memory segments. Before proceeding with the execution please note following:
 * For ASM instance, it needs to configure ASMM instead of AMM.
 * The 'pga_aggregate_target' is outside the SGA and
   you should accommodate this while calculating SGA size.
 * In case you changes the DB SGA size,
   as the new SGA will not fit in the previous HugePages configuration,
   it had better disable the whole HugePages,
   start the DB with new SGA size and run the script again.
```

And make sure that:
```
 * Oracle Database instance(s) are up and running
 * Oracle Database 11g Automatic Memory Management (AMM) is not setup
   (See Doc ID 749851.1)
 * The shared memory segments can be listed by command:
     # ipcs -m

Press Enter to proceed...

Recommended setting: vm.nr_hugepages = 603
```

## Disabling Transparent Huge Pages

Red Hat and Oracle Linux 6 have a new feature called Transparent Huge Pages (THP), which is enabled by default. THP was intended to simplify configuration of hugepages for the SAs because manual configuration of hugepages can be difficult for SAs new to Oracle. Hugepages are assigned at boot time and are usually used for highly static memory allocation of Oracle databases. THP can be dynamically set at runtime by the khugepaged thread in the kernel.

For Oracle databases, Oracle recommends disabling THP on database servers by executing the following command:

```
# echo never > /sys/kernel/mm/transparent_hugepage/enabled
```

Please refer to the Oracle document "ALERT: Disable Transparent HugePages on SLES11, RHEL6, OL6 and UEK2 Kernels" (Doc ID 1557478.1). To permanently disable transparent huge pages, add transparent_hugepage=never to the kernel boot line in /etc/grub.conf and reboot the server:

```
# cat /etc/grub.conf
# grub.conf generated by anaconda
#
# Note that you do not have to rerun grub after making changes to this file
# NOTICE:  You have a /boot partition.  This means that
#          all kernel and initrd paths are relative to /boot/, eg.
#          root (hd0,0)
#          kernel /vmlinuz-version ro root=/dev/mapper/vg_rac01-lv_root
#          initrd /initrd-[generic-]version.img
#boot=/dev/sda
default=2
timeout=5
splashimage=(hd0,0)/grub/splash.xpm.gz
hiddenmenu
title Oracle Linux Server Red Hat Compatible Kernel (2.6.32-358.23.2.el6.x86_64.debug)
        root (hd0,0)
        kernel /vmlinuz-2.6.32-358.23.2.el6.x86_64.debug ro root=/dev/mapper/vg_rac01-lv_root
        rd_NO_LUKS rd_LVM_LV=vg_rac01/lv_root LANG=en_US.UTF-8 rd_NO_MD SYSFONT=latarcyrheb-
        sun16  rd_LVM_LV=vg_rac01/lv_swap  KEYBOARDTYPE=pc KEYTABLE=us rd_NO_DM rhgb quiet
        numa=off transparent_hugepage=never crashkernel=auto
        initrd /initramfs-2.6.32-358.23.2.el6.x86_64.debug.img
```

```
title Oracle Linux Server Unbreakable Enterprise Kernel (3.8.13-16.2.1.el6uek.x86_64)
      root (hd0,0)
      kernel /vmlinuz-3.8.13-16.2.1.el6uek.x86_64 ro root=/dev/mapper/vg_rac01-lv_root
      rd_NO_LUKS rd_LVM_LV=vg_rac01/lv_root LANG=en_US.UTF-8 rd_NO_MD SYSFONT=latarcyrheb-
      sun16 rd_LVM_LV=vg_rac01/lv_swap  KEYBOARDTYPE=pc KEYTABLE=us rd_NO_DM rhgb quiet
      numa=off transparent_hugepage=never
      initrd /initramfs-3.8.13-16.2.1.el6uek.x86_64.img
title Oracle Linux Server Red Hat Compatible Kernel (2.6.32-431.el6.x86_64)
      root (hd0,0)
      kernel /vmlinuz-2.6.32-431.el6.x86_64 ro root=/dev/mapper/vg_rac01-lv_root
      rd_NO_LUKS rd_LVM_LV=vg_rac01/lv_root LANG=en_US.UTF-8 rd_NO_MD SYSFONT=latarcyrheb-
      sun16 crashkernel=auto rd_LVM_LV=vg_rac01/lv_swap  KEYBOARDTYPE=pc KEYTABLE=us
      rd_NO_DM rhgb quiet numa=off transparent_hugepage=never
      initrd /initramfs-2.6.32-431.el6.x86_64.img
```

Optionally, you can add the following lines in the /etc/rc.local file to disable THP at boot time.

```
[ -f /sys/kernel/mm/transparent_hugepage/enabled ] && echo never > /sys/kernel/mm/
transparent_hugepage/enabled
[ -f /sys/kernel/mm/transparent_hugepage/defrag ] &&  echo never > /sys/kernel/mm/
transparent_hugepage/defrag
```

# 13-3. Enabling Jumbo Frames

## Problem

You want to increase the packet size on your private network transmission unit to increase network performance. You also want to enable jumbo frames on the dedicated network for NFS or iSCSI storage performance optimizations.

## Solution

To enable jumbo frames on the Linux server, as the root user, execute the ifconfig command to set new MTU to 9000:

```
# ifconfig eth0 mtu 9000
```

Modify the network interface configuration file specific to the network interface to make the changes permanent. The following example demonstrates that by adding the parameter line MTU=9000 at the end of the network interface file, you are permanently setting jumbo frames:

```
# cat /etc/sysconfig/network-scripts/ifcfg-eth0
DEVICE=eth0
IPADDR=10.0.0.100
NETMASK=255.255.255.0
ONBOOT=yes
BOOTPROTO=none
USERCTL=no
VLAN=yes
MTU=9000
```

After you make changes to the network interface configuration file, you have to restart the network interface, eth0 in the example, by executing the `ifdown` and `ifup` commands:

```
# ifdown eth0
# ifup eth0
```

Alternatively, you can restart all the network interfaces with the `service network restart` command. Typically, you must coordinate the jumbo frame configuration with your network engineers. Jumbo switch support must be enabled on the switches, and all the switches must be enabled to support jumbo frames if you have multiple switches between the source and target database servers. The `ping` command will test end-to-end connectivity between the source and target hostnames or IPs.

Once jumbo frames are enabled for the OS and network switches, perform a simple `ping` test with the -M, do, and -s options to test jumbo frame connectivity from end to end:

```
$ ping -M do -s 8972 -c 2 dalrac01a-priv
$ ping -M do -s 8972 -c 2 dalrac01b-priv
$ ping -M do -s 8972 -c 2 dalrac02a-priv
$ ping -M do -s 8972 -c 2 dalrac02b-priv
PING dalrac01a (10.17.33.31) 8972(9000) bytes of data.
8980 bytes from dalrac01a-priv (10.17.33.31): icmp_seq=1 ttl=64 time=0.017 ms
8980 bytes from dalrac01a-priv (10.17.33.31): icmp_seq=2 ttl=64 time=0.018 ms
```

The -s option specifies the packet size. You can specify a packet size of only 8,972 bytes to the network. The remaining 28 bytes make up the header information: 20 bytes of IP header information and 8 bytes of ICMP header data. Sending a packet size larger than 8,972 bytes results in an error for the `ping` command. If you don't specify the packet size with the -s option, you will send the default packet size for the `ping` command, which happens to be 56 bytes without the ICMP header data or the IP header bytes. The example also specified the -c option to send just two iterations of the `ping` command.

The general recommendation is to enable jumbo frames for the private network interfaces for RAC configurations. When you are dealing with NFS or iSCSI disks, setting jumbo frames on the network associated with the dedicated network for NFS or iSCSI traffic significantly improves performance.

You can take advantage of the `cluvfy` command with the `healthcheck` option to verify whether jumbo frames are configured on the RAC database server. As you check for best practices, which includes the setup of jumbo frames, you can also leverage the `healthcheck` option with the –bestpractice option.

Here's a short snippet of the syntax and high-level output to the `cluvfy` command with the `healthcheck` and –bestpractice options:

```
$ cluvfy comp healthcheck -collect cluster -bestpractice -deviations
Verifying OS Best Practice
Verifying Hardware Clock synchronization at shutdown ...warning
Verifying Clusterware Best Practice\
Verifying Ethernet Jumbo Frames ...warning
Verifying disk free space for Oracle Clusterware home "/u01/app/12.1.0/grid"passed
...
...
...
```

## How It Works

In a nutshell, jumbo frames are Ethernet frames with more than 1,500 bytes of payload Maximum Transmission Unit (MTU). With jumbo frames, you can effectively increase the size of the Ethernet frame to be larger than the IEEE 802 specification for an MTU of 1,500 bytes to a value of up to 9,000 bytes. When an application such as Cluster Interconnect or the Parallel Query Engine sends a message greater than 1,500 bytes, the message is fragmented into 1,500-byte or smaller frames from one end-point to another. By setting the MTU size to 9,000 bytes, you can improve network throughput performance; because the packet size is larger, fewer packets are sent across the network for the application data, resulting in faster transfers and less CPU overhead on both the transmitting and receiving servers.

Jumbo frames should be enabled as part of your standard for Oracle RAC Interconnect. As mentioned earlier, the configuration of jumbo frames has to be enabled from end to end. Not doing it correctly results in suboptimal performance. Jumbo frames are not just used for RAC; other use cases include running Oracle Database file on NFS or even iSCSI protocols. Increasing the jumbo frames for databases running on NFS or iSCSI significantly improve performance. If your RMAN backups go to a distributed NFS, you should definitely run jumbo frames from the database server and the network attached storage (NAS) server.

Make sure that you are running Oracle's direct NFS to maximize all the performance and configuration benefits. For RAC Interconnect traffic, network interfaces correctly configured with jumbo frames improves performance by reducing the TCP and UDP overhead that occurs when large messages have to be broken up into the smaller frames of standard Ethernet. Properly setting jumbo frames is especially important if you are working with 10GB (gigE) or higher network interfaces.

# 13-4. Determining and Implementing the Right I/O Scheduler

## Problem

You want to maximize I/O potential for Oracle databases by choosing the right I/O scheduler.

## Solution

Starting from Red Hat/Oracle Linux 5, you can dynamically modify the I/O scheduler for block devices without a server reboot. For best performance, Oracle recommends the deadline scheduler for devices that are used by heavy I/O intensive requests. The deadline scheduler is highly recommended for Oracle databases to achieve higher throughput and lower latency. For flash disks or solid-state drives (SSDs), set the I/O scheduler to noop. You can dynamically set the I/O scheduler to deadline by manipulating the contents of the /sys/block/BLOCKDEVICE_NAME/queue/scheduler directory. As the root or privileged user, execute the following command for each of the disks:

```
# echo deadline > /sys/block/BLOCKDEVICE1/queue/scheduler
# echo deadline > /sys/block/BLOCKDEVICE2/queue/scheduler
```

Setting the I/O scheduler with the preceding syntax for block devices will not persist after a server reboot. Changes can be made permanent by setting the boot parameter elevator=deadline or elevator=noop for flash disks and SSDs to the active kernel in /etc/grub/grub.conf. Here's a sample grub.conf file that demonstrates how the configuration can be set at server startup:

```
default=0
timeout=5
splashimage=(hd0,0)/grub/splash.xpm.gz
hiddenmenu
```

```
title Red Hat Enterprise Linux Server (2.6.18-238.el5)
      root (hd0,0)
      kernel /vmlinuz-2.6.18-238.el5 ro root=/dev/VolGroup00/LogVol00 rhgb quiet
      elevator=deadline
      initrd /initrd-2.6.18-238.el5.img
```

If you are running the Oracle Unbreakable Enterprise Kernel (UEK), the settings for /etc/grub.conf for the I/O deadline scheduler are automatically set as default settings.

The following one-liner script can be leveraged to validate that disks are correctly configured with the right I/O scheduler. Notice from the output that the block devices are set with the deadline scheduler:

```
$ find /sys/block/*/queue -name scheduler -exec sh -c 'echo -n "$0 : "; cat $0' {} \; |tail -10
/sys/block/sda/queue/scheduler : noop anticipatory [deadline] cfq
/sys/block/sdb/queue/scheduler : noop anticipatory [deadline] cfq
/sys/block/sdc/queue/scheduler : noop anticipatory [deadline] cfq
/sys/block/sdd/queue/scheduler : noop anticipatory [deadline] cfq
/sys/block/sde/queue/scheduler : noop anticipatory [deadline] cfq
/sys/block/sdf/queue/scheduler : noop anticipatory [deadline] cfq
/sys/block/sdg/queue/scheduler : noop anticipatory [deadline] cfq
/sys/block/sdh/queue/scheduler : noop anticipatory [deadline] cfq
/sys/block/sdi/queue/scheduler : noop anticipatory [deadline] cfq
/sys/block/sr0/queue/scheduler : noop anticipatory deadline [cfq]
```

## How It Works

With Red Hat and Oracle Linux, different I/O schedulers are available with options suited to perform better under heavy Oracle database workload conditions. The default I/O scheduler shipped with Red Hat is the completely fair queuing (CFQ) scheduler, which provides a good compromise between latency and throughput. The default I/O scheduler that comes with the Oracle UEK is the deadline scheduler. The noop I/O scheduler is ideal for SSDs or flash-based systems in which the read/write head has been proven to not affect application performance. The anticipatory I/O scheduler is similar to the deadline scheduler. Although it is heuristic and can improve performance, it can also decrease performance. With the deadline I/O scheduler, hard limits are put on latency, and it guarantees a start service time for a request.

For databases running on virtualized environments such as VMware, the general recommendation is to set the I/O scheduler to noop. In a virtualized infrastructure, the hypervisor also performs I/O scheduling and optimizations. You don't want both the hypervisor and the guest OS (VM) to perform I/O scheduling; the guest OS should relinquish I/O scheduling to the hypervisor.

# 13-5. Setting Pertinent Kernel Parameters for Oracle Databases

## Problem

You want to optimize pertinent Linux kernel parameters to effectively run the Oracle database(s).

# Solution

This recipe reviews pertinent kernel parameters relevant to Oracle databases in the /etc/sysctl.conf file. In your environment, if the suggested kernel parameter value is higher than the value listed below, you should not lower the value. Range values (such as net.ipv4.ip_local_port_range or /proc/sys/net/ipv4/ip_local_port_range) should match.

The /proc/sys/net/ipv4/ip_local_port_range value defines the local port range that is used by TCP and UDP traffic. You have to set this parameter with two numbers: the first number represents the first local port allowed for TCP and UDP traffic on the server, and the second represents the last local port number. In previous releases of Oracle, the recommended values for net.ipv4.ip_local_port_range were 1024 and 65500.

Parameters such as SHMMAX should be adjusted according to the amount of physical memory on the database server. For example, you should usually tell customers that a good number to start is 1/2 or 2/3 or more of physical memory, depending on how much physical memory they have, how much PGA they have, and the number of dedicated server processes they expect. SHMALL is also derived based on physical RAM size/page size. The key thing to mention is that the value of SHMMAX is set in bytes, but the value of SHMMALL is set in pages. To determine the page size for a system, execute getconf, as shown here:

```
# getconf PAGE_SIZE
4096
```

In the following example, you opt to allocate approximately 66% of the physical memory (approximately 170GB) for SHMALL on a server with 256GB of RAM. You can use the following equation to derive the SHMALL value:

```
1024 * 1024 * 1024 * 170 /4096
kernel.shmall=44564480
```

Here's a comprehensive list of the kernel parameters modified by the Oracle-rdbms-server-12cR1-preinstall RPM:

```
# Controls the maximum number of shared memory segments, in pages
kernel.shmall = 4294967296

# oracle-rdbms-server-12cR1-preinstall setting for fs.file-max is 6815744
fs.file-max = 6815744

# oracle-rdbms-server-12cR1-preinstall setting for kernel.sem is '250 32000 100 128'
kernel.sem = 250 32000 100 128

# oracle-rdbms-server-12cR1-preinstall setting for kernel.shmmni is 4096
kernel.shmmni = 4096

# oracle-rdbms-server-12cR1-preinstall setting for kernel.shmall is 1073741824 on x86_64

# oracle-rdbms-server-12cR1-preinstall setting for kernel.shmmax is 4398046511104 on x86_64
kernel.shmmax = 4398046511104

# oracle-rdbms-server-12cR1-preinstall setting for net.core.rmem_default is 262144
net.core.rmem_default = 262144
```

```
# oracle-rdbms-server-12cR1-preinstall setting for net.core.rmem_max is 4194304
net.core.rmem_max = 4194304

# oracle-rdbms-server-12cR1-preinstall setting for net.core.wmem_default is 262144
net.core.wmem_default = 262144

# oracle-rdbms-server-12cR1-preinstall setting for net.core.wmem_max is 1048576
net.core.wmem_max = 1048576

# oracle-rdbms-server-12cR1-preinstall setting for fs.aio-max-nr is 1048576
fs.aio-max-nr = 1048576

# oracle-rdbms-server-12cR1-preinstall setting for net.ipv4.ip_local_port_range is 9000 65500
net.ipv4.ip_local_port_range = 9000 65500
```

You have to adjust the settings for SHMALL and SHMMAX according to SGA requirements. Other kernel settings set by the Oracle-rdbms-server-12cR1-preinstall RPM should be adequate for a majority of the database servers. If you have requirements for large amounts of concurrent dedicated sessions, you may have to adjust the settings for semmsl and semmns.

## How It Works

You will focus on the list of parameters that is mentioned in the solution of this recipe. Table 13-1 provides all the relevant kernel parameters for Oracle databases:

*Table 13-1. Pertinent Kernel Parameters for Oracle Databases*

| Kernel Parameter | Description |
| --- | --- |
| kernel.shmall | Represents the maximum total shared memory in 4Kb pages. |
| fs.file-max | Represents the maximum number of open files. |
| kernel.sem | Has four parameters (in order): SEMMSL, SEMMNS, SEMOPM, and SEMMNI:<br><br>• semmsl specifies the maximum number of semaphores per set.<br>• semmns specifies the maximum number of semaphores.<br>• semopm specifies the maximum operations per semop call.<br>• semmni specifies the maximum number of semaphore sets. |
| kernel.shmmni | Represents the maximum number of shared memory segments. |
| kernel.shmmax | Represents the maximum size of a single shared memory segment. We recommend a starting value of 1/2 or 2/3 of the size of physical memory (in bytes) and to go as high as 90% on some of the larger enterprise servers. |
| net.core.rmem_default | Represents the default OS receive buffer size. |
| net.core.rmem_max | Represents the maximum OS receive buffer size. |
| net.core.wmem_default | Represents the default OS send buffer size. |
| net.core.wmem_max | Represents the maximum OS send buffer size. |
| fs.aio-max-nr | Represents the total number of concurrent outstanding I/O requests. |
| net.ip_local_port_range | Represents the range of ports to be used for client connections. |

For Oracle databases 11g and above versions, set the following network–related kernel parameters in the /etc/sysctl.conf file:

- net.core.rmem_default to 262144

- net.core.wmem_default to 262144

- net.core.rmem_max to 4194304

- net.core.wmem_max to 1048576

In Linux, the kernel is designed to overcommit memory beyond its physical memory to make memory usage more efficient. The overcommit model sometimes becomes problematic when all available memory, including disk swap space, is consumed. When this state is reached, the kernel will start killing processes to stay operational. It is the job of the Linux out-of-memory (OOM) killer to sacrifice one or more processes to free up memory for the system.

For Red Hat/Oracle Linux 5 customers, it is important to set the vm.min_free_kbytes kernel parameter to protect from the OOM killer condition. In this example, you will set this to a value of 51200KB (50 MB), which will tell the kernel to reserve 50MB of memory at all times. To activate these new settings into the running kernel space, run the sysctl -p command as root.

For Red Hat/Oracle Linux 6 customers, set the panic_on_oops kernel parameter. As the kernel panics (or oops) or when a fatal bug is encountered, you will encounter potential problems with the server. If this parameter is set to 0, the kernel will attempt to continue to run with consequences. If the parameter is set to 1, the kernel will enter panic state and shut down/reboot. As the root user, execute the following command:

```
# echo 1 > /proc/sys/kernel/panic_on_oops
```

To make this kernel parameter change permanent, modify the /etc/sysctl.conf file and add the following entry:

```
kernel.panic_on_oops = 1
```

Optimizing virtual memory requires the changes to a set of kernel parameters, which impacts Oracle database performance by affecting the rate at which virtual memory is consumed and released with Oracle databases: vm.swappiness, vm.dirty_background_ratio, vm.dirty_ratio, vm.dirty_expire_centisecs, and vm.dirty_writeback_centisecs.

Some enterprise Linux SAs don't like the idea of disabling swap. The vm.swappiness parameter determines how aggressively memory pages are swapped to disk. The value can range from 0 to 100, and the default value is 60. The higher the value, the more aggressive is the rate of swapping out the physical memory when it is not active. We recommend setting the vm.swappiness parameter to 0. The Oracle-recommended value is 0 for Red Hat 6. You can monitor swap usage using native commands such as top, mem, and vmstat.

The vm.dirty_background_ratio parameter dictates the number of pages, specified in percentage, at which the pdflush background write back daemon will start writing out dirty data. The default value is 10; the Oracle recommended the value is 3.

The vm.dirty_ratio parameter dictates the number of pages, in percentage of total pages, at which a process that is generating disk writes starts writing out dirty data. This is the ratio at which dirty pages created by application disk writes will be flushed out to disk. The default value is 20; the Oracle-recommended value is 80.

The vm.dirty_expire_centisecs parameter dictates when dirty in-memory data is old enough to be eligible for writeout by the kernel flusher threads. Dirty in-memory data older than the value of this parameter will be written out the next time a flusher thread wakes up. The default value is 3000, expressed in hundredths of a second.

The vm.dirty_writeback_centisecs parameter dictates the interval when writes of dirty in-memory data are written out to disk. The default value is 500, expressed in hundredths of a second. The Oracle recommended value is 100.

In the /etc/sysctl.conf file, the following Linux kernel parameters can be set for database servers:

```
vm.swappiness = 0
vm.dirty_background_ratio = 3
vm.dirty_ratio = 80
vm.dirty_expire_centisecs = 500
vm.dirty_writeback_centisecs = 100
```

With different database workloads, you can tweak these kernel parameters as needed.

# 13-6. Configuring NTP for Oracle

## Problem

You want to configure network time protocol (NTP) to keep your server clock in sync with all the servers.

## Solution

You should synchronize your system time between your RAC nodes and even for your primary and standby database server by enabling the ntp daemon, which should be configured with the −x option to accept gradual time changes, also referred to as slewing. The slewonly option is mandatory for RACs and is also recommended for data guard configurations. To set up ntp with the −x option, modify the /etc/sysconfig/ntpd file, add the desired flag to the OPTIONS variable, and then restart the service with the service ntpd restart command:

```
# Drop root to id 'ntp:ntp' by default.
#OPTIONS="-u ntp:ntp -p /var/run/ntpd.pid -g"
OPTIONS="-x -u ntp:ntp -p /var/run/ntpd.pid"
# SYNC_HWCLOCK=no
```

Some SAs choose to update the system clock by executing the nptdate command via a scheduled job in cron, which does a brute force update of the system clock. If the system clock is off by 40 minutes, the time is immediately corrected. For RAC environments, setting the system clock with ntpdate can cause problems. As time is instantly caught up or sudden variances in time are detected, NTP can cause node evictions.

After you modify the ntpd file with the slewonly option, you have to push the files across all the database servers:

```
# for i in rac02 rac03 rac04; do scp ntpd ${i}:$PWD; done

ntpd                                    100%   255      0.3KB/s    00:00
ntpd                                    100%   255      0.3KB/s    00:00
ntpd                                    100%   255      0.3KB/s    00:00
```

You can check your current NTP configuration by checking the process status and filtering on the ntp daemon. In the following example, the ntpd service starts and checks to confirm that the settings are correct with the ps command:

```
[root@rac1 sysconfig]# service ntpd start
Starting ntpd:                                    [  OK  ]

[root@rac1 sysconfig]# ps -ef |grep -i ntp
ntp        3496    1  0 10:38 ?        00:00:00 ntpd -x -u ntp:ntp -p /var/run/ntpd.pid
root       3500 2420  0 10:39 pts/1    00:00:00 grep -i ntp
```

Set up the NTP process for time synchronization on the host to restart after a server reboot. After enabling the ntpd daemon, execute the chkconfig command to validate that it is set up to start at the appropriate run levels:

```
# chkconfig ntpd on
# chkconfig --list|grep ntpd ntpd

0:off 1:off 2:on 3:on 4:on
```

## How It Works

Time consistency across database servers is essential for every aspect of managing, troubleshooting, running, and debugging database events because everything is centered on time. You have to make sure that you have a point of reference when you are reviewing incidents and logfiles. You have to maintain an accurate system clock with NTP so that the OS time between the application server and the database server are the same. If you are also leveraging database links, you have to make sure that the source server and the remote server times are in sync.

Starting with Oracle Clusterware 11g Release 2 (11.2), Oracle provides another option for time synchronization that is intended for Oracle customers who can't leverage NTP services: Oracle Cluster Time Synchronization Service (ctssd). If you leverage NTP, Oracle ctssd starts up only in observer mode. If you don't leverage NTP, ctssd starts up in active mode and synchronizes time across all the RAC nodes. If you plan to leverage ctssd, deactivate NTP with the following commands:

```
# service ntpd stop
# chkconfig ntpd off
```

To confirm the mode in which the ctss daemon (ctssd) is working, use the following command:

```
$ crsctl check ctss
```

# 13-7. Bonding Network Interfaces

## Problem

You want to pair two network interface cards (NICs) to increase bandwidth and provide high availability.

# Solution

This recipe reviews the processes to combine multiple network interfaces (known as channel bonding or Ethernet bonding) to provide redundancy for your database server. Bonding a NIC is synonymous with port trunking and is relatively straightforward. First, you have to configure the Linux bond drivers. For example, in Red Hat 5, you must modify the /etc/modprobe.conf file to enable the bonding driver. For Red Hat 6, you must modify the /etc/modprobe.d/bonding.conf file. You must add entries for each of the logical interfaces in the modprobe.conf file that resemble the following:

```
alias bond0 bonding alias bond1 bonding
options bonding miimon=100 mode=1
```

A mode value of 0 indicates that you want a balanced round robin. A mode value of 1 indicates that you want an active backup for fault protection in which only one of the slave interfaces is active at a given time. The different slave interfaces become active only when the active slave fails. A mode value of 5 specifies that you want an adaptive transmit load balancing. Outgoing transmission will be distributed to the load of each slave interface. If one of the devices fails, the other device will assume responsibility and complete the network request. This configuration is popular because network switch support is not required. The miimon value of 100 specifies the amount of time in milliseconds when the link will be checked for failure.

In this particular solution, you are adding two bonded interfaces: one for the private interconnect and the other for the public network. You also have four network interfaces: eth0, eth1, eth2, and eth3.

If you have not bonded network interfaces before, most likely the bonding module is not loaded into the kernel. As root, execute the insmod bonding.ko command from the /lib/modules/ uname -r/kernel/ drivers/net/bonding directory to insert the module into the kernel. To confirm that the bonding module is loaded, you can leverage the lsmod command piped to the grep command, as shown here, to provide the status of the modules in the kernel:

```
# lsmod |grep -i bonding
bonding      65128  0
```

Once you confirm that the bonding module is loaded into the kernel, you can proceed by configuring the logical interfaces by creating or modifying two configuration files in the /etc/sysconfig/network-scripts directory: ifcfg-bond0 and ifcfg-bond1. The entries for ifcfg-bond0 look like this for the private network:

```
DEVICE=bond0
IPADDR=192.168.1.20
NETWORK=192.168.1.0
NETMASK=255.255.255.0
USERCTL=no
BOOTPROTO=none
ONBOOT=yes
```

You must modify the ifcfg-eth0 and ifcfg-eth1 files, which are the NICs for ifcfg-bond0. Start by modifying the ifcfg-eth0 file with these settings:

```
DEVICE=eth0
USERCTL=no
ONBOOT=yes
MASTER=bond0
SLAVE=yes
BOOTPROTO=none
```

Similarly, you can modify the ifcfg-eth1 file so it looks like what is shown here:

```
DEVICE=eth1
USERCTL=no ONBOOT=yes MASTER=bond0
SLAVE=yes
BOOTPROTO=none
```

Now you have to repeat the procedures described earlier to configure the ifcfg-bond1 interface for the public network interface. The ifcfg-bond1 interface file has to resemble this:

```
DEVICE=bond1
IPADDR=72.99.67.100
NETWORK=72.99.67.0
NETMASK=255.255.255.0
USERCTL=no
BOOTPROTO=none
ONBOOT=yes
```

The key differences between ifcfg-bond0 and ifcfg-bond1 are the IPADDR, NETWORK, and NETMASK lines. After the ifcfg-bond1 file is created, you can proceed to modify the ifcfg-eth3 and ifcfg-eth4 files. You can create these two files to look like ifcfg-eth0 and ifcfg-eth1 and modify the DEVICE and MASTER names accordingly.

To enable the newly configured bonded network, you have to bounce the networking services. You can shut down all the interfaces with the service network stop command. As the final step, you have to start the bonded network interfaces by executing the service network start command.

## How It Works

The Linux kernel comes with a bonding module that provides NIC teaming capabilities. The kernel bonding module teams multiple physical interfaces to a single logical interface.

Bonding or pairing a network is an important concept for RAC. Network interfaces that are not bonded are a single point of failure. Just as every other component of the RAC is built for redundancy, the network infrastructure must be, too.

In the /etc/modprobe.conf file, you specified options bonding miimon=100 mode=1. The miimon parameter, which stands for Media Independent Interface Monitor, represents the frequency for link monitoring. The value for miimon is specified in milliseconds (ms), is set to 0 by default, and is disabled.

The mode parameter specifies the type of configuration to be deployed. A value of 0, which is the default, indicates that a round-robin policy will be implemented, and each of the interfaces will take turns servicing requests. You can use a round-robin policy for load balancing. A value of 1 indicates that an active backup policy will be deployed. In an active backup policy, only one slave in the bond is active. One and only one device will transmit at any given moment. A value of 6 indicates adaptive load balancing.

In the ifcfg-eth[x] files, the MASTER parameter indicates the logical interface to which the particular NIC belongs. The SLAVE parameter indicates that the participating NIC is a member of bond interface. A SLAVE can belong to only one master.

# 13-8. Enabling Network Services Cache Daemon (nscd)

## Problem

You want to enable nscd to better tolerate network failures associated with NAS devices or NFS mount points.

## Solution

To enable ncsd, start by modifying the /etc/nscd.conf configuration file. You have to disable nscd options for passwd, group, and netgroup by modifying the enable-cache lines to no, as shown here:

```
# cat /etc/nscd.conf |grep enable-cache |grep -v \^# |sort -k3
enable-cache        netgroup    no
enable-cache        group       no
enable-cache        passwd      no
enable-cache        services    yes
enable-cache        hosts       yes
```

As the root or privileged user, start the nscd services with the service start nscd command. You have to enable nscd to start when the system is rebooted by issuing the following chkconfig command:

```
# chkconfig –level 345 nscd on
```

To confirm that nscd is enabled, issue the nscd command with the –g parameter, which prints the current configuration statistics. To see all valid options for nscd, pass the -? parameter.

If you performed a minimal OS install, you have to manually install nscd with the following yum command:

```
# yum –y install nscd
```

## How It Works

The nscd is a small footprint daemon that provides a caching facility for the most common name service requests. The nscd can help when you have network hiccups and minimum changes are needed to enable ncsd. Oracle database servers can house heavy network-based workloads and issue lots of name lookups NFS or in a clustered environment. The goal is to reduce latency of service requests and reduce impact on a shared infrastructure with nscd. You can also expect performance improvements when using naming services such as DNS, NIS, NIS+, LDAP.

# 13-9. Aligning Disk Partitions Correctly

## Problem

Lots of DBAs are not aware that they have to create a partition on the database disks. Correctly aligned partitions improve the performance of database workloads.

## Solution

There are several techniques to properly configure partition alignment: parted, fdisk, or sfdisk. In this example, you will focus on the parted partition editor to create a partition on a LUN that will be served to house database files for Oracle.

---

■ **Note** In Oracle Database 11g, the maximum size of an Oracle ASM disk can't be larger than 2TB. Starting with Oracle Database 12c, the maximum size of an ASM disk can be up to 32 petabytes (PB) for allocation size (AU) of 8MB. For other AU sizes, the maximum ASM disk sizes are: 4PB for 1MB AU size, 8PB for 2MB AU size, and 16PB for 4MB AU size.

---

You will see the examples using the parted command because parted can handle disk sizes larger than 2TB. For examples of leveraging the sfdisk command, please visit http://www.dbaexpert.com/blog/partition-alignment-with-sfdisk/. You can add, remove, clone, or modify partitions on the disk with the parted command. This example creates a partition alignment of 1MB with the GNU parted executable:

```
# /sbin/parted -s /dev/sdb mklabel gpt mkpart /dev/sdb1 asm1 2048s 32.0GB
```

In the preceding example, quite a number of parameters are passed. You start with the -s option, which specifies that you want to script out the command-line options instead of it being an interactive prompt. You also pass the device name that you are manipulating, followed by the gpt value for the label type, which is the GUID partition table. The mklabel option creates a new disk label for the partition table. The mkpart option tells the parted command to create a partition on the specified device name with the file system type, start points, and end points for the partition. The start and end point can be either in sectors or megabytes. The parameter 2048s represents 2048s sectors, which equates to 1MB because each sector represents 512 bytes. In the example, you chose to create a partition of 32GB in size. In your environment, you will probably create the partitions to the maximum size of the LUN.

After you create partitions for the ASM disks, double-check the settings to ensure that the partition alignment is set up correctly. To check for partition alignment on an existing device, use the following:

```
# /sbin/parted -s /dev/sdb print
Model: VMware, VMware Virtual S (scsi)
Disk /dev/sdb: 34.4GB
Sector size (logical/physical): 512B/512B
Partition Table: gpt
Number  Start   End     Size   File system  Name       Flags
1049kB  32.0GB  32.0GB                       /dev/sdb1
```

## How It Works

Misaligned ASM disks can cause suboptimal performance for Oracle database workloads. By default on Linux, the first 63 blocks are reserved for the master boot record (MBR). The first data partition starts with offset at 31.5KB, which is derived from 63 blocks multiplied by 512 bytes. The offset of 31.5KB can cause misalignment situations on many storage arrays' memory cache or RAID configurations, causing suboptimal performance due to overlapping I/Os. You want the partition offset to be 1MB or 4MB for Oracle databases.

Most importantly, use parted instead of fdisk or even sfdisk because you can create partitions for disks larger than 2TB with parted. Prior to Oracle Database 12c, you had the flexibility to use sfdisk because an ASM LUN couldn't be larger than 2TB in size. As of Oracle Database 12c, the 2TB limitation for LUN size is lifted, and you have to start migrating to commands such as parted.

■ ■ ■

# CHAPTER 14

# Working Securely Across a Network

Secure communication is a concern, particularly when sharing confidential and vital information between people. For example, English Prime Minister Winston Churchill and American President Franklin D. Roosevelt shared critical military information, such as troop movements, during World War II. To secure their voice conversations through the telephone, the SIGSALY (aka Green Hornet) was devised to encrypt and decrypt using cryptographic keys.

Today, we can't imagine anyone *not* worrying about network security. Even people who are not so technically savvy should be concerned. For instance, what if your bank's network is not secured, and a hacker steals your bank account number and PIN? Likewise, a DBA may want to connect to a Linux/Solaris server situated in a remote geographical location or another room in the building while working at the office or at home. What if a coworker is eavesdropping while that DBA is accessing sensitive data?

To address these network security concerns, version 1 of SSH was hatched in 1995, but it was replaced a year later by version 2 for security enhancements. SSH is a network protocol in which the encrypted data traverses through the network using a secure channel between computers, as illustrated in Figure 14-1. The ssh protocol replaces the older network protocols (telnet, rlogin, and rsh), and the scp command replaces the rcp command. The older protocols and commands were replaced because they lack the security feature; it just was not considered when they were initially designed.

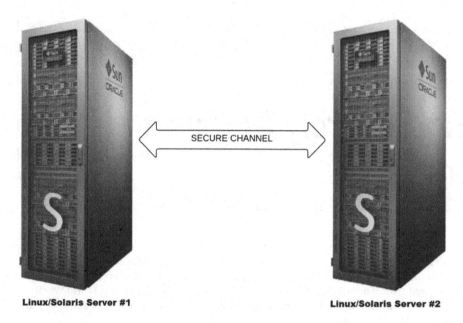

**Figure 14-1.** *SSH connection*

This chapter focuses the discussion on how to log on securely to a remote Linux/Solaris server through SSH. It also discusses how to generate the server's SSH host key, how to use the SSH public key for authentication in lieu of the username's password, and how to securely copy files between Linux/Solaris servers.

# 14-1. Setting Up SSH
## Problem

You want to configure SSH so you can have a secured and encrypted connection to your remote Linux/Solaris server.

## Solution

Before you configure SSH, ensure that you have the required packages: openssh, openssh-server, openssh-clients, and openssh-askpass. You can verify the SSH packages installed on your server by running the rpm command as follows:

```
# rpm -qa | grep -i openssh
openssh-5.3p1-94.el6.x86_64
openssh-clients-5.3p1-94.el6.x86_64
openssh-server-5.3p1-94.el6.x86_64
openssh-askpass-5.3p1-94.el6.x86_64
```

---

■ **Note**    Run the ssh -V command to check the type and version of SSH installed on your server.

---

Before you can connect to your remote Linux/Solaris server, the SSH daemon server (sshd) must be running. You can run sshd as follows:

```
# service sshd start
Starting sshd:                                          [ OK ]
```

You can also run sshd by calling the following script, which is the same script called by the previous command:

```
# /etc/rc.d/init.d/sshd start
Starting sshd:                                          [ OK ]
```

However, if sshd is already started, you can restart it as shown here. Another way is to issue the command /etc/rc.d/init.d/sshd restart:

```
# service sshd restart
Stopping sshd:                                          [ OK ]
Starting sshd:                                          [ OK ]
```

For Solaris, issue the following command to enable the ssh service, as shown here:

```
# svcadm enable network/ssh
```

To disable the ssh service, issue the following command:

```
# svcadm disable network/ssh
```

Afterward, run the following command to verify whether the ssh service is online or offline:

```
# svcs -v ssh
```

For sshd to start automatically when the Linux server is rebooted, you need to have sshd activated. You can activate sshd by using chkconfig, ntsysv, or system-config-services.

For the chkconfig command, use the --level option and provide the run level in which you want sshd to start. The following command indicates that sshd is configured to start in run levels 2, 3, 4, and 5:

```
# chkconfig --level 2345 sshd on
```

---

■ **Note**  For a discussion of the Linux system V init run levels, refer to Chapter 11.

---

For the ntsysv command, also use the --level option and specify the run levels for sshd to start. If no run levels are specified, sshd will be activated only on the current run level. The following command runs ntsysv and affects only run levels 3 and 5:

```
# ntsysv --level 35
```

---

■ **Note**  You can also launch ntsysv through the text mode setup utility by running the OS setup command and selecting System Services from the menu.

---

After you launch the ntsysv command, the screen of the text console service configuration tool will appear, as shown in Figure 14-2. Navigate by scrolling down using the arrow keys until the cursor is on sshd. The asterisk (*) inside the square brackets indicates that the status of the service is active; empty square brackets show that it is not active. (You can press the spacebar to toggle the status to become active or not active.) To save the changes, click the Tab key to highlight the Ok button and then press Enter.

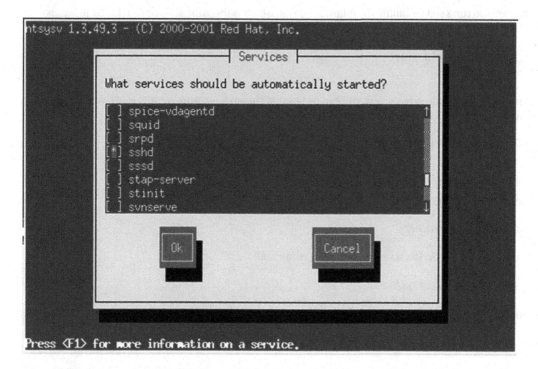

**Figure 14-2.** *Launching the ntsysv command*

Another way to activate sshd is to run the system-config-services command; you can launch this tool as follows:

```
# /usr/sbin/system-config-services
```

After you launch system-config-services, the GUI-based service configuration tool will appear, as shown in Figure 14-3. Navigate by scrolling down to the sshd service and check the adjacent box to activate it. In this dialog box, you also have the option to start, stop, and restart the sshd service. You can also check the status and PID.

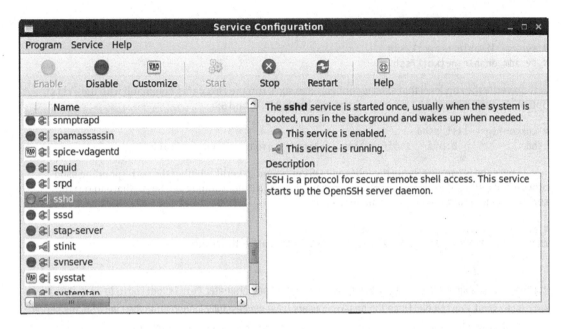

**Figure 14-3.** *Launching* system-config-services

## How It Works

By default, the required SSH packages are included in major Linux/Solaris distributions. Otherwise, you can download them from any Linux/Solaris package download site such as http://www.openssh.com.

Once the SSH packages are installed on your remote Linux/Solaris server, you can activate and run the sshd daemon, and it should be ready to accept SSH connections. You can, however, make some changes, such as modifying the default port number on which sshd should be listening.

---

■ **Note**  The default SSH port number that the Linux/Solaris server will listen on is 22. To change the default SSH port number, modify the value of the parameter Port in the /etc/ssh/sshd_config file.

---

The /etc/ssh/sshd_config file is the SSH systemwide configuration file at the Linux/Solaris server, which is the computer that you want to connect via SSH. The /etc/ssh/ssh_config file is the configuration file for the SSH client, which is the computer from which you are initiating SSH. If you make some changes to the /etc/ssh/sshd_config file, you have to reload sshd by running service sshd reload as follows:

```
[root@BLLNX2 stage]# service sshd reload
Reloading sshd:                                        [ OK ]
```

You can also run the service sshd restart command; another method is to stop and start the sshd service, which will give the same results, as follows:

```
# service sshd stop
Stopping sshd:                                         [ OK ]
# service sshd start
Starting sshd:                                         [ OK ]
```

For Solaris, run the following:

```
# svcadm disable network/ssh
# svcadm enable network/ssh
```

To verify the run level that sshd is configured to start, run the chkconfig command with the --list option. As shown here, sshd is set to start on run levels 2, 3, 4, and 5:

```
# chkconfig --list sshd
sshd              0:off   1:off   2:on   3:on   4:on   5:on   6:off
```

Once sshd is running, issue the following OS command to verify whether the corresponding sshd process is running. If there are no results, it means that sshd is not running yet. So you have to run the service sshd start command to manually start sshd:

```
# ps -ef | grep -v grep | grep ssh
root        4025    1  0 16:32 ?        00:00:00 /usr/sbin/sshd
```

---

■ **Note**    To disallow the root user to log on via SSH, set the parameter PermitRootLogin to no in the /etc/ssh/sshd_config file. Once the non-root users have successfully logged on to the Linux/Solaris server via SSH, they can then run the su - root command or run the sudo command instead.

---

# 14-2. Generating Host Keys
## Problem

The SSH host key of your remote Linux/Solaris server is lost, is corrupted, or was not generated when the SSH packages were installed or during the first run. You want to generate a new SSH host key.

## Solution

To generate a new SSH host key of the Linux/Solaris server, log on as root and run the ssh-keygen command with the -t option, which indicates the type of key to be generated. You must provide the -f option, followed by the file name of the key file. If you omit the -f option, it will create the public key for the OS account root instead of the SSH host key on the Linux/Solaris server.

The following example generates the SSH host key for the RSA type. If the files of the SSH host keys already exist, you are asked whether you want to overwrite them.

Next, you are asked to provide the passphrase:

```
root@BLSOLO2:~# ssh-keygen -t rsa -f /etc/ssh/ssh_host_rsa_key
Generating public/private rsa key pair.
/etc/ssh/ssh_host_rsa_key already exists.
Overwrite (yes/no)? yes
Enter passphrase (empty for no passphrase):
Enter same passphrase again:
Your identification has been saved in /etc/ssh/ssh_host_rsa_key.
Your public key has been saved in /etc/ssh/ssh_host_rsa_key.pub.
The key fingerprint is:
03:bc:53:70:ff:d2:c8:f5:2d:2e:6d:07:3d:3d:1a:66 root@BLSOLO2
```

To generate the SSH host key for the DSA type, run the following command:

```
root@BLSOLO2:~# ssh-keygen -t dsa -f /etc/ssh/ssh_host_dsa_key
Generating public/private dsa key pair.
/etc/ssh/ssh_host_dsa_key already exists.
Overwrite (yes/no)? yes
Enter passphrase (empty for no passphrase):
Enter same passphrase again:
Your identification has been saved in /etc/ssh/ssh_host_dsa_key.
Your public key has been saved in /etc/ssh/ssh_host_dsa_key.pub.
The key fingerprint is:
ee:0d:88:61:1a:27:20:2e:69:27:7b:bc:70:de:a2:5c root@BLSOLO2
```

■ **Note**    For security reasons, we recommend that you supply a passphrase when creating the SSH host key. This prevents non-root users from peeking on the SSH host key by running ssh-keygen with the -y option (discussed in detail in the next section).

# How It Works

The SSH host key is like a master key that encrypts and decrypts the data that traverses between the remote Linux/Solaris server and the client computer from which you want to initiate the SSH connection. This secures your connection to the remote Linux/Solaris server and eliminates vulnerability to man-in-the-middle attacks.

When creating a new SSH host key, you have to provide the type of key that corresponds to the version of SSH and the kind of encryption algorithm, which is either RSA or DSA. Both the RSA and DSA support some security method and different encryption algorithm. In terms of security, both the DSA and RSA are similar when comparing them with the same length keys. However, there is no clear winner for being fastest in encryption and decryption.

The valid values for the SSH host key are rsa1, rsa, and dsa. rsa1 refers to RSA of SSH version 1 (SSHv1); rsa and dsa are for SSH version 2 (SSHv2).

■ **Note**    If your Linux/Solaris server supports only SSHv2, set the value of the parameter Protocol to 2 in /etc/ssh/sshd_config.

To create the RSA host key, run ssh-keygen with the -t rsa option, which creates two files: /etc/ssh/ssh_host_rsa_key and /etc/ssh/ssh_host_rsa_key.pub. For the DSA host key, run -keygen with the -t dsa option, which creates /etc/ssh/ssh_host_dsa_key and /etc/ ssh/ssh_host_dsa_key.pub. Both ssh_host_rsa_key and ssh_host_dsa_key contain the private and public key, whereas ssh_host_rsa_key.pub and ssh_host_dsa_key.pub contain only the public key. The public key is used to encrypt the data; the private key is used to decrypt the data.

The first time you log on to the remote Linux/Solaris server, which is the computer you are connecting to via SSH, you are prompted to confirm the server's SSH host key fingerprint, as shown here. If you accept it, the file $HOME/.ssh/known_hosts is created on the local Linux/Solaris server, which is the computer from which you initiated the SSH connection. $HOME/.ssh/known_hosts contains the server's SSH host key.

```
oracle@BLSOL01:~$ ssh BLSOL02
The authenticity of host 'blsol02 (192.168.2.42)' can't be established.
RSA key fingerprint is 03:bc:53:70:ff:d2:c8:f5:2d:2e:6d:07:3d:3d:1a:66.
Are you sure you want to continue connecting (yes/no)? yes
Warning: Permanently added 'blsol02,192.168.2.42' (RSA) to the list of known hosts.
Password:
Last login: Thu Aug 20 23:59:50 2015 from ol6-121-rac1
Oracle Corporation      SunOS 5.11      11.2      June 2014
oracle@BLSOL02:~$
```

To determine the SSH key fingerprint on the remote Linux/Solaris server, run the ssh-keygen command with the -l option, as shown here. It verifies whether you have the correct SSH host key fingerprint of the remote Linux/Solaris server that you want to connect via SSH.

```
root@BLSOL02:~# ssh-keygen -l -f /etc/ssh/ssh_host_dsa_key.pub
1024 ee:0d:88:61:1a:27:20:2e:69:27:7b:bc:70:de:a2:5c /etc/ssh/ssh_host_dsa_key.pub
root@BLSOL02:~#
root@BLSOL02:~# ssh-keygen -l -f /etc/ssh/ssh_host_rsa_key.pub
2048 03:bc:53:70:ff:d2:c8:f5:2d:2e:6d:07:3d:3d:1a:66 /etc/ssh/ssh_host_rsa_key.pub
```

Meanwhile, to determine the SSH host key on the remote Linux/Solaris server, run the ssh-keygen command with the -y option, as shown here. For security reasons, you can be asked to provide the passphrase that you supplied when creating the SSH host key.

```
root@BLSOL02:~# ssh-keygen -y -f /etc/ssh/ssh_host_dsa_key
ssh-dss
AAAAB3NzaC1kc3MAAACBAJ2G5jV/4MHg9dG4DNb13Wrh94kbN5yUDQeW5SOPOJCzCQVpS2BnsV53L6CUQUPiNilXC
qiLVMGaJmm+GSNL4Z82zAvNekTihXa1XabdAN7hBWccaxzH7ppmNbexiZVE/63aKIN+QnsjZ+cFbrqgDN9/
10O8DKVM7AJQbyaPDbOrAAAAFQCmFbD9ei01XVMKkOzvqOpp4SwqXQAAAIBNRewVPbCM/p2GZ4PlepXnY2Etbe
UZ8WFe15gEfrTwk9lDVh1M2RBs5NRqzHe3JNNddln116fhr++tFK2/x0tG9bNbWfIUEO++gULfYDqn1Ir17L7MZ3gK1K
eELyJqtbkZKs2Ne/SAOoaZeJCOCMbi8Vs6ESkdMoSq34xbceDeugAAAIBc4ZWy84OUAb7EURncb9KJg9wLFXfYpy7
XubGGXhgfsw/z4Uect++kP8QpSYY3QynCzJ4ix3FpOyMKx4VShXKxQcYEMCNx5mnNOiLk/YmEfyeZI/
pNR7WIixvQQIjOJ0bjQRzdz2T+K3Y83S8f522N76dNVBgJmCbWOSalhwqoIw==
root@BLSOL02:~#
root@BLSOL02:~# ssh-keygen -y -f /etc/ssh/ssh_host_rsa_key
ssh-rsa AAAAB3NzaC1yc2EAAAABIwAAAQEAs/WovKxUpZw8TO3HoH4dOlYGLzQ9bbfqayRd8Me33odUzKc8loUhOAdc
k7ySzaU3fdOY+0Yt1V/CN7wKo2qKowknf2K9JDsPyztSlSZi5FcT2WU6uDlbOFnEg+VAad83ETfDQQ+Ei2s5tV24n+
QKAJd7qiAImITTfC55D/ftxpdKZL+m4Meupva6rTiagsLc7fiR4w6FYtuNI3oqaxElDuhJ3675XoTTF3FzhUj0spj
4ZLZ6nkN3mYTVyAfrrjzeHDG6N59B6O46C2zW9hCW3e0ZQ3g1sQlDaE/hScErd4JoLR8F2VnWlrjOMQx+4328/
p5C668LdPzULEuNEzXNPQ==
```

On your local client computer, run the tail command, as shown here. Check the SSH host key, which comprises the characters after ssh-rsa or ssh-dsa, and compare them against the results of the ssh-keygen -y option.

```
oracle@BLSOL01:~$ tail -1 $HOME/.ssh/known_hosts
blsol02,192.168.2.42 ssh-rsa AAAAB3NzaC1yc2EAAAABIwAAAQEAs/WovKxUpZw8TO3HoH4dOlYGLzQ9bbfqay
Rd8Me33odUzKc8loUhOAdck7ySzaU3fdOY+0Yt1V/CN7wKo2qKowknf2K9JDsPyztSlSZi5FcT2WU6uDlbOFnEg+
VAad83ETfDQQ+Ei2s5tV24n+QKAJd7qiAImITTfC55D/ftxpdKZL+m4Meupva6rTiagsLc7fiR4w6FYtuNI3oqaxElD
uhJ3675XoTTF3FzhUj0spj4ZLZ6nkN3mYTVyAfrrjzeHDG6N59B6O46C2zW9hCW3e0ZQ3g1sQlDaE/
hScErd4JoLR8F2VnWlrjOMQx+4328/p5C668LdPzULEuNEzXNPQ==
```

However, when the remote Linux/Solaris server has a duplicate hostname or IP address, you will see the following error messages the next time you log on:

```
[root@ol6-121-rac1 ~]# ssh oracle@BLSOL01
@@@@@@@@@@@@@@@@@@@@@@@@@@@@@@@@@@@@@@@@@@@@@@@@@@@@@@@@@@@@@@@
@    WARNING: REMOTE HOST IDENTIFICATION HAS CHANGED!    @
@@@@@@@@@@@@@@@@@@@@@@@@@@@@@@@@@@@@@@@@@@@@@@@@@@@@@@@@@@@@@@@
IT IS POSSIBLE THAT SOMEONE IS DOING SOMETHING NASTY!
Someone could be eavesdropping on you right now (man-in-the-middle attack)!
It is also possible that the DSA host key has just been changed.
The fingerprint for the DSA key sent by the remote host is
8d:fa:39:1e:36:a7:6a:b1:87:ea:63:1a:c0:84:4a:3d.
Please contact your system administrator.
Add correct host key in /root/.ssh/known_hosts to get rid of this message.
Offending key in /root/.ssh/known_hosts:6
DSA host key for blsol01 has changed and you have requested strict checking.
Host key verification failed.
```

To resolve this problem, you can rename $HOME/.ssh/known_hosts, but this is not advisable because you will lose the reference of the SSH host keys of the other servers. Another workaround is to edit $HOME/.ssh/known_hosts and remove the entry that corresponds to the hostname or IP address and type of SSH host key of the remote Linux/Solaris server that you want to connect via SSH. Before you edit $HOME/.ssh/known_hosts, we recommend that you make another copy of the file.

# 14-3. Logging On Securely
## Problem

You want to log on to a remote Linux/Solaris server through a secured and encrypted connection.

## Solution

On the local server, run the ssh command, followed by the hostname or IP address of the remote Linux/Solaris server that you want to connect. Afterward, supply the password of the corresponding OS user on the remote Linux/Solaris server.

In the first line of the following example, the OS prompt oracle@BLSOL01:~$ indicates that the OS username is oracle, which is logged on to the local Linux/Solaris server BLSOL01. The following ssh command connects to the remote Linux/Solaris server BLSOL02 and logs on to the same OS username oracle. You are then prompted to provide the password of the OS user on the remote Linux/Solaris server BLSOL02:

```
oracle@BLSOL01:~$ ssh BLSOL02
Password:
Last login: Wed Aug 19 18:13:50 2015 from blsol01
Oracle Corporation      SunOS 5.11      11.2      June 2014
oracle@BLSOL02:~$
```

Once you have successfully logged on, you can verify whether you are already in the remote Linux/Solaris server. In the following example, the OS prompt shows that you are now logged on as oracle on server BLSOL02. However, you can run the OS commands echo $HOSTNAME and echo $USER, as shown here, to display the hostname of the Linux/Solaris server and OS username, respectively:

```
oracle@BLSOL02:~$ echo $HOSTNAME
BLSOL02
oracle@BLSOL02:~$ echo $USER
oracle
oracle@BLSOL02:~$
```

## How It Works

Before you can run ssh on your local server, ensure that the open-ssh and openssh-clients packages are already installed. Otherwise, you can download them from any Linux/Solaris package download site, such as http://www.openssh.com.

To connect to the remote Linux/Solaris server from another UNIX/Linux computer or Mac OS, run the ssh command. If you are initiating the SSH connection from Windows, we recommend that you use the PuTTY software, as illustrated in recipe 1-1. Another option is to download and install OpenSSH for Windows.

The first time you log on to the remote Linux/Solaris server via SSH, you will be prompted to confirm the SSH host key fingerprint of the remote Linux/Solaris server, as shown here. Once you accept the SSH host key fingerprint, a row will be added in $HOME/.ssh/known_hosts of the local Linux/Solaris server, which contains the hostname, IP address, and SSH host key of the remote Linux/Solaris server.

```
oracle@BLSOL01:~$ ssh BLSOL02
The authenticity of host 'blsol02 (192.168.2.42)' can't be established.
DSA key fingerprint is 8d:fa:39:1e:36:a7:6a:b1:87:ea:63:1a:c0:84:4a:3d.
Are you sure you want to continue connecting (yes/no)? yes
Warning: Permanently added 'blsol02,192.168.2.42' (DSA) to the list of known hosts.
Password:
Last login: Wed Aug 19 18:18:37 2015 from blsol01
Oracle Corporation      SunOS 5.11      11.2      June 2014
oracle@BLSOL02:~$
```

---

■ **Note**    You can run the ssh-keygen -l -f /etc/ssh/ssh_host_rsa_key and ssh-keygen -y -f /etc/ssh/ssh_host_rsa_key commands to verify the SSH host key fingerprint and SSH host key of the server.

---

To log on to a different OS user when connecting to the remote Linux/Solaris server, you need to add the -l option followed by the username, as shown here. Notice that the prompt is oracle@BLSOL01:~$ in the first line, so the current OS username is oracle and the hostname is BLSOL01. In the last line, the prompt is [bslopuz@BLSOL02 ~]$, which shows that you are now logged in as the username bslopuz of the remote server BLSOL02:

```
oracle@BLSOL01:~$ ssh -l bslopuz BLSOL02
Password:
Last login: Wed Aug 19 15:59:33 2015 from 192.168.2.101
Oracle Corporation      SunOS 5.11      11.2      June 2014
bslopuz@BLSOL02:~$
```

Another way to connect using a different username than the one you are currently logged on with is to run the ssh bslopuz@BLSOLO command, where the username and hostname are concatenated with the @ character, as follows:

```
oracle@BLSOLO1:~$ ssh bslopuz@BLSOLO2
Password:
Last login: Wed Aug 19 18:24:15 2015 from blsolo1
Oracle Corporation      SunOS 5.11      11.2      June 2014
bslopuz@BLSOLO2:~$
```

By default, the SSH daemon server (sshd) is listening on port number 22. If the parameter Port in /etc/ssh/sshd_config on the remote Linux/Solaris server is pointing to a number other than 22, you have to add the -p option when running the ssh command, followed by the correct SSH port number, as shown here:

```
oracle@BLSOLO1:~$ ssh -p 51 ol6-121-rac1
oracle@ol6-121-rac1's password:
Last login: Wed Aug 19 18:30:37 2015 from blsolo1
[oracle@ol6-121-rac1 ~]$
```

---

■ **Note**    If you want to run an X Window application on the remote Linux/Solaris server, run the ssh command with the -X option. For additional information about running an X Window application via SSH, refer to recipe 15-5.

---

If you can't connect to your remote Linux/Solaris server via SSH, run the ping command, as shown here. It verifies whether you have a direct connection to the Linux/Solaris server. The -c3 option of the ping command means it will send requests to the remote Linux server only three times.

```
[oracle@ol6-121-rac1 ~]$ ping -c3 BLSOLO1
PING BLSOLO1 (192.168.2.41) 56(84) bytes of data.
64 bytes from BLSOLO1 (192.168.2.41): icmp_seq=1 ttl=255 time=0.452 ms
64 bytes from BLSOLO1 (192.168.2.41): icmp_seq=2 ttl=255 time=0.245 ms
64 bytes from BLSOLO1 (192.168.2.41): icmp_seq=3 ttl=255 time=0.209 ms

--- BLSOLO1 ping statistics ---
3 packets transmitted, 3 received, 0% packet loss, time 2001ms
rtt min/avg/max/mdev = 0.209/0.302/0.452/0.107 ms
```

For a Solaris server, we recommend the –s option of the ping command, which will continually send packets to the remote server, as shown here:

```
oracle@BLSOLO1:~$ ping -s BLSOLO2
PING BLSOLO2: 56 data bytes
64 bytes from BLSOLO2 (192.168.2.42): icmp_seq=0. time=0.520 ms
64 bytes from BLSOLO2 (192.168.2.42): icmp_seq=1. time=0.379 ms
64 bytes from BLSOLO2 (192.168.2.42): icmp_seq=2. time=0.290 ms
64 bytes from BLSOLO2 (192.168.2.42): icmp_seq=3. time=0.228 ms
64 bytes from BLSOLO2 (192.168.2.42): icmp_seq=4. time=0.251 ms
64 bytes from BLSOLO2 (192.168.2.42): icmp_seq=5. time=0.195 ms
^C
----BLSOLO2 PING Statistics----
6 packets transmitted, 6 packets received, 0% packet loss
round-trip (ms)  min/avg/max/stddev = 0.195/0.310/0.520/0.121
```

However, if you are passing through a proxy server before you can connect to the remote Linux/Solaris server, we recommend that you use the PuTTY software because it is easy to configure the proxy server settings (refer to recipe 1-1). If the remote Linux/Solaris server is behind a firewall, check with your SA to see whether the corresponding SSH port number is open.

To monitor the OS users connecting to the remote Linux server via SSH, check the /var/log/secure file, as shown here. This log file provides important information, such as the date and time that a particular OS user is logged on, the hostname or IP address from where the SSH connection is initiated, and the relevant messages showing why you are perhaps unable to log on.

```
[root@ol6-121-rac1 ~]# tail -f /var/log/secure
Aug 19 19:17:01 ol6-121-rac1 su: pam_unix(su-l:session): session opened for user oracle by (uid=0)
Aug 19 19:17:02 ol6-121-rac1 su: pam_unix(su-l:session): session closed for user oracle
Aug 19 19:17:04 ol6-121-rac1 sshd[5330]: Accepted password for oracle from 192.168.2.42 port 38569 ssh2
Aug 19 19:17:04 ol6-121-rac1 sshd[5330]: pam_unix(sshd:session): session opened for user oracle by (uid=0)
Aug 19 19:17:20 ol6-121-rac1 sshd[5330]: pam_unix(sshd:session): session closed for user oracle
```

■ **Note** To troubleshoot SSH connections, run the ssh command with the -v option to display debugging messages. For more debugging messages, run with the -vvv option instead. We also recommend that you review the /var/log/secure and /var/log/messages files.

# 14-4. Copying Files Securely
## Problem

You want to copy the files between Linux/Solaris servers through a secured and encrypted connection.

## Solution

Run the scp command to copy files between Linux/Solaris servers through SSH. To run the scp command, provide the source files and target files. These files can be in the local and/or remote Linux/Solaris servers. In the following example, the /home/oracle/temp/ccf_output01.log file is copied from server BLSOL01 to the same directory on server BLSOL02. You will be prompted for a password of the username on the remote Linux/Solaris server:

```
oracle@BLSOL01:~$ scp /export/home/oracle/temp/ccf_output01.log BLSOL02:/export/home/oracle/temp
Password:
ccf_output01.log      100% |****************************|  14956        00:00
```

■ **Note** The sftp command is another protocol to securely transfer files between Linux/Solaris servers. However, we excluded examples of the sftp command because the sftp protocol is not yet an Internet standard.

## How It Works

Similar to using the ssh command, you will be prompted to confirm the SSH host key fingerprint of the remote Linux/Solaris server the first time you run the scp command to securely copy files to the remote Linux/Solaris server via SSH, as shown here. Once you accept the SSH host key fingerprint, a row will be added in $HOME/.ssh/known_hosts of the local Linux/Solaris server, which contains the hostname, IP address, key type, and SSH host key of the remote Linux/Solaris server.

```
oracle@BLSOL01:~$ scp /export/home/oracle/temp/ccf_output01.log BLSOL02:/export/home/oracle/temp
The authenticity of host 'blsol02 (192.168.2.42)' can't be established.
DSA key fingerprint is 8d:fa:39:1e:36:a7:6a:b1:87:ea:63:1a:c0:84:4a:3d.
Are you sure you want to continue connecting (yes/no)? yes
Warning: Permanently added 'blsol02,192.168.2.42' (DSA) to the list of known hosts.
Password:
ccf_output01.log     100% |****************************| 14956         00:00
```

■ **Note** The scp command replaces the rcp command because the latter is not a secure way of copying files between Linux/Solaris servers, particularly when the data is traversing the Internet. We recommend that you use the scp command to safeguard your critical data.

The following is the syntax of the scp command. The hostnames can be different Linux/Solaris servers. If no hostnames are defined, the files will be copied to the same local Linux/Solaris server. The usernames may be different between the local and remote Linux/Solaris servers.

```
scp [<option>] [source_user@]source_host:]source_file
    [[target_user@]target_host:]target_file
```

Table 14-1 shows the common options of the scp command. You can run man scp to determine other options.

***Table 14-1.*** *Common Options of scp Command*

| Option | Meaning |
|--------|---------|
| P | Preserves the permission and date timestamp of the source file. |
| P | Gets the SSH port number of the remote Linux/Solaris server. |
| Q | Hides the progress meter. |
| R | Copies recursively all subdirectories and their files. |
| v | Displays debugging messages. |

To copy recursively all the files and directories, use the -r option. The following command will copy all the files and subdirectories of $HOME/temp1 of the local server BLSOL01 to a remote Linux/Solaris server BLSOL02 under the directory $HOME:

```
oracle@BLSOL01:~$ scp -r $HOME/temp1 BLSOL02:$HOME
Password:
ol6-121-rac1.localdo 100% |****************************|    54      00:00
test03.txt           100% |****************************|     0      00:00
ccf_output01.log     100% |****************************| 14956      00:00
test02.txt           100% |****************************|     0      00:00
test01.txt           100% |****************************|    29      00:00
```

Similar to using the cp command, you can use a wildcard such as the asterisk (*) to copy selected files. The following command will copy all the files with an extension of txt in the directory $HOME/temp1 on the remote Linux/Solaris server BLSOL02 to the directory $HOME/temp2 on the local Linux/Solaris server BLSOL01:

```
oracle@BLSOL01:~$ scp BLSOL02:$HOME/temp1/*.txt $HOME/temp2
Password:
ol6-121-rac1.localdo 100% |****************************|    54      00:00
test01.txt           100% |****************************|    29      00:00
test02.txt           100% |****************************|     0      00:00
test03.txt           100% |****************************|     0      00:00
```

---

■ **Note** PuTTY also provides a pscp.exe client to securely copy files from the Microsoft Windows environment to a UNIX/Linux environment. You can download pscp.exe from PuTTY's download page.

---

# 14-5. Authenticating Through Public Keys
## Problem

You want to log on to a remote Linux/Solaris server when connecting via SSH. You want to authenticate using a public key instead of typing the OS password.

## Solution

In the following example, the OS username oracle is currently logged on to the local Linux/Solaris server BLSOL01 and will log on to the remote Linux/Solaris server BLSOL02. Perform the following steps to use a public key for authentication in lieu of a password prompt:

1. On the local Linux/Solaris server BLSOL01, run the ssh-keygen command with the -t rsa option to generate the RSA public key or with -t dsa for the DSA public key. If the files of the RSA and DSA keys already exist, you will be asked whether you want to overwrite them. If no, you can skip this step, but ensure that you remember their passphrases because you will need them later. If yes, you are prompted to provide the passphrase, which is used to access the newly created private key. Afterward, the names of the private and public key files and key fingerprints are displayed.

```
oracle@BLSOL01:~$ /usr/bin/ssh-keygen -t rsa
Generating public/private rsa key pair.
Enter file in which to save the key (/export/home/oracle/.ssh/id_rsa):
Enter passphrase (empty for no passphrase):
Enter same passphrase again:
Your identification has been saved in /export/home/oracle/.ssh/id_rsa.
Your public key has been saved in /export/home/oracle/.ssh/id_rsa.pub.
The key fingerprint is:
8b:de:0e:b3:22:de:77:3b:fa:37:ff:90:96:22:8a:60 oracle@BLSOL01
```

2. On the local Linux/Solaris server BLSOL01, provide the read, write, and execute permission only to the owner for security reasons so the private and public keys are not accessible to others:

```
oracle@BLSOL01:~$ chmod 700 $HOME/.ssh
oracle@BLSOL01:~$ chmod 600 $HOME/.ssh/*
```

3. Copy the public key from the local Linux/Solaris server BLSOL01 to the remote Linux/Solaris server BLSOL02. You may need to supply the password of the OS user on the remote Linux/Solaris server BLSOL02. This public key must be from the OS username on the local Linux/Solaris server BLSOL01, which is the computer from which you want to initiate the logon to the remote Linux/Solaris server and connect via SSH.

```
oracle@BLSOL01:~$ scp $HOME/.ssh/id_rsa.pub BLSOL02:$HOME
Password:
id_rsa.pub              100% |***************************|   396      00:00
```

---

■ **Note**    We recommend that you make local copies of the key files, such as id_rsa and id_rsa.pub. In case someone mistakenly executes ssh-keygen -t rsa, at least you can always restore the original copies.

---

4. Create the directory $HOME/.ssh if not yet available on the remote Linux/Solaris server BLSOL02:

```
oracle@BLSOL02:~$ mkdir $HOME/.ssh
```

5. On the remote Linux/Solaris server BLSOL02, append the public key from the local Linux/Solaris server BLSOL01 to $HOME/.ssh/authorized_keys. Afterward, delete the key file $HOME/id_rsa.pub on the remote Linux/Solaris server BLSOL02, which you copied from the local Linux/Solaris server BLSOL01.

```
oracle@BLSOL02:~$ ls -l $HOME/.ssh/authorized_keys
/export/home/oracle/.ssh/authorized_keys: No such file or directory
oracle@BLSOL02:~$ cat $HOME/id_rsa.pub >> $HOME/.ssh/authorized_keys
oracle@BLSOL02:~$ ls -l $HOME/.ssh/authorized_keys
-rw-r--r--    1 oracle    staff         396 Aug 19 20:34 /export/home/oracle/.ssh/
authorized_keys
oracle@BLSOL02:~$ rm $HOME/id_rsa.pub
```

6. On the remote Linux/Solaris server BLSOL02, provide the read, write, and execute permission only to the owner for security reasons. Other users can't access and modify $HOME/.ssh/authorized_keys.

```
oracle@BLSOL02:~$ chmod 700 $HOME/.ssh
oracle@BLSOL02:~$ chmod 600 $HOME/.ssh/authorized_keys
oracle@BLSOL02:~$ ls -l $HOME/.ssh/authorized_keys
-rw-------   1 oracle   staff        396 Aug 19 20:34 /export/home/
oracle/.ssh/authorized_keys
```

7. After the public key is successfully appended to $HOME/.ssh/authorized_keys on the remote Linux/Solaris server BLSOL02, you can now log on without supplying the password of the OS user when connecting via SSH to the remote Linux/Solaris server BLSOL02, as shown here. Instead, you will be prompted for the passphrase, which is actually the passphrase you supplied when creating the public key on the local Linux/Solaris server BLSOL01.

```
oracle@BLSOL01:~$ ssh BLSOL02
Enter passphrase for key '/export/home/oracle/.ssh/id_rsa':
Last login: Wed Aug 19 20:31:17 2015 from blsol01
Oracle Corporation      SunOS 5.11      11.2     June 2014
```

---

■ **Note** If you immediately press Enter or Return when asked to provide the passphrase, or if you provide the passphrase incorrectly three times, you will be prompted instead for the actual password of the OS username that you want to use to log on to the remote Linux/Solaris server.

---

## How It Works

To authenticate using the public key, run the ssh-keygen command to generate the public key at the local Linux/Solaris server, which is the computer from which you are going to initiate the SSH connection. Then copy the newly generated public key and append it to the $HOME/.ssh/authorized_keys on the remote Linux/Solaris server, which is the computer from which you are going to connect via SSH.

The ssh-keygen will create the RSA and DSA key files, which are used to encrypt and decrypt the data. For RSA, use the -t rsa option command, which will create two files: $HOME/.ssh/id_rsa and $HOME/.ssh/id_rsa.pub. For DSA, use the -t dsa option, which will create $HOME/.ssh/id_dsa and $HOME/.ssh/id_dsa.pub.

$HOME/.ssh/id_rsa and $HOME/.ssh/id_dsa contain both the private key and the public key, whereas $HOME/.ssh/id_rsa.pub and $HOME/.ssh/id_dsa.pub contain just the public key. The public key is used to encrypt the data; the private key is used to decrypt the data. For security reasons, ensure that both the private key and the public key files are writable and readable only by the owner.

When creating the public key, you are prompted to provide the passphrase, which can be a string of arbitrary length. The passphrase is your password to decrypt the data. Even if the private and public keys are stolen, they are useless without the passphrase because the data can't be decrypted. So it is important that you keep the passphrase to yourself; don't share it with others.

To change the passphrase, run the ssh-keygen command with the -p option, as shown here. However, you have to supply the old passphrase before you can change it to prevent unauthorized users from changing your passphrase:

```
oracle@BLSOL01:~$ ssh-keygen -p
Enter file in which the key is (/export/home/oracle/.ssh/id_rsa):
Enter old passphrase:
Key has comment '/export/home/oracle/.ssh/id_rsa'
Enter new passphrase (empty for no passphrase):
Enter same passphrase again:
Your identification has been saved with the new passphrase.
```

Using the public key as a way to authenticate when connecting to the remote Linux/Solaris server via SSH can be a security risk. For example, if other OS users can modify your $HOME/.ssh/ authorized_keys, they can append their own public key to the said file. As a result, they can log on to your account on the remote Linux/Solaris server without needing your password.

As a security measure, we recommend that you provide a passphrase when creating the public key and not share the passphrase with anyone. Also, run the chmod 700 $HOME command, which ensures that the directories and files underneath the $HOME directory are writable, readable, and executable only by the owner. Doing so prevents other OS users to peek at and alter any files starting from your $HOME directory.

After you have successfully logged in, run the following OS commands to verify the OS username and hostname of the remote Linux/Solaris server BLSOL02, as shown here. Even though that information is sometimes obvious in the OS prompt, it's a good exercise to verify it.

```
oracle@BLSOL02:~$ echo $HOSTNAME
BLSOL02
oracle@BLSOL02:~$ echo $USER
oracle
```

# 14-6. Configuring a Promptless Logon
## Problem

You want to log on without providing the remote OS user's password and public key's passphrase when connecting through SSH to a remote Linux/Solaris server.

## Solution

In the following example, the OS username oracle is currently logged on to the local Linux/Solaris server BLSOL01 and will log on to the remote Linux/Solaris server BLSOL02. Perform the following steps to set up a promptless logon when connecting to the remote Linux/Solaris server via SSH:

1. Create the public key on the local Linux/Solaris server BLSOL01 and the OS username where you will initiate the SSH connection. For additional details, refer to recipe 14-5 because you need to perform the same steps as in that recipe.

2. Run the SSH agent and capture the output to $HOME/ssh-agent.sh:

   ```
   oracle@BLSOL01:~$ /usr/bin/ssh-agent > $HOME/ssh-agent.sh
   ```

3.  Run $HOME/ssh-agent.sh to set the environment variables SSH_AUTH_SOCK and
    SSH_AGENT_PID:

    ```
    oracle@BLSOL01:~$ source $HOME/ssh-agent.sh
    Agent pid 4566
    ```

4.  Run the ssh-add command and provide the passphrase you supplied when the
    public key was created on the local Linux/Solaris server:

    ```
    oracle@BLSOL01:~$ /usr/bin/ssh-add
    Enter passphrase for /export/home/oracle/.ssh/id_rsa:
    Identity added: /export/home/oracle/.ssh/id_rsa (/export/home/oracle/.ssh/id_rsa)
    ```

5.  As shown here, the OS username oracle on the local Linux/Solaris server
    BLSOL01 can now log on to the remote Linux/Solaris server BLSOL02 without
    providing the OS user password and the public key passphrase:

    ```
    oracle@BLSOL01:~$ ssh BLSOL02
    Last login: Wed Aug 19 20:41:48 2015 from blsol01
    Oracle Corporation      SunOS 5.11      11.2      June 2014
    oracle@BLSOL02:~$
    ```

## How It Works

In recipe 14-5, you used a public key for authentication in lieu of the OS username's password on the remote
Linux/Solaris server. However, you are asked to provide the passphrase, which is generated when the public
key was created on the local Linux/Solaris server. So you are still prompted to enter something.

For a complete promptless logon to the remote Linux/Solaris server when connecting via SSH, run the
ssh-agent and ssh-add commands. The ssh-agent command will create a socket and cache the passphrase
of the private key. It will also create a new directory under /tmp, as defined in the environment variable
SSH_AUTH_SOCK. The ssh-add command will add the RSA and DSA identities and present them to the SSH
agent. You can then log on to the remote Linux/Solaris server without any prompt for a password or passphrase.

To verify the key fingerprints, run the ssh-add command with the -l option to check what's presented
to the SSH agent. Next, run the ssh-keygen command with the -l option, followed by the path name
of the private key file. As shown here, notice that both outputs have a similar key fingerprint, which is
8b:de:0e:b3:22:de:77:3b:fa:37:ff:90:96:22:8a:60:

```
oracle@BLSOL01:~$ /usr/bin/ssh-add -l
2048 8b:de:0e:b3:22:de:77:3b:fa:37:ff:90:96:22:8a:60 /export/home/oracle/.ssh/id_rsa (RSA)

oracle@BLSOL01:~$ /usr/bin/ssh-keygen -l -f $HOME/.ssh/id_rsa
2048 8b:de:0e:b3:22:de:77:3b:fa:37:ff:90:96:22:8a:60 /export/home/oracle/.ssh/id_rsa.pub
```

To delete the identities presented to the SSH agent, run ssh-add with the -d option. To delete
everything, use the -D option instead:

```
oracle@BLSOL01:~$ /usr/bin/ssh-add -d
Identity removed: /export/home/oracle/.ssh/id_rsa (/export/home/oracle/.ssh/id_rsa.pub)
```

For a promptless logon, the critical key is to ensure that the environment variable SSH_ AUTH_SOCK is
pointing to the correct path name before connecting through SSH. Otherwise, you will be prompted again
for the passphrase once you exit from your shell or log out of the system.

A workaround is to run the `ssh-agent` command and capture the output to `$HOME/ssh-agent.sh`. Before you connect to the remote Linux/Solaris server via SSH, you must run `$HOME/ssh-agent.sh` to set the same value to the `SSH_AUTH_SOCK` environment variable. This setting should be the same as when the `ssh-agent` command was first executed.

To schedule the `ssh` or `scp` command in the `cron` job, ensure that the environment variable `SSH_AUTH_SOCK` is set correctly each time you log on to the OS username on the local Linux/Solaris server. To do this, we recommend that you add the following lines in `$HOME/.bashrc`. Notice that you send the output to `/dev/null` when you run `$HOME/ssh-agent.sh` to avoid displaying the SSH agent PID every time you log on to that OS username:

```
if [ -f $HOME/ssh-agent.sh ]; then
  source $HOME/ssh-agent.sh > /dev/null
fi
```

If you think you have configured everything correctly, but are still prompted for the passphrase, you have to troubleshoot. Begin by verifying that the OS process of the SSH agent is still active and the environment variables are set correctly. Issue the `ps -ef | grep ssh-agent` command to determine the PID of the SSH agent:

```
oracle@BLSOL01:~$ ps -ef | grep ssh-agent
 bslopuz  1639  1601   0  Aug 17 ?              0:01 /usr/bin/ssh-agent -- gnome-session
  oracle  4566     1   0 20:44:03 ?             0:00 /usr/bin/ssh-agent
```

Run the `env | grep SSH` command to display the environment variables, as shown here. The value of the `SSH_AGENT_PID` and the PID of the SSH agent should be the same. In the example, the PID is 4566:

```
oracle@BLSOL01:~$ env | grep SSH
SSH_AGENT_PID=4566
SSH_AUTH_SOCK=/tmp/ssh-XXXXoGa06i/agent.4565
```

Also, the value of the environment variable `SSH_AUTH_SOCK` should be pointing to an existing path name. To verify, run the `ls` command as follows:

```
oracle@BLSOL01:~$ ls -l /tmp/ssh-XXXXoGa06i/agent.4565
srw-------   1 oracle   staff           0 Aug 19 20:44 /tmp/ssh-XXXXoGa06i/agent.4565
```

After you have successfully logged on, run the following OS commands to verify the OS username and hostname of the remote Linux/Solaris server BLLNX2, as shown here. Even if that information is sometimes obvious in the OS prompt, it is a good exercise to verify them.

```
oracle@BLSOL02:~$ echo $HOSTNAME
BLSOL02
oracle@BLSOL02:~$ echo $USER
oracle
```

# CHAPTER 15

■ ■ ■

# Managing X Window

Many DBAs argue that most Linux/Solaris servers don't need an X Window System, even when hosting an Oracle database. In fact, previous chapters of this book show that you can manage your Oracle database on a Linux/Solaris server using a text console; you really don't need a graphical console. In recipes 10-11 and 10-12, you learned how to install the Oracle RDBMS software and how to create an Oracle database without running the Oracle Universal Installer (OUI) that requires a graphical display.

However, for DBAs planning to migrate from a Windows environment and wanting to explore Oracle Database on a Linux/Solaris environment, typing (and remembering exactly) the OS, SQL, and RMAN commands via a command line can be intimidating. If you prefer to run GUI-based programs, such as using the DBCA to create an Oracle database, this chapter is definitely for you.

To understand the concept of the X Window System in a Linux/Solaris environment, review the analogy of a client and a server in a networked environment. An X client and an X server can both be hosted on a single computer (which is an uncommon feature in a typical client/server environment) or two disparate computers on a network, as illustrated in Figure 15-1. But the terminology is backward from what many expect. An X server, for example, is what you run on your client PC to interact with your application. So the application you run on some remote machine is actually the client. The application you run locally (X Window) is actually the server.

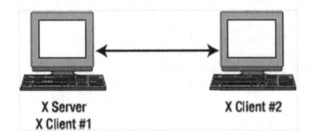

*Figure 15-1.* *X clients on local or remote Linux/Solaris servers*

This chapter shows you how to configure, start, and stop an X server; and how to redirect and secure an X display to a remote computer. You also learn how to change the look and feel when running an X terminal. If you use Windows as your client computer, you can explore OpenSSH for Windows or perhaps use Virtual Network Computing (VNC), which is discussed in detail in Chapter 16.

# 15-1. Configuring an X Server

## Problem

You want to configure an X Window server on a Linux/Solaris server to run GUI-based applications such as the DBCA to create an Oracle database.

## Solution

To set up an X Window server (often called just an *X server*) on a Linux/Solaris server, you have to edit the xorg.conf X Window configuration file, which is usually found in the /etc/X11 directory. There are two ways to edit the /etc/X11/xorg.conf file:

- Directly modify the /etc/X11/xorg.conf file

- Run the Xorg application

To configure the /etc/X11/xorg.conf file, run Xorg with the configure option, which creates a temporary configuration file called /root/xorg.conf.new. The following is the snippet of the results after running the Xorg -configure command:

```
# /usr/bin/Xorg -configure

X.Org X Server 1.14.5
Release Date: 2013-12-12
X Protocol Version 11, Revision 0
Build Operating System: SunOS 5.11 i86pc
Current Operating System: SunOS BLSOL01 5.11 11.2 i86pc
Solaris ABI: 64-bit
Current version of pixman: 0.29.2
        Before reporting problems, check http://support.oracle.com/
        to make sure that you have the latest version.
Markers: (--) probed, (**) from config file, (==) default setting,
        (++) from command line, (!!) notice, (II) informational,
        (WW) warning, (EE) error, (NI) not implemented, (??) unknown.
(==) Log file: "/var/log/Xorg.0.log", Time: Fri Nov 13 00:38:29 2015
List of video drivers:
        intel
        openchrome
        r128
        vmware
        mga
        vboxvideo
        radeon
        cirrus
        ast
        mach64
        ati
        vesa
(++) Using config file: "/root/xorg.conf.new"
(==) Using config directory: "/etc/X11/xorg.conf.d"
(==) Using system config directory "/usr/share/X11/xorg.conf.d"
```

```
Number of created screens does not match number of detected devices.
  Configuration failed.
(EE) Server terminated with error (2). Closing log file.
```

---

**■ Note** When running Xorg -configure, you might see this error message: "Fatal server error: Server is already active for display 0. If this server is no longer running, remove /tmp/.X0-lock and start again." To avoid this error, delete the file described in the error message.

---

You can then test the /root/xorg.conf.new configuration by executing the command X -config /root/xorg.conf.new. If the X server runs fine using the newly created /root/xorg.conf.new configuration file, copy that file to /etc/X11/xorg.conf.

## How It Works

When you start the X server, it reads the xorg.conf file that is located by default in the /etc/X11 directory. The /etc/X11/xorg.conf file contains configurations of the system resources, video card, keyboard, mouse, and monitor for a Linux/Solaris server running the X Window System.

You have to put in the sections that have changed into the xorg.conf file. Otherwise, the unspecified sections will use the default settings. Additional contents are also read from the files that are in the /etc/X11/xorg.conf.d directory.

In the "Solution" section, two methods were described to create and update the /etc/X11/xorg.conf file. One of the methods is to manually modify the file, which we don't recommend except when you are sure of the changes. Regardless of the method you want to pursue, make sure to back up or create another copy of the /etc/X11/xorg.conf file before you attempt to modify it. That way, you can always revert to the original settings in case the new changes don't work.

---

**■ Note** When troubleshooting X server, always check the log file /var/log/Xorg.0.log, as well as /var/log/messages for Linux and /var/adm/messages for Solaris.

---

# 15-2. Starting an X Server

## Problem

You want to start an X server on the Linux/Solaris server to run GUI-based software applications.

## Solution

For Solaris server, perform the following steps:

1.  Run the svcs command to verify the status of the GDM service.

    ```
    # svcs gdm
    STATE          STIME    FMRI
    disabled       1:25:37  svc:/application/graphical-login/gdm:default
    ```

2. If the state of GDM service is disabled, run the following command:

```
# svcadm enable gdm
```

For Linux server, there are three ways to start the X server:

- Manually run the X command.
- Run init 5 or telinit 5.
- Modify /etc/inittab and reboot the server.

The first method happens to be the most involved and requires manually starting the X server on the console of your Linux server. Follow these steps:

1. If you are prompted to log on, do so as the OS user from which you want to run the X server.

2. Run the X server by typing the X command followed by an ampersand (&), as shown in the following line of code. Make sure you add an & at the end so the X server will run in the background. That way, you can still type other OS commands in the same console session.

   ```
   $ X &
   ```

3. Press Ctrl+Alt+F7 to change to the graphical console. An x will appear in the center of a blank screen, which represents the cursor of your mouse.

4. Press Ctrl+Alt+F1 to return to the text console session.

The second method for starting an X server is to run the init 5 or telinit 5 command as root on the OS prompt. A GUI-based logon screen may appear.

The third method is to change the value of the initdefault variable to 5 in the /etc/inittab file, as shown here. But you must reboot the Linux server to effect the changes made in the /etc/inittab file.

```
id:5:initdefault:
```

---

■ **Note** To show the details of the X server, run the OS command xdpyinfo.

---

## How It Works

For Solaris server, you can run the command svcadm enable gdm to start the GDM service. If you made changes to the X Window configuration file xorg.conf, you can run the command svcadm restart gdm. To verify the status of the GDM service, issue the command svcs gdm. The following results indicate that the GDM service is online (i.e., enabled):

```
# svcs gdm
STATE          STIME    FMRI
online         11:23:58 svc:/application/graphical-login/gdm:default
```

For Linux server, if the run level is set to 5, the X server is automatically started when the Linux server is rebooted. However, if the Linux server starts with a run level 3, in which the default screen display is a text console, and you want to run some GUI-based applications such as dbca to create an Oracle Database, you have to manually start the X server on the Linux server.

You can start the X server in three ways. First, you can manually start the X server by running the X command, as demonstrated in the "Solution" section. Another method is to run either the init or telinit command and pass 5 as a parameter, but you must be root or have sudo access to run those commands. Finally, if you want X server to automatically run every time a Linux server is rebooted, you have to change the id directive in /etc/inittab to run level 5.

Because the majority of DBAs don't work in front of a server console, starting the X server is not necessary when the Linux server is booted. But if you have enough physical memory on your Linux server, we recommend that you use the third method. If the current level is 3, use either the first or second method to start the X server. We recommend the second method because it is easier and requires fewer steps than the X command.

---

■ **Note**    Running an X server on your Linux database server can pose security issues because another client can access and observe your keystrokes. For security measures, we recommend that you employ access control using xhost or tunnel X over SSH, as discussed in recipes 15-4 and 15-5.

---

The X command actually calls Xorg, as shown here:

```
# which X
/usr/bin/X
# ls -l /usr/bin/X
lrwxrwxrwx. 1 root root 4 Jan 13  2014 /usr/bin/X -> Xorg
# which Xorg
/usr/bin/Xorg
# ls -l /usr/bin/Xorg
-rwsr-xr-x. 1 root root 2274240 Nov 21  2013 /usr/bin/Xorg
```

---

■ **Note**    The X command may be in a different directory from other Linux distributions, so run the command which X to determine the exact directory.

---

Instead of running the X command to start the X server, you can run the startx command, which then invokes the X command on your behalf and also launches a graphical display manager. The default display manager of most Linux distributions is GNOME. If you prefer another graphical display manager, see recipe 15-6 on how to switch from GNOME to KDE, and vice versa.

Once an X server is already running, you can press Ctrl+Alt+F1 to change to a text console or press Alt+F7 to change to the graphical console. You can repeat these steps to go back and forth between the text and graphical consoles.

# 15-3. Stopping the X Server

## Problem

You want to stop the X server running on your Linux server. For example, you might want to save on resources such as the memory consumed by GUI-based software applications.

## Solution

For Solaris server, issue the following command:

```
# svcadm disable gdm
```

For Linux server, there are three ways to stop an X server:

- Run init 3 or telinit 3.
- Press Ctrl+Alt+Backspace.
- Modify /etc/inittab and reboot the server.

For the first method, perform the following steps to manually stop the X server on your Linux server:

1.  If the X Window system is already running, press Ctrl+Alt+F1 to change to a text console.

2.  If you are prompted to log on, do so as root.

3.  Issue either init 3 or telinit 3 to stop the X server:

    ```
    # init 3
    ```

For the second method, perform the following steps:

1.  Press Alt+F7 to change to the graphical console. If you are already on the graphical console, you can skip this step.

2.  Press Ctrl+Alt+Backspace to stop the X server.

For the third method, change the value of the initdefault variable to 3 in the /etc/inittab file, as shown here:

```
id:3:initdefault:
```

You must then reboot the Linux server to effect the changes.

## How It Works

To stop the X server in Solaris, you can issue the command svcadm disable gdm. Afterward, issue the command svcs gdm. The following results indicate that the GDM service is disabled:

```
# svcs gdm
STATE          STIME    FMRI
disabled       11:18:03 svc:/application/graphical-login/gdm:default
```

For Linux, you can stop the X server in three ways. You can manually stop the X server by running either init 3 or telinit 3 on the text console to change the current run level to 3. But you must be root or have sudo access to run these commands. If the current run level is already 3, you can press Ctrl+Alt+Backspace when you are on the graphical console. If you don't want the X server to automatically run every time the Linux server is rebooted, change the id directive to run level 3 in /etc/inittab.

The first and second methods are dependent on the current run level. If the current run level is 5 and you perform the second method, it will always return to the graphical login screen. So perform the first method if the current level is 5; otherwise, use the second method.

Issue the runlevel command to display the previous and current run levels. In the following example, the first character is N, which means that the run level is not changed yet; the second character indicates that the current run level is 5:

```
# runlevel
N 5
```

# 15-4. Displaying an X Client on a Remote Server

## Problem

You want to run an X client or a GUI-based software application on your local Linux server, but X server is not running. Instead, you want to redirect the graphical display to a remote Linux/Solaris server in which an X server is running.

## Solution

In the following example, the OS user oracle is currently logged on to the local Linux server RAC1, where you want to run an X client or a GUI-based software application, but an X server is not running. Meanwhile, the Solaris server BLSOL01 is a remote Linux server where an X server is running.

Perform the following steps to redirect the graphical display to the Solaris server BLSOL01 when running an X client or a GUI-based software application such as dbca to create an Oracle database on Linux server RAC1:

1. On the Linux server RAC1, set the OS environment variable DISPLAY to point to the Solaris server BLSOL01.

   ```
   [oracle@RAC1 ~]$ export DISPLAY=BLSOL01:0.0
   ```

2. Run dbca on the Linux server RAC1.

   ```
   [oracle@RAC1 ~]$ dbca
   ```

---

■ **Note**    If the OS environment variable DISPLAY is not set, you might see this error message: "DISPLAY not set. Set DISPLAY environment variable, then re-run." To resolve this error, make sure you set the OS environment variable DISPLAY to point to a server in which the X server is running.

---

3. Next, the Database Configuration Assistant screen will appear, as shown in Figure 15-2. Behind the screen, notice that the output of the OS command uname -a, executed on the terminal window, confirms that the Solaris server is BLSOL01.

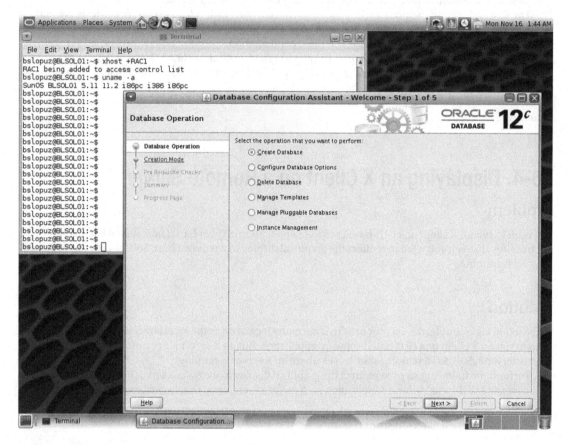

*Figure 15-2.* *Database Configuration Assistant screen*

## How It Works

You usually run an X client or GUI-based software application and have the graphical display on the local Linux/Solaris server in which you are currently logged on. But what if the X server is not running on the local Linux/Solaris server? Your option is to redirect the graphical display to another remote Linux server in which an X server is running.

However, you may experience the following error because the local Linux/Solaris server, which is the Linux server RAC1 in the example illustrated in the "Solution" section, is probably not granted access control on the remote Solaris server, which is server BLSOL01:

```
[oracle@RAC1 ~]$ dbca
No protocol specified
Error: Can't open display: BLSOL01:0.0
```

To confirm whether access has been granted, run the OS command xhost without any parameter on the Solaris server BLSOL01. If the message says "access control enabled", only authorized clients can connect. If Linux server RAC1 is not in the list, that explains why you are getting the earlier error message when running the dbca. Here's an example:

```
bslopuz@BLSOL01:~$ xhost
access control enabled, only authorized clients can connect
INET: BLSOL02
INET: RAC1
```

You can resolve this problem in two ways: run the command xhost +RAC1 from the Solaris server BLSOL01 or run the command xhost + on the Solaris server BLSOL01. Using the first approach allows only clients from the host RAC1 to connect. Here's an example:

```
bslopuz@BLSOL01:~$ xhost +RAC1
RAC1 being added to access control list
bslopuz@BLSOL01:~$ xhost
access control enabled, only authorized clients can connect
INET: RAC1
```

On the other hand, the OS command xhost + will grant access control to all servers that have direct access to BLSOL01. We don't recommend that you grant that much access because you are basically allowing access from any server. Here's an example:

```
bslopuz@BLSOL01:~$ xhost +
access control disabled, clients can connect from any host
```

To revoke access control, run the OS command xhost -RAC1 to revoke the privilege from the specific server RAC1, as shown in the following example. Notice that in the results of the first OS command, xhost without any parameters, server RAC1 is on the list. Meanwhile, after you run the OS command xhost -RAC1, server RAC1 is no longer on the list during the second time you run the OS command xhost without any parameters.

```
bslopuz@BLSOL01:~$ xhost
access control enabled, only authorized clients can connect
INET:BLSOL02
INET:RAC1
bslopuz@BLSOL01:~$ xhost -RAC1
RAC1 being removed from access control list
bslopuz@BLSOL01:~$ xhost
access control enabled, only authorized clients can connect
INET:BLSOL02
```

However, if you earlier issued the OS command, and the message says "access control disabled", clients can connect from any host when you issue the OS command xhost without any parameter. Any server, such as the Linux server RAC1, can still access the Solaris server BLSOL01, even though you have already revoked the privilege from the specific Linux server RAC1. To revoke access control from all servers, you can issue xhost -, as shown here:

```
bslopuz@BLSOL01:~$ xhost -
access control enabled, only authorized clients can connect
bslopuz@BLSOL01:~$ xhost
access control enabled, only authorized clients can connect
```

# 15-5. Tunneling X Over SSH

## Problem

You want to run an X client or a GUI-based software application on a remote Linux/Solaris server. However, you want to log on to that remote Linux server through a secured connection and have the data encrypted that is traversing between servers.

## Solution

In the following example, the OS user oracle is currently logged on to the local Linux server BLSOL01; server BLSOL02 is the remote Solaris server. Perform the following steps to connect to server BLSOL02 from server BLSOL01 through SSH and execute an X software application on server BLLNX2:

1.  On the local Solaris server BLSOL01, run ssh with the -X (uppercase X) option, as shown here. You may be prompted to provide a password of the OS user on BLSOL02.

    ```
    bslopuz@BLSOL01:~$ ssh -X BLSOL02
    Password:
    Last login: Mon Nov 16 02:17:46 2015
    Oracle Corporation        SunOS 5.11      11.2     June 2014
    ```

2.  If X11Forwarding is properly set up, the DISPLAY variable is automatically set up once you are successfully connected to the remote Linux/Solaris server, as shown here:

    ```
    bslopuz@BLSOL02:~$ echo $DISPLAY
    localhost:10.0
    ```

3.  Once you are successfully connected to server BLSOL02, you can now run an X client or GUI-based software application on server BLSOL02. To test this, we recommend that you run a simple X client, such as xeyes, as shown in Figure 15-3.

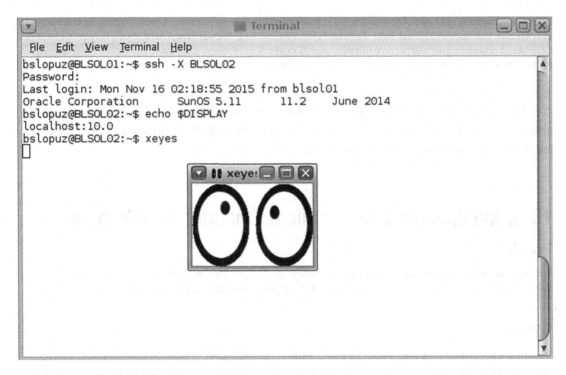

*Figure 15-3. xeyes display*

---

■ **Note**    The default port for X server is 6000. If this port is blocked, a workaround is to run ssh with the -X option to display th.plication, such as xclock or Oracle's dbca.

---

## How It Works

Recipe 15-4 allows you to redirect a graphical display to a remote Linux/Solaris server. However, the data traversing between the servers is not secured because it is not encrypted. For security reasons, we recommend that you forward or tunnel the graphical display through SSH, as shown in this recipe.

---

■ **Note**    To learn how to configure SSH tunneling using PuTTY, refer to recipe 1-1.

---

To forward the display of an X client or GUI-based software application on a remote Linux/Solaris server, run ssh with the -X (uppercase X) option. The -x (lowercase X) option disables X forwarding. However, before you can start to connect using ssh, make sure that the Secure Shell daemon, or sshd, is already running on the remote Linux/Solaris server. Otherwise, review Chapter 14, particularly recipe 14-1, which discusses in detail how to set up ssh.

When running an X client or GUI-based software application on a remote Linux/Solaris server, you may receive this message: "Warning: Remote host denied X11 forwarding." Also, if you run an X client or GUI-based software, you will receive the message "Error: Can't open display." To resolve these errors, make sure X11Forwarding is set to yes in the /etc/ssh/sshd_config file on the remote Linux/Solaris server.

---

■ **Note** To troubleshoot your SSH connection, run the ssh command with the -v option to display debugging messages. For more debugging messages, run with the -vvv option instead. We also recommend that you review the /var/log/secure and /var/log/messages files.

---

# 15-6. Manipulating the Terminal Emulator for X Windows

## Problem

You want to launch the default X terminal and change the look and feel to support different database environments: development, quality assurance, and production database environments.

## Solution

To launch an X Window terminal, you can execute the xterm command. If your OS environment variable DISPLAY is set up correctly to a Hummingbird X Server, Reflection X Server, or Cygwin X Server (or if you are running X server locally), a small white terminal will appear. This small window will probably not be adequate to support the day-to-day activities of today's DBA who supports many database environments. More than likely, you will have a larger window, a title to specify the name of the window, different colors to easily identify the environment, and a larger scroll buffer area. Here are several xterm examples you can execute in your environment to support multiple database environments:

```
xterm -sl 32000 -sb -title "Production" -geometry 128x40 -bg red -fg white &
xterm -sl 32000 -sb -title "QA" -geometry 128x40 -bg yellow -fg black &
xterm -sl 32000 -sb -title "Development" -geometry 128x40 -bg blue -fg white &
```

Each of the xterm windows is designed with different background colors with the -bg parameter to differentiate database environments. In our example, the blue window represents the development environment, the yellow window represents the QA environment, and, of course, the red window represents the production environment. DBAs should be aware of the color scheme and exercise extra caution by remembering that while in the red background, they are logged on to the production database server.

In addition to the background colors, we defined the scroll length buffer as 32,000 lines. The default scroll buffer is 64 lines above the top of the window. The scroll buffer of 32,000 lines, designated by the -sl parameter, will consume more memory on the server, but will prove to be well worth it, especially when diagnosing problems.

The title of the windows can also be defined with the -title parameter, which should be enclosed with double quotes so that you can customize titles to suit your requirements.

The dimensions of the xterm window can be managed with the -geometry parameter, which defines the window size and position. You can define a specific font, font size, and other attributes with the -font parameter. The easiest way to designate font and size attributes is to execute the xfontsel command. Executing the xfontsel command will open another X window similar to the one displayed in Figure 15-4.

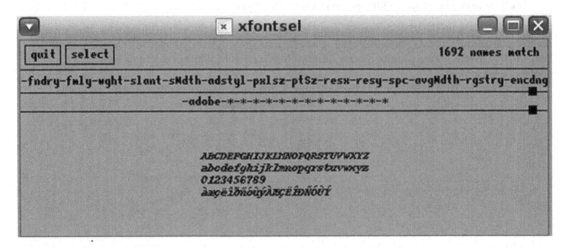

**Figure 15-4.** *xfontsel window*

When you decide on the font type and size attributes, you can click the select button and paste in another terminal with the xterm command, which will look like the following command:

```
xterm -font -adobe-courier-bold-*-*-*-12-*-*-*-*-*-*
```

Once you are satisfied with the font look and feel, you can go back to the xfontsel window and click the quit button.

Another popular parameter for xterm is the -e parameter. With the -e option, you can specify the program and arguments to run in the xterm window. Here's an example of how the -e option can be manipulated:

```
xterm -e "ssh rac3 -l root"
```

## How It Works

xterm is the standard terminal emulator that runs in X Windows. Other terminal emulators in Linux include Konsole (the default KDE terminal), GNOME Terminal (the default GNOME terminal), rxvt (a slimmed-down replacement for xterm), and Eterm. xterm is the standard de facto for terminals in all UNIX OSs. No matter whether you are running Linux, Sun Solaris, IBM AIX, or HP/UX, xterm will look and behave the same. One behavior includes the ability to copy and paste. Within an xterm window, if you highlight a word or a sentence, the highlighted portion will automatically be copied to the memory buffer. To copy the memory buffer, you simply press the middle mouse button; for a two-button mouse, the middle button is most often the trackball. You can press on the track ball to paste the contents of the memory buffer. If you have the old traditional two-button mouse, pressing both the left and right buttons at the same time will paste the memory buffer.

Similarly, if you hold the Ctrl key and simultaneously press the left, middle, or right button, you will see the following menu options:

- Press Ctrl and the left mouse button for Main Options.

- Press Ctrl and the right mouse button for VT Fonts.

- Press Ctrl and the middle mouse button for VT Options.

For example, with the VT Fonts menu, you can change the size of the font to unreadable, tiny, small, medium, large, and huge. As you change the size of the font, the window diameter will change accordingly. With the VT Options menu, you can modify simple things such as enabling or disabling scrollbars or enabling reverse video.

For assistance with the myriad of xterm arguments, you can execute the xterm -help command.

# CHAPTER 16

■ ■ ■

# Managing Remote Servers with VNC

Fewer and fewer DBAs are working in front of the console of the servers hosting their Oracle databases. It is common now to see database servers or data centers located in separate geographical areas from DBAs. For example, a database server might be hosted somewhere in New York City while the DBA is in Orlando enjoying the sunny weather.

DBAs can now easily access database servers remotely by using their preferred protocols, such as telnet, rsh, rlogin, and ssh; and by using the various tools on the market today. Some of those tools are freely available for download, particularly PuTTY and Virtual Network Computing (VNC).

Software such as PuTTY, described in Chapter 1, allows you to remotely access a server via telnet or ssh from a Windows client. PuTTY allows you to configure proxy settings and ssh port tunneling, as well as to save configurations so that you don't have to type everything each time you have to connect to the same database server.

In most cases, accessing a database server in a command-line mode via PuTTY is all you need. However, you may sometimes need to access a database server in a way that lets you run GUI-based software. For example, you may need to run Oracle's Database Configuration Assistant (DBCA) to create an Oracle database or run some other X Window System–based software. In this situation, VNC comes in handy.

VNC is a thin-client product of RealVNC, which is based in Cambridge, United Kingdom. VNC allows you to access the database server in a graphical way. This feature is useful for DBAs because Oracle requires an X server to display its Java-based screens for Oracle database installation, creation, and configuration; and also for Oracle listener setup. In other words, you can run the same GUI-based applications on your local VNC-client computer that you can actually run on the console of the database server.

To run VNC, you need two components: the server and viewer, as shown in Figure 16-1. The VNC Server component runs on the computer you want to monitor, and the VNC Viewer component runs on the computer from which you want to monitor the remote server. Both components have to be installed before you can initiate a VNC session. VNC runs on most OSs, including UNIX (such as Solaris), Linux, Windows, and Mac OS.

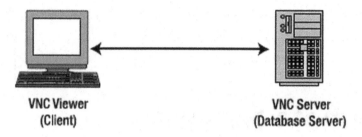

**VNC Viewer
(Client)**

**VNC Server
(Database Server)**

*Figure 16-1.* *VNC connection*

Aside from routing the output to the VNC Server, you can also route the display to other X servers that are available on the market today, such as Cygwin/X, Reflections X, and Hummingbird. However, we recommend VNC because it is freely available and is usually included by default in most Linux distributions, such as Red Hat Enterprise Linux, Novell SUSE Linux Enterprise, Oracle Enterprise Linux (OEL), and Oracle Solaris. VNC also has rich features, such as 2048-bit RSA server authentication, 128-bit or 256-bit AES session encryption, HTTP proxy, file transfer, desktop scaling, and screen sharing.

In this chapter, you will learn where to download the VNC software, how to install and configure the VNC Server on your remote Linux/Solaris database server and the VNC Viewer on your client computer, how to share and secure your VNC connection, how to configure proxy server, and how to troubleshoot VNC issues.

As you put into practice what you have read in this chapter, such as using the VNC software to access and manage your remote Linux/Solaris database server from anywhere and at any time, you will learn to appreciate the benefits provided to you as the DBA: flexibility, convenience, better collaboration with your team members, data security, and potential cost savings to your company.

# 16-1. Downloading the VNC Software
## Problem

You want to download the VNC software to allow you to manage and display the console of your remote Linux/Solaris database server from your client computer. You want to work in an X Window System environment instead of a command-line prompt.

## Solution

You need two components to run VNC: the VNC Server running on your remote Linux/Solaris database server and the VNC Viewer on your client computer. Perform the following steps to download the VNC software for the two computers:

1. Go to `https://www.realvnc.com/download/vnc/` and click the Download button that corresponds to the OS and processor type of your system, as well as the type of compressed file you want to download.

---

■ **Note** To determine the processor type of your Linux system to see whether you have x86, x64, or ia64, issue the Linux command `uname -p` or `uname -a`. For a Solaris system, run the OS command `isainfo -vk`.

---

2.  On the next screen, check the box that says "I have read and accept these terms and conditions" after you review the VNC end user license agreement.

3.  Click the Download button and save the file to a specific directory.

## How It Works

For VNC to work, you have to download and install the VNC Server on your remote Linux/Solaris database server and the VNC Viewer on your client computer. You have three different VNC editions to choose from: the Free Edition, Personal Edition, or Enterprise Edition. The Free Edition is best for individual private use, the Personal Edition is ideally suited for small-scale commercial use, and the Enterprise Edition is recommended for medium or large-scale commercial use.

By default, the Free Edition is included in most Linux distributions, such as Red Hat, SUSE, Oracle Enterprise Linux and Oracle Solaris. However, the Personal Edition and Enterprise Edition have some advantages over the Free Edition, such as encryption, authentication, and proxy server features. If you want to take advantage of these features, download the Enterprise Edition and replace the Free Edition, which is usually included as a package on your Linux distribution. Note that the Enterprise Edition and Personal Edition require a license key before you can start the VNC Server.

# 16-2. Installing the VNC Software
## Problem

You want to install the VNC Server on your remote Linux/Solaris database server and the VNC Viewer on your Windows client computer, on which you want to manage and access your remote Linux/Solaris database server.

## Solution

For VNC to work, you have to install the VNC Server on your remote Linux/Solaris database server and the VNC Viewer on your client computer. You can choose to install the VNC Server Enterprise Edition or Free Edition on your server.

First, extract the packages. Here the VNC-Server-5.2.3-Solaris-x64.pkg and VNC-Viewer-5.2.3-Solaris-x64.pkg are being extracted.

```
root@BLSOL1:~/Downloads# tar -xzvf VNC-5.2.3-Solaris-x64-PKG.tar.gz
x VNC-Server-5.2.3-Solaris-x64.pkg, 39088640 bytes, 76345 tape blocks
x VNC-Viewer-5.2.3-Solaris-x64.pkg, 8895488 bytes, 17374 tape blocks
```

To install, you must log on as root and then run the pkgadd command:

```
root@BLSOL1:~/Downloads# /usr/sbin/pkgadd -d VNC-Server-5.2.3-Solaris-x64.pkg

The following packages are available:
  1  RVNCsrv     VNC Server for Solaris
                 (i386) 5.2.3.8648

Select package(s) you wish to process (or 'all' to process
all packages). (default: all) [?,??,q]: all
```

Processing package instance <RVNCsrv> from </root/Downloads/VNC-Server-5.2.3-Solaris-x64.pkg>

VNC Server for Solaris(i386) 5.2.3.8648
Copyright (C) 2002-2015 RealVNC Ltd.  All rights reserved.
Using </> as the package base directory.
## Processing package information.
## Processing system information.
   14 package pathnames are already properly installed.
## Verifying disk space requirements.
## Checking for conflicts with packages already installed.
## Checking for setuid/setgid programs.

The following files are being installed with setuid and/or setgid
permissions:
  /usr/local/bin/Xvnc <setuid root>
  /usr/local/bin/vncserver-x11 <setuid root>

Do you want to install these as setuid/setgid files [y,n,?,q] y

This package contains scripts which will be executed with super-user
permission during the process of installing this package.

Do you want to continue with the installation of <RVNCsrv> [y,n,?] y

Installing VNC Server for Solaris as <RVNCsrv>

## Installing part 1 of 1.
/usr/lib/cups/backend/vnc
/usr/local/bin/Xvnc
/usr/local/bin/Xvnc-core
/usr/local/bin/vncinitconfig
/usr/local/bin/vnclicense
/usr/local/bin/vnclicensehelper
/usr/local/bin/vnclicensewiz
/usr/local/bin/vncpasswd
/usr/local/bin/vncpipehelper
/usr/local/bin/vncserver-virtual
/usr/local/bin/vncserver-virtuald
/usr/local/bin/vncserver-x11
/usr/local/bin/vncserver-x11-core
/usr/local/bin/vncserver-x11-serviced
/usr/local/bin/vncserverui
/usr/local/lib/vnc/get_primary_ip4
/usr/local/lib/vnc/vncelevate
/usr/local/man/man1/Xvnc.1
/usr/local/man/man1/vncinitconfig.1
/usr/local/man/man1/vnclicense.1
/usr/local/man/man1/vncpasswd.1
/usr/local/man/man1/vncserver-virtual.1

```
/usr/local/man/man1/vncserver-virtuald.1
/usr/local/man/man1/vncserver-x11-serviced.1
/usr/local/man/man1/vncserver-x11.1
/usr/share/vnc/fonts/6x13-ISO8859-1.pcf.gz
/usr/share/vnc/fonts/cursor.pcf.gz
/usr/share/vnc/fonts/fonts.alias
/usr/share/vnc/fonts/fonts.dir
/usr/share/vnc/rgb.txt
[ verifying class <server> ]
/etc/gconf/schemas/realvnc.schemas
/usr/share/applications/realvnc-vnclicensehelper.desktop
/usr/share/applications/realvnc-vnclicensewiz.desktop
/usr/share/applications/realvnc-vncserver-x11.desktop
/usr/share/icons/hicolor/48x48/apps/vnclicensewiz48x48.png
/usr/share/icons/hicolor/48x48/apps/vncserver48x48.png
/usr/share/icons/hicolor/48x48/mimetypes/application-vnclicense-key.png <symbolic link>
/usr/share/mime/packages/realvnc-vnclicensehelper.xml
[ verifying class <desktop> ]
/usr/local/doc/RVNCsvr/LICENSE_en.txt
/usr/local/doc/RVNCsvr/README
[ verifying class <doc> ]
## Executing postinstall script.
Checking for xauth... /usr/openwin/bin
WARNING: /usr/openwin/bin/xauth is not on your path.
CUPS installation not found at /opt/sfw/cups/lib/cups.
Please install CUPS from the Solaris Companion CD, then run
  vncinitconfig -enable-print
Updating /etc/pam.d/vncserver
Updating /etc/pam.conf... done
Looking for font path... /usr/X11/lib/X11/fonts/misc/:unscaled,/usr/X11/lib/X11/
fonts/100dpi/:unscaled,/usr/X11/lib/X11/fonts/75dpi/:unscaled,/usr/X11/lib/X11/fonts/misc/,
/usr/X11/lib/X11/fonts/Type1/,/usr/X11/lib/X11/fonts/100dpi/,/usr/X11/lib/X11/fonts/75dpi/,
/usr/X11/lib/X11/fonts/TrueType/,/usr/X11/lib/X11/fonts/Type1/sun/,/usr/X11/lib/X11/fonts/
F3bitmaps/ (from /etc/X11/xorg.conf).
Generating private key...done
Installed SMF manifest for VNC X11 Service-mode daemon
Start or stop the service with:
  svcadm (enable|disable) application/vncserver-x11-serviced

Installed SMF manifest for VNC Virtual-mode daemon
Start or stop the service with:
  svcadm (enable|disable) application/vncserver-virtuald

Installation of <RVNCsrv> was successful.
```

To install the VNC Viewer on your Windows client computer, you must log on as the administrator and double-click the file VNC-5.2.3-Windows.exe. Just accept the default installation directory, C:\Program Files\RealVNC\VNC Viewer, and ensure that you select at least the VNC Viewer as one of the components to install.

## How It Works

To manage and access your remote Linux/Solaris database server from your Windows client computer using the VNC software, you must install the VNC Server on your remote Linux/Solaris database server and the VNC Viewer on your Windows client computer. However, you can install the VNC Server and VNC Viewer on both computers, so you can also manage and access other servers from your Linux/Solaris database server.

# 16-3. Manually Starting and Stopping the VNC Server
## Problem

You want to manually start and stop the VNC Server on your remote Linux/Solaris database server.

## Solution

To manually start the VNC Server on your Linux/Solaris database server, type vncserver and a port number where you want the VNC Server to be listening. The port number is optional, and the default value is 1. The following example shows the VNC Server being started in its default configuration:

```
# vncserver
```

This next example shows how to specify a port number. It starts the VNC Server to listen at port number 7:

```
# vncserver :7
```

---

■ **Note**    To have a similar look and feel of your desktop as when you log on to the console of the Linux server, uncomment or add unset SESSION_MANAGER and /etc/X11/xinit/xinitrc to the $HOME/.vnc/xstartup file.

---

To manually stop the VNC Server on your Linux/Solaris database server, run the Linux command vncserver -kill and provide the same port number you used when starting the VNC Server. Here's an example:

```
# vncserver -kill :7
```

## How It Works

You start the VNC Server on your remote Linux/Solaris database server by running vncserver and a port number. Like the other Linux/Solaris daemons—such as httpd, which usually listens on port number 80, and sshd, which usually listens on 22—the VNC Server listens on port number 5901 by default. If you include a port number when running vncserver, the actual port number is plus 5900. For example, if you run vncserver :7, the VNC Server listens on port number 5907.

The first time you run VNC server Enterprise Edition on your Linux server, you must issue the command vnclicense -add <license key> to install the license key. However, the license key is not required if you are using the VNC Free Edition. For example, to add the license key, use this:

```
# /usr/bin/vnclicense -add FR464-RHDJ6-6WNF4-A4NB2-HR2YA
```

---

■ **Note**    You can purchase a VNC license at `https://www.realvnc.com/purchase/`.

---

For security reasons, you shouldn't run the VNC Server under a privileged user, such as root or oracle (in other words, the Oracle RDBMS software owner). If you run the VNC Server as root, any remote VNC user will have root privileges after they are connected to your Linux/Solaris server, and that is a security risk. Instead, you should create a new Linux/Solaris user and launch the VNC Server from that account. After remote users are connected to the server, they can su to root or oracle to perform any necessary administrative tasks.

In the following example, the groupadd command creates a new group called vncuser; the useradd command creates a new user called vncuser, and the -g option associates this user to the group vncuser. The passwd command prompts you to assign a new password for OS user vncuser:

```
# groupadd vncuser
# useradd vncuser -g vncuser
# passwd vncuser
```

---

■ **Note**    For additional details about creating OS groups and users, refer to recipes 3-12 and 3-14.

---

The first time you launch vncserver for a particular OS user, you will be prompted for a password; and the relevant VNC files, such as the security key or the private.key file, will be created in the .vnc directory under the home directory of that OS user. In the example shown here, the su command makes vncuser the current OS user, and the ls -al $HOME/.vnc command displays the files in the .vnc directory under the home directory of OS username vncuser:

```
# su - vncuser

$ ls -al $HOME/.vnc
total 28
drwxrwxr-x  2 vncuser vncuser 4096 Apr 27 01:58 .
drwx------ 29 vncuser vncuser 4096 Apr 27 02:00 ..
-rw-rw-r--  1 vncuser vncuser 5258 Apr 27 01:59 ol6-121-rac1.localdomain:9.log
-rw-rw-r--  1 vncuser vncuser    6 Apr 27 01:58 ol6-121-rac1.localdomain:9.pid
-rw-------  1 vncuser vncuser    8 Apr 27 01:56 passwd
-rwxr-xr-x  1 vncuser vncuser  654 Apr 27 01:58 xstartup
```

Subsequent restarts of the VNC Server won't ask you to set the password and won't regenerate the secure key. However, you can run the Linux/Solaris command vncpasswd to change the VNC Server password for an OS user, as shown here:

```
$ /usr/bin/vncpasswd
Password:
Verify:
```

In case you forget the port number on which the VNC Server is listening, you can run the Linux command ps -ef. The following example illustrates this. In the results, Xvnc :9 indicates that the VNC Server is listening on port number 5909:

```
$ ps -ef | grep Xvnc
vncuser 10065     1  0 01:58 ?        00:00:01 /usr/bin/Xvnc :9 -desktop ol6-121-rac1.
localdomain:9 (vncuser) -auth /home/vncuser/.Xauthority -geometry 1024x768 -rfbwait 30000
-rfbauth /home/vncuser/.vnc/passwd -rfbport 5909 -fp catalogue:/etc/X11/fontpath.d -pn
vncuser  11062 10784  0 02:02 pts/0   00:00:00 grep Xvnc
```

# 16-4. Automatically Starting the VNC Server on Linux

## Problem

You want the VNC Server to automatically start when your Linux database server is rebooted.

## Solution

Perform the following steps to ensure that the VNC Server will automatically start when your Linux database server is rebooted:

1.  Modify the /etc/sysconfig/vncservers file and insert the line
    VNCSERVERS="<port#>:<OS_user>". In the example, the VNC Server is owned by
    vncuser to listen on port number 5909:

    ```
    # cat /etc/sysconfig/vncservers
    VNCSERVERS="9:vncuser"
    ```

2.  Check the existence of the file /etc/init.d/vncserver. If it is not available,
    create the file and insert the following lines:

    ```
    #!/bin/bash
    #
    # chkconfig: - 91 35
    # description: Starts and stops vncserver. \
    #              used to provide remote X administration services.

    # Source function library.
    . /etc/init.d/functions

    # Source networking configuration.
    . /etc/sysconfig/network

    # Check that networking is up.
    [ ${NETWORKING} = "no" ] && exit 0
    unset VNCSERVERARGS
    VNCSERVERS=""
    [ -f /etc/sysconfig/vncservers ] && . /etc/sysconfig/vncservers

    prog=$"VNC server"
    ```

```
start() {
    echo -n $"Starting $prog: "
    ulimit -S -c 0 >/dev/null 2>&1
    RETVAL=0
    if [ ! -d /tmp/.X11-unix ]
    then
        mkdir -m 1777 /tmp/.X11-unix || :
        restorecon /tmp/.X11-unix 2>/dev/null || :
    fi
    NOSERV=1
    for display in ${VNCSERVERS}
    do
        NOSERV=
        echo -n "${display} "
        unset BASH_ENV ENV
        DISP="${display%%:*}"
        export USER="${display##*:}"
        export VNCUSERARGS="${VNCSERVERARGS[${DISP}]}"
        runuser -l ${USER} -c "cd ~${USER} && [ -f .vnc/passwd ] && " || \
                                "vncserver :${DISP} ${VNCUSERARGS}"
        RETVAL=$?
        [ "$RETVAL" -ne 0 ] && break
    done
    if test -n "$NOSERV"; then echo -n "no displays configured "; fi
    [ "$RETVAL" -eq 0 ] && success $"vncserver startup" || \
        failure $"vncserver start"
    echo
    [ "$RETVAL" -eq 0 ] && touch /var/lock/subsys/vncserver
}

stop() {
    echo -n $"Shutting down $prog: "
    for display in ${VNCSERVERS}
    do
        echo -n "${display} "
        unset BASH_ENV ENV
        export USER="${display##*:}"
        runuser ${USER} -c "vncserver -kill :${display%%:*}" >/dev/null 2>&1
    done
    RETVAL=$?
    [ "$RETVAL" -eq 0 ] && success $"vncserver shutdown" || \
        failure $"vncserver shutdown"
    echo
    [ "$RETVAL" -eq 0 ] && rm -f /var/lock/subsys/vncserver
}

# See how we were called.
case "$1" in
  start)
        start
        ;;
  stop)
```

```
            stop
            ;;
    restart|reload)
            stop
            sleep 3
            start
            ;;
    condrestart)
            if [ -f /var/lock/subsys/vncserver ]; then
                stop
                sleep 3
                start
            fi
            ;;
    status)
            status Xvnc
            ;;
    *)
            echo $"Usage: $0 {start|stop|restart|condrestart|status}"
            exit 1
esac
```

3.  Ensure that /etc/init.d/vncserver has an execute permission:

```
# ls -l /etc/init.d/vncserver
-rw-r--r--. 1 root root 3236 Apr 29  2013 /etc/init.d/vncserver
# chmod a+x /etc/init.d/vncserver
# ls -l /etc/init.d/vncserver
-rwxr-xr-x. 1 root root 3236 Apr 29  2013 /etc/init.d/vncserver
```

4.  Create a softlink in /etc/rc.d/rc3.d and /etc/rc.d/rc5.d:

```
# ln -s /etc/init.d/vncserver /etc/rc.d/rc5.d/S91vncserver
# ls -l /etc/rc.d/rc5.d/S91vncserver
lrwxrwxrwx 1 root root 21 Apr 27 01:46 /etc/rc.d/rc5.d/S91vncserver ->
/etc/init.d/vncserver
# ln -s /etc/init.d/vncserver /etc/rc.d/rc3.d/S91vncserver
# ls -l /etc/rc.d/rc3.d/S91vncserver
lrwxrwxrwx 1 root root 21 Apr 27 01:49 /etc/rc.d/rc3.d/S91vncserver ->
/etc/init.d/vncserver
```

5.  Enable the VNC service using the chkconfig command:

```
# chkconfig --level 35 vncserver on
# chkconfig --list | grep vnc
vncserver       0:off   1:off   2:off   3:on    4:off   5:on    6:off
```

6.  If possible, log on as root and issue the Linux command reboot to manually
    restart your Linux database server. Otherwise, you can manually restart the VNC
    service by executing the Linux command /sbin/service vncserver restart.

7.  Issue the Linux command ps -ef | grep Xvnc to verify whether the VNC Server
    started automatically after the reboot. The following is an example. In the results,
    the VNC Server is listening on port number 9 running under Linux user vncuser:

```
$ ps -ef | grep Xvnc
vncuser  10065    1  0 01:58 ?        00:00:01 /usr/bin/Xvnc :9 -desktop
ol6-121-rac1.localdomain:9 (vncuser) -auth /home/vncuser/.Xauthority -geometry
1024x768 -rfbwait 30000 -rfbauth /home/vncuser/.vnc/passwd -rfbport 5909 -fp
catalogue:/etc/X11/fontpath.d -pn
vncuser  11752 10784  0 02:10 pts/0    00:00:00 grep Xvnc
```

## How It Works

In some environments in which VNC is heavily used, you may want to automate the restart of the VNC
Server. If the VNC service is enabled at the OS level, one of the files that will be executed during the system
startup is /etc/init.d/vncserver. That script in turn reads the file /etc/ sysconfig/vncservers, which
contains the OS user under which the VNC Server will run and the port number on which the VNC Server
will listen.

---

■ **Note**    After the VNC Server is automatically started, you can still manually stop and start the VNC Server,
as discussed in recipe 16-3. You may, for example, want to manually stop the VNC Server because you lack
memory resources on the machine on which it is running.

---

# 16-5. Automatically Starting the VNC Server on Solaris
## Problem

You want the VNC Server to automatically start when the Solaris database server is rebooted.

## Solution

Perform the following steps to ensure that the VNC Server will automatically start when your Solaris
database server is rebooted:

1.  Log on as root user to the Solaris server on which you want the VNC Server to
    run.

2.  Make sure to enable the Xvnc inetd services.

    ```
    # svcadm enable xvnc-inetd
    ```

3.  Modify the /etc/services and add the following line if it is not existing yet, as
    shown here. In this example, the VNC Server will listen on port 5901:

    ```
    vnc-server   5901/tcp
    ```

4.  Run the inetadm command, as shown here:

    ```
    inetadm -m svc:/application/x11/xvnc-inetd:default exec="/usr/bin/Xvnc \\
    ```

```
    -geometry 1024x768 -inetd -query localhost -once securitytypes=none"
    user="vncuser"
```

5.  Finally, restart the xvnc-inetd:

```
svcadm restart xvnc-inetd
```

## How It Works

When a user connects to the Solaris server via the VNC client, the inetadm command allows the inetd to spawn a new VNC instance as the OS user vncuser. The VNC client session should connect to the port defined in the /etc/services as vnc-server. In the previous example, the VNC Server is listening on port 5901.

# 16-6. Starting the VNC Viewer
## Problem

You want to start the VNC Viewer on your client machine, which is either your Windows computer or another Linux server. From that client, you want to manage and access your remote Linux/Solaris database server.

## Solution

To start the VNC Viewer on a Windows computer, run the program C:\Program Files\RealVNC\VNC Viewer\vncviewer.exe or navigate to that program by selecting Start ➤ All Programs ➤ RealVNC ➤ VNC Viewer ➤ Run VNC Viewer. A connection details dialog box will display, as shown in Figure 16-2.

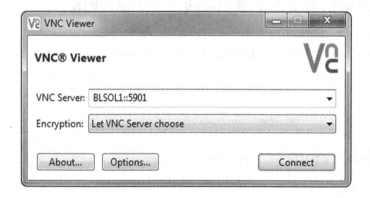

*Figure 16-2. VNC Viewer connection details*

In the connection details dialog box, provide the hostname or IP address of your remote Linux/Solaris database server, as well as the port number on which the VNC Server is listening. Click the OK button to confirm.

To start the VNC Viewer on your Linux/Solaris server, run the OS command /usr/bin/vncviewer as follows (assuming port number 1):

```
$ /usr/bin/vncviewer BLSOL:1
```

You will be prompted for a username and password, as shown in Figure 16-3. Depending on the security settings in the VNC Server, you may be prompted only for a password.

**Figure 16-3.** *VNC Viewer password prompt*

After your username and password are successfully verified, the screen of your remote Linux/Solaris database server is displayed, as shown in Figure 16-4. You can now start to access and manage your remote Linux/Solaris database server as if you were in front of the console.

**Figure 16-4.** *VNC Viewer screen display*

If you don't have the VNC Viewer installed on your client computer and you have a Java-enabled web browser, you can open the URL http://<host>:<port>, where <host> is the hostname or IP address of the VNC Server, and <port> is the port number on which the VNC Server is listening minus 100. For instance, if the IP address of the VNC Server is 192.168.2.41, and the Server is listening on port number 5901, the URL will be http://192.168.2.41:5801.

## How It Works

Before you can run the VNC Viewer on your client computer, you have to ensure that the VNC Server is running on your remote Linux/Solaris database server and listening on a specific port number. For details on how to install and start the VNC Server, review the first five recipes in this chapter.

However, if the VNC Viewer is not installed on your client computer, such as a computer in an Internet café or in an airport, you can use the VNC Viewer for Java using a Java-enabled web browser. It provides great flexibility because you are no longer confined to working in your office to perform DBA tasks. (Work from your local café instead!) But ensure that your VNC connection is secured, which you will learn more about in recipe 16-7.

---

■ **Note**    The VNC Viewer for Java is not available when connecting to the VNC server's Free Edition.

---

If you have the VNC Server Enterprise Edition running on your remote Linux/Solaris database server, you can't use the VNC Viewer Free Edition because of its security limitations. Instead, you must use the VNC Viewer Personal Edition or Enterprise Edition.

# 16-7. Securing a VNC Connection
## Problem

You want to secure your VNC connection and you want to have a good authentication method when users access the remote Linux/Solaris database server from your client computer using the VNC Viewer.

## Solution

To enhance a user's authentication and the security of your VNC connection, set the following parameters when launching the VNC Server:

- SecurityTypes: Sets the security method to employ. Valid values are None, VncAuth, RA2, and RA2ne.

- UserPasswdVerifier: Sets the method to authenticate the users. Valid values are None, VncAuth, and UnixAuth.

You can pass these parameters when manually starting your VNC Server. Here's an example:

```
$ /usr/local/bin/vncserver :9 -SecurityTypes=RA2 -UserPasswdVerifier=UnixAuth
```

You can also configure the parameters to take effect when the VNC Server is automatically started during the reboot of your remote Linux database server, as discussed in recipe 16-4. To that end, add the following lines to your /etc/sysconfig/vncservers file:

```
VNCSERVERS="9:vncuser"
VNCSERVERARGS[9]="-SecurityTypes=RA2 -UserPasswdVerifier=UnixAuth"
```

The first argument you are passing in VNCSERVERARGS corresponds to the port number on which the VNC Server is listening. In this example, the port number is 9.

## How It Works

We recommend that you use the latest version of the VNC Server Enterprise Edition because it employs 2048–bit RSA server authentication and 128–bit AES session encryption. If you use the VNC Server Free Edition, be aware that no security feature is available. However, you have to purchase a license key for the VNC Server Enterprise Edition.

---

▪ **Note**    To secure the connection to the server when you use the VNC Server Free Edition, forward the VNC connection through SSH (refer to recipe 14-7).

---

As a security measure, don't run the VNC Server as root because you don't want to allow users to have root access privilege after they connect to the server. Create another OS user with minimal privileges and run the VNC Server under that new Linux user (see recipe 16-3 for details). After remote users are connected to the server, they can su to oracle to perform any needed DBA tasks.

To encrypt a VNC connection in the VNC Server Enterprise Edition, set the SecurityTypes parameter to RA2 or RA2ne. RA2ne means that the authentication credentials will be encrypted, but subsequent connections are not. For the VNC Server Free Edition, set the SecurityTypes parameter to VncAuth.

For VNC Server Enterprise Edition, set the UserPasswdVerifier to UnixAuth instead of VncAuth. That way, the OS user's password is managed at the OS level, which requires less maintenance because you don't have to maintain two passwords: one in the VNC and the other at the OS level.

Don't set SecurityTypes or UserPasswdVerifier to None because you are then allowing any users to access the VNC Server without providing a password. It is like having no locks on your front door at home.

# 16-8. Accessing VNC via a Proxy Server
## Problem

You want to use VNC to access a remote Linux/Solaris database server that is outside your company's network, and all your Internet connections pass through a proxy server.

## Solution

Perform the following steps to configure the proxy settings in your VNC Viewer:

1.  Start the VNC Viewer (for details on starting the VNC Viewer, see recipe 16-6).

2.  Provide the appropriate hostname or IP address of the remote Linux/Solaris database server, as well as the corresponding port number where the VNC Server is listening, as shown in Figure 16-5.

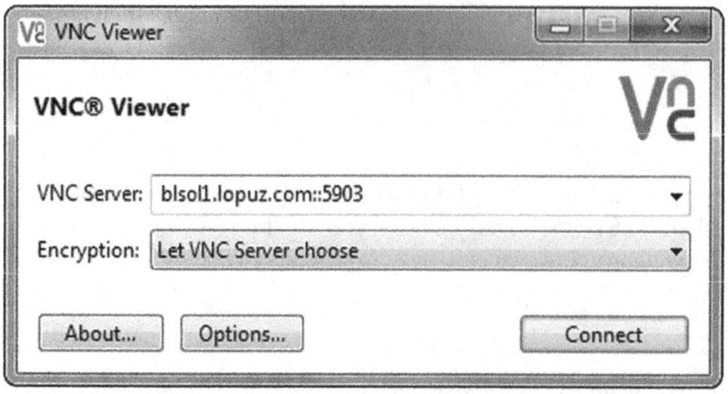

Figure 16-5. *VNC Viewer connection details*

3. Click the Options button and then the Connection tab. The VNC Viewer properties dialog box will appear, as shown in Figure 16-6.

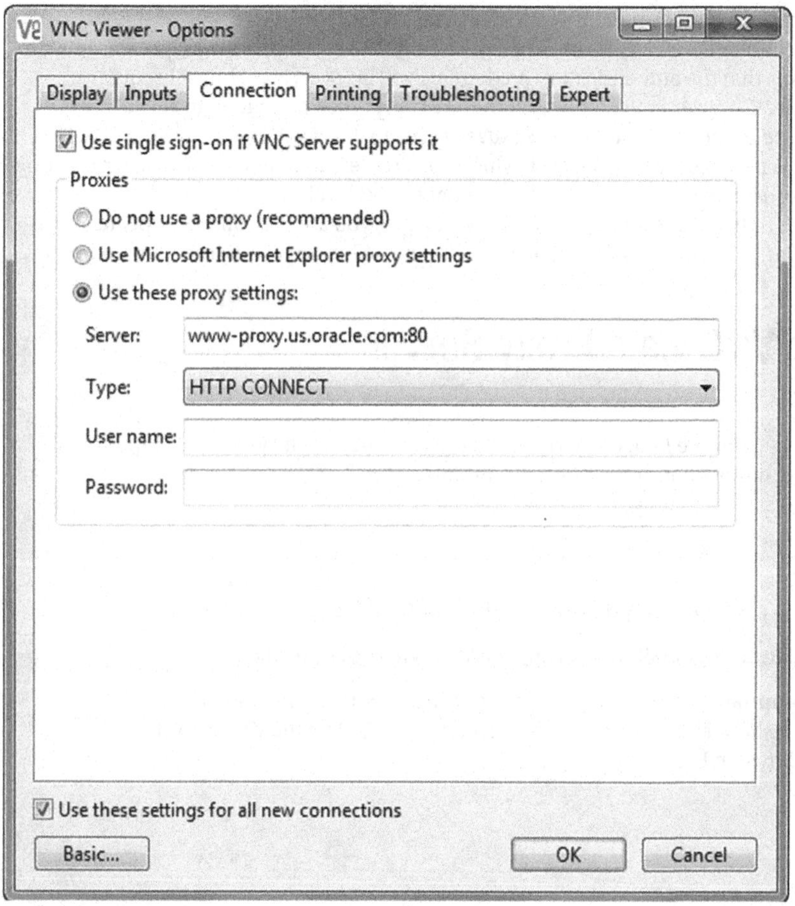

Figure 16-6. *VNC proxy server configuration*

4. In the Proxies section, select the Use These Proxy Settings radio button, and provide the appropriate hostname or IP address of the corresponding proxy server, the port number where the proxy server is listening, and the proxy type. If you have already configured a proxy setting in Microsoft Internet Explorer, select Use Microsoft Internet Explorer Proxy Settings instead.

5. Click the OK button.

6. Click the Connect button.

## How It Works

For security and performance reasons, the Internet connections of most companies that go outside their network pass through a proxy server. These servers are common for IT shops in which the DBAs access the servers of their clients or at their home while working from their office. For details about the hostname or IP address of your proxy server, its port number, and the proxy type, contact your company's system or network administrators.

To configure the proxy server setting using the VNC Viewer, you must download and use the Personal Edition or Enterprise Edition because the proxy server feature is not available in the Free Edition. The proxy server is a new feature included in VNC Viewer version 4.4, which was released in May 2008. Prior to version 4.4, you could configure SSH tunneling and the proxy server using PuTTY, as explained in recipe 1-1.

# 16-9. Running X Applications with VNC
## Problem

You want to run an X application at your remote Linux/Solaris database server, such as the Oracle DBCA, to create the Oracle database from your client computer.

## Solution

First, you have to run the VNC Viewer at your client computer. (For details on how to run the VNC Viewer, review recipe 16-6.) In the VNC Viewer, open a terminal window and log on to the OS user who will be the owner of the Oracle database:

```
$ xhost localhost
localhost being added to access control list
$ su - oracle
Password:
$ dbca
```

You will see a screen similar to Figure 16-7.

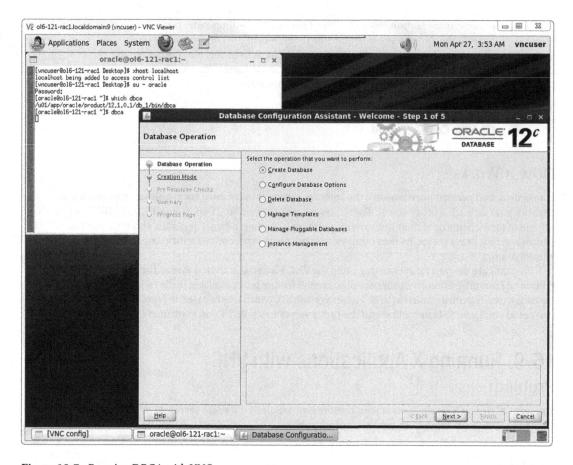

*Figure 16-7. Running DBCA with VNC*

## How It Works

Once the VNC Viewer display is available on your client machine, and you have access to the mouse and keyboard, you can then run any X application, such as Oracle's DBCA. Any X application that you run will look and feel just as if you were running it on the console of your remote Linux/Solaris database server.

# 16-10. Troubleshooting VNC

## Problem

You can't access the remote Linux/Solaris database server. You are having problems running the VNC Server or the VNC Viewer.

## Solution

When troubleshooting VNC, you may have to check the areas described in the following sections to narrow down the cause of the problem.

# VNC Server

Check that the VNC Server is running on your remote Linux/Solaris database server and is listening at the port number on which you are trying to connect. If the VNC Server does not run at all, check the parameters you are passing to the server. Check for errors such as spelling mistakes or invalid parameter values. If possible, try running the VNC Server without any parameters except for the port number and then add your parameters one at a time until you determine the culprit parameter.

---

■ **Note**    To display the VNC Server options and parameters, run the OS command `vncserver -list`.

---

You can check the log file at `$HOME/.vnc/<hostname>:<port#>.log`, where `$HOME` is the home directory of the Linux user under which the VNC Server is running, `<hostname>` corresponds to the hostname of the VNC Server, and `<port#>` represents the port on which the VNC Server is listening.

By default, the log parameter of the VNC Server is set to `*:stderr:30`. To configure the VNC Server log file, specify the VNC parameter `-log <logname>:<dest>:<level>`, where `<logname>` is the name of the log writer, `<dest>` is either `stderr` or `stdout`, and `<level>` ranges from 0 to 100. To gather extra details in the VNC Server log file, set `<level>` to 100. For example, the following command starts the VNC Server to listen on port 9 and logs extra details in the standard error file:

```
vncserver :9 -log *:stderr:100
```

You should display the VNC Server log file while you monitor incoming VNC connections. Use the `tail` command with the `-f` option for that purpose, as shown in this example:

```
bslopuz@BLSOL1:~$ tail -f /export/home/bslopuz/.vnc/BLSOL1:9.log
<14> 2015-04-27T12:18:44.206Z BLSOL1 Xvnc[22368]: SModulePrint: set printer
DELL2155-BAA060-IPv4_via_VNC_from_BLOPUZ-CA as default 1
<15> 2015-04-27T12:18:44.206Z BLSOL1 Xvnc[22368]: SystemPrinterMgr: created socket:/tmp/
.vnc-bslopuz/print.0x5760_0x2dcc53fe
<15> 2015-04-27T12:18:44.206Z BLSOL1 Xvnc[22368]: PrintDownloader:
removeFinishedPrintShare() - removing share 768365566
<15> 2015-04-27T12:18:44.206Z BLSOL1 Xvnc[22368]: FTMsgWriter: Local releasing 768365566
<15> 2015-04-27T12:18:44.207Z BLSOL1 Xvnc[22368]: PrintDownloader: startDownloading()
<15> 2015-04-27T12:18:44.207Z BLSOL1 Xvnc[22368]: PrintDownloader: startDownloading() -
nothing to download
<15> 2015-04-27T12:18:44.207Z BLSOL1 Xvnc[22368]: PrintStream: destroy (1561cd0)
<15> 2015-04-27T12:18:44.207Z BLSOL1 Xvnc[22368]: PrintDownloader: Deleted stream 1561cd0
<14> 2015-04-27T12:18:44.207Z BLSOL1 Xvnc[22368]: SConnectionST: Encodings
TRLE(15) CopyRect(1) Hextile(5) JRLE(22) JPEG(21) ZRLE(16) Zlib(6) RRE(2) Raw(0)
CursorWithAlpha(-311) Cursor(-239) DesktopSize(-223)
<14> 2015-04-27T12:18:44.207Z BLSOL1 Xvnc[22368]: SConnectionST: Current encoding TRLE
```

# VNC Viewer

To avoid any compatibility issues, ensure that the version of the VNC Viewer you use on the client computer matches the version of the VNC Server on the remote Linux/Solaris database server. For example, if the VNC Server is Enterprise Edition version 5, use VNC Viewer Enterprise Edition version 5 on the client computer.

If you still have issues with the VNC Viewer on the client computer, connect to the VNC Server using your Internet browser. Most of today's Internet browsers support Java applets, enabling you to connect. For additional information on how to start the VNC Viewer, review recipe 16-5.

## Connectivity

Verify that you can connect from your client computer to your remote Linux/Solaris database server, and vice versa. Run the ping command from the OS command prompt of your client computer. In the following example, the IP address of the remote Linux/Solaris database server is 192.168.2.41, and the client computer's IP address is 192.168.2.181:

```
C:\>ipconfig

Windows IP Configuration

Ethernet adapter Local Area Connection:

        Connection-specific DNS Suffix  . : home
        IPv4 Address. . . . . . . . . . . : 192.168.2.181
        Subnet Mask . . . . . . . . . . . : 255.255.255.0
        Default Gateway . . . . . . . . . : 192.168.2.1

Ethernet adapter VirtualBox Host-Only Network:

        Connection-specific DNS Suffix  . :
        IPv4 Address. . . . . . . . . . . : 192.168.56.1
        Subnet Mask . . . . . . . . . . . : 255.255.255.0
        Default Gateway . . . . . . . . . :

C:\>ping BLSOL1

Pinging BLSOL1 [192.168.2.41] with 32 bytes of data:
Reply from 192.168.2.41: bytes=32 time<1ms TTL=255
Reply from 192.168.2.41: bytes=32 time<1ms TTL=255
Reply from 192.168.2.41: bytes=32 time<1ms TTL=255
Reply from 192.168.2.41: bytes=32 time<1ms TTL=255

Ping statistics for 192.168.2.41:
    Packets: Sent = 4, Received = 4, Lost = 0 (0% loss),
Approximate round trip times in milli-seconds:
    Minimum = 0ms, Maximum = 0ms, Average = 0ms
```

Also, perform your tests the other way around. Try to ping the client computer from the remote Linux/Solaris database server. Here's an example:

```
root@BLSOL1:~# uname -a
SunOS BLSOL1 5.11 11.2 i86pc i386 i86pc
root@BLSOL1:~# traceroute 192.168.2.181
traceroute: Warning: Multiple interfaces found; using 192.168.2.41 @ net1
traceroute to 192.168.2.181 (192.168.2.181), 30 hops max, 40 byte packets
 1  192.168.2.181 (192.168.2.181)  0.196 ms *  0.224 ms
root@BLSOL1:~# ping 192.168.2.181
192.168.2.181 is alive
```

If you fail to make a connection using the ping command, verify that you are using the correct hostname or IP address for the VNC Server and also verify the correct port number on which the VNC Server is supposed to listen. Check for a firewall that may be blocking your connections to the remote Linux/Solaris database server from the client computer, and vice versa. If you have to connect to the remote Linux/Solaris database server through a proxy server, you have to set up your proxy server configuration. (Configuring for a proxy server is discussed in recipe 16-8.)

## How It Works

For the VNC software to work, you need the three components to function properly: the VNC Server listening at the remote Linux/Solaris database server, the VNC Viewer running at the client computer, and connectivity between the two computers. First, you have to identify the problematic area and start troubleshooting from there.

For the VNC Server, review the first five recipes in this chapter to ensure that it is installed correctly and is listening on the designated port number on your remote Linux/Solaris database server. You can also monitor the messages generated in the VNC Server log file while connections are coming to the VNC Server.

On the client computer, you have to check that the VNC Viewer is running. If the VNC Viewer is not available or not running correctly, you should connect using your Java-capable Internet browser to ensure that you are using the same versions between the VNC Server and the VNC Viewer.

Last but not least, you can use the ping command to verify connectivity between the remote Linux/ Solaris database server and the client computer. If you still can't connect, contact your system or network administrators to help you troubleshoot the connectivity issue between the remote Linux/Solaris database server and your client computer.

■ ■ ■

# RAID Concepts

In the not too distant past, a 1TB-sized database was considered to be pretty big. Currently, 1PB–2PB defines the lower boundary for a large database. In the not too distant future, *exabyte*, *zettabyte*, and *yottabyte* will become commonly bandied terms near the DBA water cooler.

As companies store more and more data, the need for disk space continues to grow. Managing database storage is a key responsibility of every database administrator. DBAs are tasked with estimating the initial size of databases, recognizing growth patterns, and monitoring disk usage. Overseeing these operations is critical to ensuring the availability of company data.

Here are some common DBA tasks associated with storage management:

- Determining disk architecture for database applications

- Planning database capacity

- Monitoring and managing growth of database files

Before more storage is added to a database server, SAs and DBAs should sit down and figure out which disk architecture offers the best availability and performance for a given budget. When working with SAs, an effective DBA needs to be somewhat fluent in the language of disk technologies. Specifically, DBAs must have a basic understanding of RAID disk technology and its implications for database performance and availability.

Even if your opinion isn't solicited in regard to disk technology, you still need to be familiar with the basic RAID configurations that will allow you to make informed decisions about database tuning and troubleshooting. This appendix discusses the fundamental information a DBA needs to know about RAID.

## Understanding RAID

As a DBA, you need to be knowledgeable about RAID designs to ensure that you use an appropriate disk architecture for your database application. RAID, which is an acronym for a Redundant Array of Inexpensive [or Independent] Disks, allows you to configure several independent disks to logically appear as one disk to the application. There are two important reasons to use RAID:

- To spread I/O across several disks, thus improving bandwidth

- To eliminate a lone physical disk as a single point of failure

If the database process that is reading and writing updates to disk can parallelize I/O across many disks (instead of a single disk), the bandwidth can be dramatically improved. RAID also allows you to configure several disks so that you never have one disk as a single point of failure. For most database systems, it is critical to have redundant hardware to ensure database availability.

The purpose of this section is not to espouse one RAID technology over another. You'll find bazillions of blogs and white papers on the subject of RAID. Each source of information has its own guru that evangelizes one form of RAID over another. All these sources have valid arguments for why their favorite flavor of RAID is the best for a particular situation.

Be wary of blanket statements regarding the performance and availability of RAID technology. For example, you might hear somebody state that RAID 5 is always better than RAID 1 for database applications. You might also hear somebody state that RAID 1 has superior fault tolerance over RAID 5. In most cases, the superiority of one RAID technology over another depends on several factors, such as the I/O behavior of the database application and the various components of the underlying stack of hardware and software. You may discover that what performs well in one scenario is not true in another; it really depends on the entire suite of technology in use.

The goal here is to describe the performance and fault tolerance characteristics of the most commonly used RAID technologies. We explain in simple terms and with clear examples how the basic forms of RAID technology work. This base knowledge enables you to make an informed disk technology decision dependent on the business requirements of your current environment. You should also be able to take the information contained in this section and apply it to the more sophisticated and emerging RAID architectures.

## Defining Array, Stripe Width, Stripe Size, Chunk Size

Before diving into the technical details of RAID, you first need to be familiar with a few terms: array, stripe width, stripe size, and chunk size.

An *array* is simply a collection of disks grouped together to appear as a single device to the application. Disk arrays allow for increased performance and fault tolerance.

The *stripe width* is the number of parallel pieces of data that can be written or read simultaneously to an array. The stripe width is usually equal to the number of disks in the array. In general (with all other factors being equal), the larger the stripe width size, the greater the throughput performance of the array. For example, you will generally see greater read/write performance from an array of twelve 32GB drives than from an array of four 96GB drives.

The *stripe size* is the amount of data you want written in parallel to an array of disks. Determining the optimal stripe size can be a highly debatable topic. Decreasing the stripe size usually increases the number of drives a file will use to store its data. Increasing the stripe size usually decreases the number of drives a file will employ to write and read to an array. The optimal stripe size depends on your database application I/O characteristics, along with the hardware and software of the system.

---

■ **Note**  The stripe size is usually a configurable parameter that can be dynamically configured by the storage administrator. Contrast that with the stripe width, which can be changed only by increasing or decreasing the physical number of disks.

---

The *chunk size* is the subset of the stripe size. The chunk size (also called the *striping unit*) is the amount of data written to each disk in the array as part of a stripe size.

Figure A-1 shows a 4KB stripe size that is being written to an array of four disks (a stripe width of 4). Each disk gets a 1KB chunk written to it.

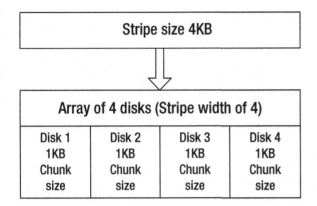

*Figure A-1.* *A 4KB stripe of data is written to four disks as 1KB chunks*

The chunk size can have significant performance effects. An inappropriate chunk size can result in I/O being concentrated on single disks within the array. If this happens, you may end up with an expensive array of disks that perform no better than a single disk.

What's the correct chunk size to use for database applications? It depends somewhat on the average size of I/O your databases generates. Typically, database I/O consists of several simultaneous and small I/O requests. Ideally, each small I/O request should be serviced by one disk, with the multiple I/O requests spread out across all disks in the array. So in this scenario, you want your chunk size to be a little larger than the average database I/O size.

---

■ **Tip** You'll have to test your particular database and disk configuration to determine which chunk size results in the best I/O distribution for a given application and its average I/O size.

---

# RAID 0

RAID 0 is commonly known as *striping*, which is a technique that writes chunks of data across an array of disks in a parallel fashion. Data is also read from disks in the same way, which allows several disks to participate in the read/write operations. The idea behind striping is that simultaneous access to multiple disks will have greater bandwidth than I/O to a single disk.

---

■ **Note** One disk can be larger than the other disks in a RAID 0 device (and the additional space is still used). However, this is not recommended because I/O will be concentrated on the large disk where more space is available.

---

Figure A-2 demonstrates how RAID 0 works. This RAID 0 disk array physically comprises four disks. Logically, it looks like one disk (/mount01) to the application. The stripe of data written to the RAID 0 device consists of 16 bits: 0001001000110100. Each disk receives a 4-bit chunk of the stripe.

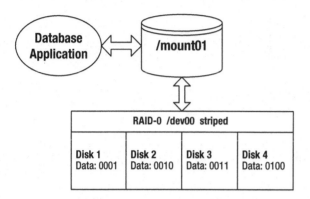

**Figure A-2.** *Four-disk RAID 0 striped device*

With RAID 0, your realized disk capacity is the number of disks times the size of the disk. For example, if you have four 100GB drives, the overall realized disk capacity available to the application is 400GB. In this sense, RAID 0 is a very cost-effective solution.

RAID 0 also provides excellent I/O performance. It allows for simultaneous reading and writing on all disks in the array. This spreads out the I/O, which reduces disk contention, alleviates bottlenecks, and provides excellent I/O performance.

The huge downside to RAID 0 is that it doesn't provide any redundancy. If one disk fails, the entire array fails. Therefore, you should never use RAID 0 for data you consider to be critical. You should use RAID 0 only for files that you can easily recover and only when you don't require a high degree of availability.

---

■ **Tip**   One way to remember what RAID 0 means is that it provides "0" redundancy. You get zero fault tolerance with RAID 0. If one disk fails, the whole array of disks fails.

---

# RAID 1

RAID 1 is commonly known as *mirroring*, which means that each time data is written to the storage device, it is physically written to two (or more) disks. In this configuration, if you lose one disk of the array, you still have another disk that contains a byte-for-byte copy of the data.

Figure A-3 shows how RAID 1 works. The mirrored disk array is composed of two disks. Disk 1b is a copy (mirror) of Disk 1a. As the data bits 0001 are written to Disk 1a, a copy of the data is also written to Disk 1b. Logically, the RAID 1 array of two disks looks like one disk (/mount01) to the application.

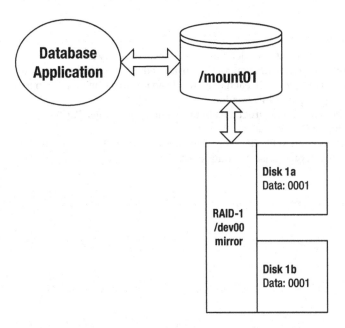

**Figure A-3.** *RAID 1 two-disk mirror*

Write performance with RAID 1 takes a little longer (than a single disk) because data must be written to each participating mirrored disk. However, read bandwidth is increased because of parallel access to data contained in the mirrored array.

RAID 1 is popular because it is simple to implement and provides fault tolerance. You can lose one mirrored disk and still continue operations as long as there is one surviving member. One downside to RAID 1 is that it reduces the amount of realized disk space available to the application. Although typically there are only two disks in a mirrored array, you can have more than two disks in a mirror. The realized disk space in a mirrored array is the size of the disk.

Here's the formula for calculating realized disk space for RAID 1:

```
Number of mirrored arrays * Disk Capacity
```

For example, suppose that you have four 100GB disks and you want to create two mirrored arrays with two disks in each array. The realized available disk space is calculated as shown here:

```
2 arrays * 100 gigabytes = 200 gigabytes
```

Another way of formulating it is as follows:

```
(Number of disks available / number of disks in the array) * Disk Capacity
```

This formula also shows that the amount of disk space available to the application is 200GB:

```
(4 / 2) * 100 gigabytes = 200 gigabytes
```

---

■ **Tip**   One way to remember the meaning of RAID 1 is that it provides 100% redundancy. You can lose one member of the RAID 1 array and still continue operations.

---

# Generating Parity

Before discussing the next levels of RAID, it is important to understand the concept of *parity* and how it is generated. RAID 4 and RAID 5 configurations use parity information to provide redundancy against a single disk failure. For a three-disk RAID 4 or RAID 5 configuration, each write results in two disks being written to in a striped fashion, with the third disk storing the parity information.

Parity data contains the information needed to reconstruct data in the event one disk fails. Parity information is generated from an XOR (exclusive OR) operation.

Table A-1 describes the inputs and outputs of an XOR operation. The table reads as follows: if one and only one of the inputs is a 1, the output will be a 1; otherwise, the output is a 0.

***Table A-1.*** *Behavior of an XOR Operation*

| Input A | Input B | Output |
|---------|---------|--------|
| 1 | 1 | 0 |
| 1 | 0 | 1 |
| 0 | 1 | 1 |
| 0 | 0 | 0 |

For example, from the first row in Table A-1, if both bits are a 1, the output of an XOR operation is a 0. From the second and third rows, if one bit is a 1 and the other bit is a 0, the output of an XOR operation is a 1. The last row shows that if both bits are a 0, the output is a 0.

A slightly more complicated example will help clarify this concept. In the example shown in Figure A-4, there are three disks. Disk 1 is written 0110, and Disk 2 is written 1110. Disk 3 contains the parity information generated by the output of an XOR operation on data written to Disk 1 and Disk 2.

| | | |
|---|---|---|
| **Disk 1**<br>Data: 0110 | **Disk 2**<br>Data: 1110 | **Disk 3 (parity)**<br>Data: 1000 |

***Figure A-4.*** *Disk 1 XOR Disk 2 = Disk 3 (parity)*

How was the 1000 parity information calculated? The first two bits of the data written to Disk 1 and Disk 2 are a 0 and a 1; therefore, the XOR output is a 1. The second two bits are both 1, so the XOR output is a 0. The third sets of bits are both 1, and the output is a 0. The fourth bits are both zeros, so the output is a 0.

This discussion is summarized here in equation form:

```
Disk1 XOR Disk2 = Disk3 (parity disk)
----- --- ----- -----
0110  XOR 1110  = 1000
```

How does parity allow for the recalculation of data in the event of a failure? For this example, suppose that you lose Disk 2. The information on Disk 2 can be regenerated by taking an XOR operation on the parity information (Disk 3) with the data written to Disk 1. An XOR operation of 0110 and 1000 yields 1110 (which was originally written to Disk 2). This discussion is summarized here in equation form:

```
Disk1 XOR Disk3 = Disk2
----- --- ----- -----
0110  XOR 1000  = 1110
```

You can perform an XOR operation with any number of disks. Suppose that you have a four-disk configuration. Disk 1 is written 0101, Disk 2 is written 1110, and Disk 3 is written 0001. Disk 4 contains the parity information, which is the result of Disk 1 XOR Disk 2 XOR Disk 3:

```
Disk1 XOR Disk2 XOR Disk3 = Disk4 (parity disk)
----- --- ---- --- ----- -----
0101  XOR 1110  XOR 0001  = 1010
```

Suppose that you lose Disk 2. To regenerate the information on Disk 2, you perform an XOR operation on Disk 1, Disk 3, and the parity information (Disk 4), which results in 1110:

```
Disk1 XOR Disk3 XOR Disk4 = Disk2
----- --- ----- --- ----- -----
0101  XOR 0001  XOR 1010  = 1110
```

You can always regenerate the data on the drive that becomes damaged by performing an XOR operation on the remaining disks with the parity information. RAID 4 and RAID 5 technologies use parity as a key component for providing fault tolerance. These parity-centric technologies are described in the next two sections.

# RAID 4

RAID 4, which is sometimes referred to as *dedicated parity*, writes a stripe (in chunks) across a disk array. One drive is always dedicated for parity information. A RAID 4 configuration minimally requires three disks: two disks for data and one for parity. The term *RAID 4* does not mean there are four disks in the array; there can be three or more disks in a RAID 4 configuration.

Figure A-5 shows a four-disk RAID 4 configuration. Disk 4 is the dedicated parity disk. The first stripe consists of the data 000100100011. Chunks of data 0001, 0010, and 0011 are written to Disks 1, 2, and 3, respectively. The parity value of 0000 is calculated and written to Disk 4.

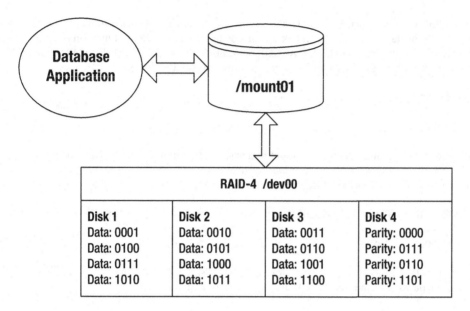

**Figure A-5.** *Four-disk RAID 4 dedicated parity device*

RAID 4 uses an XOR operation to generate the parity information. For each stripe in Figure A-5, the parity information is generated as follows:

```
Disk1 XOR Disk2 XOR Disk3 = Parity
----- --- ----- --- ----- ------
0001  XOR 0010  XOR 0011  = 0000
0100  XOR 0101  XOR 0110  = 0111
0111  XOR 1000  XOR 1001  = 0110
1010  XOR 1011  XOR 1100  = 1101
```

---

■ **Tip**    Refer to the previous "Generating Parity" section for details on how an XOR operation works.

---

RAID 4 requires that parity information be generated and updated for each write, so the writes take longer in a RAID 4 configuration than a RAID 0 write. Reading from a RAID 4 configuration is fast because the data is spread across multiple drives (and potentially multiple controllers).

With RAID 4, you get more realized disk space than you do with RAID 1. The RAID 4 amount of disk space available to the application is calculated with this formula:

```
(Number of disks - 1) * Disk Capacity
```

For example, if you have four 100GB disks, the realized disk capacity available to the application is calculated as shown here:

```
(4 -1) * 100 gigabytes = 300 gigabytes
```

In the event of a single disk failure, the remaining disks of the array can continue to function. For example, suppose that Disk 1 fails. The Disk 1 information can be regenerated with the parity information, as shown here:

```
Disk2 XOR Disk3 XOR Parity = Disk1
----- --- ----- --- ------    -----
0010  XOR 0011  XOR 0000   = 0001
0101  XOR 0110  XOR 0111   = 0100
1000  XOR 1001  XOR 0110   = 0111
1011  XOR 1100  XOR 1101   = 1010
```

During a single disk failure, RAID 4 performance will be degraded because the parity information is required for generating the data on the failed drive. Performance will return to normal levels after the failed disk has been replaced and its information regenerated. In practice, RAID 4 is seldom used because of the inherent bottleneck with the dedicated parity disk.

## RAID 5

RAID 5, which is sometimes referred to as *distributed parity*, is similar to RAID 4 except that RAID 5 interleaves the parity information among all the drives available in the disk array. A RAID 5 configuration minimally requires three disks: two for data and one for parity. The term *RAID 5* does not mean there are five disks in the array; there can be three or more disks in a RAID 5 configuration.

Figure A-6 shows a four-disk RAID 5 array. The first stripe of data consists of 000100100011. Three chunks of 0001, 0010, and 0011 are written to Disks 1, 2, and 3; the parity of 0000 is written to Disk 4. The second stripe writes its parity information to Disk 1, the third stripe writes its parity to Disk 2, and so on.

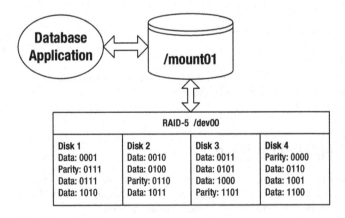

**Figure A-6.** *Four-disk RAID 5 distributed parity device*

RAID 5 uses an XOR operation to generate the parity information. For each stripe in Figure A-6, the parity information is generated as follows:

```
0001    XOR 0010   XOR 0011    = 0000
0100    XOR 0101   XOR 0110    = 0111
0111    XOR 1000   XOR 1001    = 0110
1010    XOR 1011   XOR 1100    = 1101
```

---

▧ **Tip**    Refer to the previous "Generating Parity" section for details on how an XOR operation works.

---

Like RAID 4, RAID 5 writes suffer a slight write performance hit because of the additional update required for the parity information. RAID 5 performs better than RAID 4 because it spreads the load of generating and updating parity information to all disks in the array. For this reason, RAID 5 is almost always preferred over RAID 4.

RAID 5 is popular because it combines good I/O performance with fault tolerance and cost effectiveness. With RAID 5, you get more realized disk space than you do with RAID 1. The RAID 5 amount of disk space available to the application is calculated with this formula:

```
(Number of disks - 1) * Disk Capacity
```

Using the previous formula, if you have four 100GB disks, the realized disk capacity available to the application is calculated as follows:

```
(4 -1) * 100 gigabytes = 300 gigabytes
```

RAID 5 provides protection against a single disk failure through the parity information. If one disk fails, the information from the failed disk can always be recalculated from the remaining drives in the RAID 5 array. For example, suppose that Disk 3 fails; the remaining data on Disk 1, Disk 2, and Disk 4 can regenerate the required Disk 3 information as follows:

```
DISK1 XOR DISK2 XOR DISK4 = DISK3
----- --- ----- --- -----   -----
0001  XOR 0010  XOR 0000  = 0011
0111  XOR 0100  XOR 0110  = 0101
0111  XOR 0110  XOR 1001  = 1000
1010  XOR 1011  XOR 1100  = 1101
```

During a single disk failure, RAID 5 performance will be degraded because the parity information is required for generating the data on the failed drive. Performance will return to normal levels after the failed disk has been replaced and its information regenerated.

# Building Hybrid (Nested) RAID Devices

The RAID 0, RAID 1, and RAID 5 architectures are the building blocks for more sophisticated storage architectures. Companies that need better availability can combine these base RAID technologies to build disk arrays with better fault tolerance. Some common hybrid RAID architectures are as follows:

- RAID 0+1 (striping and then mirroring)
- RAID 1+0 (mirroring and then striping)
- RAID 5+0 (RAID 5 and then striping)

These configurations are sometimes referred to as *hybrid* or *nested* RAID levels. Much like Lego blocks, you can take the underlying RAID architectures and snap them together for some interesting configurations that have performance, fault tolerance, and cost advantages and disadvantages. These technologies are described in detail in the following sections.

■ **Note**    Some degree of confusion exists about the naming standards for various RAID levels. The most common industry standard for nested RAID levels is that RAID A+B means that RAID level A is built first and then RAID level B is layered on top of RAID level A. This standard is not consistently applied by all storage vendors. You have to carefully read the specifications for a given storage device to ensure that you understand which level of RAID is in use.

# RAID 0+1

RAID 0+1 is a disk array that is first striped and then mirrored (a mirror of stripes). Figure A-7 shows an eight-disk RAID 0+1 configuration. Disks 1 through 4 are written to in a striped fashion. Disks 5 through 8 are a mirror of Disks 1 through 4.

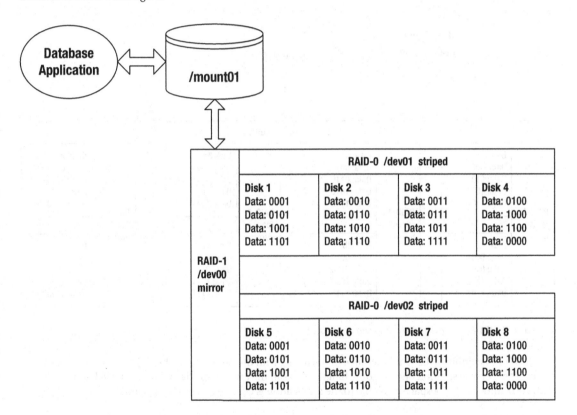

*Figure A-7.*  *RAID 0+1 striped and then mirrored device*

RAID 0+1 provides the I/O benefits of striping while providing the sturdy fault tolerance of a mirrored device. This is a relatively expensive solution because only half the disks in the array comprise your usable disk space. The RAID 0+1 amount of disk space available to the application is calculated with this formula:

```
(Number of disks in stripe) * Disk Capacity
```

Using the previous formula, if you have eight 100GB drives with four drives in each stripe, the realized disk capacity available to the application is calculated as follows:

```
4 * 100 gigabytes = 400 gigabytes
```

The RAID 0+1 configuration can survive multiple disk failures only if the failures occur within one stripe. RAID 0+1 cannot survive two disk failures if one failure is in one stripe (/dev01) and the other disk failure is in the second stripe (/dev02).

## RAID 1+0

RAID 1+0 is a disk array that is first mirrored and then striped (a stripe of mirrors). Figure A-8 displays an eight-disk RAID 1+0 configuration. This configuration is also commonly referred to as RAID 10.

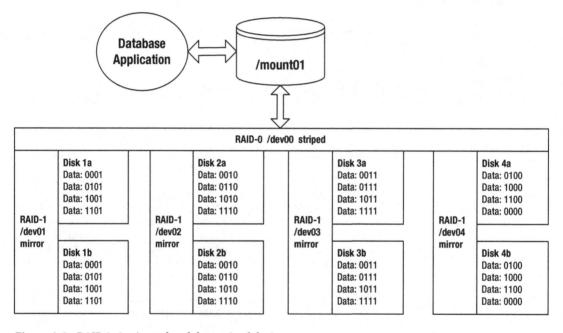

**Figure A-8.** *RAID 1+0 mirrored and then striped device*

RAID 1+0 combines the fault tolerance of mirroring with the performance benefits of striping. This is a relatively expensive solution because only half the disks in the array comprise your usable disk space. The RAID 1+0 amount of disk space available to the application is calculated with this formula:

```
(Number of mirrored devices) * Disk Capacity
```

For example, if you start with eight 100GB drives, and you build four mirrored devices of two disks each, the overall realized capacity to the application is calculated as follows:

```
4 * 100 gigabytes = 400 gigabytes
```

Interestingly, the RAID 1+0 arrangement provides much better fault tolerance than RAID 0+1. Analyze Figure A-8 carefully. The RAID 1+0 hybrid configuration can survive a disk failure in each stripe and can also survive one disk failure within each mirror. For example, in this configuration, Disk 1a, Disk 2b, Disk 3a, and Disk 4b could fail; but the overall device would continue to function because of the mirrors in Disk 1b, Disk 2a, Disk 3b, and Disk 4a.

Likewise, an entire RAID 1+0 stripe could fail, and the overall device would continue to function because of the surviving mirrored members. For example, Disk 1b, Disk 2b, Disk 3b, and Disk 4b could fail; but the overall device would continue to function because of the mirrors in Disk 1a, Disk 2a, Disk 3a, and Disk 4a.

Many articles, books, and storage vendor documentation confuse the RAID 0+1 and RAID 1+0 configurations (they refer to one when really meaning the other). It is important to understand the differences in fault tolerance between the two architectures. If you're architecting a disk array, ensure that you use the one that meets your business needs.

Both RAID 0+1 and RAID 1+0 architectures possess the excellent performance attributes of striped storage devices without the overhead of generating parity. Does RAID 1+0 perform better than RAID 0+1 (and vice versa)? Unfortunately, we have to waffle a bit (no pun intended) on the answer to this question: it depends. Performance characteristics are dependent on items such as the configuration of the underlying RAID devices, amount of cache, number of controllers, I/O distribution of the database application, and so on. We recommend that you perform an I/O load test to determine which RAID architecture works best for your environment.

# RAID 5+0

RAID 5+0 is a set of disk arrays placed in a RAID 5 configuration and then striped. Figure A-9 displays the architecture of an eight-disk RAID 5+0 configuration.

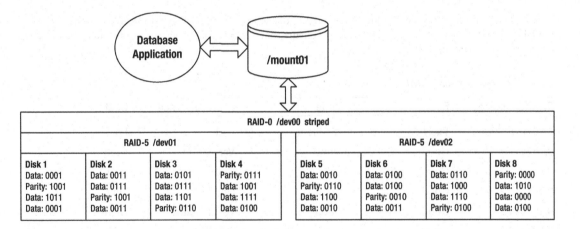

**Figure A-9.** *RAID 5+0 (RAID 5 and then striped) device*

RAID 5+0 is sometimes referred to as *striping parity*. The read performance is slightly less than the other hybrid (nested) approaches. The write performance is good, however, because each stripe consists of a RAID 5 device. Because this hybrid is underpinned by RAID 5 devices, it is more cost effective than the RAID 0+1 and RAID 1+0 configurations. The RAID 5+0 amount of disk space available to the application is calculated with this formula:

```
(Number of disks - number of disks used for parity) * Disk Capacity
```

For example, if you have eight 100GB disks with four disks in each RAID 5 device, the total realized capacity would be calculated as shown here:

```
(8 - 2) * 100 gigabytes = 600 gigabytes
```

RAID 5+0 can survive a single disk failure in either RAID 5 device. However, if there are two disk failures in one RAID 5 device, the entire RAID 5+0 device will fail.

# Determining Disk Requirements

Which RAID technology is best for your environment? It depends on your business requirements. Some storage gurus recommend RAID 5 for databases; others argue that RAID 5 should never be used. There are valid arguments on both sides of the fence. You may be part of a shop that already has a group of storage experts who predetermine the underlying disk technology without input from the DBA team. Ideally, you want to be involved with architecture decisions that affect the database, but realistically that does not always happen.

Or you might be in a shop that is constrained by cost and might conclude that a RAID 5 configuration is the only viable architecture. For your database application, you'll have to determine the cost–effective RAID solution that performs well while also providing the required fault tolerance. This will most likely require you to work with your storage experts to monitor disk performance and I/O characteristics.

---

■ **Tip**    Refer to Chapter 8 for details on how to use tools such as `iostat` and `sar` to monitor disk I/O behavior.

---

Table A-2 summarizes the various characteristics of each RAID technology. These are general guidelines, so test the underlying architecture to ensure that it meets your business requirements before you implement a production system.

***Table A-2.***  *Comparison of RAID Technologies*

| Disk Technology | Read | Write | Fault Tolerance | Cost |
|---|---|---|---|---|
| RAID 0 | Excellent | Excellent | Bad | Low |
| RAID 1 | Good | Slow | Very Good | High |
| RAID 4 | Good | Good | Good | Low |
| RAID 5 | Good | Good | Good | Low |
| RAID 0+1 | Good | Good | Very Good | High |
| RAID 1+0 | Good | Good | Excellent | High |
| RAID 5+0 | Good | Good | Good | Medium |

Table A-2 is intended only to provide general heuristics for determining the appropriate RAID technology for your environment. There will be some technologists who might disagree with some of these general guidelines. From our experience, there are often two very opposing RAID opinions, and both have valid points of view.

Some variables that are unique to a particular environment also influence the decision about the best solution. For this reason, it can be difficult to determine exactly which combination of chunk, stripe size, stripe width, underlying RAID technology, and storage vendor will work best over a wide variety of database applications. If you have the resources to test every permutation under every type of I/O load, you probably can determine the perfect combination of the previously mentioned variables.

Realistically, few shops have the time and money to exercise every possible storage architecture for each database application. You'll have to work with your SA and storage vendor to architect a cost-effective solution for your business that performs well over a variety of database applications.

---

■ **Caution**   Using RAID technology *doesn't* eliminate the need for a backup and recovery strategy. You should always have a strategy in place to ensure that you can restore and recover your database. You should periodically test your backup and recovery strategy to make sure it protects you if all disks fail (because of a fire, earthquake, tornado, avalanche, grenade, hurricane, and so on).

---

# Capacity Planning

DBAs are often involved with disk storage capacity planning. They have to ensure that adequate disk space will be available, both initially and for future growth, when the database server disk requirements are first spec'ed out (specified). When using RAID technologies, you have to be able to calculate the actual amount of disk space that will be available given the available disks.

For example, when the SA says that there are *x* number of type Y disks configured with a given RAID level, you have to calculate whether there will be enough disk space for your database requirements.

Table A-3 details the formulas used to calculate the amount of available disk space for each RAID level.

***Table A-3.***  *Calculating the Amount of RAID Disk Space Realized*

| Disk Technology | Realized Disk Capacity |
| --- | --- |
| RAID 0 (striped) | Num Disks in Stripe * Disk Size |
| RAID 1 (mirrored) | Num Mirrored Arrays * Disk Size |
| RAID 4 (dedicated parity) | (Num Disks – 1) * Disk Size |
| RAID 5 (distributed parity) | (Num Disks – 1) * Disk Size |
| RAID 0+1 (striped and then mirrored) | Num Disks in Stripe * Disk Size |
| RAID 1+0 (mirrored and then striped) | Num Mirrored Arrays * Disk Size |
| RAID 5+0 (RAID 5 and then striped) | (Num Disks – Num Parity Disks) * Disk Size |

Be sure to include future database growth requirements in your disk space calculations. Also consider the amount of disk space needed for files such as database transaction logs and database binaries, as well as the space required for database backups (keep in mind that you may want to keep multiple days' worth of backups on disk).

---

■ **Tip**   A good rule of thumb is to always keep one database backup on disk, back up the database backup files to tape, and then move the backup tapes offsite. You will have the good performance that is required for routine backup and recovery tasks and protection against complete disasters.

---

# Server Log Files

Server log files contain informational messages about the kernel, applications, and services running on a system. These files can be very useful for troubleshooting and debugging system-level issues. DBAs often look in the system log files as a first step in diagnosing server issues. Even if you're working with competent SAs, you can still save time and gain valuable insights into the root cause of a problem by inspecting these log files.

This appendix covers managing Linux and Solaris log files. You'll learn about the basic information contained in the log files and the tools available to rotate the logs.

## Managing Linux Log Files

Most of the system log files are located in the /var/log directory. There is usually a log file for a specific application or service. For example, the cron utility has a log file named cron (no surprise) in the /var/log directory. Depending on your system, you may need root privileges to view certain log files.

The log files will vary somewhat by the version of the OS and the applications running on your system. Table B-1 contains the names of some of the more common log files and their descriptions.

*Table B-1.* *Typical Linux Log Files and Descriptions*

| Log File Name | Purpose |
| --- | --- |
| /var/log/boot.log | System boot messages |
| /var/log/cron | cron utility log file |
| /var/log/maillog | Mail server log file |
| /var/log/messages | General system messages |
| /var/log/secure | Authentication log file |
| /var/log/wtmp | Login records |
| /var/log/yum.log | yum utility log file |

■ **Note**    Some utilities can have their own subdirectory under the /var/log directory.

## Rotating Log Files

The system log files will continue to grow unless they are somehow moved or removed. Moving and removing log files is known as *rotating* the log files, which means that the current log file is renamed, and a new log file is created.

Most Linux systems use the `logrotate` utility to rotate the log files. This tool automates the rotation, compression, removal, and mailing of log files. Typically, you'll rotate your log files so that they don't become too large and cluttered with old data. You should delete log files that are older than a certain number of days.

By default, the `logrotate` utility is automatically run from the `cron` scheduling tool on most Linux systems. Here's a typical listing of the contents of the `/etc/crontab` file:

```
SHELL=/bin/bash
PATH=/sbin:/bin:/usr/sbin:/usr/bin
MAILTO=root
HOME=/
# run-parts
01 * * * * root run-parts /etc/cron.hourly
02 4 * * * root run-parts /etc/cron.daily
22 4 * * 0 root run-parts /etc/cron.weekly
42 4 1 * * root run-parts /etc/cron.monthly
```

Notice that the `/etc/crontab` uses the `run-parts` utility to run all scripts located within a specified directory. For example, when `run-parts` inspects the `/etc/cron.daily` directory, it finds a file named `logrotate` that calls the `logrotate` utility. Listed here are the contents of a typical `logrotate` script:

```
#!/bin/sh
/usr/sbin/logrotate /etc/logrotate.conf
EXITVALUE=$?
if [ $EXITVALUE != 0 ]; then
    /usr/bin/logger -t logrotate "ALERT exited abnormally with [$EXITVALUE]"
fi
exit 0
```

The behavior of the `logrotate` utility is governed by the `/etc/logrotate.conf` file. Here's a listing of a typical `/etc/logrotate.conf` file:

```
# see "man logrotate" for details
# rotate log files weekly
weekly
# keep 4 weeks worth of backlogs
rotate 4
# create new (empty) log files after rotating old ones
create
# uncomment this if you want your log files compressed
#compress
# RPM packages drop log rotation information into this directory
include /etc/logrotate.d
# no packages own wtmp -- we'll rotate them here
/var/log/wtmp {
    monthly
    create 0664 root utmp
    rotate 1
}
# system-specific logs may be also be configured here.
```

By default, the logs are rotated weekly on most Linux systems, and four weeks' worth of logs are preserved. These are designated by the lines weekly and rotate 4 in the /etc/ logrotate.conf file. You can change the values within the /etc/logrotate.conf file to suit the rotating requirements of your environment.

If you list the files in the /var/log directory, notice that some log files end with an extension of .1 or .gz. This indicates that the logrotate utility is running on your system.

You can manually run the logrotate utility to rotate the log files. Use the -f option to force a rotation, even if logrotate doesn't think it is necessary:

```
# logrotate -f /etc/logrotate.conf
```

Application-specific logrotate configurations are stored in the /etc/logrotate.d directory. Change directories to the /etc/logrotate.d directory and list some typical application logs on a Linux server:

```
# cd /etc/logrotate.d
# ls
acpid  cups  mgetty  ppp  psacct  rpm  samba  syslog  up2date  yum
```

## Setting Up a Custom Log Rotation

The logrotate utility is sometimes perceived as a utility only for SAs. However, any user on the system can use logrotate to rotate log files for applications for which they have read/write permissions on the log files. For example, as the oracle user, you can use logrotate to rotate your database alert.log file.

Here are the steps for setting up a job to rotate the alert log file of an Oracle database:

1. Create a configuration file named alert.conf in the directory $HOME/config (create the config directory if it doesn't already exist):

   ```
   /oracle/RMDB1/admin/bdump/*.log {
   daily
   missingok
   rotate 7
   compress
   mail oracle@localhost
   }
   ```

2. In the preceding configuration file, the first line specifies the location of the log file. The asterisk (wildcard) tells logrotate to look for any file with the extension of .log in that directory. The daily keyword specifies that the log file should be rotated on a daily basis. The missingok keyword specifies that logrotate should not throw an error if it doesn't find any log files. The rotate 7 keyword specifies that the log files should be kept for seven days. The compress keyword compresses the rotated log file. Finally, a status e-mail is sent to the local oracle user on the server.

3. Create a cron job to automatically run the job on a daily basis:

   ```
   0 9 * * * /usr/sbin/logrotate -f -s /home/oracle/config/alrotate.status
   /home/oracle/config/alert.conf
   ```

---

■ **Note**    The previous two lines of code should be one line in your cron table (the code didn't fit nicely on this page on one line).

---

4.  The cron job runs the logrotate utility every day at 9 a.m. The -s (status) option directs the status file to the specified directory and file. The configuration file used is /home/oracle/config/alert.conf.

5.  Manually test the job to see whether it rotates the alert log correctly. Use the -f switch to force logrotate to do a rotation:

```
$ /usr/sbin/logrotate -f -s /home/oracle/config/alrotate.status \
/home/oracle/config/alert.conf
```

As shown in the previous steps, you can use the logrotate utility to set up log rotation jobs.
Compare using logrotate instead of writing a custom shell script such as the one described in recipe 10-8.

## Monitoring Log Files

Many Linux systems have graphical interfaces for monitoring and managing the log files. As a DBA, you often need to look only at a specific log file when trying to troubleshoot a problem. In these scenarios, it is usually sufficient to manually inspect the log files with a text editor such as vi or a paging utility such as more or less.

You can also monitor the logs with the logwatch utility. You can modify the default behavior of logwatch by modifying the logwatch.conf file. Depending on your Linux system, the logwatch.conf file is usually located in a directory named /etc/log.d. To print the default log message details, use the --print option:

```
# logwatch --print
```

Many SAs set up a daily job to be run that automatically e-mails the logwatch report to a specified user. Usually this functionality is implemented as a script located in the /etc/cron.daily directory. The name of the script will vary by Linux system. Typically, these scripts are named something like 0logwatch or 00-logwatch.

# Managing Solaris Log Files

The Solaris OS logs can be found under the /var directory. Table B-2 documents the names and purpose of commonly used log files in a Solaris environment.

*Table B-2.* *Typical Solaris Log Files*

| Log File Name | Purpose |
| --- | --- |
| /var/adm/messages | General-purpose, catch-all file for system messages |
| /var/adm/sulog | Records each attempt to use the su command |
| /var/cron/log | Contains entries for cron jobs running on the server |
| /var/log/syslog | Logging output from various system utilities (e.g., mail) |

## Viewing System Message Log Files

The syslogd daemon automatically records various system errors, warnings, and faults in message log files. You can use the dmesg command to view the most recently generated system-level messages. For example, run the following as the root user:

```
# dmesg
```

Here's some sample output:

```
Apr  1 12:27:56 sb-gate su: [ID 810491 auth.crit] 'su root' failed for mt...
Apr  2 11:14:09 sb-gate sshd[15969]: [ID 800047 auth.crit] monitor fatal: protocol error...
```

The /var/adm directory contains several log directories and files. The most recent system log entries are in the /var/adm/messages file. Periodically (typically every 10 days), the contents of the messages file are rotated and renamed to messages.N. For example, you should see a messages.0, messages.1, messages.2, and messages.3 file (older files are deleted). Use the following command to view the current messages file:

```
# more /var/adm/messages
```

If you want to view all logged messages, enter the following command:

```
# more /var/adm/messages*
```

## Rotating Solaris Log Files

You can rotate logs in a Solaris environment via the logadm utility, which is a very flexible and powerful tool that you can use to manage your log files. The logadm utility is called from the root user's cron table. Here's an example:

```
10 3 * * * /usr/sbin/logadm
```

This code shows that the logadm utility is called once per day at 3:10 a.m. The logadm utility will rotate files based on information in the /etc/logadm.conf file. Although you can manually modify this file, the recommended approach to modifying the /etc/logadm.conf file is via the logadm utility.

A short example will help illustrate how to add an entry. This next line of code instructs the logadm utility to add an entry with the -w switch:

```
# logadm -w /orahome/logs/mylog.log -C 8 -c -p 1d -t '/orahome/logs/mylog.log.$n' -z 1
```

Now if you inspect the contents of the /etc/logadm.conf file, the prior line has been added to the file:

```
/orahome/logs/mylog.log -C 8 -c -p 1d -t '/orahome/logs/mylog.log.$n' -z 1
```

The preceding line of code instructs logadm to rotate the /orahome/logs/mylog.log file. The -C 8 switch specifies that it should keep eight old versions before deleting the oldest file. The -c switch instructs the file to be copied and truncated (and not moved). The -p 1d switch specifies that the log file should be rotated on a daily basis. The -t switch provides a template for the rotated log file name. The -z 1 switch specifies that the number 1 rotated log should be compressed.

You can validate your entry by running logadm with the -V switch. Here's an example:

```
# logadm -V
```

You can also force an immediate execution of the entry via the -p now switch:

```
# logadm -p now /orahome/logs/mylog.log
```

After running the preceding command, you should see that your log has been rotated:

```
# cd /orahome/logs
# ls -altr
-rw-r--r--  1 root      root        0 Apr  5 16:40 mylog.log.0
-rw-r--r--  1 root      root        0 Apr  5 16:40 mylog.log
```

To remove an entry from the /etc/logadm.conf file, use the -r switch. Here's an example:

```
# logadm -r /orahome/logs/mylog.log
```

# Summary

Server log files are often the first places to look when you experience performance and security issues. These files contain messages that help diagnose and troubleshoot problems. Because log files tend to grow very fast, it is important to understand how to rotate the logs, which ensures that they are archived, compressed, and deleted at regular intervals.

On Linux systems, use the logrotate utility to rotate log files; on Solaris servers, use the logadm utility.

# Index

**⟨IOUG⟩** *For the Complete Technology & Database Professional*
independent oracle users group

**IOUG** represents the **voice of Oracle technology and database professionals** - empowering you to be **more productive in your business** and career by **delivering education,** sharing **best practices** and providing technology direction and **networking opportunities.**

## Context, Not Just Content

IOUG is dedicated to helping our members become an #IOUGenius by staying on the cutting-edge of Oracle technologies and industry issues through practical content, user-focused education, and invaluable networking and leadership opportunities:

- *SELECT Journal* is our quarterly publication that provides in-depth, peer-reviewed articles on industry news and best practices in Oracle technology

- Our #IOUGenius blog highlights a featured weekly topic and provides content driven by Oracle professionals and the IOUG community

- Special Interest Groups provide you the chance to collaborate with peers on the specific issues that matter to you and even take on leadership roles outside of your organization

- COLLABORATE is our once-a-year opportunity to connect with the members of not one, but three, Oracle users groups (IOUG, OAUG and Quest) as well as with the top names and faces in the Oracle community.

### Who we are...

... more than 20,000 database professionals, developers, application and infrastructure architects, business intelligence specialists and IT managers

... a community of users that share experiences and knowledge on issues and technologies that matter to you and your organization

Interested? Join IOUG's community of Oracle technology and database professionals at **www.ioug.org/Join.**

Independent Oracle Users Group | phone: (312) 245-1579 | email: membership@ioug.org
330 N. Wabash Ave., Suite 2000, Chicago, IL 60611

Printed in the United States
By Bookmasters